FORD V8
ENGINE REBUILDING MANUAL

Senior Vice President	Ronald A. Hoxter
Publisher & Editor-In-Chief	Kerry A. Freeman, S.A.E.
Executive Editors	Dean F. Morgantini, S.A.E., W. Calvin Settle, Jr., S.A.E.
Managing Editor	Nick D'Andrea
Senior Editors	Jacques Gordon, Michael L. Grady, Debra McCall, Ben Greisler, Kevin M. G. Maher, Richard J. Rivele, S.A.E., Richard T. Smith, Jim Taylor, Ron Webb
Project Managers	Martin J. Gunther, Will Kessler, A.S.E., Richard Schwartz
Production Manager	Andrea Steiger
Product Systems Manager	Robert Maxey
Director of Manufacturing	Mike D'Imperio
Authors	Rich Rivele and Ron Webb

CHILTON BOOK COMPANY

ONE OF THE **DIVERSIFIED PUBLISHING COMPANIES,**
A PART OF **CAPITAL CITIES/ABC, INC.**

Manufactured in USA
© 1996 Chilton Book Company
Chilton Way, Radnor, PA 19089
ISBN 0-8019-8793-8
Library of Congress Catalog Card No. 96-83982
1234567890 5432109876

Contents

1 GETTING STARTED

1-2 PRELIMINARIES
1-25 SPECIFICATIONS CHARTS

2 SETTING UP SHOP

2-2 THE WORK AREA
2-9 UNDERSTANDING THE BASICS

3 EQUIPPING YOUR SHOP

3-2 SUPPLIES AND EQUIPMENT
3-6 TOOLS
3-26 FASTENERS

4 THE ENGINE

4-2 THE HARD WORK STARTS

5 THE REBUILDING PROCESS

5-2 DISASSEMBLY
5-47 PARTS CLEANING
5-52 INSPECTION
5-64 REPAIR AND REFINISHING
5-73 PUTTING IT ALL BACK TOGETHER
5-102 SPECIFICATIONS CHARTS

6 FINISHING THE JOB

6-2 ENGINE INSTALLATION
6-9 TUNE-UP PROCEDURES
6-19 SPECIFICATIONS CHARTS

Contents

6-36 GLOSSARY

6-41 MASTER INDEX

GLOSSARY

MASTER INDEX

SAFETY NOTICE

Proper service and repair procedures are vital to the safe, reliable operation of all motor vehicles, as well as the personal safety of those performing repairs. This manual outlines procedures for servicing and repairing vehicles using safe, effective methods. The procedures contain many NOTES, CAUTIONS and WARNINGS which should be followed along with standard procedures to eliminate the possibility of personal injury or improper service which could damage the vehicle or compromise its safety.

It is important to note that the repair procedures and techniques, tools and parts for servicing motor vehicles, as well as the skill and experience of the individual performing the work vary widely. It is not possible to anticipate all of the conceivable ways or conditions under which vehicles may be serviced, or to provide cautions as to all of the possible hazards that may result. Standard and accepted safety precautions and equipment should be used when handling toxic or flammable fluids, and safety goggles or other protection should be used during cutting, grinding, chiseling, prying, or any other process that can cause material removal or projectiles.

Some procedures require the use of tools specially designed for a specific purpose. Before substituting another tool or procedure, you must be completely satisfied that neither your personal safety, nor the performance of the vehicle will be endangered.

Although information in this manual is based on industry sources and is complete as possible at the time of publication, the possibility exists that some car manufacturers made later changes which could not be included here. While striving for total accuracy, Chilton Book Company cannot assume responsibility for any errors, changes or omissions that may occur in the compilation of this data.

PART NUMBERS

Part numbers listed in this reference are not recommendation by Chilton for any product by brand name. They are references that can be used with interchange manuals and aftermarket supplier catalogs to locate each brand supplier's discrete part number.

SPECIAL TOOLS

Special tools are recommended by the vehicle manufacturer to perform their specific job. Use has been kept to a minimum, but where absolutely necessary, they are referred to in the text by the part number of the tool manufacturer. These tools can be purchased, under the appropriate part number, from your local dealer or regional distributor, or an equivalent tool can be purchased locally from a tool supplier or parts outlet. Before substituting any tool for the one recommended, read the SAFETY NOTICE at the top of this page.

ACKNOWLEDGMENTS

The Chilton Book Company expresses appreciation to Ford Motor Co. and Mardinly Enterprise, Havertown, PA, for their generous assistance in producing this manual.

PRELIMINARIES
ACCESSORY DRIVE BELTS 1-18
AIR CONDITIONING 1-21
CAN YOU DO IT? 1-2
DOES THE ENGINE NEED
 REBUILDING? 1-4
FORD ENGINES 1-3
GETTING AN ENGINE 1-3
HOSES 1-18
IS THE ENGINE WORTH
 REBUILDING? 1-4
LOCATION 1-2
PARTS 1-4
PREPARING THE WORK AREA 1-2
SPARK PLUG WIRES 1-17
SPARK PLUGS 1-10
TIMING BELTS 1-18
TO REBUILD OR NOT TO
 REBUILD 1-2
WHAT TYPE OF ENGINE? 1-2
SPECIFICATIONS CHARTS
STANDARD (ENGLISH) TO METRIC
 CONVERSION CHARTS 1-25

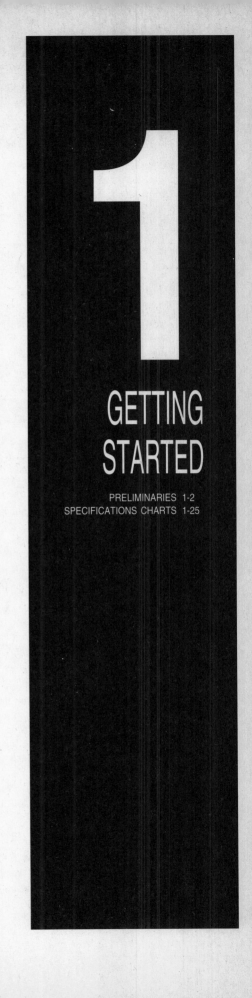

1

GETTING STARTED

PRELIMINARIES 1-2
SPECIFICATIONS CHARTS 1-25

PRELIMINARIES

To Rebuild or Not to Rebuild

That's a good question. The fact that you're looking at this book means that you're seriously considering it. In most cases, people decide to rebuild as a project, not out of necessity. If you are planning the job as a project, you'll probably do a better job than if you are working under the pressure of replacing a non-working engine in a vehicle that you are forced to do without in the meantime. The more relaxed and less hurried you are, the more fun you'll have. Things that may go wrong will have less of an impact since you'll have time to correct them. Delays won't be as stressful.

We've tried to gear the writing of this book towards the average do-it-yourselfer who has no specialized mechanical knowledge. An experienced mechanic in a well equipped shop doesn't need this book. We will prepare you for the job, take you through it step-by-step and make sure that you complete your rebuild successfully.

Can You Do It?

Probably the first real question you're asking yourself is, 'Can I really do this?' The answer is, sure, why not?

You don't have to be an experienced mechanic to rebuild an engine successfully. Really! If you have a basic set of hand tools — ratchets, sockets, wrenches, feeler gauges — and are at all familiar with their use, and, if you have or can get a few special tools, you should have few, if any, real problems.

Physical strength doesn't have much of a bearing on your ability to complete the job either. There is not a lot of heavy lifting involved. A friend is always helpful for lifting items such as manifolds and cylinder heads. Besides, anyone trying to lift heavy parts without either human or mechanical help is just asking for an injury. Using your head is always better than abusing your back!

Location

Hopefully, you have a garage or workshop. You can do the job in your basement, but that's not a good idea for several reasons among which are the job of getting heavy engine parts in and out of the basement, and the presence of flammable chemicals. Therefore, this book will assume that you're working in your garage.

Now, just about any garage will do. It doesn't have to be huge or especially well equipped. If your garage is at all like most peoples' it's more a storage room than anything else. Some garages are so junked up that you can barely walk from one side to the other. So, your first job is to clean the mess up.

You're going to need a clean work area with uncluttered floor space. You're also going to need at least one good, strong workbench, the top of which should be about 3 ft. x 6 ft., at least. Also, you'll need storage shelves to handle the parts, both used and new, as you remove, clean and install them.

Cleanliness is an important factor throughout the job, as is an uncluttered floor. You're going to be working around a large heavy engine, mounted on a workstand, so you don't need anything which would cause you to trip, or knock over the engine stand. You also don't need oil and grease on the floor, which can cause an accident, or worse, which you can track into the house!

Along with space and cleanliness are:

1. At least two 5 lbs. fire extinguishers suitable for chemical and electrical fires
2. A good electrical system which can handle the load of power tools
3. Bright, comfortable lighting
4. Adequate ventilation and
5. If working in the winter, a safe heating system.

Preparing the Work Area

Okay, get rid of the junk! Most of it you don't really need and some of it you probably didn't even know you had. Have a real garage sale! I'll let you handle that. You don't need my advice. If you're like most of us, you never throw anything away, so, just close your eyes and get it over with!

Okay, you're done? Good, let's get busy!

What Type of Engine?

Obviously, since you have this book, you'll want a Ford V8. That gives you about 20 choices! The primary determining factor will be the vehicle. If you want to do an even-up replacement, that is, you have a 302 and want to replace it with a 302, there's no decision to make. However, if you want to upgrade horsepower and torque there are several limiting factors.

1. The size of the engine compartment
2. The positions of the mounts
3. The bolt pattern of the transmission housing or clutch housing
4. The front suspension load limits, and, if you're really going up in engine size
5. The ability of the driveline and axle to take the torque

In other words, if you have a 302 Mustang you probably can't put a 460 in it without prohibitively expensive and time consuming work. That's going from a small block 60° V8 to a big block 90° V8. The engine compartment, mounts, transmission, suspension, driveline and axle will all have to be altered.

However, if you have a 302 F-150 pickup, a 460 conversion isn't such a bad thing. There's plenty of engine compartment room, mount adapter kits are available and transmission adapter kits are popular as are transmissions with big block bolt patterns. Heavy duty front springs are inexpensive and the driveline should take the additional torque without modification.

Your situation will fall somewhere in that range. To help you out, there are several companies that supply engine conversion kits, the most experienced of which is Advance Adapters Inc.

Also, check your state's emission laws regarding replacement engines. The engine you install in your vehicle may have to meet the emission regulations pertaining the the year of vehicle manufacture. So, if you have a 1982 car or truck and you want to rebuild and install a 429SCJ in it, you may have to extensively modify the engine to meet the emission requirements of your 1982 vehicle; something the engine wasn't designed for.

Ford Engines

As noted above, there are about 20 different Ford V8s, not counting those designed exclusively for medium and heavy duty trucks, nor do we include flat-heads like the venerable 239.

These engine range in displacement from 255 cubic inches to 460 cubic inches. Briefly, by displacement and years manufactured, they are:
- 255, 1979-82
- 260, 1962-64
- 289, 1963-68
- 302, 1968 to present
- 302 Boss, 1969-70
- 351W, 1969 to present
- 351C, 1970-74
- 351 Boss, 1970-74
- 351M, 1975-85
- 352, 1960-66
- 390, 1961-71
- 400, 1971-81
- 406, 1962-63
- 410, 1966-67
- 427, 1963-68
- 428, 1966-70
- 429 STD, 1968-73
- 429 CJ, 1969-70
- 429 SCJ, 1969-70
- 429 Boss (S), 1969
- 429 Boss (T), 1969-70
- 460, 1969 to present

All these engines fall into four engine families: two small block families, the 90° V and the 335 Series; and two big block families, the 385 Series and the FE Series.

90° V SMALL BLOCK

The 90° Series include the 255, 260, 289, 302 and 351W. The W stands for Windsor, the plant at which the engine is assembled. Except for the 351W, these engines are nearly identical and most parts interchange. The 351W is considerably different.

335 SERIES SMALL BLOCK

The 335 series include the 351C (C is for Cleveland), the 351M (M is for Modified Cleveland) and the 400. The 351M began life in 1975 and shares the same bore and stroke as all other 351s, but not much else. The M and C engines share almost no interchangeable parts. The 400 is a 351M with a longer stroke. The 351M and 400 share almost all parts.

FE SERIES BIG BLOCK

This group includes the 352, 390, 406, 410, 427 and 428 cid engines. All these engines share most parts with little or no modification. Obvious exceptions would be pistons and rings.

385 SERIES BIG BLOCK

This series is perhaps the most sought-after since it is made up of the 429 and 460. Rebuilds of these engines make for some extremely high horsepower and torque ratings. These two engines share most parts with the major exceptions being valve and pistons size differences. One interesting note is that the 351M/400 and the 429/460 use the same bellhousing bolt pattern, making upgrades from the smaller engines much easier!

Getting an Engine

If you're going to rebuild a worn or damaged engine you already have, step one is taken care of. Just be certain that the engine is rebuildable. Short of a cracked block, it should be. A good rule of thumb would be to remove a cylinder head and check the ridge at the top of the cylinders. An obvious, pronounced ridge would indicate that the cylinders may be worn beyond reboring and the engine may not be suitable for rebuilding. A cracked block may be obvious..........external leaks, visible cracks, etc., or may be harder to detect. Something which we will discuss later.

If you are beginning a project engine, and you need something to start with, you have several choices:

1. Go to your local junkyards, now called Automotive Parts Recyclers, and hunt for a good, rebuildable engine. Most junkyards are reputable and will tell you the type and year vehicle the engine came from. Many times the engine will still be in the car or truck and you can see it before you buy it. Buying this type of engine will usually also get you all the attached parts such as alternator, carburetor, fuel pump, power steering pump, starter, flywheel and many more. These parts can be used on your rebuilt engine, saved as spares, or used as cores (trade-ins) when you purchase new parts. Junkyard engines can run anywhere between $100.00 and $500.00 dollars.

2. Shop around your local auto parts retailers or rebuilders for a short block or bare block. A short block will be a reconditioned block, bored up to 0.030 in. overbore and comes with new core plugs and a crankshaft installed with ne bearings. All other parts will have to be purchased separately. The short block will cost over $500.00. A bare block is just what it sounds like: a clean, reconditioned, empty block with new core plugs.

3. Purchase a long block from your local rebuilder or parts retailer. A long block will usually come with a crankshaft, pistons and rings, and a camshaft and timing chain and gear set. Long blocks can cost $1500.00 or more. Also, long blocks don't really allow for rebuilding. You will simply be assembling them with the additional parts you'll have to buy.

Parts

For the purposes of this book, let's assume that you're going to purchase and rebuild a recycled (junkyard) engine as a project. You may have the idea that you'll replace everything. That's not a good philosophy unless you have lots of money and can't think of anything else to do with it. With rare exceptions, there are many perfectly good, reusable parts in any engine.

The best (cheapest) place to look for parts would be automotive parts catalogs. Check specialty magazines such as Motor Trend or Four Wheeler for aftermarket vendors. The ads in many of these magazines will contain descriptions and prices as well as ordering information. Delivery is timely and the quality is, usually, high with name brand parts being used.

If you like to see what you're buying first, or don't do catalog shopping, shop around at your local automotive aftermarket retailers for the best selection and quality.

There are many ways to buy parts. Complete rebuild kits are available which contain just about every part that you can think of. However, as stated above, you may not need all these parts. Rebuilding kits with various levels of parts are available. The fewer parts supplied, the less the cost. A good compromise is the kit which supplies all the gaskets and seals along with rings, main bearings, rod bearings, timing chain and gears, and an oil pump. This kit is probably the first thing to order, since these are parts which are replaced, no matter what the circumstances.

Don't decide on such major parts as pistons, rods, crankshaft or camshafts until the engine has been disassembled and the components inspected.

Is the Engine Worth Rebuilding?

The question of whether or not an engine is worth rebuilding is largely a subjective matter and one of personal worth. Is the engine a popular one, or is it an obsolete model? Are parts available? Will it get acceptable gas mileage once it is rebuilt? Is the car it's being put into worth keeping? Would it be less expensive to buy a new engine or a used engine from a junkyard? Or would it be simpler and less expensive to buy another car? If you have considered all these matters and more and have still decided to rebuild the engine, then it is time to decide if you need to rebuild it.

Does the Engine Need Rebuilding?

The usual yardstick for determining whether or not an engine needs rebuilding is mileage. As a very rough guideline, this is a useful method. Most engine rebuilders would consider 100,000 miles as the maximum mileage an average engine can go without a rebuild. The significant word here is average. There is absolutely no reason why a carefully maintained engine cannot easily exceed 100,000 miles and still provide excellent service. Conversely, a poorly maintained or abused engine will never get to 100,000 miles without help. This book, will omit discussion of the mileage factor and concentrate on the symptoms of an engine in trouble.

ISOLATING ENGINE PROBLEMS AND DETERMINING THEIR SEVERITY

Oil Consumption Problems

An engine's oil consumption is probably the single best indicator of the engine's internal condition. An engine's internal parts are tightly fitted, and an inevitable amount of wear occurs as the engine accumulates mileage. Because oil is used as the lubricating agent between the moving parts, excessive wear will invariably result in excessive oil consumption. The consequent question is, what constitutes excessive oil consumption? Any engine, no matter how new or how carefully built, will consume a certain amount of oil. Most rebuilders agree that an engine that uses no more than one quart of oil every 1000 miles is in good condition. This is essentially an optimum figure. An engine can use far more oil than this and still function on a daily basis. Just because the engine continues to run, however, does not mean that it does not need attention.

There are two ways an engine can lose oil. It can be leaking large amounts of oil due to a faulty gasket or external seal, or it can be losing oil 'out of the tailpipe.' The first condition is easy to spot. Simply park the car over a clean, dry area and let it idle for a short time. If any oil accumulates on the floor, the engine is leaking. Once you have fixed the leak, you can look for other causes of oil consumption.

Major internal oil consumption problems are generally caused by either worn or broken piston rings or severely worn valve guides. If oil can get past the oil control ring, it will enter the combustion chamber and be burned along with the fuel/air mixture. It can also be blown right past the rings into the crankcase, creating a condition called blow-by. Before the advent of emission controls, blow-by was vented from the crankcase into the atmosphere by means of a road draft tube or a crankcase vent. Emission-controlled engines have sealed crankcase ventilation systems, and vent excessive blow-by through the PCV valve, into the air cleaner, and eventually back into the combustion chamber. Oil that is at least partially burned in the combustion chamber along with the fuel/air mixture is responsible for the blue smoke that comes from the tailpipe of an engine that needs an overhaul. When you see this kind of 'death smoke' coming from an engine, you know it is time for an overhaul. Ways to isolate and determine piston ring condition will be discussed later in this chapter.

Severely worn valve guides are the other major internal cause of excessive oil consumption. A worn valve guide will allow oil to get past the valve stem and into the combustion chamber or into the exhaust port. In either case, excessive amounts of oil will be lost. Generally speaking, by the time valve guides wear to this extent, the piston rings will be badly worn as well. In fact, rings frequently wear out before valve guides, depending on how often the oil is changed. But do not mistake worn valve stem seals for worn valve guides. Worn seals will create exactly the same conditions as worn guides. So always check the seals before worrying about the guides, especially if the engine has less than 75,000 miles on it. Ways to spot worn guides and seals will be discussed later in this chapter.

Whether it is caused by worn rings, worn valve guides, or anything else, the bottom line on oil consumption is this: if the engine is using a quart or more of oil every 500 miles, it needs some very careful attention. If you discover that the cause of the oil consumption is an internal problem, it is time for a rebuild.

Engine Noises and Their Possible Causes

One of the most common reasons for rebuilding an engine is unusual or excessive engine noise. It is, however, extremely difficult to diagnose engine condition from noises alone. Engine noises are a useful indicator of engine condition, provided other factors, such as oil consumption, test instrument results, and performance loss problems are taken into account. This section will help you to determine which engine noises indicate serious trouble and which do not.

ACCESSORY NOISES

If the engine begins to make an unusual noise, the very, first things to check are the engine accessories. Water pumps, alternators, air pumps, and air-conditioning compressors can all make noises that are easily mistaken for more serious engine noises. There is only one sure way to check possible accessory noises, and that is to remove the belt that drives that particular accessory. Of course, most belts drive more than one accessory, but at least you will have narrowed the field. Worn bushings or bearings in any of these accessories will often make a knocking noise that easily can be mistaken for a more serious knock. If you have removed all the belts and the noises remain, the noise is not in the accessories.

CRANKSHAFT OR BOTTOM END NOISES

Crankshaft noises are generally much heavier in volume and tone than other engine noises. They will also occur at engine speed; that is, the noise will rise and fall in perfect synchronization with engine speed. Worn crankshaft bearings will produce an audible knock when the engine is idling, especially if the idle is uneven. If you suspect a bottom end noise, disconnect each spark plug lead one at a time and listen for changes in the noise. If the noise decreases or goes away with a particular plug disconnected, you have located the cylinder and/or bearing with the noise.

PISTON NOISES OR PISTON SLAP

Piston slap is caused by excessive clearance between the piston skirt and the cylinder wall. Generally, piston slap decreases as the engine warms up and the piston expands, so listen for it when the engine is cold. As a general rule, piston slap will create a hollow dull sound, much lower in intensity than a crankshaft noise. A more accurate test of piston slap is to accelerate the engine from low speed under a load; that is, apply a lot of throttle, but do not shift to a lower gear. If the noise increases in intensity, you have located the problem.

You can also check for piston slap by disconnecting each spark plug in turn, or by retarding the spark. If all of the pistons have excessive clearance, retarding the spark should reduce the noise by reducing the load on the pistons. Disconnecting the spark plug leads will do the same thing for each individual piston. Keep in mind, however, that other engine noises are also affected by these operations.

It is sometimes possible to temporarily eliminate piston and ring noises by pouring a small amount of very heavy oil into the cylinder (through the spark plug holes). Crank the engine

over (coil wire disconnected) until the oil works past the rings. Start the engine. If the noise has gone away, piston slap is the probable diagnosis.

PISTON PIN NOISES

Excessive piston pin clearance will frequently create a sharp metallic noise or clatter that is usually most audible when the engine is idling. You can check for excessive pin clearance in the same manner as you do for piston slap. Retard the spark and listen for any reduction in the noise. Generally, retarding the spark will reduce the intensity of the knock. Then short out each spark plug in turn. If the piston pin is worn, the sharp metallic knock should become more, not less, pronounced in that particular cylinder. Remember that the same problem exists here that exists with all other internal engine noises: if one component is worn out other components are probably worn out and making noise as well. So keep in mind that the engine is likely making more than one noise, especially if it has well over 100,000 miles on it.

VALVE TRAIN NOISES

Because the camshaft and all related valve train components operate at one-half crankshaft speed, any noise coming from the valve train will occur at one-half the frequency of other noises. If the engine is equipped with hydraulic valve lifters, a sharp rapping or clicking noise probably indicates a worn or collapsed lifter. A somewhat lighter noise may indicate excessive clearance between the rocker arm and the valve stem. Sometimes this clearance is adjustable, and sometimes it is not. (This is only the case with hydraulic lifters; solid lifter valve trains are always adjustable.) Engines equipped with solid lifters will inevitably make a certain amount of noise. It is simply a question of experience and familiarity with a particular engine that will enable you to determine whether or not the noise is excessive.

It is much easier to detect valve train noises with a mechanic's stethoscope or a large, long screwdriver. Place the tip of the screwdriver or stethoscope against the valve cover. Any valve train noises will be greatly amplified. Place the stethoscope against the valve cover at regular intervals along its length, and you may be able to isolate the noise.

If you definitely suspect a valve train noise, and have an engine that is equipped with adjustable rockers, the next step is to remove the valve cover or camshaft cover and check the valve clearance. The valve clearance should be checked as a normal part of a good tune-up anyway.

If you find that the valve clearances are correct and you still hear excessive valve train noises, the engine may have severely worn lifters or a worn camshaft. If you cannot adjust the excessive clearance out of the valve train, the engine's rocker arms are probably worn out. And remember that worn rockers usually mean worn valve stems or lifters as well.

CONNECTING ROD BEARING NOISES

Connecting rod bearing noises are similar to main bearing noises in that they occur in exact synchronization with engine speed. However, they are much lighter in intensity than main bearing noises. In terms of noise intensity, they fall somewhere between valve train noises and main bearing noises. Check for rod bearing noises by shorting out each cylinder in turn and listening for a reduction in the noise. Remember, you may not

ENGINE NOISES

Possible Cause	Correction

NOISY VALVES

Constant loud clacking, light clicking or intermittent noise indicates faulty hydraulic valve lifters (tappets), or mal-adjusted mechanical tappets.

Possible Cause	Correction
1. High or low oil level in crankcase.	Check for correct oil level.
2. Low oil pressure.	Check engine oil level.
3. Dirt in tappets.	Clean tappets.
4. Bend push rods.	Install new push rods.
5. Worn rocker arms.	Inspect oil supply to rockers.
6. Worn tappets.	Install new tappets.
7. Worn valve guides.	Replace guides if removable or ream and install new valves.
8. Excessive run-out of valve seats or valve faces.	Grind valve seats and valves.
9. Incorrect tappet lash.	Adjust to specifications.

CONNECTING ROD NOISE

A metallic knock when idling or retarding engine speed, which disappears under load indicates worn or loose connecting rod bearings. The bearing at fault can be found by shorting out the spark plugs one at a time. The noise will disappear when the cylinder with the faulty bearing is shorted out.

Possible Cause	Correction
1. Insufficient oil supply	Check engine oil level.
2. Low oil pressure.	Check engine oil level.
3. Thin or diluted oil.	Change oil to correct viscosity.
4. Excessive bearing clearance.	Measure bearings for correct clearance or failures.
5. Connecting rod journals out-of-round.	Remove crankshaft and regrind journals.
6. Misaligned connecting rods.	Remove bent connecting rods.

MAIN BEARING NOISE

A main bearing knock is more of a bump than a knock, and it can be located by shorting out the plugs near it. The noise is loudest when the engine is "lugging" (pulling hard at slow speed). The sound is heavier and more dull than a connecting rod knock.

Possible Cause	Correction
1. Insufficient oil supply.	Check engine oil level. Inspect oil pump relief valve damper and spring.
2. Low oil pressure.	Check engine oil level.
3. Thin or diluted oil.	Change the oil to correct viscosity.
4. Excessive bearing clearance.	Check the bearings for correct clearances or failures.
5. Excessive end-play.	Check thrust main bearing for wear on flanges.
6. Crankshaft journals out-of-round or worn.	Remove crankshaft and regrind journals.
7. Loose flywheel.	Tighten correctly.

OTHER ENGINE NOISES

Possible Cause	Correction
1. A sharp rap at idle speed indicates a loose piston pin. The pin at fault can be found by shorting out the spark plugs one at a time. The noise will disappear when the cylinder with the faulty pin is shorted out.	Replace piston pin.
2. A flat slap, when advancing engine speed under load, indicates a loose piston.	Replace piston and rebore cylinder block if necessary.

be able to eliminate the noise entirely, but you will be able to reduce it considerably. A stethoscope or long screwdriver held against the block is a big help, provided you can reach it.

DETONATION AND PREIGNITION

Detonation and preignition are not the same thing, but both can create the same symptoms, and both can severely damage an engine's performance. In addition, both can create a rapid metallic rattle, generally called 'ping' or 'spark knock.' Preignition occurs when the combustion process is initiated by any source other than the spark plug. In other words, preignition is caused by the presence of any hot spot in the combustion chamber. A piece of glowing carbon, the sharp edge of a valve, a hot spot on the piston crown--any of these can cause premature ignition of the fuel/air mixture. As a result, the fuel/air mixture ignites while the piston is on the way up in the cylinder on the compression stroke. The resultant pressure attempts to force the piston back down while it is still trying to come up. This places a tremendous load on the piston, connecting rod, and the bearings, as well as resulting in a sharp knocking sound.

To understand detonation, you must remember that the ignition of the fuel/air mixture is not an explosion, but a very rapid, controlled burning process. The spark plug ignites the fuel/air mixture, which spreads very rapidly out in a specific pattern. This is what occurs during normal ignition of the fuel/air charge. Detonation occurs when part of the charge auto-ignites from excessive combustion chamber heat and pressure. This explosion spreads out and meets the oncoming flame front created by normal ignition. The resultant collision creates extremely high combustion chamber pressures, places great strain on the piston, connecting rod and bearings, eats away metal where it occurs, and causes a sharp knocking sound.

A number of things can cause preignition or detonation, including excessive carbon deposits or poor quality fuel. For the purposes of this book, it should be noted that excessively high combustion chamber temperatures or pressures can be detected by a careful spark plug analysis. If the engine is pinging or rattling, and you suspect it might be preignition or detonation, the first thing to do is to analyze the spark plugs and give the car a good tune-up. Pay particular attention to

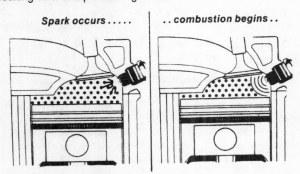
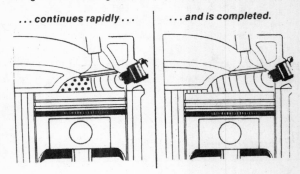

Normal combustion (Courtesy Champion Spark Plug Co.)

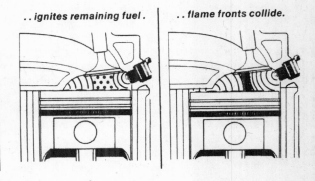

Preignition (Courtesy Champion Spark Plug Co.)

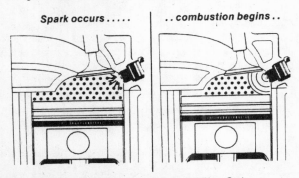
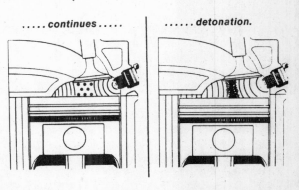

Detonation (Courtesy Champion Spark Plug Co.)

87931002

correct ignition timing and spark plug heat range. In the end, you may find that the car is pinging and rattling simply because of poor quality gas, a common problem today.

If you find that the car is in a good state of tune, and you have switched to high octane gas but still have rattling noises coming from the engine, the problem may be excessive carbon deposits on the valves or on the tops of the pistons. There are gasoline additives on the market that will loosen carbon deposits. It is not uncommon, however, for these additives to work all too well, loosening the carbon from the piston crown and the valves and allowing it to bounce around in the combustion chamber. The point to remember is that carbon is a symptom of a problem rather than the problem itself. This does not mean that carbon buildup cannot cause problems, only that simply getting rid of the carbon does not necessarily solve the problem. Frequently, carbon deposits are caused by vehicle usage: if you do a lot of low-speed driving and stop-and-go driving, you stand a good chance of developing carbon deposits in the engine.

Carbon deposits can also be caused by worn piston rings or valve stems, allowing oil to get into the combustion chamber where a certain amount of it will be glazed onto the valves or the piston crown by combustion chamber heat. Carbon deposits can cause knocks that easily may be mistaken for more serious noises. The only positive way to determine whether or not the engine has developed excessive carbon deposits is to remove the cylinder heads, but that is going far beyond simple diagnosis.

PERFORMANCE LOSS PROBLEMS AND POSSIBLE CAUSES

▶ See Figure 1

The possible causes of poor performance are almost limitless, but this book will discuss only serious internal engine problems that will directly and obviously affect engine performance. If, for instance, the engine is using a lot more gas and showing serious power losses, it could have a blown head gasket or a warped cylinder head. If the engine is using coolant but there is no leak, that may also indicate a blown head gasket or warped head. Check for the presence of water in the oil or oil in the water. If coolant is getting into the oil supply, oil on the dipstick will be whitish and foamy. The presence of oil in the cooling system will be immediately obvious because there will be an oily scum apparent when the radiator cap is removed. Use a pressure tester to locate any coolant leaks.

Burned valves will definitely affect an engine's performance. Keep in mind, however, that larger, more powerful engines show less effect from a burned valve than a small engine. In other words, a burned valve on a four-cylinder car is immediately apparent, but you may not notice the power loss on a large V8. A compression test will reveal a burned valve. Vacuum gauge readings will also detect burned valves, assuming that the engine is in a good state of tune to begin with.

A worn timing chain or a worn camshaft can also drastically affect performance, yet not be noticeable when the engine is idling. Unfortunately, it is almost impossible to detect this problem with external diagnosis. A badly worn timing chain may

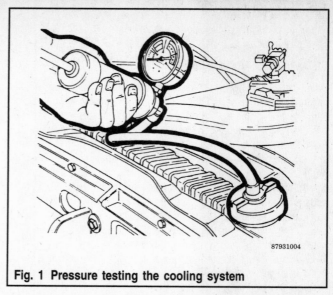

87931004

Fig. 1 Pressure testing the cooling system

give a late valve timing reading on the vacuum gauge, but it is entirely possible that it may not.

USING TEST INSTRUMENTS TO DETERMINE ENGINE CONDITION

Test instruments are the most reliable and accurate way to determine an engine's condition. There are three very important tests that you must perform on any engine before you decide to rebuild it. They are the vacuum gauge readings, compression test results, and spark plug analysis.

Vacuum Gauge Readings
▶ See Figure 2

A vacuum gauge simply measures how well the engine is pumping air. To use it, locate a vacuum gauge fitting on the intake manifold and connect the vacuum gauge to the fitting. Variations in atmospheric pressure will affect vacuum gauge readings, so remember that the action of the needle is more important than the actual reading.

Checking Engine Compression
▶ See Figure 3

A noticeable lack of engine power, excessive oil consumption and/or poor fuel mileage measured over an extended period are all indicators of internal engine wear. Worn piston rings, scored or worn cylinder bores, blown head gaskets, sticking or burnt valves and worn valve seats are all possible culprits here. A check of each cylinder's compression will help you locate the problems.

As mentioned earlier, a screw-in type compression gauge is more accurate that the type you simply hold against the spark plug hole, although it takes slightly longer to use. It's worth it to obtain a more accurate reading. Follow the procedures below.

1. Warm up the engine to normal operating temperature.
2. Remove all the spark plugs.
3. Disconnect the high tension lead from the ignition coil and ground it.

Normal engine

Late ignition timing

Stuck throttle valve, leaking intake manifold or carburetor gaskets

Leaking head gasket

Worn valve guides

Burnt or leaking valves

Sticking valves

Weak valve springs

Carburetor needs adjustment

Late valve timing

Choked muffler

Normal engine—(opened and closed throttle, rings and valves OK)

87931003

Fig. 2 Analyzing the engine with a vacuum gauge

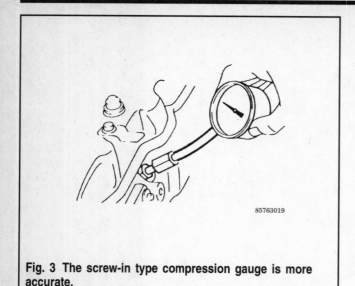

Fig. 3 The screw-in type compression gauge is more accurate.

4. Screw the compression gauge into the no.1 spark plug hole until the fitting is snug.

✳✳WARNING

Be careful not to crossthread the plug hole. On aluminum cylinder heads use extra care, as the threads in these heads are easily ruined.

5. Fully open the throttle either by operating the carburetor throttle linkage by hand or by having an assistant floor the accelerator pedal.

6. While you read the compression gauge, ask the assistant to crank the engine two or three times in short bursts using the ignition switch or a remote starter switch.

7. Read the compression gauge at the end of each series of cranks, and record the highest of these readings. Repeat this procedure for each of the engine's cylinders. Compare the highest reading of each cylinder.

The difference between any two cylinders should be no more than 12-14 pounds.

8. If a cylinder is unusually low, pour a tablespoon of clean engine oil into the cylinder through the spark plug hole and repeat the compression test. If the compression comes up after adding the oil, it appears that the cylinder's piston rings or bore are damaged or worn. If the pressure remains low, the valves may not be seating properly (a valve job is needed), or the head gasket may be blown near that cylinder. If compression in any two adjacent cylinders is low, and if the addition of oil doesn't help the compression, there is leakage past the head gasket. Oil and coolant water in the combustion chamber can result from this problem. There may be evidence of water droplets on the engine dipstick when a head gasket has blown.

CHECKING THE RESULTS

Now that you have all your compression readings, it is time to decide what they mean. Depending on the engine, you may observe readings anywhere from 80 to 200 or even 250 psi. Specific readings, however, are not as important as the spread between cylinders. In other words, no one cylinder should be appreciably lower than any other. All cylinder readings should be within a range of 25 percent. If, for example, the highest reading is 100 psi and the lowest is 75 psi, the compression readings are within tolerance.

If the compression readings do not fall within this range, the first thing to do is to perform a 'wet test.' Squirt a teaspoonful or two of heavy oil into the cylinder and give it a couple of minutes to seep down around the rings. Then recheck the compression. If the readings improve appreciably, the piston rings (at least) are worn out. You may also have worn pistons and cylinder bores.

If you discover two adjacent cylinders with low compression, chances are that there is a blown head gasket or a warped cylinder head--probably a blown gasket-between the two cylinders. Keep in mind that there should be other indications of a blown head gasket, such as water in the oil or oil in the water. It is also possible for a blown head gasket to affect only one cylinder. Run the engine to operating temperature and then carefully remove the radiator cap. If you see a lot of bubbles, that is another indication of a blown gasket.

If compression buildup is erratic on any of the cylinders, the problem could be sticky valves. Check for this condition by removing the valve or camshaft cover and connecting a timing light to the spark plug lead of the suspect cylinder. Aim the timing light at the valves of the cylinder in question. Loosen the distributor and vary the timing gradually in order to observe the motion of the valve or valves. If the valve appears to be operating erratically, it could possibly be sticking. Keep in mind that it is a tricky test (not to mention a messy one), and it takes a lot of experience to detect a sticky valve.

Spark Plugs

▶ **See Figure 4**

A typical spark plug consists of a metal shell surrounding a ceramic insulator. A metal electrode extends downward through the center of the insulator and protrudes a small distance. Located at the end of the plug and attached to the side of the outer metal shell is the side electrode. The side electrode bends in at a 90 degree angle so that its tip is even with, and parallel to, the tip of the center electrode. The distance between these two electrodes (measured in thousandths of an inch) is called the spark plug gap. The spark plug does not actually produce a spark but merely provides a gap across which the current can arc. The coil produces anywhere from 20,000 to 40,000 volts which travels to the distributor where it is distributed through the spark plug wires to the spark plugs. The current passes along the center electrode and jumps the gap to the side electrode, and, in so doing, ignites the air/fuel mixture in the combustion chamber.

SPARK PLUG HEAT RANGE

▶ **See Figure 5**

Spark plug heat range is the ability of the plug to dissipate heat. The longer the insulator (or the farther it extends into the engine), the hotter the plug will operate; the shorter the insulator the cooler it will operate. A plug that absorbs little heat and remains too cool will quickly accumulate deposits of oil and carbon since it is not hot enough to burn them off. This leads to plug fouling and consequently to misfiring. A plug that ab-

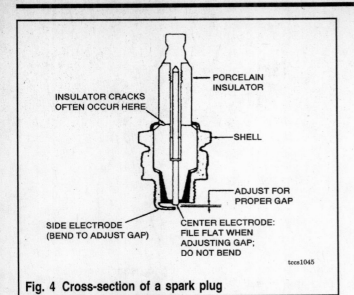

Fig. 4 Cross-section of a spark plug

INSULATOR CRACKS OFTEN OCCUR HERE

PORCELAIN INSULATOR

SHELL

ADJUST FOR PROPER GAP

SIDE ELECTRODE (BEND TO ADJUST GAP)

CENTER ELECTRODE: FILE FLAT WHEN ADJUSTING GAP; DO NOT BEND

tccs1045

THE SHORTER THE PATH, THE FASTER THE HEAT IS DISSIPATED AND THE COOLER THE PLUG

HEAVY LOADS, HIGH SPEEDS

SHORT Insulator Tip
Fast Heat Transfer
LOWER Heat Range
COLD PLUG

THE LONGER THE PATH, THE SLOWER THE HEAT IS DISSIPATED AND THE HOTTER THE PLUG

SHORT TRIP STOP-AND-GO

LONG Insulator Tip
Slow Heat Transfer
HIGHER Heat Range
HOT PLUG

tccs1046

Fig. 5 Spark plug heat range

sorbs too much heat will have no deposits, but, due to the excessive heat, the electrodes will burn away quickly and in some instances, preignition may result. Preignition takes place when plug tips get so hot that they glow sufficiently to ignite the fuel/air mixture before the actual spark occurs. This early ignition will usually cause a pinging sound during low speeds and heavy loads.

The general rule of thumb for choosing the correct heat range when picking a spark plug is: if most of your driving is long distance, high speed travel, use a colder plug; if most of your driving is stop and go, use a hotter plug. Original equipment plugs are compromise plugs, but most people never have occasion to change their plugs from the factory-recommended heat range.

REMOVAL

◆ **See Figures 6 and 7**

When you're removing spark plugs, you should work on one at a time. Don't start by removing the plug wires all at once because unless you number them, or they're going to get mixed up. On some models though, it will be more convenient for you to remove all the wires before you start to work on the plugs. If this is necessary, take a minute before you begin and number the wires with tape before you take them off. The time you spend doing this will pay off later when it comes time to reconnect the wires to the plugs.

1. Disconnect the negative battery cable from the negative battery terminal.

2. Twist the spark plug boot slightly in either direction to break loose the seal, then remove the boot from the plug. You may also use a plug wire removal tool designed especially for this purpose. Do not pull on the wire itself or you may separate the plug connector from the end of the wire. When the wire has been removed, take a wire brush and clean the area around the plug. An evaporative spray cleaner such as those designed for brake applications will also work well. Make sure

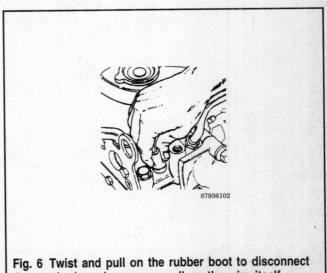

87936102

Fig. 6 Twist and pull on the rubber boot to disconnect the spark plug wires; never pull on the wire itself

that all the foreign material is removed so that none will enter the cylinder after the plug has been removed.

➡**If you have access to a compressor, use the air hose to blow all material away from the spark plug bores before loosening the plug. Always protect your eyes with safety glasses when using compressed air.**

3. Remove the plug using the proper size socket, extensions, and universals as necessary. Be careful to hold the socket or the extension close to the plug with your free hand as this will help lessen the possibility of applying a shear force which might snap the spark plug in half.

4. If removing the plug is difficult, drip some penetrating oil on the plug threads, allow it to work, then remove the plug. Also, be sure that the socket is straight on the plug, especially on those hard to reach plugs. Again, if the socket is cocked to one side, a shear force may be applied to the plug and could snap the plug in half.

INSPECTION

▶ **See Figures 8, 9 and 10**

Check the plugs for deposits and wear. If they are not going to be replaced, clean the plugs thoroughly. Remember that any kind of deposit will decrease the efficiency of the plug. Plugs can be cleaned on a spark plug cleaning machine, which can sometimes be found in service stations, or you can do an acceptable job of cleaning with a stiff brush. If the plugs are cleaned, the electrodes must be filed flat. Use an ignition points file, not an emery board or the like, which will leave deposits. The electrodes must be filed perfectly flat with sharp edges; rounded edges reduce the spark plug voltage by as much as 50%.

Check and adjust the spark plug gap immediately before installation. The ground electrode (the L-shaped one connected to the body of the plug) must be parallel to the center electrode and the specified size gauge (see Tune-Up Specifications in Chapter 6) should pass through the gap with a slight drag.

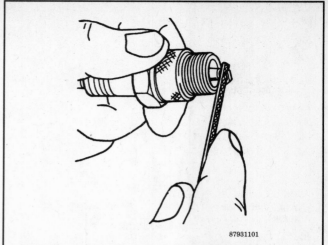

Fig. 8 Spark plugs that are in good condition can be filed and re-used

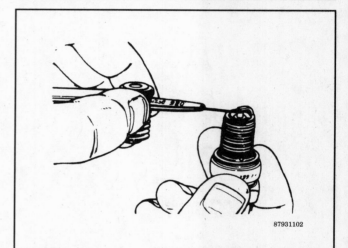

Fig. 9 Always use a wire gauge to check the electrode gap on used plugs

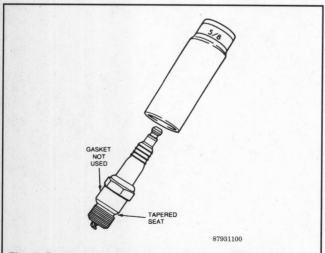

Fig. 7 Remove the spark plug using a suitable socket and driver

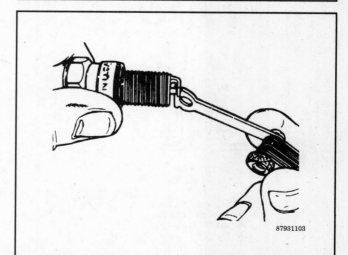

Fig. 10 Adjust the gap by bending the side electrode very slightly towards or away from the center electrode

Always check the gap on new plugs, too; since they are not always set correctly at the factory.

➡**NEVER adjust the gap on a used platinum type spark plug.**

Do not use a flat feeler gauge when measuring the gap on used plugs, because the reading may be inaccurate. The ground electrode on a used plug is often rounded on the face closest to the center electrode. A flat gauge will not be able to accurately measure this distance as well as a wire gauge. Most gapping tools usually have a bending tool attached. This tool may be used to adjust the side electrode until the proper distance is obtained. Never attempt to move or bend the center electrode or spark plug damage will likely occur. Also, be careful not to bend the side electrode too far or too often; if it is overstressed it may weaken and break off within the engine, requiring removal of the cylinder head to retrieve it.

CHECKING SPARK PLUGS

▶ **See Figure 11**

The single most accurate indicator of the engine's condition is the firing end of the spark plugs. Although the spark plug has no moving parts. It is exposed to more stress than any other engine part. It is required to deliver a high-voltage spark thousands of times a minute, at precisely timed intervals, under widely varying conditions. Because it is inside the combustion chamber, it is exposed to the corrosive effects from chemical additives in fuel and oil and to extremes of temperature and pressure. The terminal end may be as cold as ice, but the firing tip will be exposed to flame temperatures in excess of 3000°F (1650°C).

READING SPARK PLUGS

A close examination of spark plugs will provide many clues to the condition of an engine. Keeping the plugs in order according to cylinder location will make the diagnosis even more effective and accurate. The following diagrams illustrate some of the conditions that spark plugs will reveal.

APPEARANCE

▶ **See Figure 12**

This plug is typical of one operating normally. The insulator nose varies from a light tan to grayish color with slight electrode wear. The presence of slight deposits is normal on used plugs and will have no adverse effect or engine performance. The spark plug heat range is correct for the engine and the engine is running correctly.

tccs2135

Fig. 12 A normally worn spark plug should have light tan or grey deposits on the firing tip

CAUSE

Properly running engine.

RECOMMENDATION

Before reinstalling this plug, the electrodes should be cleaned and filed square. Set the gap to specifications If the plug has been in service for more than 10,000 to 12,000 miles, the entire set should probably be replaced with a fresh set of the same heat range.

APPEARANCE

▶ **See Figure 13**

The firing end of the plug is covered with a wet, oily coating.

Tracking Arc
High voltage arcs between a fouling deposit on the insulator tip and spark plug shell. This ignites the fuel/air mixture at some point along the insulator tip, retarding the ignition timing which causes a power and fuel loss.

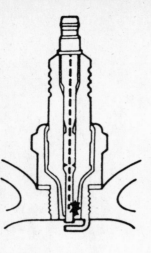

Wide Gap
Spark plug electrodes are worn so that the high voltage charge cannot arc across the electrodes. Improper gapping of electrodes on new or "cleaned" spark plugs could cause a similar condition. Fuel remains unburned and a power loss results.

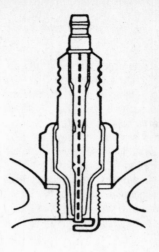

Flashover
A damaged spark plug boot, along with dirt and moisture, could permit the high voltage charge to short over the insulator to the spark plug shell or the engine. AC's buttress insulator design helps prevent high voltage flashover.

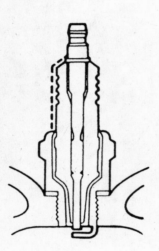

Fouled Spark Plug
Deposits that have formed on the insulator tip may become conductive and provide a "shunt" path to the shell. This prevents the high voltage from arcing between the electrodes. A power and fuel loss is the result.

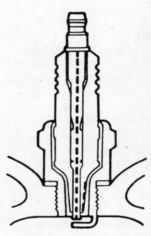

Bridged Electrodes
Fouling deposits between the electrodes "ground out" the high voltage needed to fire the spark plug. The arc between the electrodes does not occur and the fuel air mixture is not ignited. This causes a power loss and exhausting of raw fuel.

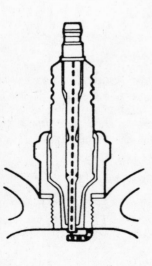

Cracked Insulator
A crack in the spark plug insulator could cause the high voltage charge to "ground out." Here, the spark does not jump the electrode gap and the fuel air mixture is not ignited. This causes a power loss and raw fuel is exhausted.

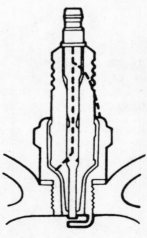

tccs2001

Fig. 11 Used spark plugs which show damage may indicate engine problems

tccs2138

Fig. 13 An oil fouled spark plug indicates an engine with worn piston rings and/or bad valve seals allowing excessive oil to enter the combustion chamber

CAUSE

The problem is poor oil control. On high-mileage engines, oil is leaking past the rings or valve guides into the combustion chamber. A common cause also is a plugged PCV valve, and a ruptured fuel pump diaphragm also can cause this condition. Oil-fouled plugs such as these are often found in new or recently overhauled engines, before normal oil control is achieved, and can be cleaned and reinstalled.

RECOMMENDATION

A hotter spark plug may temporarily relieve the problem, but the engine is probably in need of repair.

APPEARANCE

▶ See Figure 14

Carbon fouling is easily identified by the presence of dry, soft, black, sooty deposits.

tccs2136

Fig. 14 A carbon fouled plug, identified by soft, sooty, black deposits, may indicate an improperly tuned engine. Check the air cleaner, ignition components and engine control systems

CAUSE

Changing the heat range can often lead to carbon fouling, as can prolonged slow, stop-and-start driving. If the heat range is correct, carbon fouling can be attributed to a rich fuel mixture, sticking choke, clogged air cleaner, worn breaker points, retarded timing, or low compression. If only one or two plugs are carbon-fouled, check for corroded or cracked wires on the affected plugs. Also look for cracks in the distributor cap between the towers of affected cylinders.

RECOMMENDATION

After the problem is corrected, these plugs can be cleaned and reinstalled if not worn severely.

APPEARANCE

▶ See Figure 15

Splash deposits occur in varying degrees as spotty deposits on the insulator.

tccs2140

Fig. 15 A bridged gap or almost bridged spark plug, identified by a build-up of deposits between the electrodes, caused by excessive carbon or oil build-up on the plug

tccs2139

Fig. 16 This plug has been left in the engine too long causing an excessive gap between the electrodes. Plugs with an excessive gap can cause misfiring, stumble, poor fuel economy and a lack of power

CAUSE

By-products of combustion have accumulated on pistons and valves because of a delayed tune-up. Following tune-up or during hard acceleration, the deposits loosen and are thrown against the hot surface of the plug. If sufficient deposits accumulate, misfiring can occur.

RECOMMENDATION

These plugs can be cleaned, gapped, and reinstalled.

APPEARANCE

▶ See Figure 16

Excessive gap.

CAUSE

During hard, fast acceleration, plug temperatures rise suddenly. Deposits from normal combustion have no chance to burn off; instead, they melt on the insulator forming an electrically conductive coating that causes misfiring.

RECOMMENDATION

Glazed plugs are not easily cleaned. They should be replaced with a fresh set of plugs of the correct heat range. If the condition recurs, using plugs with a heat range one step colder may cure the problem.

APPEARANCE

▶ See Figure 17

Detonation is usually characterized by a broken plug insulator.

Fig. 17 A physically damaged spark plug may be evidence of severe detonation in that cylinder. Watch that cylinder carefully since continued detonation will not only damage the plug, but could also damage the engine

CAUSE

A portion of the fuel charge will begin to burn spontaneously from the increased heat following ignition. The explosion that results applies extreme pressure to engine components, frequently damaging spark plugs and pistons.

Detonation can result from over-advanced ignition timing, inferior gasoline (low octane), lean fuel/air mixture, poor carburetion, engine lugging, or an increase in compression ratio due to combustion chamber deposits or engine modification.

RECOMMENDATION

Replace the plugs after correcting the problem.

Spark Plug Wires

TESTING

▶ **See Figures 18 and 19**

Visually check the spark plug cables for burns cuts, or breaks in the insulation. Check the boots and the nipples on the distributor cap and coil. Replace any damaged wiring.

Every 50,000 miles (80,000 Km) or 60 months, the resistance of the wires should be checked with an ohmmeter. Wires with excessive resistance will cause misfiring, and may make the engine difficult to start in damp weather.

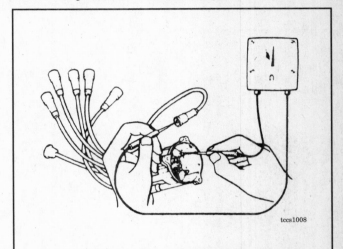

Fig. 18 Checking plug wire resistance through the distributor cap with an ohmmeter

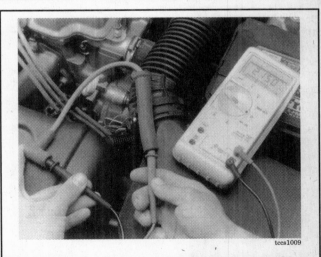

Fig. 19 Checking individual plug wire resistance with an digital ohmmeter

Accessory Drive Belts

INSPECTION

▶ **See Figures 20, 21, 22, 23 and 24**

Inspect the belts for signs of glazing or cracking. A glazed belt will be perfectly smooth from slippage, while a good belt will have a slight texture of fabric visible. Cracks will usually start at the inner edge of the belt and run outward. All worn or damaged drive belts should be replaced immediately. It is best to replace all drive belts at one time, as a preventive maintenance measure, during this service operation.

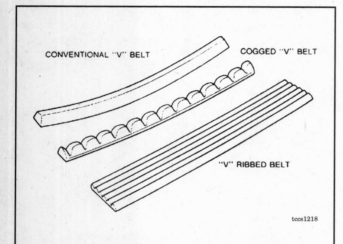

Fig. 20 There are typically 3 types of accessory drive belts found on vehicles today

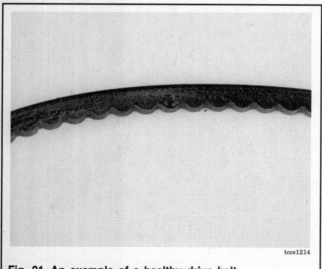

Fig. 21 An example of a healthy drive belt

Timing Belts

INSPECTION

▶ **See Figures 25, 26, 27, 28, 29 and 30**

Timing belts are found with increasing frequency on most domestic and imported vehicles. It is important to periodically check the condition of the timing belt, but when overhauling and engine equipped with a timing belt, always change it. A broken timing belt can cause major internal damage.

Hoses

INSPECTION

▶ **See Figures 31, 32, 33 and 34**

Upper and lower radiator hoses along with the heater hoses should be checked for deterioration, leaks and loose hose clamps at least every 15,000 miles (24,000 km). It is also wise to check the hoses periodically in early spring and at the beginning of the fall or winter when you are performing other maintenance. A quick visual inspection could discover a weakened hose which might have left you stranded if it had remained unrepaired.

Whenever you are checking the hoses, make sure the engine and cooling system are cold. Visually inspect for cracking, rotting or collapsed hoses, and replace as necessary. Run your hand along the length of the hose. If a weak or swollen spot is noted when squeezing the hose wall, the hose should be replaced.

REMOVAL & INSTALLATION

1. Remove the radiator pressure cap.

❋❋CAUTION

Never remove the pressure cap while the engine is running, or personal injury from scalding hot coolant or steam may result. If possible, wait until the engine has cooled to remove the pressure cap. If this is not possible, wrap a thick cloth around the pressure cap and turn it slowly to the stop. Step back while the pressure is released from the cooling system. When you are sure all the pressure has been released, use the cloth to turn and remove the cap.

2. Position a clean container under the radiator and/or engine draincock or plug, then open the drain and allow the cooling system to drain to an appropriate level. For some upper hoses, only a little coolant must be drained. To remove

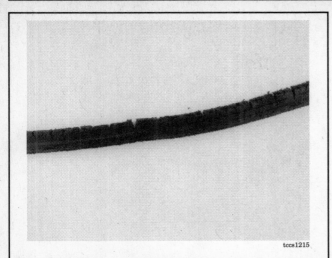

Fig. 22 Deep cracks in this belt will cause flex, building up heat that will eventually lead to belt failure

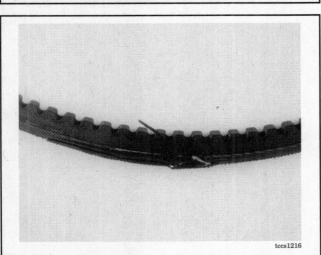

Fig. 23 The cover of this belt is worn, exposing the critical reinforcing cords to excessive wear

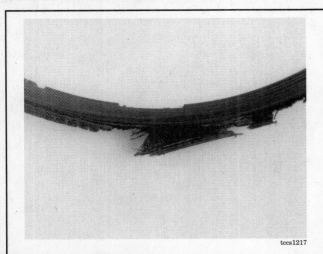

Fig. 24 Installing too wide a belt can result in serious belt wear and/or breakage

Fig. 25 Do not bend, twist or turn the timing belt inside out. Never allow oil, water or steam to contact the belt

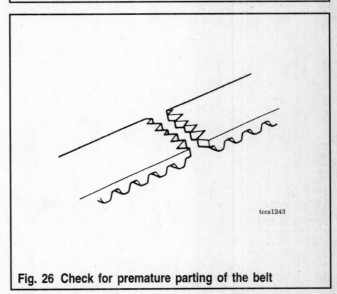

Fig. 26 Check for premature parting of the belt

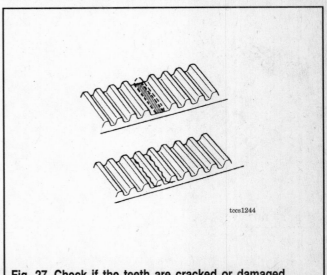

Fig. 27 Check if the teeth are cracked or damaged

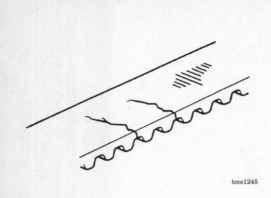

Fig. 28 Look for noticeable cracks or wear on the belt face

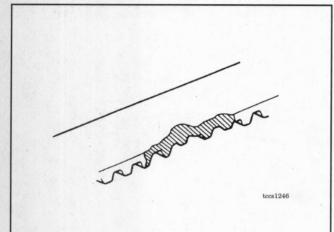

Fig. 29 You may only have damage on one side of the belt; if so, the guide could be the culprit

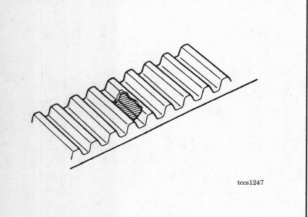

Fig. 30 Foreign materials can get in between the teeth and cause damage

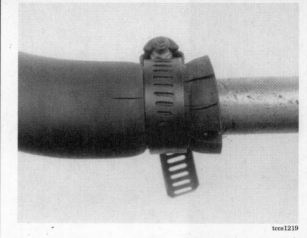

Fig. 31 The cracks developing along this hose are a result of age-related hardening

Fig. 32 A hose clamp that is too tight can cause older hoses to separate and tear on either side of the clamp

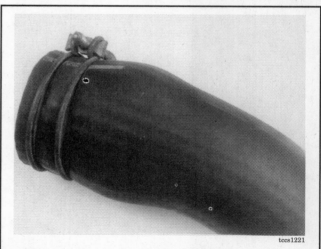

Fig. 33 A soft spongy hose (identifiable by the swollen section) will eventually burst and should be replaced

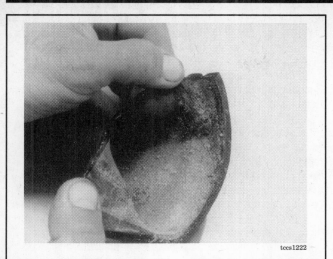

tccs1222

Fig. 34 Hoses are likely to deteriorate from the inside if the cooling system is not periodically flushed

hoses positioned lower on the engine, such as a lower radiator hose, the entire cooling system must be emptied.

✳✳CAUTION

When draining coolant, keep in mind that cats and dogs are attracted by ethylene glycol antifreeze, and are quite likely to drink any that is left in an uncovered container or in puddles on the ground. This will prove fatal in sufficient quantity. Always drain coolant into a sealable container. Coolant may be reused unless it is contaminated or several years old.

3. Loosen the hose clamps at each end of the hose requiring replacement. Clamps are usually either of the spring tension type (which require pliers to squeeze the tabs and loosen) or of the screw tension type (which require screw or hex drivers to loosen). Pull the clamps back on the hose away from the connection.

4. Twist, pull and slide the hose off the fitting, taking care not to damage the neck of the component from which the hose is being removed.

➡**If the hose is stuck at the connection, do not try to insert a screwdriver or other sharp tool under the hose end in an effort to free it, as the connection and/or hose may become damaged. Heater connections especially may be easily damaged by such a procedure. If the hose is to be replaced, use a single-edged razor blade to make a slice along the portion of the hose which is stuck on the connection, perpendicular to the end of the hose. Do not cut deep so as to prevent damaging the connection. The hose can then be peeled from the connection and discarded.**

5. Clean both hose mounting connections. Inspect the condition of the hose clamps and replace them, if necessary.

To install:

6. Dip the ends of the new hose into clean engine coolant to ease installation.

7. Slide the clamps over the replacement hose, then slide the hose ends over the connections into position.

8. Position and secure the clamps at least ¼ in. (6.35mm) from the ends of the hose. Make sure they are located beyond the raised bead of the connector.

9. Close the radiator or engine drains and properly refill the cooling system with the clean drained engine coolant or a suitable mixture of ethylene glycol coolant and water.

10. If available, install a pressure tester and check for leaks. If a pressure tester is not available, run the engine until normal operating temperature is reached (allowing the system to naturally pressurize), then check for leaks.

✳✳CAUTION

If you are checking for leaks with the system at normal operating temperature, BE EXTREMELY CAREFUL not to touch any moving or hot engine parts. Once temperature has been reached, shut the engine OFF, and check for leaks around the hose fittings and connections which were removed earlier.

Air Conditioning

➡**Be sure to consult the laws in your area before servicing the air conditioning system. In most areas, it is illegal to perform repairs involving refrigerant unless the work is done by a certified technician. Also, it is quite likely that you will not be able to purchase refrigerant without proof of certification.**

SAFETY PRECAUTIONS

There are two major hazards associated with air conditioning systems and they both relate to the refrigerant gas. First, the refrigerant gas (R-12 or R-134a) is an extremely cold substance. When exposed to air, it will instantly freeze any surface it comes in contact with, including your eyes. The other hazard relates to fire (if your vehicle is equipped with R-12. Although normally non-toxic, the R-12 gas becomes highly poisonous in the presence of an open flame. One good whiff of the vapor formed by burning R-12 can be fatal. Keep all forms of fire (including cigarettes) well clear of the air conditioning system.

Because of the inherent dangers involved with working on air conditioning systems, these safety precautions must be strictly followed.

• Avoid contact with a charged refrigeration system, even when working on another part of the air conditioning system or vehicle. If a heavy tool comes into contact with a section of tubing or a heat exchanger, it can easily cause the relatively soft material to rupture.

• When it is necessary to apply force to a fitting which contains refrigerant, as when checking that all system couplings are securely tightened, use a wrench on both parts of the fitting involved, if possible. This will avoid putting torque on refrigerant tubing. (It is also advisable to use tube or line wrenches when tightening these flare nut fittings.)

➡**R-12 refrigerant is a chlorofluorocarbon which, when released into the atmosphere, can contribute to the depletion of the ozone layer in the upper atmosphere. Ozone filters out harmful radiation from the sun.**

• Do not attempt to discharge the system without the proper tools. Precise control is possible only when using the service gauges and a proper A/C refrigerant recovery station. Wear protective gloves when connecting or disconnecting service gauge hoses.

• Discharge the system only in a well ventilated area, as high concentrations of the gas which might accidentally escape can exclude oxygen and act as an anesthetic. When leak testing or soldering, this is particularly important, as toxic gas is formed when R-12 contacts any flame.

• Never start a system without first verifying that both service valves are properly installed, and that all fittings throughout the system are snugly connected.

• Avoid applying heat to any refrigerant line or storage vessel. Charging may be aided by using water heated to less than 125°F (50°C) to warm the refrigerant container. Never allow a refrigerant storage container to sit out in the sun, or near any other source of heat, such as a radiator or heater.

• Always wear goggles to protect your eyes when working on a system. If refrigerant contacts the eyes, it is advisable in all cases to consult a physician immediately.

• Frostbite from liquid refrigerant should be treated by first gradually warming the area with cool water, and then gently applying petroleum jelly. A physician should be consulted.

• Always keep refrigerant drum fittings capped when not in use. If the container is equipped with a safety cap to protect the valve, make sure the cap is in place when the can is not being used. Avoid sudden shock to the drum, which might occur from dropping it, or from banging a heavy tool against it. Never carry a drum in the passenger compartment of a vehicle.

• Always completely discharge the system into a suitable recovery unit before painting the vehicle (if the paint is to be baked on), or before welding anywhere near refrigerant lines.

• When servicing the system, minimize the time that any refrigerant line or fitting is open to the air in order to prevent moisture or dirt from entering the system. Contaminants such as moisture or dirt can damage internal system components. Always replace O-rings on lines or fittings which are disconnected. Prior to installation coat, but do not soak, replacement O-rings with suitable compressor oil.

GENERAL SERVICING PROCEDURES

➡It is recommended, and possibly required by law, that a qualified technician perform the following services.

❋❋WARNING

Some of the vehicles covered by this manual may be equipped with R-134a refrigerant systems, rather than R-12. Be ABSOLUTELY SURE what type of system you are working on before attempting to add refrigerant. Use of the wrong refrigerant or oil will cause damage to the system.

The most important aspect of air conditioning service is the maintenance of a pure and adequate charge of refrigerant in the system. A refrigeration system cannot function properly if a significant percentage of the charge is lost. Leaks are common because the severe vibration encountered underhood in an

automobile can easily cause a sufficient cracking or loosening of the air conditioning fittings; allowing, the extreme operating pressures of the system to force refrigerant out.

The problem can be understood by considering what happens to the system as it is operated with a continuous leak. Because the expansion valve regulates the flow of refrigerant to the evaporator, the level of refrigerant there is fairly constant. The receiver/drier stores any excess refrigerant, and so a loss will first appear there as a reduction in the level of liquid. As this level nears the bottom of the vessel, some refrigerant vapor bubbles will begin to appear in the stream of liquid supplied to the expansion valve. This vapor decreases the capacity of the expansion valve very little as the valve opens to compensate for its presence. As the quantity of liquid in the condenser decreases, the operating pressure will drop there and throughout the high side of the system. As the refrigerant continues to be expelled, the pressure available to force the liquid through the expansion valve will continue to decrease, and, eventually, the valve's orifice will prove to be too much of a restriction for adequate flow even with the needle fully withdrawn.

At this point, low side pressure will start to drop, and a severe reduction in cooling capacity, marked by freeze-up of the evaporator coil, will result. Eventually, the operating pressure of the evaporator will be lower than the pressure of the atmosphere surrounding it, and air will be drawn into the system wherever there are leaks in the low side.

Because all atmospheric air contains at least some moisture, water will enter the system mixing with the refrigerant and oil. Trace amounts of moisture will cause sludging of the oil, and corrosion of the system. Saturation and clogging of the filter/drier, and freezing of the expansion valve orifice will eventually result. As air fills the system to a greater and greater extent, it will interfere more and more with the normal flows of refrigerant and heat.

From this description, it should be obvious that much of the repairman's focus in on detecting leaks, repairing them, and then restoring the purity and quantity of the refrigerant charge. A list of general rules should be followed in addition to all safety precautions:

• Keep all tools as clean and dry as possible.

• Thoroughly purge the service gauges/hoses of air and moisture before connecting them to the system. Keep them capped when not in use.

• Thoroughly clean any refrigerant fitting before disconnecting it, in order to minimize the entrance of dirt into the system.

• Plan any operation that requires opening the system beforehand, in order to minimize the length of time it will be exposed to open air. Cap or seal the open ends to minimize the entrance of foreign material.

• When adding oil, pour it through an extremely clean and dry tube or funnel. Keep the oil capped whenever possible. Do not use oil that has not been kept tightly sealed.

• Purchase refrigerant intended for use only in automatic air conditioning systems.

• Completely evacuate any system that has been opened for service, or that has leaked sufficiently to draw in moisture and air. This requires evacuating air and moisture with a good vacuum pump for at least one hour. If a system has been open for a considerable length of time it may be advisable to evacuate the system for up to 12 hours (overnight).

- Use a wrench on both halves of a fitting that is to be disconnected, so as to avoid placing torque on any of the refrigerant lines.
- When overhauling a compressor, pour some of the oil into a clean glass and inspect it. If there is evidence of dirt, metal particles, or both, flush all refrigerant components with clean refrigerant before evacuating and recharging the system. In addition, if metal particles are present, the compressor should be replaced.
- Schrader valves may leak only when under full operating pressure. Therefore, if leakage is suspected but cannot be located, operate the system with a full charge of refrigerant and look for leaks from all Schrader valves. Replace any faulty valves.

Additional Preventive Maintenance

USING THE SYSTEM

The easiest and most important preventive maintenance for your A/C system is to be sure that it is used on a regular basis. Running the system for five minutes each month (no matter what the season) will help assure that the seals and all internal components remain lubricated.

ANTIFREEZE

▶ See Figure 35

In order to prevent heater core freeze-up during A/C operation, it is necessary to maintain a proper antifreeze protection. Use a hand-held antifreeze tester (hydrometer) to periodically check the condition of the antifreeze in your engine's cooling system.

➡ Antifreeze should not be used longer than the manufacturer specifies.

RADIATOR CAP

For efficient operation of an air conditioned vehicle's cooling system, the radiator cap should have a holding pressure which meets manufacturer's specifications. A cap which fails to hold these pressures should be replaced.

Fig. 35 An antifreeze tester can be use to determine the freezing and boiling level of the coolant in your vehicle

CONDENSER

Any obstruction of or damage to the condenser configuration will restrict the air flow which is essential to its efficient operation. It is therefore a good rule to keep this unit clean and in proper physical shape.

➡ Bug screens which are mounted in front of the condenser (unless they are original equipment) are regarded as obstructions.

CONDENSATION DRAIN TUBE

This single molded drain tube expels the condensation, which accumulates on the bottom of the evaporator housing, into the engine compartment. If this tube is obstructed, the air conditioning performance can be restricted and condensation buildup can spill over onto the vehicle's floor.

SYSTEM INSPECTION

➡ R-12 refrigerant is a chlorofluorocarbon which, when released into the atmosphere, can contribute to the depletion of the ozone layer in the upper atmosphere. Ozone filters out harmful radiation from the sun.

The easiest and often most important check for the air conditioning system consists of a visual inspection of the system components. Visually inspect the air conditioning system for refrigerant leaks, damaged compressor clutch, compressor drive belt tension and condition, plugged evaporator drain tube, blocked condenser fins, disconnected or broken wires, blown fuses, corroded connections and poor insulation.

A refrigerant leak will usually appear as an oily residue at the leakage point in the system. The oily residue soon picks up dust or dirt particles from the surrounding air and appears greasy. Through time, this will build up and appear to be a heavy dirt impregnated grease. Most leaks are caused by damaged or missing O-ring seals at the component connections, damaged charging valve cores or missing service gauge port caps.

For a thorough visual and operational inspection, check the following:

1. Check the surface of the radiator and condenser for dirt, leaves or other material which might block air flow.
2. Check for kinks in hoses and lines. Check the system for leaks.
3. Make sure the drive belt is under the proper tension. When the air conditioning is operating, make sure the drive belt is free of noise or slippage.
4. Make sure the blower motor operates at all appropriate positions, then check for distribution of the air from all outlets with the blower on **HIGH**.

➡ Keep in mind that under conditions of high humidity, air discharged from the A/C vents may not feel as cold as expected, even if the system is working properly. This is because the vaporized moisture in humid air retains heat more effectively than does dry air, making the humid air more difficult to cool.

5. Make sure the air passage selection lever is operating correctly. Start the engine and warm it to normal operating

temperature, then make sure the hot/cold selection lever is operating correctly.

DISCHARGING, EVACUATING AND CHARGING

Discharging, evacuating and charging the air conditioning system must be performed by a properly trained and certified mechanic in a facility equipped with refrigerant recovery/recycling equipment that meets SAE standards for the type of system to be serviced.

If you don't have access to the necessary equipment, we recommend that you take your vehicle to a reputable service station to have the work done. If you still wish to perform repairs on the vehicle, have them discharge the system, then take your vehicle home and perform the necessary work. When you are finished, return the vehicle to the station for evacuation and charging. Just be sure to cap ALL A/C system fittings immediately after opening them and keep them protected until the system is recharged.

ENGLISH TO METRIC CONVERSION: MASS (WEIGHT)

Current mass measurement is expressed in pounds and ounces (lbs. & ozs.). The metric unit of mass (or weight) is the kilogram (kg). Even although this table does not show conversion of masses (weights) larger than 15 lbs, it is easy to calculate larger units by following the data immediately below.

To convert ounces (oz.) to grams (g): multiply th number of ozs. by 28
To convert grams (g) to ounces (oz.): multiply the number of grams by .035

To convert pounds (lbs.) to kilograms (kg): multiply the number of lbs. by .45
To convert kilograms (kg) to pounds (lbs.): multiply the number of kilograms by 2.2

lbs	kg	lbs	kg	oz	kg	oz	kg
0.1	0.04	0.9	0.41	0.1	0.003	0.9	0.024
0.2	0.09	1	0.4	0.2	0.005	1	0.03
0.3	0.14	2	0.9	0.3	0.008	2	0.06
0.4	0.18	3	1.4	0.4	0.011	3	0.08
0.5	0.23	4	1.8	0.5	0.014	4	0.11
0.6	0.27	5	2.3	0.6	0.017	5	0.14
0.7	0.32	10	4.5	0.7	0.020	10	0.28
0.8	0.36	15	6.8	0.8	0.023	15	0.42

ENGLISH TO METRIC CONVERSION: TEMPERATURE

To convert Fahrenheit (F) to Celsius (°C): take number of °F and subtract 32; multiply result by 5; divide result by 9

To convert Celsius (°C) to Fahrenheit (°F): take number of °C and multiply by 9; divide result by 5; add 32 to total

Fahrenheit (F)	Celsius (C)	Celsius (C)	Fahrenheit (F)	Fahrenheit (F)	Celsius (C)	Celsius (C)	Fahrenheit (F)	Fahrenheit (F)	Celsius (C)	Celsius (C)	Fahrenheit (F)
°F	°C	°C	°F	°F	°C	°C	°F	°F	°C	°C	°F
−40	−40	−38	−36.4	80	26.7	18	64.4	215	101.7	80	176
−35	−37.2	−36	−32.8	85	29.4	20	68	220	104.4	85	185
−30	−34.4	−34	−29.2	90	32.2	22	71.6	225	107.2	90	194
−25	−31.7	−32	−25.6	95	35.0	24	75.2	230	110.0	95	202
−20	−28.9	−30	−22	100	37.8	26	78.8	235	112.8	100	212
−15	−26.1	−28	−18.4	105	40.6	28	82.4	240	115.6	105	221
−10	−23.3	−26	−14.8	110	43.3	30	86	245	118.3	110	230
−5	−20.6	−24	−11.2	115	46.1	32	89.6	250	121.1	115	239
0	−17.8	−22	−7.6	120	48.9	34	93.2	255	123.9	120	248
1	−17.2	−20	−4	125	51.7	36	96.8	260	126.6	125	257
2	−16.7	−18	−0.4	130	54.4	38	100.4	265	129.4	130	266
3	−16.1	−16	3.2	135	57.2	40	104	270	132.2	135	275
4	−15.6	−14	6.8	140	60.0	42	107.6	275	135.0	140	284
5	−15.0	−12	10.4	145	62.8	44	112.2	280	137.8	145	293
10	−12.2	−10	14	150	65.6	46	114.8	285	140.6	150	302
15	−9.4	−8	17.6	155	68.3	48	118.4	290	143.3	155	311
20	−6.7	−6	21.2	160	71.1	50	122	295	146.1	160	320
25	−3.9	−4	24.8	165	73.9	52	125.6	300	148.9	165	329
30	−1.1	−2	28.4	170	76.7	54	129.2	305	151.7	170	338
35	1.7	0	32	175	79.4	56	132.8	310	154.4	175	347
40	4.4	2	35.6	180	82.2	58	136.4	315	157.2	180	356
45	7.2	4	39.2	185	85.0	60	140	320	160.0	185	365
50	10.0	6	42.8	190	87.8	62	143.6	325	162.8	190	374
55	12.8	8	46.4	195	90.6	64	147.2	330	165.6	195	383
60	15.6	10	50	200	93.3	66	150.8	335	168.3	200	392
65	18.3	12	53.6	205	96.1	68	154.4	340	171.1	205	401
70	21.1	14	57.2	210	98.9	70	158	345	173.9	210	410
75	23.9	16	60.8	212	100.0	75	167	350	176.7	215	414

tccs1c01

ENGLISH TO METRIC CONVERSION: LENGTH

To convert inches (ins.) to millimeters (mm): multiply number of inches by 25.4

To convert millimeters (mm) to inches (ins.): multiply number of millimeters by .04

Inches		Decimals	Milli-meters	Inches to millimeters		Inches		Decimals	Milli-meters	Inches to millimeters	
				inches	mm					inches	mm
	1/64	0.051625	0.3969	0.0001	0.00254		33/64	0.515625	13.0969	0.6	15.24
	1/32	0.03125	0.7937	0.0002	0.00508	17/32		0.53125	13.4937	0.7	17.78
	3/64	0.046875	1.1906	0.0003	0.00762		35/64	0.546875	13.8906	0.8	20.32
1/16		0.0625	1.5875	0.0004	0.01016	9/16		0.5625	14.2875	0.9	22.86
	5/64	0.078125	1.9844	0.0005	0.01270		37/64	0.578125	14.6844	1	25.4
	3/32	0.09375	2.3812	0.0006	0.01524	19/32		0.59375	15.0812	2	50.8
	7/64	0.109375	2.7781	0.0007	0.01778		39/64	0.609375	15.4781	3	76.2
1/8		0.125	3.1750	0.0008	0.02032	5/8		0.625	15.8750	4	101.6
	9/64	0.140625	3.5719	0.0009	0.02286		41/64	0.640625	16.2719	5	127.0
	5/32	0.15625	3.9687	0.001	0.0254	21/32		0.65625	16.6687	6	152.4
	11/64	0.171875	4.3656	0.002	0.0508		43/64	0.671875	17.0656	7	177.8
3/16		0.1875	4.7625	0.003	0.0762	11/16		0.6875	17.4625	8	203.2
	13/64	0.203125	5.1594	0.004	0.1016		45/64	0.703125	17.8594	9	228.6
	7/32	0.21875	5.5562	0.005	0.1270	23/32		0.71875	18.2562	10	254.0
	15/64	0.234375	5.9531	0.006	0.1524		47/64	0.734375	18.6531	11	279.4
1/4		0.25	6.3500	0.007	0.1778	3/4		0.75	19.0500	12	304.8
	17/64	0.265625	6.7469	0.008	0.2032		49/64	0.765625	19.4469	13	330.2
	9/32	0.28125	7.1437	0.009	0.2286	25/32		0.78125	19.8437	14	355.6
	19/64	0.296875	7.5406	0.01	0.254		51/64	0.796875	20.2406	15	381.0
5/16		0.3125	7.9375	0.02	0.508	13/16		0.8125	20.6375	16	406.4
	21/64	0.328125	8.3344	0.03	0.762		53/64	0.828125	21.0344	17	431.8
	11/32	0.34375	8.7312	0.04	1.016	27/32		0.84375	21.4312	18	457.2
	23/64	0.359375	9.1281	0.05	1.270		55/64	0.859375	21.8281	19	482.6
3/8		0.375	9.5250	0.06	1.524	7/8		0.875	22.2250	20	508.0
	25/64	0.390625	9.9219	0.07	1.778		57/64	0.890625	22.6219	21	533.4
	13/32	0.40625	10.3187	0.08	2.032	29/32		0.90625	23.0187	22	558.8
	27/64	0.421875	10.7156	0.09	2.286		59/64	0.921875	23.4156	23	584.2
7/16		0.4375	11.1125	0.1	2.54	15/16		0.9375	23.8125	24	609.6
	29/64	0.453125	11.5094	0.2	5.08		61/64	0.953125	24.2094	25	635.0
	15/32	0.46875	11.9062	0.3	7.62	31/32		0.96875	24.6062	26	660.4
	31/64	0.484375	12.3031	0.4	10.16		63/64	0.984375	25.0031	27	690.6
1/2		0.5	12.7000	0.5	12.70						

ENGLISH TO METRIC CONVERSION: TORQUE

To convert foot-pounds (ft. lbs.) to Newton-meters: multiply the number of ft. lbs. by 1.3

To convert inch-pounds (in. lbs.) to Newton-meters: multiply the number of in. lbs. by .11

in lbs	N-m	in lbs	N-m	in lbs	N-m	in lbs	N-m	in lbs	N-m
0.1	0.01	1	0.11	10	1.13	19	2.15	28	3.16
0.2	0.02	2	0.23	11	1.24	20	2.26	29	3.28
0.3	0.03	3	0.34	12	1.36	21	2.37	30	3.39
0.4	0.04	4	0.45	13	1.47	22	2.49	31	3.50
0.5	0.06	5	0.56	14	1.58	23	2.60	32	3.62
0.6	0.07	6	0.68	15	1.70	24	2.71	33	3.73
0.7	0.08	7	0.78	16	1.81	25	2.82	34	3.84
0.8	0.09	8	0.90	17	1.92	26	2.94	35	3.95
0.9	0.10	9	1.02	18	2.03	27	3.05	36	4.0/

tccs1c02

ENGLISH TO METRIC CONVERSION: TORQUE

Torque is now expressed as either foot-pounds (ft./lbs.) or inch-pounds (in./lbs.). The metric measurement unit for torque is the Newton-meter (Nm). This unit—the Nm—will be used for all SI metric torque references, both the present ft./lbs. and in./lbs.

ft lbs	N-m	ft lbs	N-m	ft lbs	N-m	ft lbs	N-m
0.1	0.1	33	44.7	74	100.3	115	155.9
0.2	0.3	34	46.1	75	101.7	116	157.3
0.3	0.4	35	47.4	76	103.0	117	158.6
0.4	0.5	36	48.8	77	104.4	118	160.0
0.5	0.7	37	50.7	78	105.8	119	161.3
0.6	0.8	38	51.5	79	107.1	120	162.7
0.7	1.0	39	52.9	80	108.5	121	164.0
0.8	1.1	40	54.2	81	109.8	122	165.4
0.9	1.2	41	55.6	82	111.2	123	166.8
1	1.3	42	56.9	83	112.5	124	168.1
2	2.7	43	58.3	84	113.9	125	169.5
3	4.1	44	59.7	85	115.2	126	170.8
4	5.4	45	61.0	86	116.6	127	172.2
5	6.8	46	62.4	87	118.0	128	173.5
6	8.1	47	63.7	88	119.3	129	174.9
7	9.5	48	65.1	89	120.7	130	176.2
8	10.8	49	66.4	90	122.0	131	177.6
9	12.2	50	67.8	91	123.4	132	179.0
10	13.6	51	69.2	92	124.7	133	180.3
11	14.9	52	70.5	93	126.1	134	181.7
12	16.3	53	71.9	94	127.4	135	183.0
13	17.6	54	73.2	95	128.8	136	184.4
14	18.9	55	74.6	96	130.2	137	185.7
15	20.3	56	75.9	97	131.5	138	187.1
16	21.7	57	77.3	98	132.9	139	188.5
17	23.0	58	78.6	99	134.2	140	189.8
18	24.4	59	80.0	100	135.6	141	191.2
19	25.8	60	81.4	101	136.9	142	192.5
20	27.1	61	82.7	102	138.3	143	193.9
21	28.5	62	84.1	103	139.6	144	195.2
22	29.8	63	85.4	104	141.0	145	196.6
23	31.2	64	86.8	105	142.4	146	198.0
24	32.5	65	88.1	106	143.7	147	199.3
25	33.9	66	89.5	107	145.1	148	200.7
26	35.2	67	90.8	108	146.4	149	202.0
27	36.6	68	92.2	109	147.8	150	203.4
28	38.0	69	93.6	110	149.1	151	204.7
29	39.3	70	94.9	111	150.5	152	206.1
30	40.7	71	96.3	112	151.8	153	207.4
31	42.0	72	97.6	113	153.2	154	208.8
32	43.4	73	99.0	114	154.6	155	210.2

tccs1c03

ENGLISH TO METRIC CONVERSION: FORCE

Force is presently measured in pounds (lbs.). This type of measurement is used to measure spring pressure, specifically how many pounds it takes to compress a spring. Our present force unit (the pound) will be replaced in SI metric measurements by the Newton (N). This term will eventually see use in specifications for electric motor brush spring pressures, valve spring pressures, etc.

To convert pounds (lbs.) to Newton (N): multiply the number of lbs. by 4.45

lbs	N	lbs	N	lbs	N	oz	N
0.01	0.04	21	93.4	59	262.4	1	0.3
0.02	0.09	22	97.9	60	266.9	2	0.6
0.03	0.13	23	102.3	61	271.3	3	0.8
0.04	0.18	24	106.8	62	275.8	4	1.1
0.05	0.22	25	111.2	63	280.2	5	1.4
0.06	0.27	26	115.6	64	284.6	6	1.7
0.07	0.31	27	120.1	65	289.1	7	2.0
0.08	0.36	28	124.6	66	293.6	8	2.2
0.09	0.40	29	129.0	67	298.0	9	2.5
0.1	0.4	30	133.4	68	302.5	10	2.8
0.2	0.9	31	137.9	69	306.9	11	3.1
0.3	1.3	32	142.3	70	311.4	12	3.3
0.4	1.8	33	146.8	71	315.8	13	3.6
0.5	2.2	34	151.2	72	320.3	14	3.9
0.6	2.7	35	155.7	73	324.7	15	4.2
0.7	3.1	36	160.1	74	329.2	16	4.4
0.8	3.6	37	164.6	75	333.6	17	4.7
0.9	4.0	38	169.0	76	338.1	18	5.0
1	4.4	39	173.5	77	342.5	19	5.3
2	8.9	40	177.9	78	347.0	20	5.6
3	13.4	41	182.4	79	351.4	21	5.8
4	17.8	42	186.8	80	355.9	22	6.1
5	22.2	43	191.3	81	360.3	23	6.4
6	26.7	44	195.7	82	364.8	24	6.7
7	31.1	45	200.2	83	369.2	25	7.0
8	35.6	46	204.6	84	373.6	26	7.2
9	40.0	47	209.1	85	378.1	27	7.5
10	44.5	48	213.5	86	382.6	28	7.8
11	48.9	49	218.0	87	387.0	29	8.1
12	53.4	50	224.4	88	391.4	30	8.3
13	57.8	51	226.9	89	395.9	31	8.6
14	62.3	52	231.3	90	400.3	32	8.9
15	66.7	53	235.8	91	404.8	33	9.2
16	71.2	54	240.2	92	409.2	34	9.4
17	75.6	55	244.6	93	413.7	35	9.7
18	80.1	56	249.1	94	418.1	36	10.0
19	84.5	57	253.6	95	422.6	37	10.3
20	89.0	58	258.0	96	427.0	38	10.6

tccs1c04

ENGLISH TO METRIC CONVERSION: LIQUID CAPACITY

Liquid or fluid capacity is presently expressed as pints, quarts or gallons, or a combination of all of these. In the metric system the liter (l) will become the basic unit. Fractions of a liter would be expressed as deciliters, centiliters, or most frequently (and commonly) as milliliters.

To convert pints (pts.) to liters (l): multiply the number of pints by .47
To convert liters (l) to pints (pts.): multiply the number of liters by 2.1
To convert quarts (qts.) to liters (l): multiply the number of quarts by .95

To convert liters (l) to quarts (qts.): multiply the number of liters by 1.06
To convert gallons (gals.) to liters (l): multiply the number of gallons by 3.8
To convert liters (l) to gallons (gals.): multiply the number of liters by .26

gals	liters	qts	liters	pts	liters
0.1	0.38	0.1	0.10	0.1	0.05
0.2	0.76	0.2	0.19	0.2	0.10
0.3	1.1	0.3	0.28	0.3	0.14
0.4	1.5	0.4	0.38	0.4	0.19
0.5	1.9	0.5	0.47	0.5	0.24
0.6	2.3	0.6	0.57	0.6	0.28
0.7	2.6	0.7	0.66	0.7	0.33
0.8	3.0	0.8	0.76	0.8	0.38
0.9	3.4	0.9	0.85	0.9	0.43
1	3.8	1	1.0	1	0.5
2	7.6	2	1.9	2	1.0
3	11.4	3	2.8	3	1.4
4	15.1	4	3.8	4	1.9
5	18.9	5	4.7	5	2.4
6	22.7	6	5.7	6	2.8
7	26.5	7	6.6	7	3.3
8	30.3	8	7.6	8	3.8
9	34.1	9	8.5	9	4.3
10	37.8	10	9.5	10	4.7
11	41.6	11	10.4	11	5.2
12	45.4	12	11.4	12	5.7
13	49.2	13	12.3	13	6.2
14	53.0	14	13.2	14	6.6
15	56.8	15	14.2	15	7.1
16	60.6	16	15.1	16	7.6
17	64.3	17	16.1	17	8.0
18	68.1	18	17.0	18	8.5
19	71.9	19	18.0	19	9.0
20	75.7	20	18.9	20	9.5
21	79.5	21	19.9	21	9.9
22	83.2	22	20.8	22	10.4
23	87.0	23	21.8	23	10.9
24	90.8	24	22.7	24	11.4
25	94.6	25	23.6	25	11.8
26	98.4	26	24.6	26	12.3
27	102.2	27	25.5	27	12.8
28	106.0	28	26.5	28	13.2
29	110.0	29	27.4	29	13.7
30	113.5	30	28.4	30	14.2

tccs1c05

ENGLISH TO METRIC CONVERSION: PRESSURE

The basic unit of pressure measurement used today is expressed as pounds per square inch (psi). The metric unit for psi will be the kilopascal (kPa). This will apply to either fluid pressure or air pressure, and will be frequently seen in tire pressure readings, oil pressure specifications, fuel pump pressure, etc.

To convert pounds per square inch (psi) to kilopascals (kPa): multiply the number of psi by 6.89

Psi	kPa	Psi	kPa	Psi	kPa	Psi	kPa
0.1	0.7	37	255.1	82	565.4	127	875.6
0.2	1.4	38	262.0	83	572.3	128	882.5
0.3	2.1	39	268.9	84	579.2	129	889.4
0.4	2.8	40	275.8	85	586.0	130	896.3
0.5	3.4	41	282.7	86	592.9	131	903.2
0.6	4.1	42	289.6	87	599.8	132	910.1
0.7	4.8	43	296.5	88	606.7	133	917.0
0.8	5.5	44	303.4	89	613.6	134	923.9
0.9	6.2	45	310.3	90	620.5	135	930.8
1	6.9	46	317.2	91	627.4	136	937.7
2	13.8	47	324.0	92	634.3	137	944.6
3	20.7	48	331.0	93	641.2	138	951.5
4	27.6	49	337.8	94	648.1	139	958.4
5	34.5	50	344.7	95	655.0	140	965.2
6	41.4	51	351.6	96	661.9	141	972.2
7	48.3	52	358.5	97	668.8	142	979.0
8	55.2	53	365.4	98	675.7	143	985.9
9	62.1	54	372.3	99	682.6	144	992.8
10	69.0	55	379.2	100	689.5	145	999.7
11	75.8	56	386.1	101	696.4	146	1006.6
12	82.7	57	393.0	102	703.3	147	1013.5
13	89.6	58	399.9	103	710.2	148	1020.4
14	96.5	59	406.8	104	717.0	149	1027.3
15	103.4	60	413.7	105	723.9	150	1034.2
16	110.3	61	420.6	106	730.8	151	1041.1
17	117.2	62	427.5	107	737.7	152	1048.0
18	124.1	63	434.4	108	744.6	153	1054.9
19	131.0	64	441.3	109	751.5	154	1061.8
20	137.9	65	448.2	110	758.4	155	1068.7
21	144.8	66	455.0	111	765.3	156	1075.6
22	151.7	67	461.9	112	772.2	157	1082.5
23	158.6	68	468.8	113	779.1	158	1089.4
24	165.5	69	475.7	114	786.0	159	1096.3
25	172.4	70	482.6	115	792.9	160	1103.2
26	179.3	71	489.5	116	799.8	161	1110.0
27	186.2	72	496.4	117	806.7	162	1116.9
28	193.0	73	503.3	118	813.6	163	1123.8
29	200.0	74	510.2	119	820.5	164	1130.7
30	206.8	75	517.1	120	827.4	165	1137.6
31	213.7	76	524.0	121	834.3	166	1144.5
32	220.6	77	530.9	122	841.2	167	1151.4
33	227.5	78	537.8	123	848.0	168	1158.3
34	234.4	79	544.7	124	854.9	169	1165.2
35	241.3	80	551.6	125	861.8	170	1172.1
36	248.2	81	558.5	126	868.7	171	1179.0

THE WORK AREA
  FLOOR SPACE AND WORKING
    HEIGHT 2-2
  SHOP SAFETY 2-5
  STORAGE AREAS 2-2
UNDERSTANDING THE BASICS
  ADD-ON ELECTRICAL
    EQUIPMENT 2-13
  BATTERY, STARTING AND
    CHARGING SYSTEMS 2-12
  UNDERSTANDING ELECTRICITY 2-9

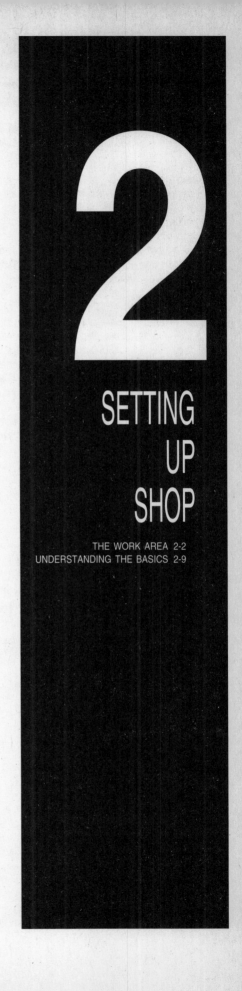

2

SETTING UP SHOP

THE WORK AREA 2-2
UNDERSTANDING THE BASICS 2-9

THE WORK AREA

Floor Space and Working Height

The average one car garage will give you more than enough work space. A floor plan of 16 ft. X 12 ft. is more than sufficient for shelving, work benches, tool shelves or boxes and parts storage areas. 12 X 16 works out to 192 square feet. You may think that this sounds like a lot of room, but when you start building shelves, and constructing work benches almost most half of that can be eaten up!

Also, you may wonder why a lot of floor space is needed. There are several reasons, not the least of which is the safety factor. You'll be working around a large, heavy, metal object mounted on a work stand. The work stand has wheels so that it can be moved to allow easy work angles. The work stand allows the engine to be rotated for the same reason and the work stand has legs and supports that take up floor space. Accidents can happen! Even the best engine stand can tip over; you can easily trip over a work stand leg or drop a heavy part or tool. You'll need room to take evasive action!

Most garages have concrete floors. The engine and stand can weigh 800 lbs. or more when fully assembled. Engine stands have small steel wheels which roll best on smooth concrete. If your garage floor has cracks with raised sections or blocks with deep grooves, you may have a problem. The wheels can hang up on these cracks or grooves causing the whole thing to tip over.

As for working height, overhead clearance is necessary for the engine crane. To lift an engine from or install an engine in a vehicle, the crane cane need as much as 10 ft. overhead. If you don't have this much room, you might want to lift the engine out of or into the vehicle outside an roll it to or from the garage mounted on an engine dolly. DON'T roll the crane any great distance with the engine suspended! A tip over or crane damage can easily occur. Plus, once an engine starts swinging on the crane boom, it's tough to control.

Storage Areas

SHELVES

▶ See Figures 1, 2 and 3

You can't have enough shelf space. Adequate shelf space means that you don't have to stack anything on the floor, where it would be in the way.

Shelves aren't tough. You can make your own or buy modular or prefab units. The best modular units are those made of interlocking shelves and uprights of ABS plastic. They're lightweight and easy to assemble, and their load-bearing capacity is more than sufficient. Also, they are not subject the rust or rot as are wood and metal shelves.

Probably the cheapest and best shelves are ones that you make yourself from one inch shelving with 2X4 uprights. You can make them as long, wide and high as you want. For at least the uprights, use pressure treated wood. Its resistance to rot is more than worth the additional cost.

87932001

Fig. 1 Typical home-made wood shelves, crammed with stuff. These shelves are made from spare ⁵⁄₄ x 6 in. pressure treated decking

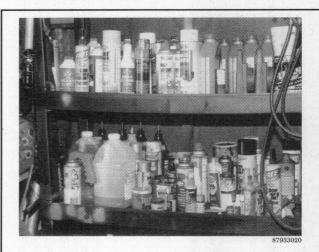

87933020

Fig. 2 Modular plastic shelves, such as these are inexpensive, weather-proof and easy to assemble

TOOL CHESTS

▶ See Figures 4 and 5

There are many types and sizes of tool chests. Their greatest advantage is that they can hold a lot of tools, securely, in a relatively small area. If you decide that you need one, make sure that you buy one that's big enough and mobile enough for the work area. Also, you get what you pay for, so purchase a good brand name. It will last a lifetime.

WORK BENCHES

▶ See Figure 6

As with the shelving, work benches can be either store-bought or home-made. The store-bought work benches can be

Fig. 3 These shelves were made from the frame of old kitchen cabinets

Fig. 4 Different types of mobile, steel tool chests

Fig. 5 A good tool chest has several drawers, each designed to hold a different type tool

87933512

Fig. 6 Homemade workbenches

steel or precut wood kits. Either are fine and are available at most building supply stores or through tool catalogs.

Home-made benches, as with the shelves have the advantage of being made-to-fit your workshop. A free-standing workbench is best, as opposed to one attached to an outside wall. The free-standing bench can take more abuse since it doesn't transfer the shock or vibration to wall supports.

A good free-standing workbench should be constructed using 4X4 pressure treated wood as legs, 2X6 planking as header boards and ¾ inch plywood sheathing as a deck. Diagonal supports can be 2X4 studs and it's always helpful to construct a full size ¾ inch plywood shelf under the bench. Not only can you use the shelf for storage but it gives great rigidity to the whole bench structure. Assembling the bench with screws rather than nails takes longer but adds strength and gives you the ability to take the whole thing apart if you ever want to move it.

LIGHTING

▶ **See Figures 7 and 8**

The importance of adequate lighting can't be over emphasized. Good lighting is not only a convenience but a safety feature. If you can see what your working on you're less likely to make mistakes, have a wrench slip or trip over an obstacle. On most engines, everything is about the same color and usually dirty. During disassembly, a lot of frustration can be avoided if you can see all the bolts, some of which may be hidden or obscured.

For overhead lighting, at least 2 twin tube 36 inch fluorescent shop lights should be in place. Most garages are wired with standard light bulbs attached to the wall studs at intervals. Four or five of these lights, at about a 6 foot height combined with the overhead lighting should suffice. However, no matter where the lights are, your body is going to block some of it so a droplight or clip-on type work light is a great idea. These lights can be mounted on the engine stand, or even the engine itself.

Fig. 7 At least two of this type of twin tube fluorescent light is essential

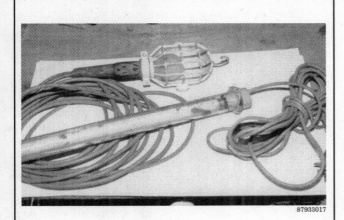

Fig. 8 Two types of droplights. Incandescent and fluorescent

VENTILATION

At one time or another, be working with chemicals which may require adequate ventilation. Now, just about all garages have a big car-sized door and all sheds or workshops have a door. In bad weather the door will have to be closed so at least one window that opens is a necessity. An exhaust fan or regular ventilation fan is a great help, especially in hot weather.

HEATERS

If you live in an area where the winters are cold, as do most of us, it's nice to have some sort of heat where we work. If your workshop or garage is attached to the house, you'll probably be okay. If your garage or shop is detached, then a space heater of some sort — electric, propane or kerosene

— will be necessary. NEVER run a space heater in the presence of flammable vapors! When running a space heater, always allow for some means of venting the carbon monoxide!

ELECTRICAL REQUIREMENTS

Obviously, your workshop should be wired according to all local codes. As to what type of service you need, that depends on your electrical load. If you have a lot of power equipment and maybe a refrigerator, TV, stereo or whatever, not only do you have a great shop, but your amperage requirements may exceed your wiring's capacity. If you are at all in doubt, consult your local electrical contractor.

Shop Safety

▶ **See Figures 9, 10, 11 and 12**

It is virtually impossible to anticipate all of the hazards involved with automotive maintenance and service but care and common sense will prevent most accidents.

The rules of safety for mechanics range from 'don't smoke around gasoline' to 'use the proper tool for the job.' The trick to avoiding injuries is to develop safe work habits and take every possible precaution.

Do's

• Do keep a fire extinguisher and first aid kit within easy reach.
• Do wear safety glasses or goggles when cutting, drilling, grinding, or prying, even if you have 20/20 vision. If you wear glasses for the sake of vision, then they should be made of hardened glass that can serve also as safety glasses, or wear safety glasses over your regular glasses.
• Do shield your eyes whenever you work around the battery. Batteries contain sulfuric acid; in case of contact with the eyes or skin, flush the area with water or a mixture of water and baking soda and get medical attention immediately.

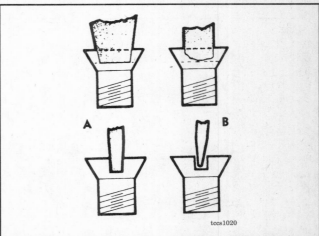

Fig. 9 Screwdrivers should be kept in good condition to prevent injury or damage which could result if the blade slips from the screw

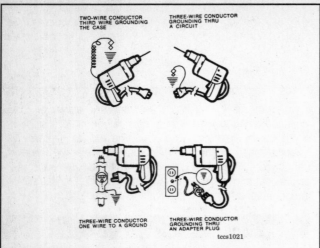

Fig. 10 Power tools should always be properly grounded

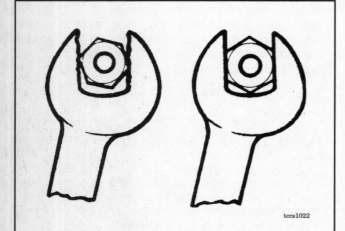

Fig. 11 Using the correct size wrench will help prevent the possibility of rounding-off a nut

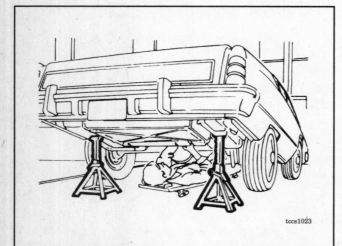

Fig. 12 NEVER work under a vehicle unless it is supported using safety stands (jackstands)

• Do use safety stands for any under-truck service. Jacks are for raising vehicles; safety stands are for making sure the vehicle stays raised until you want it to come down. Whenever the vehicle is raised, block the wheels remaining on the ground and set the parking brake.

• Do use adequate ventilation when working with any chemicals. Like carbon monoxide, the asbestos dust resulting from brake lining wear can be poisonous in sufficient quantities.

• Do disconnect the negative battery cable when working on the electrical system. The primary ignition system can contain up to 40,000 volts.

• Do follow manufacturer's directions whenever working with potentially hazardous materials. Both brake fluid and antifreeze are poisonous if taken internally.

• Do properly maintain your tools. Loose hammerheads, mushroomed punches and chisels, frayed or poorly grounded electrical cords, excessively worn screwdrivers, spread wrenches (open end), cracked sockets, slipping ratchets, or faulty droplight sockets can cause accidents.

• Do use the proper size and type of tool for the job being done.

• Do when possible, pull on a wrench handle rather than push on it, and adjust your stance to prevent a fall.

• Do be sure that adjustable wrenches are tightly adjusted on the nut or bolt and pulled so that the face is on the side of the fixed jaw.

• Do select a wrench or socket that fits the nut or bolt. The wrench or socket should sit straight, not cocked.

• Do strike squarely with a hammer. Avoid glancing blows.

• Do set the parking brake and block the drive wheels if the work requires that the engine be running.

Don't's

• Don't run an engine in a garage or anywhere else without proper ventilation — EVER! Carbon monoxide is poisonous; it takes a long time to leave the human body and you can build up a deadly supply of it in your system by simply breathing in a little every day. You may not realize you are slowly poisoning yourself. Always use proper vents, window, fans or open the garage door.

• Don't work around moving parts while wearing a necktie or other loose clothing. Short sleeves are much safer than long, loose sleeves and hard-toed shoes with neoprene soles protect your toes and give a better grip on slippery surfaces. Jewelry such as watches, fancy belt buckles, beads or body adornment of any kind is not safe working around a truck. Long hair should be hidden under a hat or cap.

• Don't use pockets for toolboxes. A fall or bump can drive a screwdriver deep into your body. Even a wiping cloth hanging from the back pocket can wrap around a spinning shaft or fan.

• Don't smoke when working around gasoline, cleaning solvent or other flammable material.

• Don't smoke when working around the battery. When the battery is being charged, it gives off explosive hydrogen gas.

• Don't use gasoline to wash your hands; there are excellent soaps available. Gasoline removes all the natural oils from the skin so that bone dry hands will such up oil and grease.

• Don't service the air conditioning system unless you are equipped with the necessary tools and training. The refrigerant,

R-12, is extremely cold and when exposed to the air, will instantly freeze any surface it comes in contact with, including your eyes. Although the refrigerant is normally non-toxic, R-12 becomes a deadly poisonous gas in the presence of an open flame. One good whiff of the vapors from burning refrigerant can be fatal.

• Don't ever use a bumper jack (the jack that comes with the vehicle) for anything other than changing tires! If you are serious about maintaining your truck yourself, invest in a hydraulic floor jack of at least 1½ ton capacity. It will pay for itself many times over through the years.

SAFETY EQUIPMENT

▶ See Figures 13 and 14

Fire Extinguishers

There are many types of safety equipment. The most important of these is the fire extinguisher. You'll be well off with two 5 lbs. extinguishers rated for oil, chemical and wood.

Fig. 14 A good, all-purpose fire extinguisher

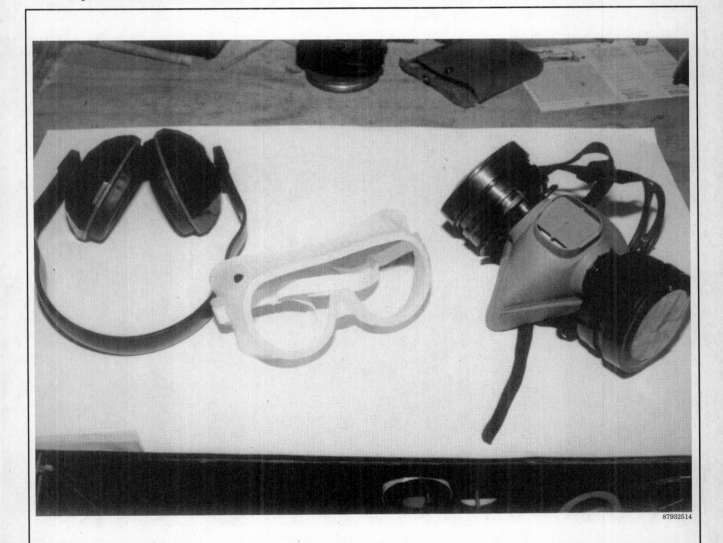

Fig. 13 Three essential pieces of safety equipment. Left to right: ear protectors, safety goggles and respirator

First Aid

Next you'll need a good first aid kit. Any good kit which can purchase from the local drug store will be fine. It's a good idea, in addition, to have something easily accessible in the event of a minor injury, such a hydrogen peroxide or other antiseptic that can be poured onto or applied to a wound immediately.

Work Gloves

▶ See Figure 15

Unless you think scars on your hands are cool, enjoy pain and like wearing bandages, get a good pair of work gloves. Canvass or leather are the best. And yes, I realize that there are some jobs involving small parts that can't be done while wearing work gloves. These jobs are not the ones usually associated with hand injuries.

A good pair of rubber gloves such as those usually associated with dish washing is also a great idea. There are some liquids such as solvent and penetrants that don't belong on your skin. Avoid burns and rashes. Wear these gloves.

And lastly, an option. If you're tired of being greasy and dirty all the time, go to the drug store and buy a box of disposable latex gloves like medical professionals wear. You can handle greasy parts, perform small tasks, wash parts, etc. all without getting dirty! These gloves take a surprising amount of abuse without tearing and aren't expensive. Note however, that it has been reported that some people are allergic to the latex.

Work Boots

It's up to you, but I think that a good, comfortable pair of steel-toed work boots is a sensible idea. Primarily because heavy parts always get dropped sooner or later. A manifold can do significant damage to a sneaker-clad foot.

Good work boots also provide better support — you're going to be on your feet a lot — are oil-resistant, and they keep your feet warm and dry.

Eye Protection

Don't begin this, or for that matter any, job without a good pair of work goggles or impact resistant glasses! When doing any kind of work, it's all too easy to avoid eye injury through

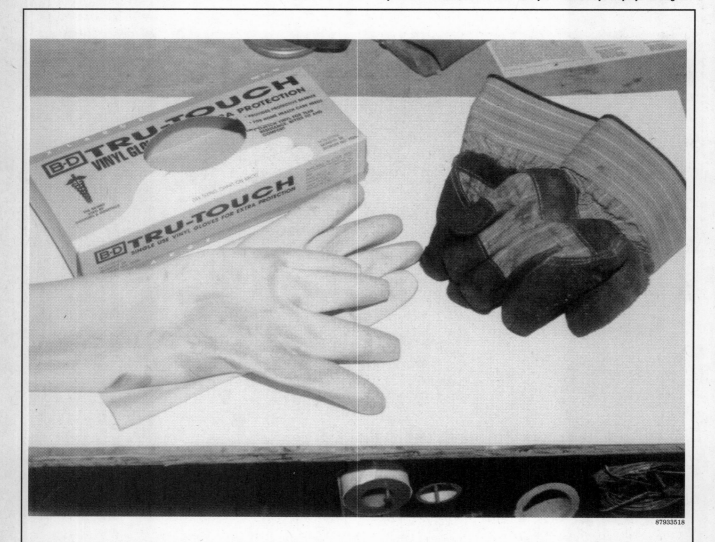

Fig. 15 Three different types of work gloves. The box contains latex gloves

this simple precaution. And don't just buy eye protection and leave it on the shelf. Wear it all the time! Things have a habit of breaking, chipping, splashing, spraying, splintering and flying around. And, for some reason, your eye is always in the way!

Ear Protection

Often overlooked is hearing protection. Power equipment is noisy! Loud noises damage your ears. It's as simple as that!

The simplest and cheapest form of ear protection is a pair of noise-reducing ear plugs. Cheap insurance for your ears. And, they even come with their own, cute little carrying case.

More substantial, more protection and more money is a good pair of noise reducing ear muffs. They protect from all but the loudest sounds. Hopefully those are sounds that you'll never encounter since they're usually associated with disasters or rock concerts.

Work Clothes

Everyone has 'work clothes'. Usually this consists of old jeans and a shirt that has seen better days. That's fine. In addition, a denim work apron is a nice accessory. It's rugged, can hold some tools, and you don't feel bad wiping your hands or tools on it. That's what it's for.

UNDERSTANDING THE BASICS

To do a good job when performing any automotive work, you have to be capable of more than just turning a wrench. When you get around to installing and trying to start your new engine, a lot of things can go wrong. Among the most mysterious is the electrical system. Read the following paragraphs to gain some basic start on understanding automotive electrical systems.

Understanding Electricity

For any electrical system to operate, there must be a complete circuit. This simply means that the power flow from the battery must make a full circle. When an electrical component is operating, power flows from the battery to the components, passes through the component (load) causing it to function, and returns to the battery through the ground path of the circuit. This ground may be either another wire or a metal part of the vehicle (depending upon how the component is designed).

BASIC CIRCUITS

▶ See Figure 16

Perhaps the easiest way to visualize a circuit is to think of connecting a light bulb (with two wires attached to it) to the battery. If one of the two wires was attached to the negative post (-) of the battery and the other wire to the positive post (+), the circuit would be complete and the light bulb would illuminate. Electricity could follow a path from the battery to the bulb and back to the battery. It's not hard to see that with longer wires on our light bulb, it could be mounted anywhere on the vehicle. Further, one wire could be fitted with a switch so that the light could be turned on and off. Various other items could be added to our primitive circuit to make the light flash, become brighter or dimmer under certain conditions, or advise the user that it's burned out.

Ground

Some automotive components are grounded through their mounting points. The electrical current runs through the chassis of the vehicle and returns to the battery through the ground (-) cable; if you look, you'll see that the battery ground cable connects between the battery and the body of the vehicle.

Load

▶ See Figure 17

Every complete circuit must include a 'load" (something to use the electricity coming from the source). If you were to connect a wire between the two terminals of the battery (DON'T do this, but take out word for it) without the light bulb, the battery would attempt to deliver its entire power supply from one pole to another almost instantly. This is a short circuit. The electricity is taking a short cut to get to ground and is not being used by any load in the circuit. This sudden and uncontrolled electrical flow can cause great damage to other components in the circuit and can develop a tremendous amount of heat. A short in an automotive wiring harness can develop sufficient heat to melt the insulation on all the surrounding wires and reduce a multiple wire cable to one sad lump of plastic and copper. Two common causes of shorts are broken insulation (thereby exposing the wire to contact with surrounding metal surfaces or other wires) or a failed switch (the pins inside the switch come out of place and touch each other).

Switches and Relays

Some electrical components which require a large amount of current to operate also have a relay in their circuit. Since these circuits carry a large amount of current (amperage or amps), the thickness of the wire in the circuit (wire gauge) is also greater. If this large wire were connected from the load to the control switch on the dash, the switch would have to carry the high amperage load and the dash would be twice as large to accommodate wiring harnesses as thick as your wrist. To prevent these problems, a relay is used. The large wires in the circuit are connected from the battery to one side of the relay and from the opposite side of the relay to the load. The relay is normally open, preventing current from passing through the circuit. An additional, smaller wire is connected from the relay to the control switch for the circuit. When the control switch is turned on, it grounds the smaller wire to the relay and completes its circuit. The main switch inside the relay closes, sending power to the component without routing the main power through the inside of the vehicle. Some common circuits which may use relays are the horn, headlights, starter and rear window defogger systems.

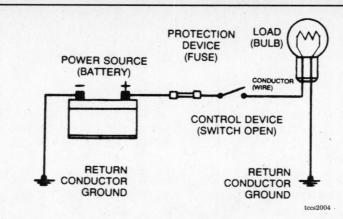

Fig. 16 Here is an example of a simple automotive circuit. When the switch is closed, power from the positive battery terminal flows through the fuse, then the switch and to the load (light bulb), the light illuminates and then, the circuit is completed through the return conductor and the vehicle ground. If the light did not work, the tests could be made with a voltmeter or test light at the battery, fuse, switch or bulb socket

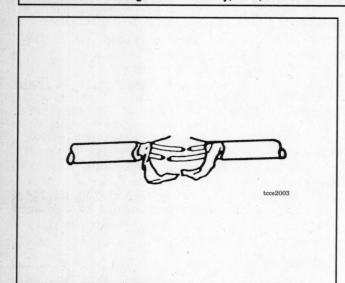

Fig. 17 Damaged insulation can allow wires to break (causing an open circuit) or touch (causing a short)

Protective Devices

It is possible for larger surges of current to pass through the electrical system of your vehicle. If this surge of current were to reach the load in the circuit, it could burn it out or severely damage it. To prevent this, fuses, circuit breakers and/or fusible links are connected into the supply wires of the electrical system. These items are nothing more than a built-in weak spot in the system. It's much easier to go to a known location (the fusebox) to see why a circuit is inoperative than to dissect 15 feet of wiring under the dashboard, looking for what happened.

When an electrical current of excessive power passes through the fuse, the fuse blows (the conductor melts) and breaks the circuit, preventing the passage of current and protecting the components.

A circuit breaker is basically a self repairing fuse. It will open the circuit in the same fashion as a fuse, but when either the

short is removed or the surge subsides, the circuit breaker resets itself and does not need replacement.

A fuse link (fusible link or main link) is a wire that acts as a fuse. One of these is normally connected between the starter relay and the main wiring harness under the hood. Since the starter is usually the highest electrical draw on the vehicle, an internal short during starting could direct about 130 amps into the wrong places. Consider the damage potential of introducing this current into a system whose wiring is rated at 15 amps and you'll understand the need for protection. Since this link is very early in the electrical path, it's the first place to look if nothing on the vehicle works, but the battery seems to be charged and is properly connected.

TROUBLESHOOTING

▶ **See Figures 18, 19 and 20**

Electrical problems generally fall into one of three areas:
• The component that is not functioning is not receiving current.
• The component is receiving power but is not using it or is using it incorrectly (component failure).
• The component is improperly grounded.

The circuit can be can be checked with a test light and a jumper wire. The test light is a device that looks like a pointed screwdriver with a wire on one end and a bulb in its handle. A jumper wire is simply a piece of wire with alligator clips or special terminals on each end. If a component is not working, you must follow a systematic plan to determine which of the three causes is the villain.

1. Turn ON the switch that controls the item not working.

➡**Some items only work when the ignition switch is turned ON.**

2. Disconnect the power supply wire from the component.
3. Attach the ground wire of a test light or a voltmeter to a good metal ground.
4. Touch the end probe of the test light (or the positive lead of the voltmeter) to the power wire; if there is current in the wire, the light in the test light will come on (or the voltme-

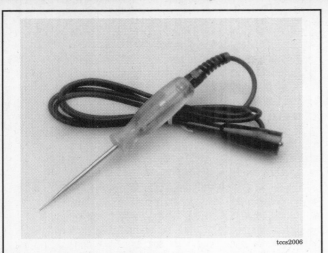

Fig. 18 A 12 volt test light is useful when checking parts of a circuit for power

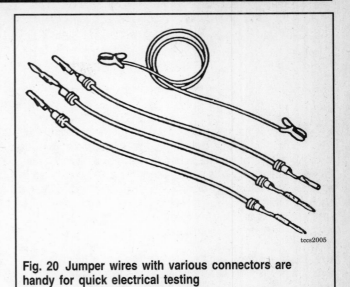

Fig. 20 Jumper wires with various connectors are handy for quick electrical testing

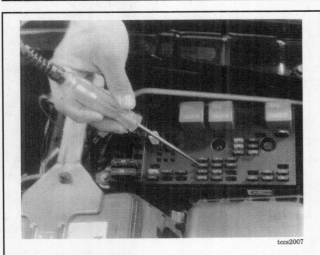

Fig. 19 Here, someone is checking a circuit by making sure there is power to the component's fuse

ter will indicate the amount of voltage). You have now established that current is getting to the component.

5. Turn the ignition or dash switch **OFF** and reconnect the wire to the component.

If there was no power, then the problem is between the battery and the component. This includes all the switches, fuses, relays and the battery itself. The next place to look is the fusebox; check carefully either by eye or by using the test light across the fuse clips. The easiest way to check is to simply replace the fuse. If the fuse is blown, and upon replacement, immediately blows again, there is a short between the fuse and the component. This is generally (not always) a sign of an internal short in the component. Disconnect the power wire at the component again and replace the fuse; if the fuse holds, the component is the problem.

✳✳WARNING

DO NOT test a component by running a jumper wire from the battery UNLESS you are certain that it operates on 12 volts. Many electronic components are designed to oper-

ate with less voltage and connecting them to 12 volts could destroy them. Jumper wires are best used to bypass a portion of the circuit (such as a stretch of wire or a switch) that DOES NOT contain a resistor and is suspected to be bad.

If all the fuses are good and the component is not receiving power, find the switch for the circuit. Bypass the switch with the jumper wire. This is done by connecting one end of the jumper to the power wire coming into the switch and the other end to the wire leaving the switch. If the component comes to life, the switch has failed.

✳✳WARNING

Never substitute the jumper for the component. The circuit needs the electrical load of the component. If you bypass it, you will cause a short circuit.

Checking the ground for any circuit can mean tracing wires to the body, cleaning connections or tightening mounting bolts for the component itself. If the jumper wire can be connected to the case of the component or the ground connector, you can ground the other end to a piece of clean, solid metal on the vehicle. Again, if the component starts working, you've found the problem.

A systematic search through the fuse, connectors, switches and the component itself will almost always yield an answer. Loose and/or corroded connectors, particularly in ground circuits, are becoming a larger problem in modern vehicles. The computers and on-board electronic (solid state) systems are highly sensitive to improper grounds and will change their function drastically if one occurs.

Remember that for any electrical circuit to work, ALL the connections must be clean and tight.

Battery, Starting and Charging Systems

BASIC OPERATING PRINCIPLES

Battery

The battery is the first link in the chain of mechanisms which work together to provide cranking of the automobile engine. In most modern vehicles, the battery is a lead/acid electrochemical device consisting of six 2v subsections (cells) connected in series so the unit is capable of producing approximately 12v of electrical pressure. Each subsection consists of a series of positive and negative plates held a short distance apart in a solution of sulfuric acid and water.

The two types of plates are of dissimilar metals. This sets-up a chemical reaction, and it is this reaction which produces current flow from the battery when its positive and negative terminals are connected to an electrical accessory such as a lamp or motor. The continued transfer of electrons would eventually convert the sulfuric acid to water, and make the two plates identical in chemical composition. As electrical energy is removed from the battery, its voltage output tends to drop. Thus, measuring battery voltage and battery electrolyte composition are two ways of checking the ability of the unit to supply power. During engine cranking, electrical energy is removed from the battery. However, if the charging circuit is in good condition and the operating conditions are normal, the power removed from the battery will be replaced by the alternator which will force electrons back through the battery, reversing the normal flow, and restoring the battery to its original chemical state.

Starting System

The battery and starting motor are linked by very heavy electrical cables designed to minimize resistance to the flow of current. Generally, the major power supply cable that leaves the battery goes directly to the starter, while other electrical system needs are supplied by a smaller cable. During starter operation, power flows from the battery to the starter and is grounded through the vehicle's frame/body or engine and the battery's negative ground strap.

The starter is a specially designed, direct current electric motor capable of producing a great amount of power for its size. One thing that allows the motor to produce a great deal of power is its tremendous rotating speed. It drives the engine through a tiny pinion gear (attached to the starter's armature), which drives the very large flywheel ring gear at a greatly reduced speed. Another factor allowing it to produce so much power is that only intermittent operation is required of it. Thus, little allowance for air circulation is necessary, and the windings can be built into a very small space.

The starter solenoid is a magnetic device which employs the small current supplied by the start circuit of the ignition switch. This magnetic action moves a plunger which mechanically engages the starter and closes the heavy switch connecting it to the battery. The starting switch circuit usually consists of the starting switch contained within the ignition switch, a neutral safety switch or clutch pedal switch, and the wiring necessary to connect these in series with the starter solenoid or relay.

The pinion, a small gear, is mounted to a one way drive clutch. This clutch is splined to the starter armature shaft. When the ignition switch is moved to the **START** position, the solenoid plunger slides the pinion toward the flywheel ring gear via a collar and spring. If the teeth on the pinion and flywheel match properly, the pinion will engage the flywheel immediately. If the gear teeth butt one another, the spring will be compressed and will force the gears to mesh as soon as the starter turns far enough to allow them to do so. As the solenoid plunger reaches the end of its travel, it closes the contacts that connect the battery and starter, then the engine is cranked.

As soon as the engine starts, the flywheel ring gear begins turning fast enough to drive the pinion at an extremely high rate of speed. At this point, the one-way clutch begins allowing the pinion to spin faster than the starter shaft so that the starter will not operate at excessive speed. When the ignition switch is released from the starter position, the solenoid is de-energized, and a spring pulls the gear out of mesh interrupting the current flow to the starter.

Some starters employ a separate relay, mounted away from the starter, to switch the motor and solenoid current on and off. The relay replaces the solenoid electrical switch, but does not eliminate the need for a solenoid mounted on the starter used to mechanically engage the starter drive gears. The relay is used to reduce the amount of current the starting switch must carry.

Charging System

The automobile charging system provides electrical power for operation of the vehicle's ignition system, starting system and all electrical accessories. The battery serves as an electrical surge or storage tank, storing (in chemical form) the energy originally produced by the engine driven generator. The system also provides a means of regulating output to protect the battery from being overcharged and to avoid excessive voltage to the accessories.

The storage battery is a chemical device incorporating parallel lead plates in a tank containing a sulfuric acid/water solution. Adjacent plates are slightly dissimilar, and the chemical reaction of the two dissimilar plates produces electrical energy when the battery is connected to a load such as the starter motor. The chemical reaction is reversible, so that when the generator is producing a voltage (electrical pressure) greater than that produced by the battery, electricity is forced into the battery, and the battery is returned to its fully charged state.

Newer automobiles use alternating current generators or alternators, because they are more efficient, can be rotated at higher speeds, and have fewer brush problems. In an alternator, the field usually rotates while all the current produced passes only through the stator winding. The brushes bear against continuous slip rings. This causes the current produced to periodically reverse the direction of its flow. Diodes (electrical one way valves) block the flow of current from traveling in the wrong direction. A series of diodes is wired together to permit the alternating flow of the stator to be rectified back to 12 volts DC for use by the vehicle's electrical system.

The voltage regulating function is performed by a regulator. The regulator is often built in to the alternator; this system is termed an integrated or internal regulator.

Fusible Links

The fuse link is a short length of special, Hypalon (high temperature) insulated wire, integral with the engine compartment wiring harness and should not be confused with standard wire. It is several wire gauges smaller than the circuit which it protects. Under no circumstances should a fuse link replacement repair be made using a length of standard wire cut from bulk stock or from another wiring harness.

To repair any blown fuse link use the following procedure:

1. Determine which circuit is damaged, its location and the cause of the open fuse link. If the damaged fuse link is one of three fed by a common No. 10 or 12 gauge feed wire, determine the specific affected circuit.

2. Disconnect the negative battery cable.

3. Cut the damaged fuse link from the wiring harness and discard it. If the fuse link is one of three circuits fed by a single feed wire, cut it out of the harness at each splice end and discard it.

4. Identify and procure the proper fuse link with butt connectors for attaching the fuse link to the harness.

➡**Heat shrink tubing must be slipped over the wire before crimping and soldering the connection.**

5. To repair any fuse link in a 3-link group with one feed:

a. After cutting the open link out of the harness, cut each of the remaining undamaged fuse links close to the feed wire weld.

b. Strip approximately ½ in. (13mm) of insulation from the detached ends of the two good fuse links. Insert two wire ends into one end of a butt connector, then carefully push one stripped end of the replacement fuse link into the same end of the butt connector and crimp all three firmly together.

➡**Care must be taken when fitting the three fuse links into the butt connector as the internal diameter is a snug fit for three wires. Make sure to use a proper crimping tool. Pliers, side cutters, etc. will not apply the proper crimp to retain the wires and withstand a pull test.**

c. After crimping the butt connector to the three fuse links, cut the weld portion from the feed wire and strip approximately ½ in. (13mm) of insulation from the cut end. Insert the stripped end into the open end of the butt connector and crimp very firmly.

d. To attach the remaining end of the replacement fuse link, strip approximately ½ in. (13mm) of insulation from the wire end of the circuit from which the blown fuse link was removed, and firmly crimp a butt connector or equivalent to the stripped wire. Then, insert the end of the replacement link into the other end of the butt connector and crimp firmly.

e. Using rosin core solder with a consistency of 60 percent tin and 40 percent lead, solder the connectors and the wires at the repairs then insulate with electrical tape or heat shrink tubing.

6. To replace any fuse link on a single circuit in a harness, cut out the damaged portion, strip approximately ½ in. (13mm) of insulation from the two wire ends and attach the appropriate replacement fuse link to the stripped wire ends with two proper size butt connectors. Solder the connectors and wires, then insulate.

7. To repair any fuse link which has an eyelet terminal on one end such as the charging circuit, cut off the open fuse link behind the weld, strip approximately ½ in. (13mm) of insulation from the cut end and attach the appropriate new eyelet fuse link to the cut stripped wire with an appropriate size butt connector. Solder the connectors and wires at the repair, then insulate.

8. Connect the negative battery cable to the battery and test the system for proper operation.

➡**Do not mistake a resistor wire for a fuse link. The resistor wire is generally longer and has print stating, 'Resistor-don't cut or splice."**

When attaching a single No. 16, 17, 18 or 20 gauge fuse link to a heavy gauge wire, always double the stripped wire end of the fuse link before inserting and crimping it into the butt connector for positive wire retention.

Add-On Electrical Equipment

The electrical system in your vehicle is designed to perform under reasonable operating conditions without interference between components. Before any additional electrical equipment is installed, it is recommended that you consult your dealer or a reputable repair facility that is familiar with the vehicle and its systems.

If the vehicle is equipped with mobile radio equipment and/or mobile telephone, it may have an effect upon the operation of any on-board computer control modules. Radio Frequency Interference (RFI) from the communications system can be picked up by the vehicle's wiring harnesses and conducted into the control module, giving it the wrong messages at the wrong time. Although well shielded against RFI, the computer should be further protected by taking the following measures:

• Install the antenna as far as possible from the control module. For instance, if the module is located behind the center console area, then the antenna should be mounted at the rear of the vehicle.

• Keep the antenna wiring a minimum of eight inches away from any wiring running to control modules and from the module itself. NEVER wind the antenna wire around any other wiring.

• Mount the equipment as far from the control module as possible. Be very careful during installation not to drill through any wires or short a wire harness with a mounting screw.

• Insure that the electrical feed wire(s) to the equipment are properly and tightly connected. Loose connectors can cause interference.

• Make certain that the equipment is properly grounded to the vehicle. Poor grounding can damage expensive equipment.

Troubleshooting Basic Starting System Problems

Problem	Cause	Solution
Starter motor rotates engine slowly	• Battery charge low or battery defective	• Charge or replace battery
	• Defective circuit between battery and starter motor	• Clean and tighten, or replace cables
	• Low load current	• Bench-test starter motor. Inspect for worn brushes and weak brush springs.
	• High load current	• Bench-test starter motor. Check engine for friction, drag or coolant in cylinders. Check ring gear-to-pinion gear clearance.
Starter motor will not rotate engine	• Battery charge low or battery defective	• Charge or replace battery
	• Faulty solenoid	• Check solenoid ground. Repair or replace as necessary.
	• Damaged drive pinion gear or ring gear	• Replace damaged gear(s)
	• Starter motor engagement weak	• Bench-test starter motor
	• Starter motor rotates slowly with high load current	• Inspect drive yoke pull-down and point gap, check for worn end bushings, check ring gear clearance
	• Engine seized	• Repair engine
Starter motor drive will not engage (solenoid known to be good)	• Defective contact point assembly	• Repair or replace contact point assembly
	• Inadequate contact point assembly ground	• Repair connection at ground screw
	• Defective hold-in coil	• Replace field winding assembly
Starter motor drive will not disengage	• Starter motor loose on flywheel housing	• Tighten mounting bolts
	• Worn drive end busing	• Replace bushing
	• Damaged ring gear teeth	• Replace ring gear or driveplate
	• Drive yoke return spring broken or missing	• Replace spring
Starter motor drive disengages prematurely	• Weak drive assembly thrust spring	• Replace drive mechanism
	• Hold-in coil defective	• Replace field winding assembly
Low load current	• Worn brushes	• Replace brushes
	• Weak brush springs	• Replace springs

tccs2c01

FASTENERS
  BOLTS AND SCREWS 3-28
  LOCKWASHERS 3-29
  NUTS 3-28
  SCREW AND BOLT
    TERMINOLOGY 3-29
  STUDS 3-28
SUPPLIES AND EQUIPMENT
  CHEMICALS 3-2
  FLUID DISPOSAL 3-2
TOOLS
  AIR TOOLS AND
    COMPRESSORS 3-21
  ELECTRIC POWER TOOLS 3-21
  ENGINE TOOLS 3-22
  HANDS TOOLS 3-6
  SHOP CRANES, DOLLIES, JACKS
    AND ENGINE STANDS 3-22
  SPECIAL TOOLS 3-20

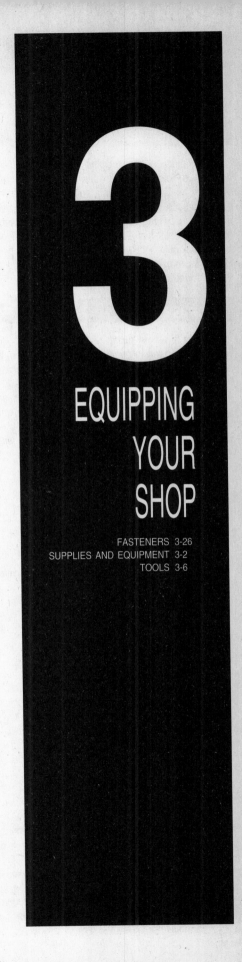

3

EQUIPPING YOUR SHOP

FASTENERS 3-26
SUPPLIES AND EQUIPMENT 3-2
TOOLS 3-6

SUPPLIES AND EQUIPMENT

Fluid Disposal

Used fluids such as engine oil, transmission fluid, antifreeze and brake fluid are hazardous wastes and must be disposed of properly. Before draining any fluids, consult with your local authorities; in many areas waste oil, etc. is being accepted as a part of recycling programs. A number of service stations and auto parts stores are also accepting waste fluids for recycling.

Be sure of the recycling center's policies before draining any fluids, as many will not accept different fluids that have been mixed together.

Chemicals

There is a whole range of chemicals that you'll be needing. The most common types are, lubricants, penetrants and sealers. Keep these handy, on some convenient shelf. You'll be using each type throughout the rebuild.

When a particular chemical is not being used, keep it capped, upright and in a safe place. These substances may be flammable or irritants or caustic and should always be stored properly, used properly and handled with care. Always read and follow all label directions and wear hand and eye protection!

Lubricants and Penetrants

▶ **See Figure 1**

In this category you'll need:
• Clean engine oil. Whatever you use regularly in your engine will be fine.
• Lithium grease.
• Chassis lube
• Assembly lube
• Silicone grease
• Silicone spray
• Penetrating oil

Clean engine oil is used to coat most bolts, screws and nuts prior to installation. This is always a good practice since the less friction there is on a fastener, the less chance there will be of breakage and crossthreading. Also, an oiled bolt will give a truer torque value and be less likely to rust or seize. An obvious exception would be exhaust manifold bolts or studs. These are not oiled.

Lithium grease, chassis lube and silicone grease can all be used pretty much interchangeably. All can be used for coating rust-prone fasteners and for facilitating the assembly of parts which are a tight fit. Silicone grease is the most versatile and should always be used on the inside of spark plug wire boots as a release agent.

Silicone spray is a good lubricant for hard-to-reach places and parts that shouldn't be gooped up with grease.

Penetrating oil may turn out to be one of your best friends during disassembly. The most familiar penetrating oils are Liquid Wrench® and WD-40®. These products have hundreds of uses. For your purposes, they are vital!

Before disassembling any part, check the fasteners. If any appear rusted, soak them thoroughly with the penetrant and let them stand while you do something else. This simple act can save you hours of tedious work trying to extract a broken bolt or stud.

Assembly lube. There are several types of this product available. Essentially it is a heavy bodied lubricant used for coating moving parts prior to assembly. The idea is that is stays in place until the engine starts for the first time and dissolves in the engine oil as oil pressure is achieved. This way, expensive parts receive needed protection until everything is working.

Sealants

▶ **See Figure 2**

Sealants are an indispensible part of almost all automotive work. The purpose of sealants is to establish a leak-proof bond between or around assembled parts. Most sealers are used in conjunction with gaskets, but some are used instead of conventional gasket material in newer engines.

The most common sealers are the non-hardening types such as Permatex®No.2 or its equivalents. These sealers are applied to the mating surfaces of each part to be joined, then a gasket is put in place and the parts are assembled.

One very helpful type of non-hardening sealer is the 'high tack' type. This type is a very sticky material which holds the gasket in place while the parts are being assembled. This stuff is really a good idea when you don't have enough hands or fingers to keep everything where it should be.

The stand-alone sealers are the RTV (Room Temperature Vulcanizing) silicone gasket makers. On may newer engines, this material is used instead of a gasket. In those instances, a gasket amy not be available or, because of the shape of the mating surfaces, a gasket shouldn't be used. This stuff, when used in conjunction with a conventional gasket, produces the surest bonds.

It does have its limitations though. When using this material, you will have a time limit. It starts to set-up within 15 minutes or so, so you have to assemble the parts without delay. In addition, when squeezing the material out of the tube, don't drop any glops into the engine. The stuff will form and set and travel around the oil gallery, possibly plugging up a passage. Also, most types are not fuel-proof. Check the tube for all cautions.

Cleaners

▶ **See Figures 3, 4 and 5**

You'll have two types of cleaners to deal with: parts cleaners and hand cleaners.

The parts cleaners are for the engine; the hand cleaners are for you.

There are many good, non-flammable, biodegradable parts cleaners on the market. These cleaning agents are safe for you, the parts and the environment. Therefore, there is no

87933516

Fig. 1 Penetrants and lubricants

reason to use flammable, caustic or toxic substances to clean your parts or tools.

As far as hand cleaners go, the waterless types are the best. They have always been efficient at cleaning, but left behind a pretty smelly odor. Recently though, just about all of them have eliminated the odor and added stuff that actually smells good. Make sure that you pick one that contains lanolin or some other moisture-replenishing additive. Cleaners not only remove grease and oil but also skin oil.

One other note: most women know this already but most men don't. Use a hand lotion when you're all cleaned up. It's okay. Real men DO use hand lotion!

Shop Towels

▶ **See Figure 6**

One of the most important elements in doing shop work is a good supply of shop towels. Paper towels just don't cut it! Most auto parts stores sell packs of shop towels, usually 50-100 in a pack. They are relatively cheap and can be washed over and over. Always keep them handy.

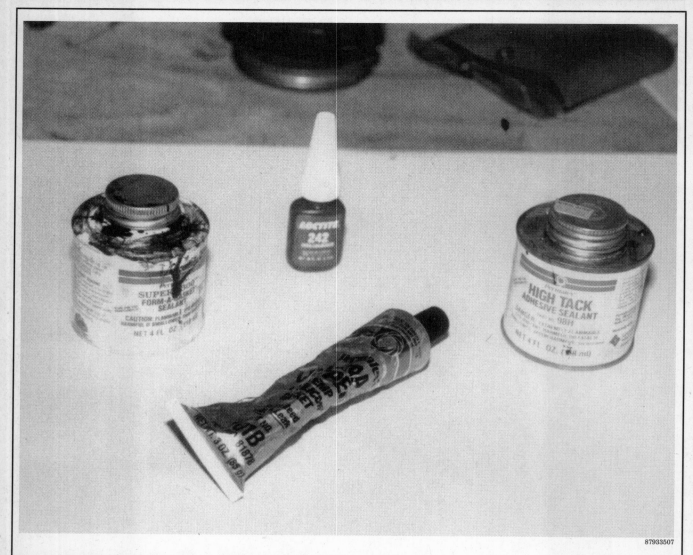

87933507

Fig. 2 Sealants are essential. These four types are all that you'll need

Fig. 3 Three types of cleaners. Some are caustic; some are not

87933508

87933018

Fig. 4 This is one type of hand cleaner that not only works well but smells pretty good too

87932003

Fig. 5 Along with cleaners, you'll need clean-up material. The best thing for all types of spills is 'kitty litter'

TOOLS

▶ **See Figures 7, 8, 9 and 10**

Every do-it-yourselfer loves to accumulate tools. So gathering the tools necessary for engine work can be real fun!

When buying tools, the saying 'You get what you pay for' is absolutely true! Don't go cheap! Any hand tool that you buy should be drop forged and/or chrome vanadium. These two qualities tell you that the tool is strong enough for the job. With any tool, power or not, go with a name that you've heard of before, or, that is recommended buy your local professional retailer. Let's go over a list of tools that you'll need.

87933065

Fig. 6 A pack of shop towels

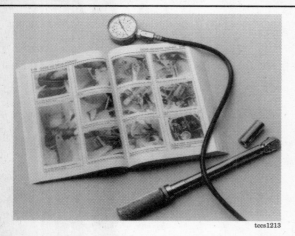

tccs1213

Fig. 7 The most important tool you need to do the job is the proper information, so always have a Chilton Total Car Care manual handy

Hands Tools

Socket sets

▶ **See Figures 11, 12, 13 and 14**

Socket sets are the most basic, necessary hand tools for engine work. For our purposes, socket sets come in three drive sizes: ¼ inch, ⅜ inch and ½ inch. Drive size refers to the size of the drive lug on the ratchet, breaker bar or speed handle.

You'll need a good ½ inch set since this size drive lug assure that you won't break a ratchet or socket. Also, torque wrenches with a torque scale high enough are all ½ inch drive. The socket set that you'll need should range is sizes from 7/16 inch through 1 inch.

A ⅜ set is very handy to have since it allows you to get into tight places that the larger drive ratches can't. Also, this size set gives you a range of smaller sockets which are still strong enough for heavy duyt work.

¼ inch drive sets aren't really necessary or applicable for engine work, but they're good to have for other, light work around the car or house. Besides, they're tools...you NEED them!

As for the sockets themselves, they come in standard and deep lengths, standard and thin walled and 6 and 12 point.

Standard length sockets are good for just about all jobs, however, some stud-head bolts, hard-to-reach bolts, nuts on long studs, etc., require the deep sockets.

Thin-walled sockets are not too common and aren't usually needed in engine work. They are exactly what you think, sockets made with thinner wall to fit into tighter places. They don't have the wall strength of a standard socket, of course, but their usefulness in a tight spot can make them worth it.

6 and 12 points. This refers to how many sides are in the socket itself. Each has advantages. The 6 point socket is stronger and less prone to slipping which would strip a bolt head or nut. 12 point sockets are more common, usually less expensive and can operate better in tight places where the ratchet handle can't swing far.

Torque Wrenches
▶ **See Figure 15**

In most applications, a torque wrench can be used to assure proper installation of a fastener. Torque wrenches come in various designs and most automotive supply stores will carry a variety to suit your needs. A torque wrench should be used any time we supply a specific torque value for a fastener. A torque wrench can also be used if you are following the general guidelines in the accompanying charts. Keep in mind that because there is no worldwide standardization of fasteners, the charts are a general guideline and should be used with caution. Again, the general rule of "if you are using the right tool for the job, you should not have to strain to tighten a fastener" applies here.

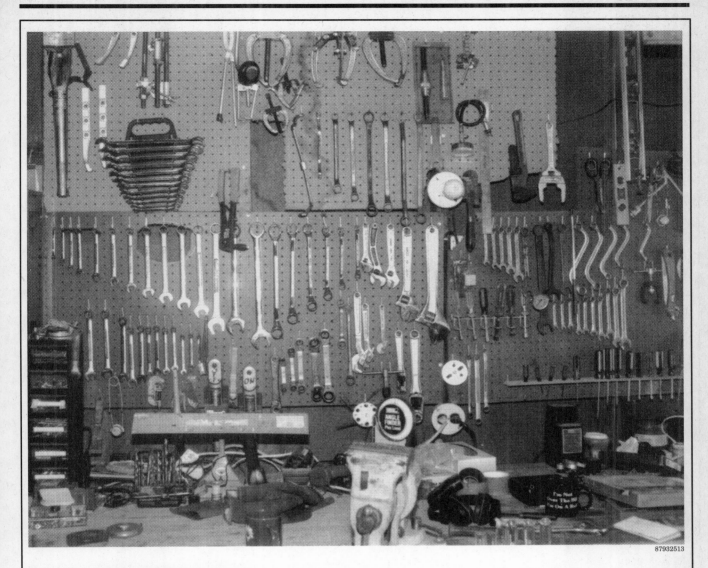

Fig. 8 The well-stocked garage pegboard

BEAM TYPE

▶ See Figure 16

The beam type torque wrench is one of the most popular types. It consists of a pointer attached to the head that runs the length of the flexible beam (shaft) to a scale located near the handle. As the wrench is pulled, the beam bends and the pointer indicates the torque using the scale.

CLICK (BREAKAWAY) TYPE

▶ See Figure 17

Another popular design of torque wrench is the click type. To use the click type wrench you pre-adjust it to a torque setting. Once the torque is reached, the wrench has a reflex signalling feature that causes a momentary breakaway of the torque wrench body, sending an impulse to the operator's hand.

PIVOT HEAD TYPE

▶ See Figure 18

Some torque wrenches (usually of the click type) may be equipped with a pivot head which can allow it to be used in areas of limited access. BUT, it must be used properly. To hold a pivot head wrench, grasp the handle lightly, and as you pull on the handle, it should be floated on the pivot point. If the handle comes in contact with the yoke extension during the process of pulling, there is a very good chance the torque readings will be inaccurate because this could alter the wrench

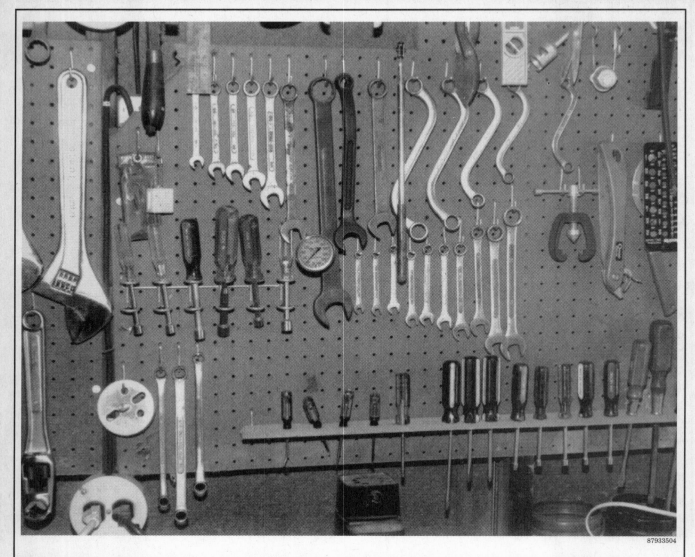

87933504

Fig. 9 You can arrange the pegboard any way you like, but it's best to hang the most used tools closest to you

87932007

Fig. 10 A good set of handy storage cabinets for fasteners and small parts makes any job easier

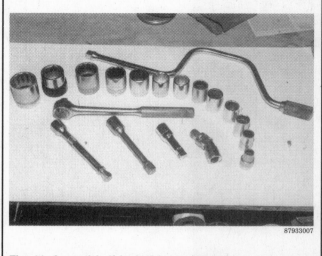

87933007

Fig. 11 A good half inch drive socket set

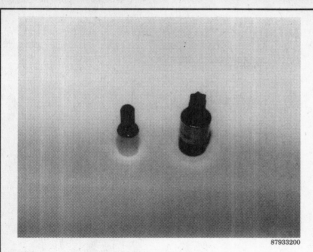

Fig. 12 Left, a hex drive socket; right, a Torx drive socket

Fig. 13 Two types of drive adapters and a swivel (U-joint) adapter

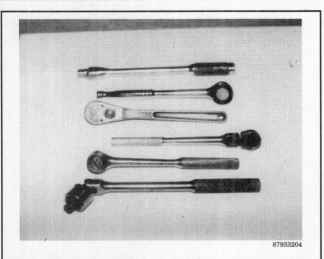

Fig. 14 Ratchets come in all sizes from rigid to swivel-headed

loading point. The design of the handle is usually such as to make it inconvenient to deliberately misuse the wrench.

➡ It should be mentioned that the use of any U-joint, wobble or extension will have an effect on the torque readings, no matter what type of wrench you are using. For the most accurate readings, install the socket directly on the wrench driver. If necessary, straight extensions (which hold a socket directly under the wrench driver) will have the least effect on the torque reading. Avoid any extension that alters the length of the wrench from the handle to the head/driving point (such as a crow's foot). U-joint or Wobble extensions can greatly affect the readings; avoid their use at all times.

RIGID CASE (DIRECT READING)

▶ See Figure 19

A rigid case or direct reading torque wrench is equipped with a dial indicator to show torque values. One advantage of these wrenches is that they can be held at any position on the wrench without affecting accuracy. These wrenches are often preferred because they tend to be compact, easy to read and have a great degree of accuracy.

TORQUE ANGLE METERS

▶ See Figure 20

Because the frictional characteristics of each fastener or threaded hole will vary, clamp loads which are based strictly on torque will vary as well. In most applications, this variance is not significant enough to cause worry. But, in certain applications, a manufacturer's engineers may determine that more precise clamp loads are necessary (such is the case with many aluminum cylinder heads). In these cases, a torque angle method of installation would be specified. When installing fasteners which are torque angle tightened, a predetermined seating torque and standard torque wrench are usually used first to remove any compliance from the joint. The fastener is then tightened the specified additional portion of a turn measured in degrees. A torque angle gauge (mechanical protractor) is used for these applications.

Breaker Bars

Breaker bars are long handles with a drive lug. Their main purpose is to provide extra turning force when breaking loose tight bolts or nuts. They come in all drive sizes and lengths. Always wear gloves when using a breaker bar

Speed Handles

▶ See Figure 21

Speed handles are tools with a drive lug and angled turning handle which allow you to quickly remove or install a bolt or nut. They don't, however have much torque ability. You might consider one when installing a number of similar bolts such as head bolts or main bearing cap nuts.

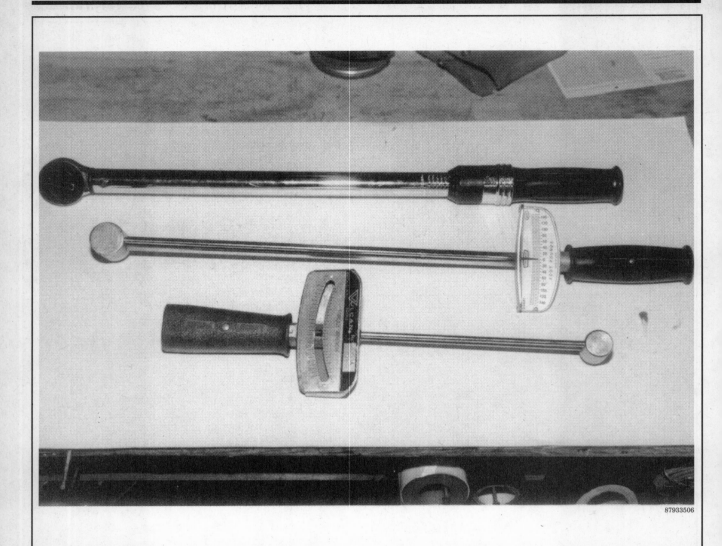

87933506

Fig. 15 Three types of torque wrenches. Top to bottom: a half inch drive clicker type, a half inch drive beam type and a three-eights in drive beam type that read in inch lbs.

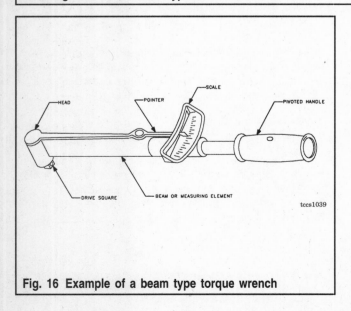

HEAD POINTER SCALE PIVOTED HANDLE DRIVE SQUARE BEAM OR MEASURING ELEMENT

tccs1039

Fig. 16 Example of a beam type torque wrench

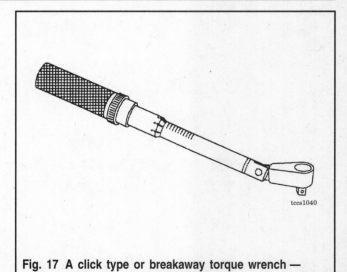

tccs1040

Fig. 17 A click type or breakaway torque wrench — note this one has a pivoting head

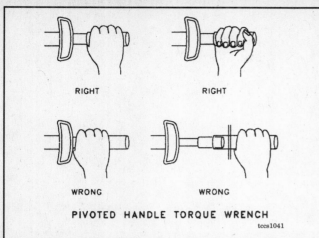

Fig. 18 Torque wrenches with pivoting heads must be grasped and used properly to prevent an incorrect reading

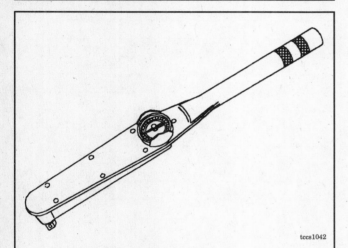

Fig. 19 The rigid case (direct reading) torque wrench uses a dial indicator to show torque

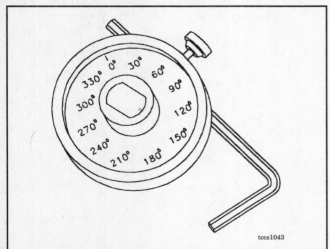

Fig. 20 Some specifications require the use of a torque angle meter (mechanical protractor)

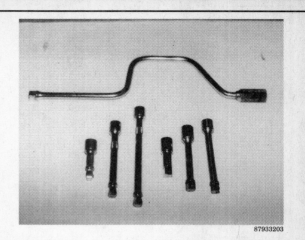

Fig. 21 A speed driver and drive extensions. The three extensions on the left are called 'wobble' extensions since they allow some lateral movement

Wrenches

▶ See Figures 22, 23, 24 and 25

Basically, there are 3 kinds of fixed wrenches: open end, box end, and combination.

Open end wrenches have 2-jawed end ends at each end of the wrench. These wrenches are able to fit onto just about any nut or bolt. They are extremely versatile but have one major drawback. They can slip on a worn or rounded bolt head or nut and cause bleeding knuckles and a useless fastener.

Box-end wrenches have a 360° circular jaw at each end of the wrench. They come in both 6 and 12 point versions just like sockets and each type has the same advantages and disadvantages as sockets.

Combination wrenches have the best of both. They have a 2-jawed open end and a box end. These wrenches are probably the most versatile.

As for sizes, you'll need a range of ¼ inch through 1 inch. As for numbers, you'll need 2 of each size, since, in many instances, one wrench holds the nut while the other turns the bolt. On most fasteners, the nut and bolt are the same size.

One extremely valuable type of wrench is the adjustable wrench. An adjustable wrench has a fixed upper jaw and a moveable lower jaw. The lower jaw is moved by turning a threaded drum. The advantage of an adjustable wrench is its ability to be adjusted to just about any size fastener. The main drawback of an adjustable wrench is the lower jaw's tendency to move slightly under heavy pressure. This can cause the wrench to slip. Adjustable wrenches come in a large range of sizes, measured by the wrench length.

Pliers

▶ See Figure 26

At least 2 pair of standard pliers is an absolute necessity. Pliers are simply mechanical fingers. They are, more than anything, an extension of your hand.

INCHES	DECIMAL		DECIMAL	MILLIMETERS
1/8"	.125		.118	3mm
3/16"	.187		.157	4mm
1/4"	.250		.236	6mm
5/16"	.312		.354	9mm
3/8"	.375		.394	10mm
7/16"	.437		.472	12mm
1/2"	.500		.512	13mm
9/16"	.562		.590	15mm
5/8"	.625		.630	16mm
11/16"	.687		.709	18mm
3/4"	.750		.748	19mm
13/16"	.812		.787	20mm
7/8"	.875		.866	22mm
15/16"	.937		.945	24mm
1"	1.00		.984	25mm

87933106

Fig. 22 Comparison of U.S. measure and metric wrench sizes

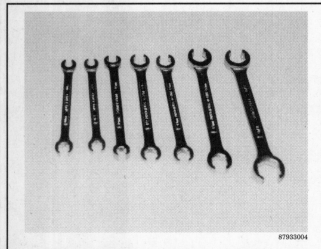

87933004

Fig. 23 Flarenut wrenches. They are useful for turning nuts mounted on tubing

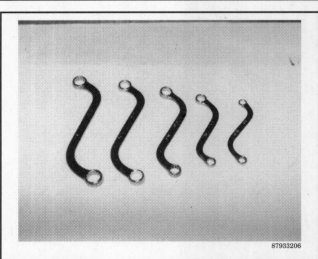

87933206

Fig. 24 These S-shaped wrenches are called obstruction wrenches

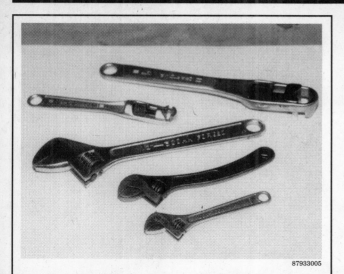

Fig. 25 Several types and sizes of adjustable wrenches

In addition to standard pliers there are the slip-joint, multi-position pliers such as ChannelLock® pliers and locking pliers, such as Vise Grips®.

Slip joint pliers are extremely valuable in grasping oddly sized parts and fasteners. Just make sure that you don't use them instead of a wrench too often since they can easily round off a bolt head or nut.

Locking pliers are usually used for gripping bolt or stud that can't be removed conventionally. You can get locking pliers in square jawed, needle-nosed and pipe-jawed. Pipe jawed have slightly curved jaws for gripping more than just pipes. Locking pliers can rank right up behind duct tape as the handy-man's best friend.

Screwdrivers

You can't have too many screwdrivers. Screwdrivers are either standard or Phillips. Standard blades come in various sizes and thicknesses for all types of slotted fasteners. Phillips screwdrivers come in three sizes: No. 1, 2 and 3; 3 being the largest. Screwdrivers can be purchased separately or in sets.

Hammers

▶ **See Figure 27**

You always need a hammer — for just about any kind of work. For engine work, you need a ball-peen hammer for using drivers and other like tools, a plastic hammer for hitting things safely, and a soft-faced dead-blow hammer for hitting things safely and hard.

Other Common Tools

▶ **See Figures 28, 29, 30 and 31**

There are a lot of other tools that every workshop should have for automotive work. The include:
- Chisels
- Punches
- Files
- Hacksaw
- Bench Vise
- Tap and Die Set
- Gasket scraper
- Putty Knife
- Screw/Bolt Extractors
- Pry Bar

Chisel, punches and files are repair tools. There uses will come up during the rebuilding operation.

Chisel, punches and files are repair tools. There uses will come up during the rebuilding operation.

Hacksaws have just one use, cutting things off. You may wonder why you'd need one for something as precise as engine work, but the chances are you will. Among other things, guide studs for parts installation can be made from old bolts with their heads cut off.

A large bench vise — 4 inch capacity is good — is essential. A vise is needed to hold anything being worked on.

A tap and die set might be something you've never needed, but you can't get along without it when rebuilding. It's a good rule, when everything is apart, to run clean-up all threads, on bolts, screws and threaded holes. Also, you'll likely run across a situation in which stripped threads will be encountered. The tap and die set will handle that for you.

Gasket scrapers are just what you'd think, tools made for scraping old gasket material off of parts. You don't absolutely need one. Old gasket material can be remove with a putty knife or single edge razor blade. However, putty knives may not be sharp enough for some really stuck gaskets and razor blades have a knack of breaking just when you don't want them to, inevitably slicing the nearest body part!

Putty knives really do have a use in automotive work. Just because you remove all the bolts from a rocker cover or oil pan doesn't mean it's going to come off. Most of the time, the gasket and sealer will hold it tightly. Lightly driving a putty knife at various points between the two parts will break the seal without damage to the parts.

A small — 8-10 inches long — pry bar is extremely useful for removing stuck parts such as cylinder heads, timing cases, intake manifolds, etc. NEVER, NEVER, use a screwdriver as a pry bar! Screwdrivers are not meant for prying. Screwdrivers, used for prying, can break, sending the broken shaft flying!

Screw/bolt extractors are used for removing broken bolts or studs that have broke off flush with the surface of the part. Their function will be explained in Chapter 4.

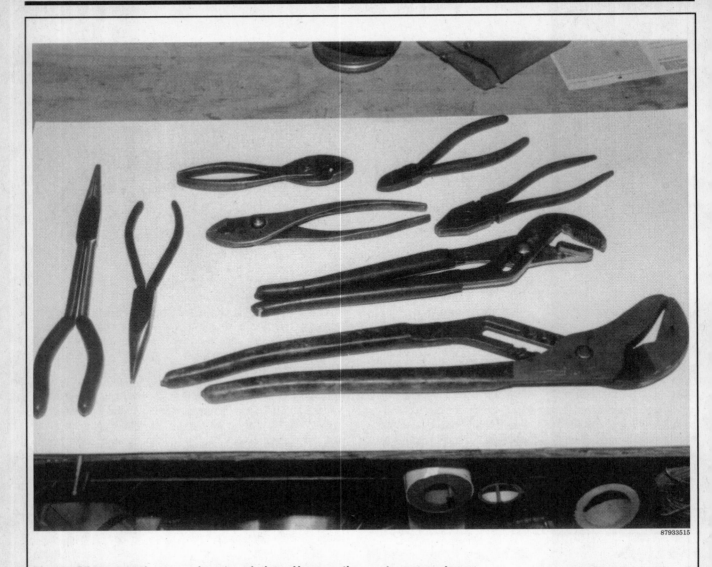

87933515

Fig. 26 Pliers come in many shapes and sizes. Here are the most common types

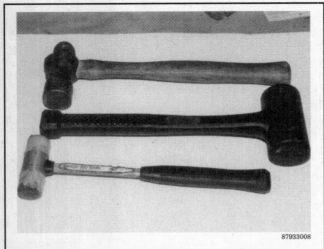

87933008

Fig. 27 Three types of hammers. Top to bottom: ball peen, rubber dead-blow, and plastic

87933069

Fig. 28 A good quality, heavy-duty bench vise, like this 5½ in. type, with reversible jaws, is ideal for shop work

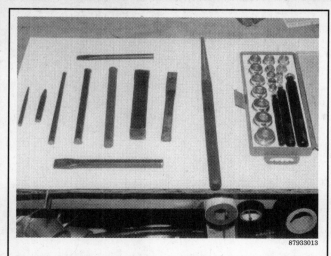

Fig. 29 Punches, chisels and drivers can be purchased separately or in sets

Fig. 30 Two good tap and die sets; US measure (left) and metric

Automotive Tools

In addition to the common hand tools, there are a number of tools designed specifically for automotive work. They are:

- ring groove cleaner
- piston ring compressor
- piston ring spreader
- valve spring compressor
- valve lifter magnet
- oil filter wrench
- cylinder hone
- ridge reamer
- valve lapper
- 2 in. 2-jaw puller
- 2-jaw pullers
- 3-jaw pullers
- damper puller set
- O-Ring Picks

Piston Ring Expander
▶ **See Figure 32**

The piston ring spreader is used for removing and installing the rings. Unlike piston ring compressors, a piston ring installer is not absolutely necessary. But if you are a little doubtful of your ability, you should get one. They are not that expensive (certainly not as much as a new set of rings), and they will add immeasurably to your peace of mind.

Ring Groove Cleaner

The ring groove cleaner is used for cleaning the ring grooves in the pistons after the rings are removed. Some engine rebuilders will say that a ring groove cleaner is not necessary; that an old piece of broken piston ring will work just as well. While a broken piston ring will accomplish the same thing, it will take three times as long, and you will wear your hands out. Buy the ring groove cleaner.

Piston Ring Compressor

There are two basic types of ring compressor. The most common utilizes an allen wrench to activate the compression process. The other uses a pliers. The ring compressor is used for pushing the rings within the ring grooves so that the piston can be installed in the cylinder. This tool is indispensable. There is simply no way to get a ringed piston into the cylinder without a compressor. It's use will be discussed further in Chapter 5.

Cylinder Hone or Glaze Breaker

There are two types of cylinder hones: those that follow the existing bore (spring-loaded or ball-type hones) and those that remain rigid and cut their own path. Rigid hones are used to hone cylinders that have a pronounced amount of wear and out-of-roundness. Spring-loaded or ball-type hones are used for cylinders that are not as badly worn or to get a good cross-hatch pattern on a recently rebored cylinder. Ball-type hones are generally acknowledged to give a better result, but they are not as versatile as the spring-loaded type because each particular ball-type hone will only fit a certain range of bore sizes.

Ridge Reamer
▶ **See Figure 33**

A ridge reamer is the sort of tool you will not know you are going to need until you get the cylinder heads off the engine. Engines with well over 100,000 miles on them sometimes won't have a ridge, and some with 50,000 miles on them will. A cylinder ridge is a combination of unworn cylinder bore and some carbon buildup. Because the top piston ring cannot get all the way to the top of the cylinder, there will always be a slight (or not so slight) amount of unworn bore here. It has to be removed before you can remove the pistons from the engine. A ridge reamer is essentially a cutting tool designed to do this particular job. The cutter can be expanded to fit a variety of bore sizes.

Most ridge reamers have 3 or 4 cutting blades. The tool is placed in the top of a cylinder and turned with a wrench to remove the ridge caused by cylinder wear.

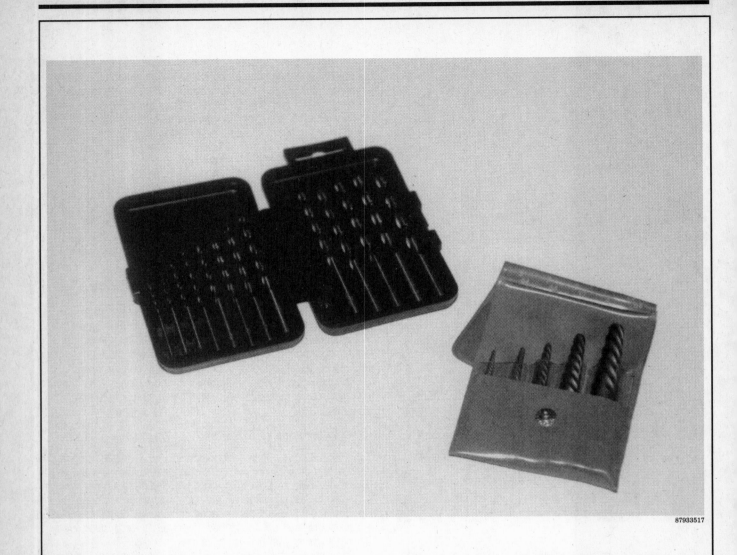

87933517

Fig. 31 A set of drill bits and a set of screw extractors

Valve Lappers

▶ See Figure 34

The valve lapper is basically a handle with a suction cup. When installing reground or new valves, the valve lapper is used, in conjunction with lapping compound, to effectively mate the valves with their seats in the head. The precise use will be explained in Chapter 5.

Pullers

▶ See Figures 35 and 36

The 2- and 3-jawed pullers are used mainly for removing bearings, gears and sprockets, although you'll find they come in handy for a number of other things. Pullers come in various sizes. We'd recommend that you have 2 in., 4 in., 6 in., and 8 in. pullers.

The damper puller is essential for removing the crankshaft damper. You can't do the job without it. Complete instructions are supplied with the damper kit.

Gauges and Testers

▶ See Figures 37, 38 and 39

- spark plug gauge
- 30 in. machinist's straightedge
- 40-piece flat feeler gauge set
- starter/alternator tester
- auto-ranging, digital multi-tester
- Tach/Dwell/Voltmeter
- vacuum gauge
- vacuum pump
- timing light
- compression tester

Everybody knows what a spark plug gauge set is. But, if you don't, it's used for checking the gap between the spark plug's center and ground electrodes.

The machinist's straightedge is used to check the flatness of cylinder heads, block surfaces and intake manifold surfaces. You'll need one that is at least 30 inches long.

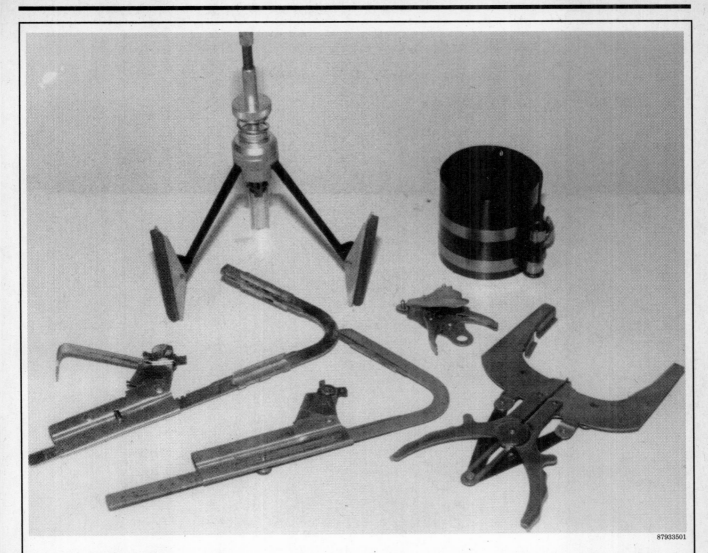

Fig. 32 An assortment of piston-related tools. From the top, clockwise: cylinder hone, piston ring compressor, ring expanders, and 2 types of ring groove cleaners

A set of flat feeler gauges is needed to measure the gap between parts where gapping is critical or part of the part's function. A 40-piece set will give you all the feelers that you'll ever need.

Micrometers and Calipers

Outside Micrometers

Outside micrometers are used to check the diameters of such components as the pistons and crankshaft. The most common type of micrometer reads in 1/1000 of an inch. Micrometers that use a vernier scale can estimate to 1/10 of an inch. The illustrations show the various part names.

Micrometers and calipers are devices used to make extremely precise measurements. The success of any rebuild is dependent, to a great extent on the ability to check the size and fit of components as specified by the engine manufacturer. These measurements are made in thousandths and ten-thousandths of an inch.

A micrometer is an instrument made up of a precisely machined spindle which is rotated in a fixed nut, opening and closing the distance between the end of the spindle and a fixed anvil.

To make a measurement, you back off the spindle until you can place the piece to be measured between the spindle and anvil. You then rotate the spindle until the part is contacted by both the spindle and anvil. The measurement is then found by reading the gradations in the handle of the micrometer.

Here's the hard part. I'll try to explain how to read a micrometer. The spindle is threaded. Most micrometers use a thread pitch of 40 threads per inch. One complete revolution of the spindle move the spindle toward or away from the anvil 0.025 in. ($\frac{1}{40}$ in.).

The fixed part of the handle (called, the sleeve) is marked with 40 gradations per inch of handle length, so each line is 0.025 in. apart. Okay so far?

Every 4th line is marked with a number. The first long line marked 1 represents 0.100 in., the second is 0.200 in., and so on.

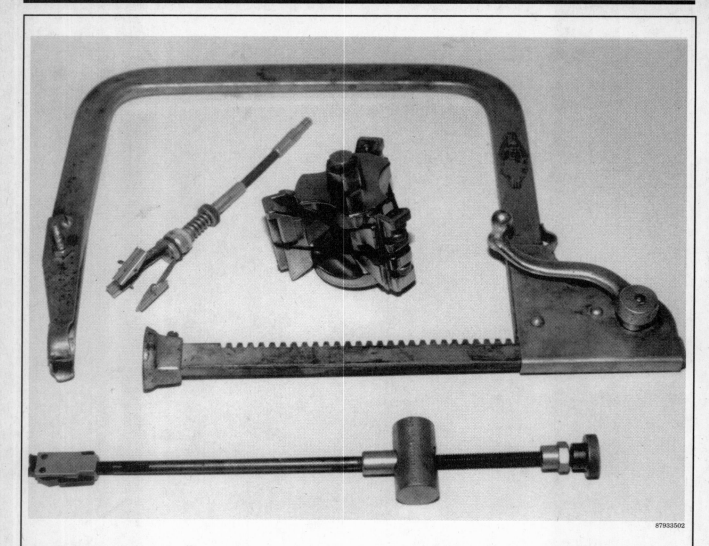

Fig. 33 More special tools. The big thing is a valve spring compressor. Positioned within it are a small hone (left) and a ridge reamer. Underneath is a lifter puller.

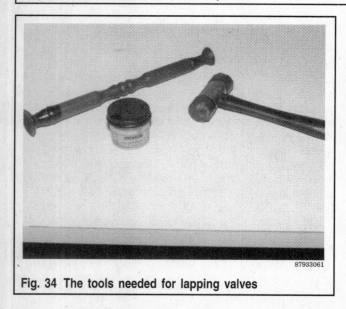

Fig. 34 The tools needed for lapping valves

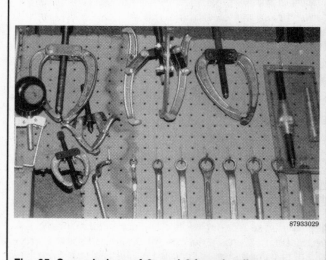

Fig. 35 Several sizes of 2- and 3-jawed pullers

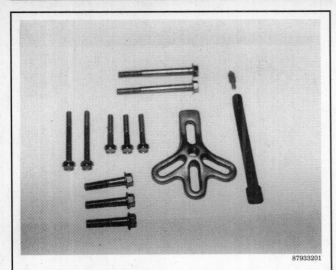

Fig. 36 The various parts of a damper puller

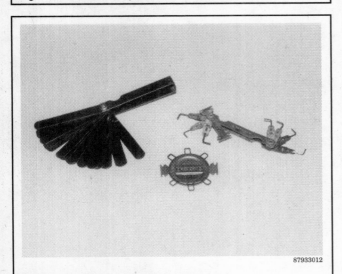

Fig. 37 Flat and round feeler gauges

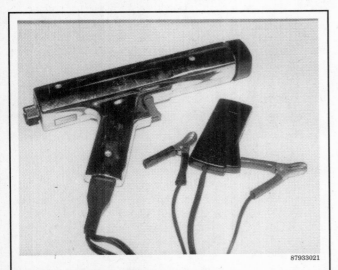

Fig. 38 A typical inductive timing light

The part of the handle that turns is called the thimble. The beveled end of the thimble is marked with gradations, each of which corresponds to 0.001 in. and, usually, every 5th line is numbered.

Turn the thimble until the 0 lines up with the 0 on the sleeve. Now, rotate the thimble one complete revolution and look at the sleeve. You'll see that one complete thimble revolution moved the thimble 0.025 in. down the sleeve.

To read the micrometer, multiply the number of gradations exposed on the sleeve by 0.025 and add that to the number of thousandths indicated by the thimble line that is lined up with the horizontal line on the sleeve. So, if you've measured a part and there are 6 vertical gradations exposed on the sleeve and the 7th gradation on the thimble is lined up with the horizontal line on the sleeve, the thickness of the part is 0.157 in. (6 x 0.025 = 0.150 . Add to that 0.007 representing the 7 lines on the thimble and you get 0.157). See?

If you didn't understand that, try the instructions that come with the micrometer or ask someone that knows, to show you how to work it.

Inside Micrometers

Inside micrometers are used to measure the distance between two parallel surfaces. In engine rebuilding work, the inside mike measures cylinder bore wear, connecting rod big end wear, and block main bearing bore sizes. Inside mikes are graduated the same way as outside mikes and are read the same way as well.

Remember that an inside mike must be absolutely perpendicular to the work being measured. When you measure with an inside mike, rock the mike gently from side to side and tip it back and forth slightly so that you span the widest part of the bore. Just to be on the safe side, take several readings. It takes a certain amount of experience to work any mike with confidence.

Metric Micrometers

Metric micrometers are read in the same way as inch micrometers, except that the measurements are in millimeters. Each line on the main scale equals 1 mm. Each fifth line is stamped 5, 10, 15, and so on. Each line on the thimble scale equals 0.01 mm. It will take a little practice, but if you can read an inch mike, you can read a metric mike.

Inside and Outside Calipers

Inside and outside calipers are useful devices to have if you need to measure something quickly and precise measurement is not necessary. Simply take the reading and then hold the calipers on an accurate steel rule.

DIAL INDICATORS

A dial indicator is a gauge that utilizes a dial face and a needle to register measurements. There is a movable contact arm on the dial indicator. When the arms moves, the needle rotates on the dial. Dial indicators are calibrated to show readings in thousandths of an inch and typically, are used to measure end play and runout on camshafts, crankshafts, gears, and so on.

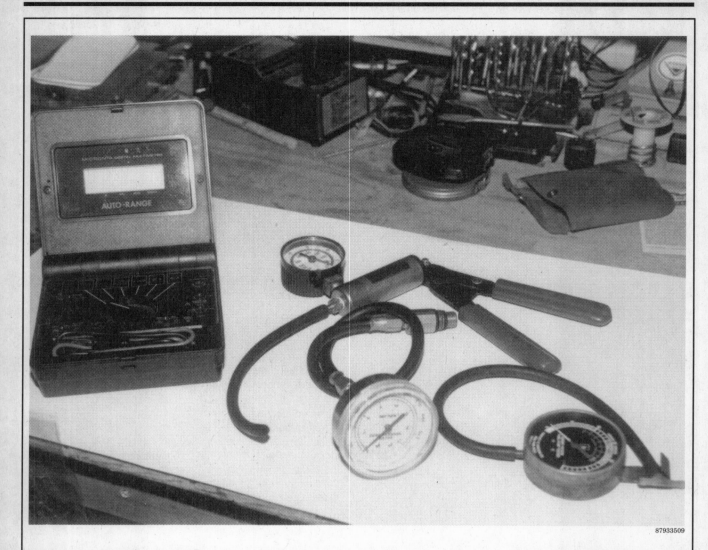

Fig. 39 Several types of test equipment. Left to right: digital multi-tester, vacuum pump, compression tester and vacuum gauge

Dial indicators are quite easy to use, although they are relatively expensive. A variety of mounting devices are available so that the indicator can be used in a number of situations. Make certain that the contact arm is always parallel to the movement of the work being measured.

TELESCOPING GAUGES

A telescope gauge is used to measure the inside of bores, connecting rod big ends, and so on. They can take the place of an inside mike for some of these jobs. Simply insert the gauge in the hole to be measured and lock the plungers after they have contacted the walls. Remove the tool and measure across the plungers with an outside micrometer.

PLASTIGAGE®

Plastigage is a sort of soft plastic that will flatten out to predetermined widths when subjected to torquing. These widths will equal a specific clearance. Plastigage is normally used to check main and rod-bearing clearance. It is sold in a paper sleeve that also doubles as the scale upon which it is measured. The scale reads out in thousandths of an inch. The most common type is green Plastigage which is used to measure clearances from 0.001 to 0.003 in. Its use will be discussed later, in Chapter 5.

Special Tools

Normally, the use of special factory tools is avoided for repair procedures, since these are not readily available for the do-it-yourself mechanic. When it is possible to perform the job with more commonly available tools, it will be pointed out, but occasionally, a special tool was designed to perform a specific function and should be used. Before substituting another tool, you should be convinced that neither your safety nor the performance of the vehicle will be compromised.

Special tools can usually be purchased from an automotive parts store or from your dealer. In some cases special tools may be available directly from the tool manufacturer.

Electric Power Tools

♦ **See Figures 40 and 41**

Power tools are most often associated with wood working. However, there are a few which are very helpful in automotive work.

The most common and most useful power tool is the bench grinder. You'll need a grinder with a grinding stone on one side and a wire brush wheel on the other. The brush wheel is indispensible for cleaning parts and the stone can be used to remove rough surfaces and for reshaping, where necessary.

Almost as useful as the bench grinder is the drill. Drills can come in very handy when a stripped or broken fastener is encountered. See Chapter 4 for their uses.

Power ratchets and impact wrenches can come in very handy. Power ratchets can save a lot of time and muscle when removing and installing long bolts or nuts on long studs, especially where there is little room to swing a manual ratchet.

Electric impact wrenches can be invaluable in a lot of automotive work, especially wheel lugs and axle shaft nuts. They don't have much use on engines, though.

Air Tools and Compressors

♦ **See Figures 43 and 44**

Air-powered tools are not necessary for engine work. They are, however, useful for speeding up many jobs and for general clean-up of parts. If you don't have air tools, and you want them, be prepared for an initial outlay of a lot of money.

The first thing you need is a compressor. Compressors are available in electrically driven and gas engine driven models. As long as you have electricity, you don't need a gas engine driven type.

The common shop-type air compressor is a pump mounted on a tank. The pump compresses air and forces it into the tank where it is stored until you need it. The compressor automatically turns the pump on when the air pressure in the tank falls below a certain preset level.

There are all kinds of air powered tools, including ratchets, impact wrenches, saws, drills, sprayers, nailers, scrapers, riveters, grinders and sanders. In general, air powered tools are much cheaper than their electric counterparts.

When deciding what size compressor unit you need, you'll be driven by two factors: the psi (pounds per square inch) capacity of the unit and the deliver rate in cfm (cubic feet per minute). For example, most air powered ratchets require 90 psi at 4 to 5 cfm to operate at peak efficiency. Grinders and saws may require up to 7 cfm at 90 psi. So, before buying the compressor unit, decide what types of tools you'll want so that you don't short-change yourself on the compressor purchase.

If you decide that a compressor and air tools isn't for you, you can have the benefit of air pressure rather cheaply. Purchase an air storage tank, available in sizes up to 20 gallons at most retail stores that sell aut products. These storage tanks can safely store air pressure up to 125 psi and come with a high pressure nozzle for cleaning things and an air chuck for filling tires. The tank can be filled using the common tire-type air compressor.

Fig. 40 Three types of common power tools useful in your work. Left to right: a hand-held grinder, drill and impact wrench

Fig. 41 The bench grinder may be the most frequently used power tool, since it's used for cleaning just about every part removed from the engine

Fig. 42 This is about the best size and type compressor set for the do-it-yourselfer. It operates off ordinary house current and provides all the air pressure you'll need

Fig. 43 An air storage tank

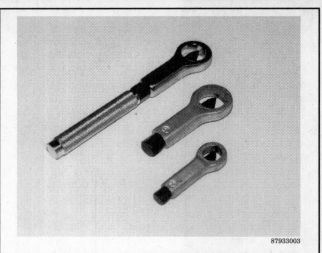

Fig. 44 A really handy tool is the nut splitter. When a frozen nut simply won't budge, use one of these

Engine Tools

▶ See Figure 44

You're not going to need too many tools that are used just for engine work. Among them, the most used are:
- Piston ring expander
- Piston ring compressor
- Valve spring compressor
- Ridge reamer
- 2-jawed puller
- 3-jawed puller
- slide hammer
- dial indicator
- micrometer
- feeler gauges
- calipers
- compression tester
- vacuum gauge
- vacuum pump

The use of of the piston ring tools will be explained in Chapter 5. Essentially they are absolute necessities for removing and installing the rings.

The ridge reamer is used for removing the ridge in a cylinder caused by excessive wear.

The valve spring compressor grasps the valve face and levers the spring downward allowing the valve spring keepers to be removed.

Pullers and slide hammers are needed for removing gears, bearings, and sprockets from shafts or bores.

Feelers, micrometers, calipers, compression testers, vacuum gauges and vacuum pumps are measuring tools. Their uses will be explained in Chapter 5 and 6.

Shop Cranes, Dollies, Jacks and Engine Stands

SHOP CRANES

▶ See Figure 45

Your shop crane should be of at least 1 ton capacity. A crane with adjustable legs is preferable. Adjustable legs allow you to get closer to the vehicle. The further away the base of the crane is, the further out you have to extend the boom, reducing the lifting capacity.

All cranes have booms which adjust in a telescoping fashion. The more adjustable your crane is, the easier the removal or installation will be.

Stands and cranes can be taken apart for storage. They are available at a lot of tool retailers or through tool catalogs.

ENGINE DOLLY

▶ See Figure 46

An engine dolly is a relatively simple device. Most are made of bolted-together lengths of angle iron in a size and shape to support an engine. The device is mounted on heavy swiveling casters to allow you to roll it around the garage. You can easily make one yourself using an old bed frame.

ENGINE STANDS

▶ See Figure 47

You can't do the overhaul without an engine stand. The engine stand holds the engine up off the floor, about waist high, and allows you to rotate the engine 360° for easy access to all parts.

Whatever engine stand you get should be at least of 750 lbs. capacity. The lighter capacity stands have three wheels or

Fig. 45 A 4,000 lb. capacity shop crane with adjustable legs and boom

'legs'. The heavier capacity stands have 4 wheels or legs. The 4-wheel stands are less likely to tip over.

JACKS AND JACKSTANDS

▶ See Figures 48 and 49

Your vehicle was supplied with a jack for emergency road repairs. This jack is fine for changing a flat tire or other short term procedures not requiring you to go beneath the vehicle. For any real work, you MUST use a floor jack.

Never place the jack under the radiator, engine or transmission components. Severe and expensive damage will result when the jack is raised. Additionally, never jack under the floorpan or bodywork; the metal will deform.

Whenever you plan to work under the vehicle, you must support it on jackstands or ramps. Never use cinder blocks or stacks of wood to support the vehicle, even if you're only going to be under it for a few minutes. Never crawl under the vehicle when it is supported only by the tire-changing jack or other floor jack.

➡ **Always position a block of wood or small rubber pad on top of the jack or jackstand to protect the lifting point's finish when lifting or supporting the vehicle.**

Small hydraulic, screw, or scissors jacks are satisfactory for raising the vehicle. Drive-on trestles or ramps are also a handy and safe way to both raise and support the vehicle. Be careful though, some ramps may be too steep to drive your vehicle onto without scraping the front bottom panels. Never support the vehicle on any suspension member (unless specifically instructed to do so by a repair manual) or by an underbody panel.

Fig. 46 A good engine dolly, capable of holding 1,000 lbs.

Fig. 47 An engine on a workstand, in the shop

JACKING PRECAUTIONS

The following safety points cannot be overemphasized:
• Always block the opposite wheel or wheels to keep the vehicle from rolling off the jack.
• When raising the front of the vehicle, firmly apply the parking brake.
• When the drive wheels are to remain on the ground, leave the vehicle in gear to help prevent it from rolling.
• Always use jackstands to support the vehicle when you are working underneath. Place the stands beneath the vehicle's jacking brackets. Before climbing underneath, rock the vehicle a bit to make sure it is firmly supported.

87933573

Fig. 48 Floor jacks come in all sizes and capacities. Top is a large 2¼ ton models; underneath is a compact 2 ton model

FASTENERS

▶ **See Figures 50 and 51**

Although there are a great variety of fasteners found in the modern car or truck, the most commonly used retainer is the threaded fastener (nuts, bolts, screws, studs, etc). Most threaded retainers may be reused, provided that they are not damaged in use or during the repair. Some retainers (such as stretch bolts or torque prevailing nuts) are designed to deform when tightened or in use and should not be reinstalled.

Whenever possible, we will note any special retainers which should be replaced during a procedure. But you should always inspect the condition of a retainer when it is removed and replace any that show signs of damage. Check all threads for rust or corrosion which can increase the torque necessary to achieve the desired clamp load for which that fastener was originally selected. Additionally, be sure that the driver surface of the fastener has not been compromised by rounding or other damage. In some cases a driver surface may become only partially rounded, allowing the driver to catch in only one

direction. In many of these occurrences, a fastener may be installed and tightened, but the driver would not be able to grip and loosen the fastener again. (This could lead to frustration down the line should that component ever need to be disassembled again).

If you must replace a fastener, whether due to design or damage, you must ALWAYS be sure to use the proper replacement. In all cases, a retainer of the same design, material and strength should be used. Markings on the heads of most bolts will help determine the proper strength of the fastener. The same material, thread and pitch must be selected to assure proper installation and safe operation of the vehicle afterwards.

Thread gauges are available to help measure a bolt or stud's thread. Most automotive and hardware stores keep gauges available to help you select the proper size. In a pinch, you can use another nut or bolt for a thread gauge. If the bolt you are replacing is not too badly damaged, you can select a

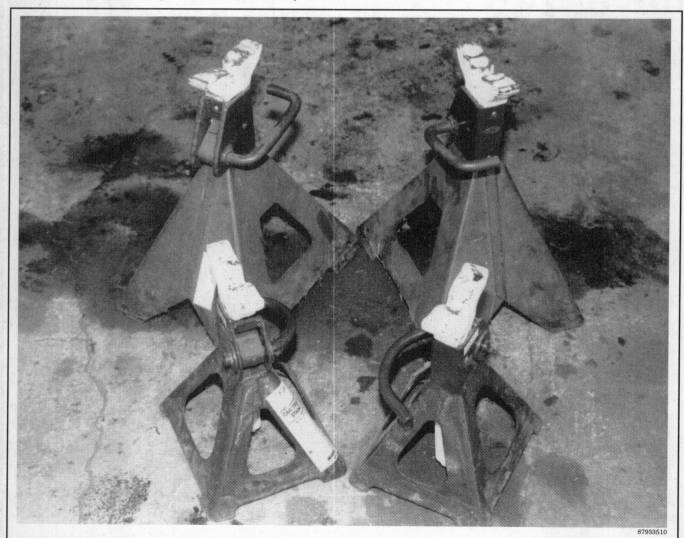

87933510

Fig. 49 Jackstands are necessary for holding your vehicle up off the ground. Top are 6 ton models; bottom are 4 ton models

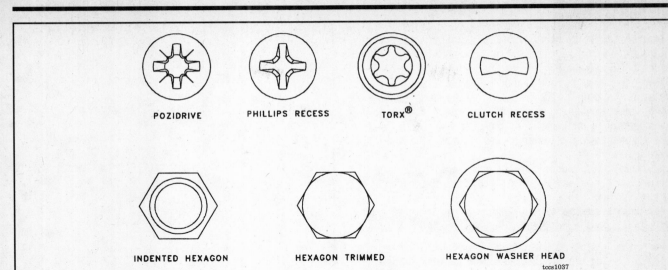

POZIDRIVE   PHILLIPS RECESS   TORX®   CLUTCH RECESS

INDENTED HEXAGON   HEXAGON TRIMMED   HEXAGON WASHER HEAD

tccs1037

Fig. 50 Here are a few of the most common screw/bolt driver styles

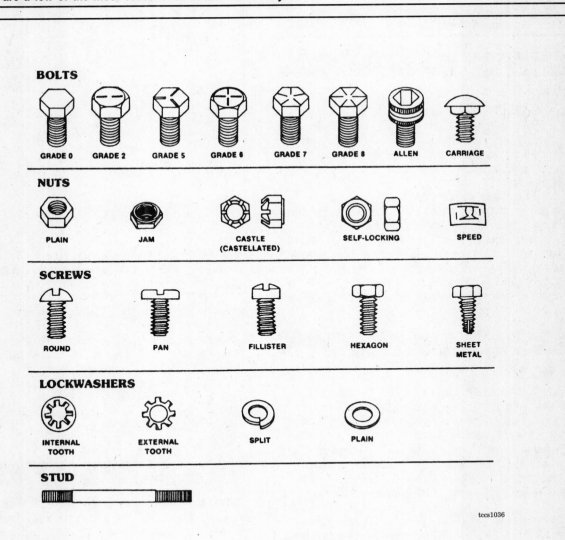

BOLTS

GRADE 0   GRADE 2   GRADE 5   GRADE 6   GRADE 7   GRADE 8   ALLEN   CARRIAGE

NUTS

PLAIN   JAM   CASTLE (CASTELLATED)   SELF-LOCKING   SPEED

SCREWS

ROUND   PAN   FILLISTER   HEXAGON   SHEET METAL

LOCKWASHERS

INTERNAL TOOTH   EXTERNAL TOOTH   SPLIT   PLAIN

STUD

tccs1036

Fig. 51 There are many different types of threaded retainers found on vehicles

match by finding another bolt which will thread in its place. If you find a nut which threads properly onto the damaged bolt, then use that nut to help select the replacement bolt. If however, the bolt you are replacing is so badly damaged (broken or drilled out) that its threads cannot be used as a gauge, you might start by looking for another bolt (from the same assembly or a similar location on your vehicle) which will thread into the damaged bolt's mounting. If so, the other bolt can be used to select a nut; the nut can then be used to select the replacement bolt.

In all cases, be absolutely sure you have selected the proper replacement. Don't be shy, you can always ask the store clerk for help.

❊❊WARNING

Be aware that when you find a bolt with damaged threads, you may also find the nut or drilled hole it was threaded into has also been damaged. If this is the case, you may have to drill and tap the hole, replace the nut or otherwise repair the threads. NEVER try to force a replacement bolt to fit into the damaged threads.

Bolts and Screws

▶ **See Figure 52**

Technically speaking, bolts are hexagon head or cap screws. For the purposes of this book, however, cap screws will be called bolts because that is the common terminology for them. Both bolts and screws are turned into drilled or threaded holes to fasten two parts together. Frequently, bolts require a nut on the other end, but this is not always the case. Screws seldom, if ever, require a nut on the other end.

Screws are supplied with slotted or Phillips heads. For obvious reasons, screws are not generally used where a great deal of torque is required. Most of the screws you will encounter will be used to retain components, such as the camshaft cover or other components, where strength is not a factor. Screw sizes are designated as 8-32, 10-32, or 1/4-32. The first number indicates the minor diameter, and the second number indicates the number of threads per inch.

Nuts

▶ **See Figure 53**

Nuts have only one use: they simply hold the other end of the bolt and, thereby, hold the two parts together. There are a variety of nuts used on cars, but a standard hexagon head (six-sided) nut is the most common.

Castellated and slotted nuts are designed for use with a cotter pin and are usually used when it is extremely important that the nuts do not work loose (in wheel bearings, for example). Other nuts are self-locking nuts that have a slot cut in the side.

When the nut is tightened, the separated sections pull together and lock the nut onto the bolt. Interference nuts have a collar of soft metal or fiber. The bolt cuts threads in the soft

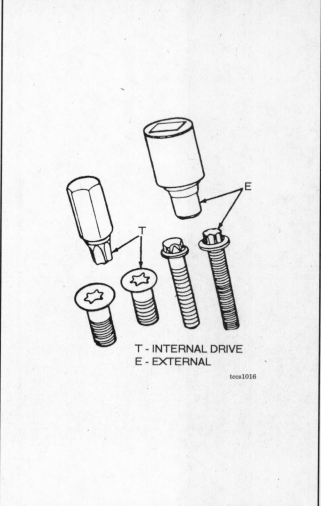

T - INTERNAL DRIVE
E - EXTERNAL

tccs1016

Fig. 52 Special fasteners such as these Torx® head bolts are used by manufacturers to discourage people from working on vehicles without the proper tools

material which then jams in the threads and prevents the nut and bolt from working loose.

A jam nut is a second hexagon nut that is used to hold the first nut in place. They are usually found where some type of adjustment is needed. valve trains, for instance.

Pawlnuts are single thread nuts that provide some locking action when they have been turned down on the nut.

Speed nuts are simply rectangular bits of sheet metal that are pushed down over a bolt, screw, or stud to provide locking action.

Studs

Studs are simply pieces of threaded rod. They are similar to bolts and screws in their thread configuration, but they have no heads. One end is turned into a threaded hole and the other end is generally secured by same type of nut. Unless the nut is self-locking, a lockwasher or jam nut is generally used underneath it.

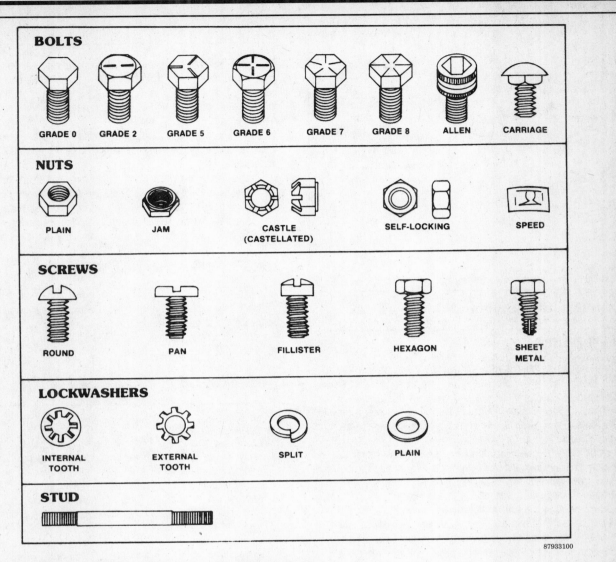

Fig. 53 Various types of fasteners found in automotive applications

Lockwashers

Lockwashers are a form of washer. They may be either split or toothed, and they are always installed between a nut or screwhead and the actual part being held. The split washer is crushed flat and locks the nut in place by spring tension. The toothed washer provides many edges to improve the locking effect and is usually used on smaller bolts and screws.

Screw and Bolt Terminology

Bolts and screws are identified by type, major diameter, minor diameter, pitch or threads per inch, class, length, thread length, and the size of the wrench required.

MAJOR DIAMETER

▶ **See Figure 54**

This is the widest diameter of the bolt as measured from the top of the threads on one side to the top of the threads on the other side.

MINOR DIAMETER

This is the diameter obtained by measuring from the bottom of the threads on one side of the bolt to the bottom of the threads on the other side. In other words, it is the diameter of the bolt if it does not have any threads.

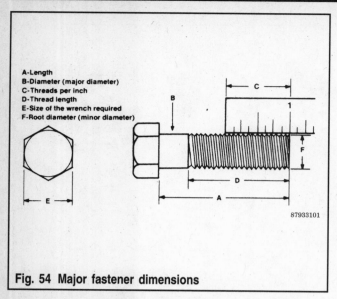

A-Length
B-Diameter (major diameter)
C-Threads per inch
D-Thread length
E-Size of the wrench required
F-Root diameter (minor diameter)

87933101

Fig. 54 Major fastener dimensions

PITCH OR THREADS PER INCH

▶ See Figure 55

Thread pitch is the distance between the top of one thread to the top of the next. It is simply the distance between one thread and the next. There are two types of threads in general use today. Unified National Coarse thread, and Unified National Fine. These are usually known simply as either fine or coarse thread.

Anyone who has been working on cars for any length of time can tell the difference between the two simply by looking at the screw, bolt, or nut. The only truly accurate way to determine thread pitch is to use a thread pitch gauge. There are some general rules to remember, however.

Coarse thread screws and bolts are used frequently when they are being threaded into aluminum or cast iron because the finer threads tend to strip more easily in these materials. Also, as a bolt or screw's diameter increases, thread pitch becomes greater.

THREAD CLASS

Thread class is a measure of the operating clearance between the internal nut threads and the external threads of the bolt. There are three classes of fit, 1, 2, or 3. In addition, there are letter designations to designate either internal (class A) or external (class B) threads.

Class 1 threads are a relatively loose fit and are used when ease of assembly and disassembly are of paramount importance.

Class 2 bolts are most commonly encountered in automotive applications and give an accurate, but not an overly tight, fit.

Class 3 threads are used when utmost accuracy is needed. You might find a class 3 bolt and nut combination on an airplane, but you won't encounter them very often on a car.

LENGTH AND THREAD LENGTH

Screw length is the length of the bolt or screw from the bottom of the head to the bottom of the bolt or screw. Thread length is exactly that, the length of the threads. The illustrations show this in greater detail.

Types or Grades of Bolts and Screws

▶ See Figure 56

The tensile strength of bolts and screws varies widely. Standards for these fasteners have been established by the Society of Automotive Engineers (SAE). Distinctive markings on the head of the bolt will identify its tensile strength.

These outward radiating lines are normally called points. A bolt with no points on the head is a grade 1 or a grade 2 bolt. This type of bolt is suitable for applications in which only a low-strength bolt is necessary.

On the other hand, a grade 5 bolt is found in a number of automotive applications and has double the tensile strength of a grade 2 bolt. A grade 5 bolt will have three embossed lines or points on the head.

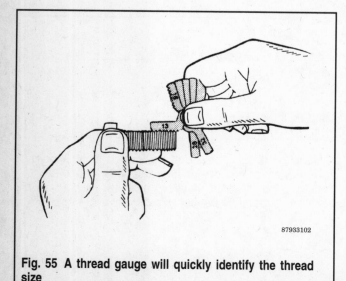

87933102

Fig. 55 A thread gauge will quickly identify the thread size

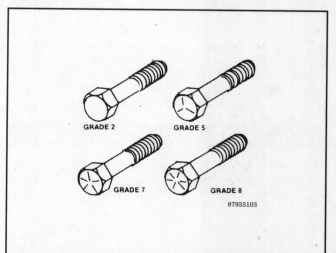

GRADE 2   GRADE 5

GRADE 7   GRADE 8

87933103

Fig. 56 Markings on U.S. measure bolts indicate the relative strength of the bolt

Grade 8 bolts are the best and are frequently called aircraft grade bolts. Grade 8 bolts have six points on the head.

METRIC BOLTS

▶ **See Figures 57, 58, 59 and 60**

While metric bolts may seem to be the same as their U.S. measure counterparts, they definitely are not. The pitch on a metric bolt is different from that of an U.S. measure bolt. It is entirely possible to start a metric bolt into a hole with U.S. measure threads and run it down a few turns. Then it is going to bind. Recognizing the problem at this point is not going to do much good. It is also possible to run a metric nut down on an U.S. measure bolt and find that it is too loose to provide sufficient strength.

Metric bolts are marked in a manner different from that of U.S. measure bolts. Most metric bolts have a number stamped on the head. This metric grade marking won't be an even number, but something like 4.6 or 10.9. The number indicates the relative strength of the bolt. The higher the number, the greater the strength of the bolt. Some metric bolts are also marked with a single-digit number to indicate the bolt strength. Metric bolt sizes are also identified in a manner different from that of U.S. measure fasteners.

If, for example, a metric bolt were designated 14 x 2, that would mean that the major diameter is 14 mm (.56 in.), and that the thread pitch is 2 mm (.08 in.). More important, metric bolts are not classified by number of threads per inch, but by the distance between the threads, and the distance between threads does not quite correspond to number of threads per inch. For example, 2 mm between threads is about 12.7 threads per inch.

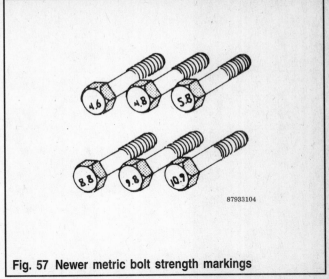

Fig. 57 Newer metric bolt strength markings

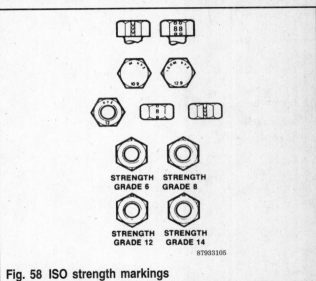

Fig. 58 ISO strength markings

	Mark	Class		Mark	Class
Hexagon head bolt	Bolt head No. (4) 4— 5— 6— 7— 8— 9— 10— 11—	4T 5T 6T 7T 8T 9T 10T 11T	Stud bolt	No mark	4T
	No mark	4T		Grooved	6T
Hexagon flange bolt w/ washer hexagon bolt	 No mark	4T			
Hexagon head bolt	 Two protruding lines	5T			
Hexagon flange bolt w/ washer hexagon bolt	 Two protruding lines	6T	Welded bolt		4T
Hexagon head bolt	 Three protruding lines	7T			
Hexagon head bolt	 Four protruding lines	8T			

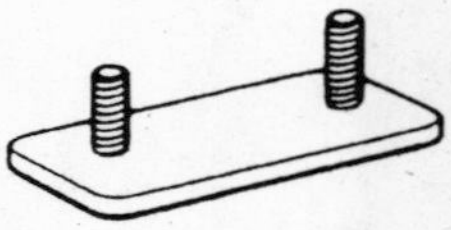

tccs1240

Fig. 59 Metric bolt strength indicator marks

THE HARD WORK STARTS
  BEFORE DISASSEMBLY 4-22
  BUDGETING YOUR TIME 4-22
  CLEANING THE ENGINE 4-21
  CLEARING THE WAY 4-4
  ENGINE REMOVAL 4-6
  FASTENERS 4-2
  FLYWHEEL/FLEX PLATE AND RING
    GEAR 4-21
  STORING PARTS 4-2
  THE ENGINE DOLLY 4-21

4

THE ENGINE

THE HARD WORK STARTS 4-2

THE HARD WORK STARTS

Before you start the actual hand-on work, let's go over a few work rules.

There are 3 common mistakes in mechanical work:

• Incorrect order of assembly, disassembly or adjustment. When taking something apart or putting it together, doing things in the wrong order usually just cost you extra time; however, it CAN break something. Read the entire procedure before beginning disassembly. Do everything in the order in which the instructions say you should do it, even if you can't immediately see a reason for it. When you're taking apart something that is very intricate (for example, a carburetor), you might want to draw a picture of how it looks when assembled at one point in order to make sure you get everything back in its proper position. (We will supply exploded view whenever possible). When making adjustments, especially tune-up adjustments, do them in order; often, one adjustment affects another, and you cannot expect satisfactory results unless each adjustment is made only when it cannot be changed by any order.

• Overtorquing (or undertorquing). While it is more common for over-torquing to cause damage, undertorquing can cause a fastener to vibrate loose causing serious damage. Especially when dealing with aluminum parts, pay attention to torque specifications and utilize a torque wrench in assembly. If a torque figure is not available, remember that if you are using the right tool to do the job, you will probably not have to strain yourself to get a fastener tight enough. The pitch of most threads is so slight that the tension you put on the wrench will be multiplied many, many times in actual force on what you are tightening. A good example of how critical torque is can be seen in the case of spark plug installation, especially where you are putting the plug into an aluminum cylinder head. Too little torque can fail to crush the gasket, causing leakage of combustion gases and consequent overheating of the plug and engine parts. Too much torque can damage the threads, or distort the plug which changes the spark gap. There are many commercial products available for ensuring that fasteners won't come loose, even if they are not torqued just right (a very common brand is Loctite®). If you're worried about getting something together tight enough to hold, but loose enough to avoid mechanical damage during assembly, one of these products might offer substantial insurance. Read the label on the package and make sure the products is compatible with the materials, fluids, etc. involved before choosing one.

• Crossthreading. This occurs when a part such as a bolt is screwed into a nut or casting at the wrong angle and forced. Cross threading is more likely to occur if access is difficult. It helps to clean and lubricate fasteners, and to start threading with the part to be installed going straight in. Then, start the bolt, spark plug, etc. with your fingers. If you encounter resistance, unscrew the part and start over again at a different angle until it can be inserted and turned several turns without much effort. Keep in mind that many parts, especially spark plugs, used tapered threads so that gentle turning will automatically bring the part you're treading to the proper angle if you don't force it or resist a change in angle. Don't put a wrench on the part until its's been turned a couple of turns by hand. If you suddenly encounter resistance, and the part has not seated fully, don't force it. Pull it back out and make sure it's clean and threading properly.

Always take your time and be patient; the further you go, the more confident you will become.

Storing Parts

Above all, I can't emphasize too strongly the necessity of a neat and orderly disassembly. Even if you are an experienced mechanic, parts can get mislaid, misidentified and just plain lost.

Start with an indelible marker, lots of cans and/or boxes and tags. Each time a part is removed, label it and store it safely. 'Parts' includes all fasteners (bolts, nuts, screws, washers). Bolts and nuts may look alike and not be alike. Similar looking bolts may be different lengths or thread count. Lockwashers may be required in some places and not in others. Everything should go back exactly where it came from.

Fasteners

The term fasteners refers to the bolts, nuts, screws, pins, and washers that hold everything together. These components come in all sizes shapes and grades. It is extremely important to have the correct size and grade fastener for the job.

REPLACING FASTENERS

Whenever you remove a bolt, screw or nut, check its condition. Wipe it off with a shop rag and clean it up with a wire brush or brush wheel. Check the threads for signs of stripping, stretching or breakage. Check the shaft of the bolt or screw for rust, cracks or pitting. If everything looks okay, the fastener can be used again. If you are at all suspicious of the condition of any part, fasteners included, replace it. When replacing a fastener, always use the exact same size and type.

NEVER use a substitute bolt or screw of a lower grade or unknown grade. Markings on the bolt head will tell you what the grade is. The grading indicates the bolt's strength. See the accompanying chart for a complete explanation of fastener grading.

Often, the length of a particular bolt or screw is critical. Never replace a bolt or screw with one that is longer. A lot of bolts and screw are threaded into blind holes. A bolt that is too long won't secure the part. Worse still, a bolt that is a few threads too long may look or feel tight but actually won't be, resulting in engine trouble later on.

When removing a fastener, consider how long it's been in place. If it's been in there a while it's bound to be rusted and/or seized. Always use a liberal amount of penetrating oil on and around a rusted fastener, or for that matter, all the fasteners from an old engine.

Keep in mind that old, rusted fasteners will probably be hard to remove, even with all your preparation. So, don't get impatient and force something that doesn't want to move. When trying to unscrew a stubborn, old bolt, use the breaker bar and apply gradually increasing force until the bolt or nut begins to move. At this point, apply a little more penetrating oil. The oil can now get under the bolt head and maybe onto the threads. WEAR HEAVY GLOVES for when the bolt or nut breaks free.

➡️Before any assembly takes place, always clean up (chase) the threads of any fastener or threaded hole with your tap and die set. This simple procedure makes assembly much easier and reduces the risk of crossthreading, stripping or breakage.

Broken Bolts or Studs

I'm sure this won't happen to you, but if you know anyone who happens to come across a broken bolt or stud or who is unfortunate enough to break one, here's what to do.

There are tools called stud extractors. If, after breakage, the is a piece of the bolt or stud still visible, the stud extractors can grab a hold of it and continue the unscrewing process.

Or, if the shaft of the bolt or stud is thick enough, you can file a notch in the end for a screwdriver.

Or, you may be able to grab the shaft of the bolt or stud with a pair of locking pliers, such as ViseGrips®.

However, if the bolt or stud is broken off flush with the surface of the part, a tool kit called screw extractors or 'Easy-Outs' is available. These tools are coarsely threaded reamers with left-hand threads. To use them, you drill a tap hole down through the shaft of the offending bolt or stud and screw the extractor into it. The extractor tightens in the direction of bolt loosening, turn the bolt out.

If all the above methods don't work, which sometimes happens, your only recourse is to complete drill out the stud or bolt, CAREFULLY! Don't over-drill! Usually when you drill out enough of the bolt or stud the rest will come out easily. What will probably happen as a result of all this drilling is that you'll do some damage to the threads in the hole. If the damage isn't too severe, you can clean up the threads with a tap and die set, using the proper sized tap. If the threads are completely destroyed, go on to the next paragraph.

REPAIRING DAMAGED THREADS

▶ See Figures 1, 2, 3, 4 and 5

Several methods of repairing damaged threads are available. Heli-Coil® (shown here), Keenserts® and Microdot® are among the most widely used. All involve basically the same principle — drilling out stripped threads, tapping the hole and installing a prewound insert — making welding, plugging and oversize fasteners unnecessary.

Two types of thread repair inserts are usually supplied: a standard type for most - Inch Coarse, Inch Fine, Metric Course and Metric Fine thread sizes and a spark lug type to fit most spark plug port sizes. Consult the individual manufacturer's catalog to determine exact applications. Typical thread repair kits will contain a selection of prewound threaded inserts, a tap (corresponding to the outside diameter threads of the insert) and an installation tool. Spark plug inserts usually differ because they require a tap equipped with pilot threads and a

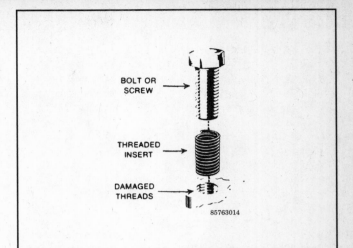

Fig. 1 Damaged bolt holes can be repaired with thread insert kits

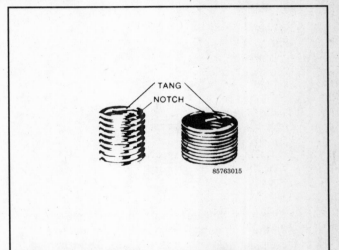

Fig. 2 Standard thread repair insert (left) and spark plug thread insert (right)

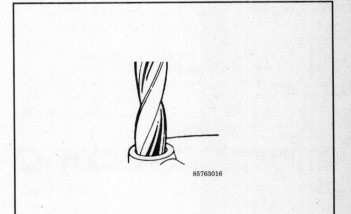

Fig. 3 Drill out the damaged threads with specified drill. Drill completely through the hole or to the bottom of a blind hole.

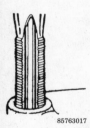

Fig. 4 With the tap supplied, tap the hole to receive the thread insert. Keep the tap well oiled and back it out frequently to avoid clogging the threads.

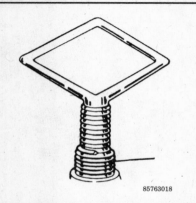

Fig. 5 Screw the threaded insert onto the installation tool until the tang engages the slot. Screw the insert into the tapped hole until it is ¼-½ turn below the top surface. After installation break off the tang with a hammer and punch.

combined reamer/tap section. Most manufacturers also supply blister-packed thread repair inserts separately in addition to a master kit containing a variety of taps and inserts plus installation tools.

Before effecting a repair to a threaded hole, remove any snapped, broken or damaged bolts or studs. Penetrating oil can be used to free frozen threads. The offending item can be removed with locking pliers or with a screw or stud extractor. After the hole is clear, the thread can be repaired, as shown in the series of accompanying illustrations.

Clearing the Way

Before removing the engine, there are a few parts that have to come out. They are:

Carburetor or Throttle Body

The main reason that you'll remove this now is to prevent its being damaged by the lifting chain. To remove the carburetor or throttle body, tag and disconnect the fuel and vacuum lines, and the linkage. Remove the holddown bolts or nuts and lift the unit off. Store it safely on a shelf.

Radiator

▶ See Figures 6, 7, 8, 9, 10 and 11

1. Disconnect the negative battery cable and drain the engine cooling system.

✳✳CAUTION

When draining the coolant, keep in mind that cats and dogs are attracted by the ethylene glycol antifreeze, and are quite likely to drink any that is left in an uncovered container or in puddles on the ground. This will prove fatal in sufficient quantity. Always drain the coolant into a sealable container. Coolant should be reused unless it is contaminated or several years old.

2. As necessary, remove the fan, the upper fan shroud and/or the upper support.

➡If the fan is removed on vehicle equipped with a clutch type fan, be sure to keep it in an upright position to prevent the fluid from leaking.

3. Disconnect upper and lower hoses.
4. If equipped with an automatic transmission, disconnect and plug the oil cooler lines. The lines should be plugged to prevent system contamination or excessive fluid loss.
5. Lift radiator straight up and out of the vehicle.

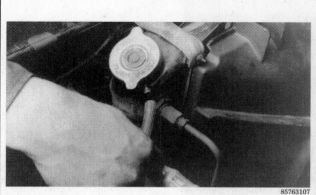

Fig. 6 Removing the overflow hose

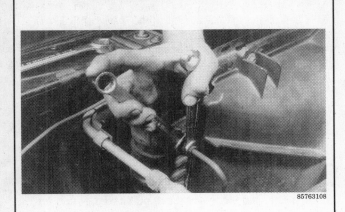

Fig. 7 Loosening the transmission cooler lines

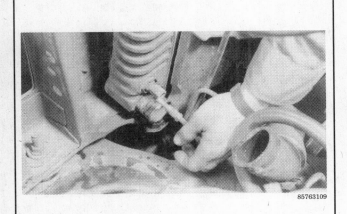

Fig. 8 Disconnecting the transmission cooler lines

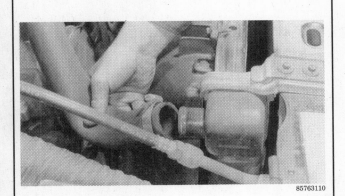

Fig. 9 Disconnecting the upper hose from the radiator

Fig. 10 Removing the upper radiator support bolts

Fig. 11 Removing the radiator. It might be a good idea to unbolt the fan shroud from the radiator first

Condenser

✳✳CAUTION

Consult your local laws concerning refrigerant discharge and recycling. In many areas it may be illegal for anyone but a certified technician to service the A/C system. Always use an approved recovery station when discharging the air conditioning.

1. Discharge the air conditioning system into a suitable recovery station.
2. Remove the upper radiator shroud.
3. Disconnect the air conditioning lines at the condenser. Plug all openings to prevent system contamination
4. Pull the condenser out from the top.

Power Steering Pumps

1. Disconnect the pressure line from the pump.
2. Loosen the pump bracket nuts and remove the drive belt. On the 8-302 with a serpentine drive belt, remove belt tension by lifting the tensioner out of position.
3. Remove the nuts and lift out the pump/bracket assembly.
4. If a new pump or bracket is being installed, you'll have to remove the pulley from the present pump. This is best done with a press and adapters.

Quick-Connect Pressure Line

Some pumps will have a quick-connect fitting for the pressure line. This fitting may, under certain circumstances, leak and/or be improperly engaged resulting in unplanned disconnection.

The leak is usually caused by a cut O-ring, imperfections in the outlet fitting inside diameter, or an improperly machined O-ring groove.

Improper engagement can be caused by an improperly machined tube end, tube nut, snapring, outlet fitting or gear port.

If a leak occurs, the O-ring should be replaced with new O-rings. Special O-rings are made for quick-disconnect fittings. Standard O-rings should never be used in their place. If the new O-rings do not solve the leak problem, replace the outlet fitting. If that doesn't work, replace the pressure line.

Improper engagement due to a missing or bent snapring, or improperly machined tube nut, may be corrected with a Ford snapring kit made for the purpose. If that doesn't work, replace the pressure hose.

When tightening a quick-connect tube nut, always use a tube nut wrench; never use an open-end wrench! Use of an open-end wrench will result in deformation of the nut! Tighten quick-connect tube nuts to 15 ft. lbs. maximum.

Swivel and/or endplay of quick-connect fittings is normal.

Starter

Before removing the engine, you'll have to remove the starter. Starter removal on some models may necessitate the removal of the front support which runs from the corner of the frame to the front crossmember. If so, loosen the mounting bolt which attaches the support the frame first, then remove the crossmember bolt and swing the support out of the way.

1. Disconnect the negative battery cable.
2. Raise and support the vehicle safely using jackstands.

➡If access to the wiring is difficult, the starter may be partially lowered before disconnecting it, but be careful not to stretch or damage the wiring.

3. Disconnect all wiring from the starter solenoid. Replace each nut as the connector is removed, as thread sizes differ from connector to connector. Note or tag the wiring positions for installation purposes.
4. If equipped, remove the front bracket from the starter. On engines with a solenoid heat shield, remove the front bracket upper bolt and detach the bracket from the starter.

5. Remove the starter mounting bolts. If a starter shim tab can be seen protruding out from between the mating surfaces of the starter and the block, remove the outer bolt first, then loosen the inner bolt. With the outer bolt removed and the inner loosened, most shims may be grasped and pulled from the top of the starter at this point. Once the bolts are removed, lower the starter front end first, and remove the unit from the car.

Engine Removal

♦ **See Figures 12, 13, 14, 15, 16, 17, 18, 19, 20, 21, 22, 23 and 24**

➡**Obviously, this section applies only if you are removing an engine for rebuild. If you have purchased an old engine, short block, bare block or whatever, skip it.**

We've included engine removal instructions for some of the most popular Ford cars and trucks. If your particular vehicle isn't mentioned here, check the local book stores for a Chilton book that would cover whatever vehicle you have.

Removing an engine from a vehicle could be the hardest part of the whole job. The first thing you should do is remove the hood.

For this job, you'll need a helper. Hoods are heavy and awkward.

The first step in removing the hood it to outline the position of the hinges on the hood with an indelible marker. If you don't do this, you'll have a hard time getting the hood to close properly when you install it. So:

1966-86 Pickups and Bronco

1. Outline the hood positions and slowly start removing the hood-to-hinge retaining bolts. At this point, your helper should be supporting the hood.
2. Remove the bolts evenly, side-to-side, leaving one bolt loosely in place.
3. Now, position yourself at the last bolt, with your helper on the other side. Remove the bolt and lift off the hood.

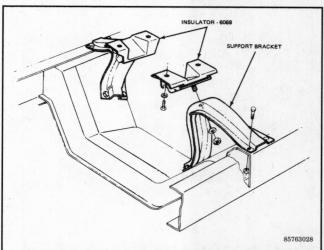

Fig. 12 Engine front mounts for a 1976-79 F-100-150 with the 8-302 or 351W

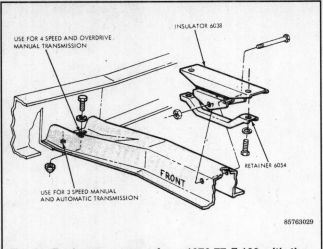

Fig. 13 Engine rear mount for a 1976-77 F-100 with the 8-302

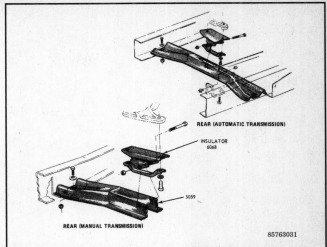

Fig. 15 Engine rear mounts for a 1976 F-150-350 with the 8-360 or 390

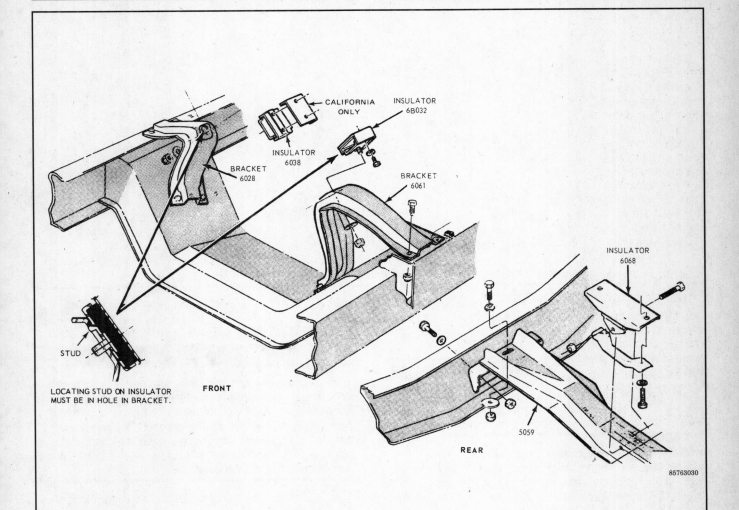

Fig. 14 Engine front mounts for a 1976 F-150-350 with the 8-360 or 390

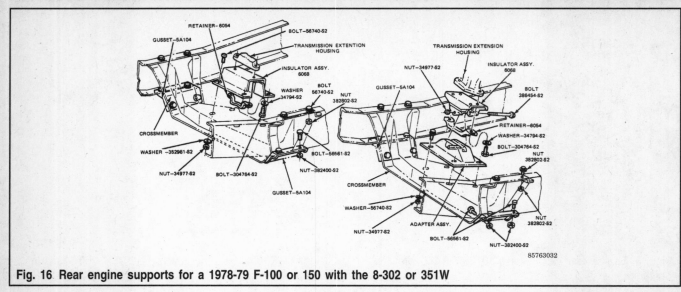

Fig. 16 Rear engine supports for a 1978-79 F-100 or 150 with the 8-302 or 351W

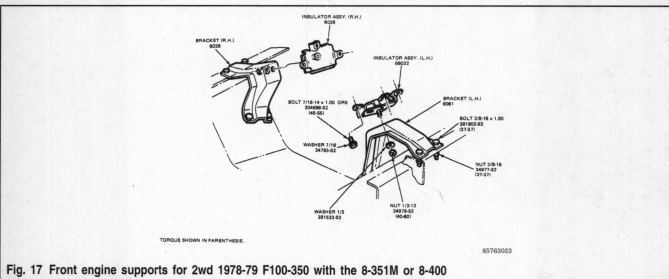

Fig. 17 Front engine supports for 2wd 1978-79 F100-350 with the 8-351M or 8-400

The best way to store the hood is standing up on its back end. Place wood blocks on the floor and place the hood on the blocks. This will protect the paint and keep the metal out of the wet.

✳✳WARNING

Disconnect the negative battery cable(s) before beginning any work. Always label all disconnected hoses, vacuum lines and wires, to prevent incorrect reassembly.

➡You should be able to remove just about any engine without disconnecting the refrigerant lines. In any event, don't disconnect any air conditioning lines; escaping refrigerant will freeze any surface it contacts, including skin and eyes and is an environmental hazard. If you have to disconnect the refrigerant lines, have the system discharged professionally by someone with a recovery system.

Okay, you have the hood off and safely out of the way, so let's go.

4. Drain the cooling system and crankcase.

✳✳CAUTION

When draining the coolant, keep in mind that cats and dogs are attracted by the ethylene glycol antifreeze, and are quite likely to drink any that is left in an uncovered container or in puddles on the ground. This will prove fatal in sufficient quantity. Always drain the coolant into a sealable container. Coolant should be reused unless it is contaminated or several years old.

5. Disconnect the battery cables and alternator wiring. Tag the wires.

6. On carbureted engines, remove the air cleaner and intake duct assembly, plus the crankcase ventilation hose. On fuel injected engines, remove the air intake hoses. Remove the PCV tube and carbon canister hose.

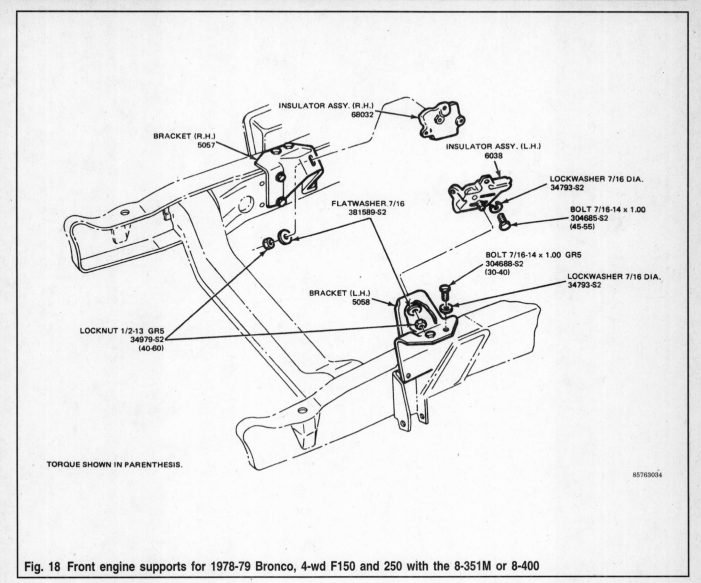

INSULATOR ASSY. (R.H.)
68032

BRACKET (R.H.)
5057

INSULATOR ASSY. (L.H.)
6038

LOCKWASHER 7/16 DIA.
34793-S2

BOLT 7/16-14 x 1.00
304685-S2
(45-55)

FLATWASHER 7/16
381589-S2

BOLT 7/16-14 x 1.00 GR5
304688-S2
(30-40)

LOCKWASHER 7/16 DIA.
34793-S2

BRACKET (L.H.)
5058

LOCKNUT 1/2-13 GR5
34979-S2
(40-60)

TORQUE SHOWN IN PARENTHESIS.

85763034

Fig. 18 Front engine supports for 1978-79 Bronco, 4-wd F150 and 250 with the 8-351M or 8-400

7. Disconnect the upper and lower radiator hoses.

➡**It's probably not necessary to disconnect any air conditioning lines. Sufficient clearance can be gained simply by dismounting the compressor and laying it aside. If, for some reason, sufficient clearance cannot be achieved, perform the next 2 steps.**

8. Have the air conditioning system discharged by someone with a refrigerant recover system.

9. Disconnect the refrigerant lines at the compressor. Cap all openings immediately.

10. If you have an automatic transmission, disconnect the automatic transmission oil cooler lines.

11. Remove the fan shroud and lay it over the fan.

12. Remove the retaining bolts at each of the 4 corners of the shroud, if so equipped, and position the shroud over the fan, clear of the radiator.

13. Disconnect the upper and lower hoses from the radiator.

14. Remove the radiator retaining bolts or the upper supports and lift the radiator from the vehicle.

15. Remove the fan shroud, fan, spacer, pulley and belt.

16. Remove the alternator pivot and adjusting bolts. Remove the alternator.

17. Disconnect the oil pressure sending unit lead from the sending unit. Tag it.

18. Disconnect the fuel tank-to-pump fuel line at the fuel pump and plug or clamp the line.

19. Disconnect the accelerator linkage and speed control linkage at the carburetor.

20. Disconnect the automatic transmission kick-down rod and remove the return spring, if so equipped.

21. Disconnect the power brake booster vacuum hose. Tag it.

22. Disconnect the heater hoses from the water pump and intake manifold or tee (EFI).

23. Disconnect the temperature sending unit wire from the sending unit. Tag it.

24. Remove the 4 carburetor attaching nuts and lift off the carburetor. This isn't absolutely necessary, but the carburetor can be damaged by the chains attached to the crane.

25. Remove the upper bellhousing-to-engine attaching bolts.

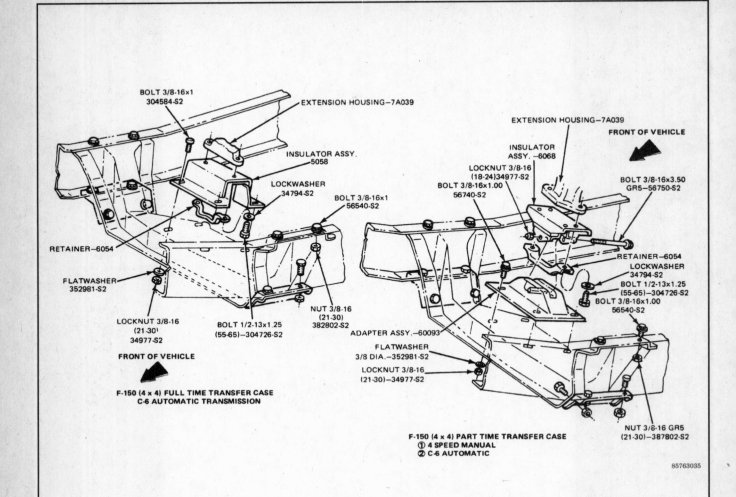

Fig. 19 Rear engine supports for 4wd 1978-79 Bronco, F150 and 250 with the 8-351M or 8-400

26. Remove the wiring harness from the left rocker arm cover and position the wires out of the way.

27. Disconnect the ground strap from the cylinder block.

28. Disconnect the air conditioning compressor clutch wire. Tag it.

29. Unbolt the air conditioning compressor and move it out of the way. Secure it in this position with rope or wires.

30. Raise the front of the vehicle and disconnect the starter cable from the starter.

31. Remove the starter.

32. Disconnect the exhaust pipes from the exhaust manifolds.

33. Disconnect the engine mounts from the brackets on the frame.

34. On vehicles with automatic transmissions, remove the converter inspection plate and remove the torque converter-to-flywheel attaching bolts. To get to all of the bolts, you'll have to turn the engine by hand.

35. Remove the remaining bellhousing-to-engine attaching bolts.

36. Lower the vehicle and support the transmission with a jack.

37. Attach the engine crane. Some engines have lifting eyes built in under manifold bolts. Most don't. Most cranes come equipped with lifting eyes. These are installed under existing bolts. Good places are at the alternator mounting bolt hole in the block and in any of the manifold bolts or threaded holes in the manifold at the opposite rear of the engine.

➡**Now you'll be happy that you invested in the load equalizer.**

38. Raise the engine slightly and carefully pull it forward and out of the transmission. Using the load equalizer to angle the engine, lift the engine out of the engine compartment.

✳✳WARNING

This is one of the most dangerous parts! The engine will suddenly break free, most of the time. Don't try to catch it if it starts to lurch or swing. Guide it carefully. You can't rebuild the engine if your hand is broken.

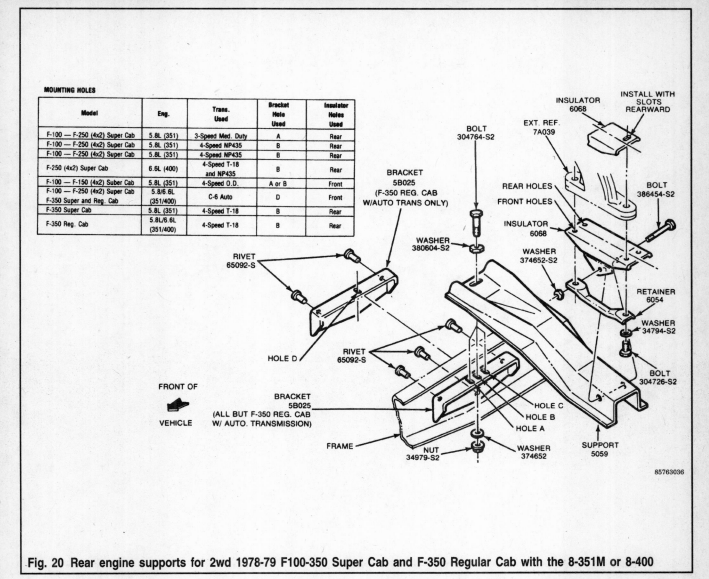

MOUNTING HOLES

Model	Eng.	Trans. Used	Bracket Hole Used	Insulator Holes Used
F-100 — F-250 (4x2) Super Cab	5.8L (351)	3-Speed Med. Duty	A	Rear
F-100 — F-250 (4x2) Super Cab	5.8L (351)	4-Speed NP435	B	Rear
F-100 — F-250 (4x2) Super Cab	5.8L (351)	4-Speed NP435	B	Rear
F-250 (4x2) Super Cab	6.6L (400)	4-Speed T-18 and NP435	B	Rear
F-100 — F-150 (4x2) Suber Cab	5.8L (351)	4-Speed O.D.	A or B	Front
F-100 — F-250 (4x2) Super Cab F-350 Super and Reg. Cab	5.8/6.6L (351/400)	C-6 Auto	D	Front
F-350 Super Cab	5.8L (351)	4-Speed T-18	B	Rear
F-350 Reg. Cab	5.8L/6.6L (351/400)	4-Speed T-18	B	Rear

Fig. 20 Rear engine supports for 2wd 1978-79 F100-350 Super Cab and F-350 Regular Cab with the 8-351M or 8-400

39. Clearing the front of the vehicle, especially if you have a truck, may require lowering the front end significantly; even taking the front wheels off and lowering the front end to the ground may be necessary.

1987-96 Pickups and Bronco

8-5.0L, 8-5.7L

1. Remove the hood.
2. Drain the cooling system and crankcase.

✳✳CAUTION

When draining the coolant, keep in mind that cats and dogs are attracted by the ethylene glycol antifreeze, and are quite likely to drink any that is left in an uncovered container or in puddles on the ground. This will prove fatal in sufficient quantity. Always drain the coolant into a sealable container. Coolant should be reused unless it is

contaminated or several years old. The EPA warns that prolonged contact with used engine oil may cause a number of skin disorders, including cancer! You should make every effort to minimize your exposure to used engine oil. Protective gloves should be worn when changing the oil. Wash your hands and any other exposed skin areas as soon as possible after exposure to used engine oil. Soap and water, or waterless hand cleaner should be used.

3. Disconnect the battery and alternator cables.
4. On carbureted engines, remove the air cleaner and intake duct assembly, plus the crankcase ventilation hose. On fuel injected engines, remove the air intake hoses, PCV tube and carbon canister hose.
5. Disconnect the upper and lower radiator hoses.
6. Discharge the air conditioning system.
7. Disconnect the refrigerant lines at the compressor. Cap all openings immediately.
8. If so equipped, disconnect the automatic transmission oil cooler lines.
9. Remove the fan shroud and lay it over the fan.

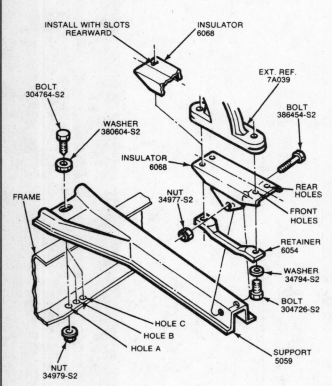

MOUNTING HOLES

Model	W.B.	Engine	Trans	Frame Hole User	Insulator Holes Used
F-100	116"	5.8L (351)	3-Speed Med. Duty	A	Rear
F-100 — 250	133"	5.8L (351)	3-Speed Med. Duty	B	Front
F-100	116"/133"	5.8L (351)	4-Speed T-18	C	Front
F-150	133"	5.8L (351)	4-Speed T-18	C	Front
F-250	133"	5.8L & 6.6L (351 & 400)	4-Speed T-18	C	Front
F-100	116"/133"	5.8L (351)	4-Speed NP-435	C	Front
F-150	133"	5.8L (351)	4-Speed NP-435	C	Front
F-250	133"	5.8L & 6.6L (351 & 400)	4-Speed NP-435	C	Front
F-100	133"	5.8L (351)	4-Speed O.D.	A	Front
F-100 -- F-150	116"/133"	5.8L & 6.6L (351 & 400)	C-6 Auto	C	—
F-250	133"	5.8L & 6.6L (351 & 400)	C-6 Auto	C	—

85763037

Fig. 21 Rear engine supports for 2wd 1978-79 F100-250 Regular Cab with the 8-351M or 8-400

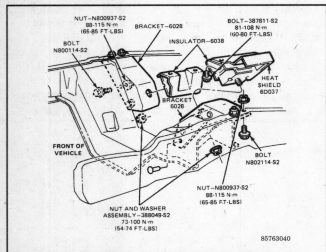

85763040

Fig. 22 Front engine mounts for 1980-86 F-series and Bronco with the 8-255, 8-302 or 8-351W

10. Remove the radiator and fan, shroud, fan, spacer, pulley and belt.

11. Remove the alternator pivot and adjusting bolts. Remove the alternator.

12. Disconnect the oil pressure sending unit lead from the sending unit.

13. Disconnect the fuel tank-to-pump fuel line at the fuel pump and plug the line.

14. On trucks with EFI, disconnect the chassis fuel line at the fuel rails.

15. Disconnect the accelerator linkage and speed control linkage at the carburetor or throttle body.

16. Disconnect the automatic transmission kick-down rod and remove the return spring, if so equipped.

17. Disconnect the power brake booster vacuum hose.

18. On EFI models, disconnect the throttle bracket from the upper intake manifold and swing it out of the way with the cables still attached.

19. Disconnect the heater hoses from the water pump and intake manifold or tee (EFI).

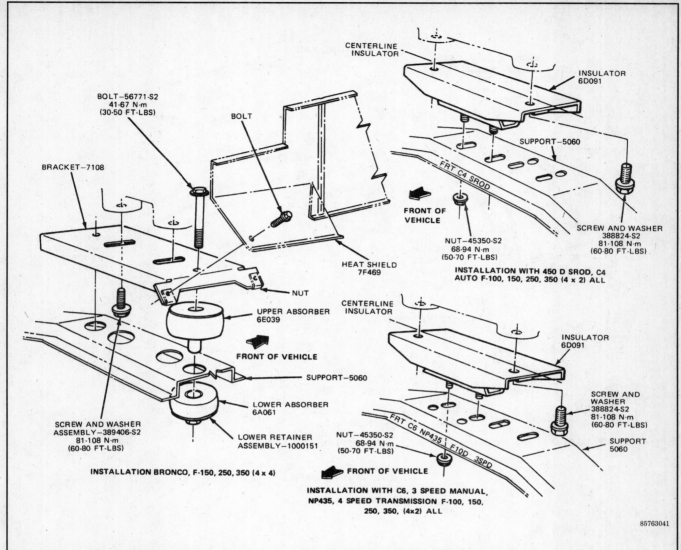

BOLT—56771-S2
41-67 N·m
(30-50 FT-LBS)

BOLT

BRACKET—7108

CENTERLINE INSULATOR

INSULATOR 6D091

SUPPORT—5060

FRT C4 SROD

FRONT OF VEHICLE

NUT—45350-S2
68-94 N·m
(50-70 FT-LBS)

SCREW AND WASHER
388824-S2
81-108 N·m
(60-80 FT-LBS)

INSTALLATION WITH 450 D SROD, C4 AUTO F-100, 150, 250, 350 (4 x 2) ALL

HEAT SHIELD 7F469

NUT

UPPER ABSORBER 6E039

FRONT OF VEHICLE

SUPPORT—5060

LOWER ABSORBER 6A061

SCREW AND WASHER ASSEMBLY—389406-S2
81-108 N·m
(60-80 FT-LBS)

LOWER RETAINER ASSEMBLY—1000151

INSTALLATION BRONCO, F-150, 250, 350 (4 x 4)

CENTERLINE INSULATOR

INSULATOR 6D091

SCREW AND WASHER 388824-S2
81-108 N·m
(60-80 FT-LBS)

FRT C6 NP435   F10D 3SPD

NUT—45350-S2
68-94 N·m
(50-70 FT-LBS)

SUPPORT 5060

FRONT OF VEHICLE

INSTALLATION WITH C6, 3 SPEED MANUAL, NP435, 4 SPEED TRANSMISSION F-100, 150, 250, 350, (4x2) ALL

85763041

Fig. 23 Rear engine mounts for 1980-83 F-series and Bronco with the 8-255, 8-302 or 8-351W

20. Disconnect the temperature sending unit wire from the sending unit.

21. Remove the upper bellhousing-to-engine attaching bolts.

22. Remove the wiring harness from the left rocker arm cover and position the wires out of the way.

23. Disconnect the ground strap from the cylinder block.

24. Disconnect the air conditioning compressor clutch wire.

25. Raise the front of the truck and disconnect the starter cable from the starter.

26. Remove the starter.

27. Disconnect the exhaust pipe from the exhaust manifolds.

28. Disconnect the engine mounts from the brackets on the frame.

29. On trucks with automatic transmissions, remove the converter inspection plate and remove the torque converter-to-flywheel attaching bolts.

30. Remove the remaining bellhousing-to-engine attaching bolts.

31. Lower the vehicle and support the transmission with a jack.

32. Install an engine lifting device.

33. Raise the engine slightly and carefully pull it out of the transmission. Lift the engine out of the engine compartment.

8-7.5L

1. Remove the hood.
2. Drain the cooling system.

✳✳CAUTION

When draining the coolant, keep in mind that cats and dogs are attracted by the ethylene glycol antifreeze, and are quite likely to drink any that is left in an uncovered container or in puddles on the ground. This will prove fatal in sufficient quantity. Always drain the coolant into a sealable container. Coolant should be reused unless it is contaminated or several years old.

3. Disconnect the negative battery cable from the block.
4. Remove the air cleaner assembly.
5. Remove the crankcase ventilation hose.
6. Remove the canister hose.

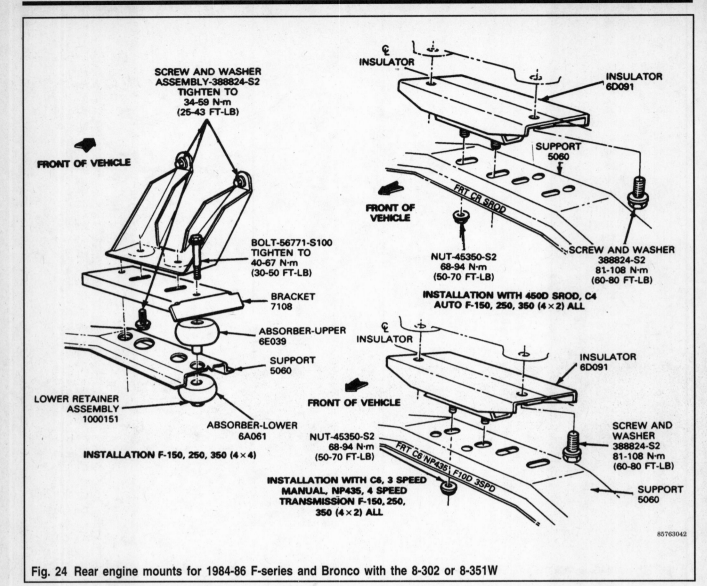

SCREW AND WASHER ASSEMBLY-388824-S2 TIGHTEN TO 34-59 N·m (25-43 FT-LB)

FRONT OF VEHICLE

BOLT-56771-S100 TIGHTEN TO 40-67 N·m (30-50 FT-LB)

BRACKET 7108

ABSORBER-UPPER 6E039

SUPPORT 5060

LOWER RETAINER ASSEMBLY 1000151

ABSORBER-LOWER 6A061

INSTALLATION F-150, 250, 350 (4×4)

INSULATOR

INSULATOR 6D091

SUPPORT 5060

FRONT OF VEHICLE

FRT CR SROD

NUT-45350-S2 68-94 N·m (50-70 FT-LB)

SCREW AND WASHER 388824-S2 81-108 N·m (60-80 FT-LB)

INSTALLATION WITH 450D SROD, C4 AUTO F-150, 250, 350 (4×2) ALL

INSULATOR

INSULATOR 6D091

FRONT OF VEHICLE

SCREW AND WASHER 388824-S2 81-108 N·m (60-80 FT-LB)

NUT-45350-S2 68-94 N·m (50-70 FT-LB)

FRT C6 NP435 F10D 3SPD

INSTALLATION WITH C6, 3 SPEED MANUAL, NP435, 4 SPEED TRANSMISSION F-150, 250, 350 (4×2) ALL

SUPPORT 5060

85763042

Fig. 24 Rear engine mounts for 1984-86 F-series and Bronco with the 8-302 or 8-351W

7. Disconnect the upper and lower radiator hoses.

8. Disconnect the transmission oil cooler lines from the radiator.

9. Disconnect the engine oil cooler lines at the oil filter adapter.

✳✳WARNING

Don't disconnect the lines at the quick-connect fittings behind or at the oil cooler. Disconnecting them may permanently damage them.

10. Discharge the air conditioning system.

11. Disconnect the refrigerant lines at the compressor. Cap the openings at once!

12. Disconnect the refrigerant lines at the condenser. Cap the openings at once!

13. Remove the condenser.

14. Remove the fan shroud from the radiator and position it up, over the fan.

15. Remove the radiator.

16. Remove the fan shroud.

17. Remove the fan, belts and pulley from the water pump.

18. Remove the compressor.

19. Remove the power steering pump from the engine, if so equipped, and position it to one side. Do not disconnect the fluid lines.

20. Disconnect the fuel pump inlet line from the pump and plug the line.

21. Disconnect the oil pressure sending unit wire at the sending unit.

22. Remove the alternator drive belts and disconnect the alternator from the engine, positioning it aside.

23. Disconnect the ground cable from the right front corner of the engine.

24. Disconnect the heater hoses.

25. Remove the transmission fluid filler tube attaching bolt from the right side valve cover and position the tube out of the way.

26. Disconnect all vacuum lines at the rear of the intake manifold.

27. Disconnect the speed control cable at the carburetor, if so equipped.

28. Disconnect the accelerator rod and the transmission kickdown rod and secure them out of the way.

29. Disconnect the engine wiring harness at the connector on the fire wall. Disconnect the primary wire at the coil.

30. Remove the upper flywheel housing-to-engine bolts.

31. Raise the vehicle and disconnect the exhaust pipes at the exhaust manifolds.

32. Disconnect the starter cable and remove the starter. Bring the starter forward and rotate the solenoid outward to remove the assembly.

33. Remove the access cover from the converter housing and remove the flywheel-to-converter attaching nuts.

34. Remove the lower the converter housing-to-engine attaching bolts.

35. Remove the engine mount through bolts attaching the rubber insulator to the frame brackets.

36. Lower the vehicle and place a jack under the transmission to support it.

37. Remove the converter housing-to-engine block attaching bolts (left side).

38. Remove the coil and bracket assembly from the intake manifold.

39. Attach an engine lifting device and carefully take up the weight of the engine.

40. Move the engine forward to disengage it from the transmission and slowly lift it from the truck.

1971-96 Full-Sized Vans

5.0L, 5.7L

1. Remove the engine cover.
2. Drain the cooling system and crankcase.

✳✳CAUTION

When draining the coolant, keep in mind that cats and dogs are attracted by the ethylene glycol antifreeze, and are quite likely to drink any that is left in an uncovered container or in puddles on the ground. This will prove fatal in sufficient quantity. Always drain the coolant into a sealable container. Coolant should be reused unless it is contaminated or several years old.The EPA warns that prolonged contact with used engine oil may cause a number of skin disorders, including cancer! You should make every effort to minimize your exposure to used engine oil. Protective gloves should be worn when changing the oil. Wash your hands and any other exposed skin areas as soon as possible after exposure to used engine oil. Soap and water, or waterless hand cleaner should be used.

3. Disconnect the battery and alternator cables.
4. Remove the air intake hoses, PCV tube and carbon canister hose.

5. Disconnect the upper and lower radiator hoses.
6. Discharge the air conditioning system.
7. Disconnect the refrigerant lines at the compressor. Cap all openings immediately.
8. If so equipped, disconnect the automatic transmission oil cooler lines.
9. Remove the fan shroud and lay it over the fan.
10. Remove the radiator and fan, shroud, fan, spacer, pulley and belt.
11. Remove the grille.
12. Remove the gravel deflector.
13. Remove the bumper.
14. Remove the upper grille support bracket.
15. Remove the hood lock support.
16. Remove the alternator pivot and adjusting bolts. Remove the alternator.
17. Disconnect the oil pressure sending unit lead from the sending unit.
18. Disconnect the fuel tank-to-pump fuel line at the fuel pump and plug the line.
19. Disconnect the chassis fuel line at the fuel rails.
20. Disconnect the accelerator linkage and speed control linkage at the throttle body.
21. Disconnect the automatic transmission kick-down rod and remove the return spring, if so equipped.
22. Disconnect the power brake booster vacuum hose.
23. Disconnect the throttle bracket from the upper intake manifold and swing it out of the way with the cables still attached.
24. Disconnect the heater hoses from the water pump and intake manifold or tee.
25. Disconnect the temperature sending unit wire from the sending unit.
26. Remove the upper bellhousing-to-engine attaching bolts.
27. Remove the wiring harness from the left rocker arm cover and position the wires out of the way.
28. Disconnect the ground strap from the cylinder block.
29. Disconnect the air conditioning compressor clutch wire.
30. Raise the front of the van and disconnect the starter cable from the starter.
31. Remove the starter.
32. Disconnect the exhaust pipe from the exhaust manifolds.
33. Disconnect the engine mounts from the brackets on the frame.
34. On vans with automatic transmissions, remove the converter inspection plate and remove the torque converter-to-flywheel attaching bolts.
35. Remove the remaining bellhousing-to-engine attaching bolts.
36. Lower the vehicle and support the transmission with a jack.
37. Install an engine lifting device.
38. Raise the engine slightly and carefully pull it out of the transmission. Lift the engine out of the engine compartment.

8-7.5L

1. Remove the hood and engine cover.

2. Drain the cooling system.

✳✳CAUTION

When draining the coolant, keep in mind that cats and dogs are attracted by the ethylene glycol antifreeze, and are quite likely to drink any that is left in an uncovered container or in puddles on the ground. This will prove fatal in sufficient quantity. Always drain the coolant into a sealable container. Coolant should be reused unless it is contaminated or several years old.

3. Disconnect the negative battery cable from the block.
4. Remove the air cleaner assembly.
5. Remove the crankcase ventilation hose.
6. Remove the canister hose.
7. Disconnect the upper and lower radiator hoses.
8. Disconnect the transmission oil cooler lines from the radiator.
9. Disconnect the engine oil cooler lines at the oil filter adapter.

✳✳WARNING

Don't disconnect the lines at the quick-connect fittings behind or at the oil cooler. Disconnecting them may permanently damage them.

10. Discharge the air conditioning system.
11. Disconnect the refrigerant lines at the compressor. Cap the openings at once!
12. Disconnect the refrigerant lines at the condenser. Cap the openings at once!
13. Remove the condenser.
14. Remove the fan shroud from the radiator and position it up, over the fan.
15. Remove the radiator.
16. Remove the fan shroud.
17. Remove the bumper and grille.
18. Remove the fan, belts and pulley from the water pump.
19. Remove the compressor.
20. Remove the power steering pump from the engine, if so equipped, and position it to one side. Do not disconnect the fluid lines.
21. Disconnect the fuel pump inlet line from the pump and plug the line.
22. Disconnect the oil pressure sending unit wire at the sending unit.
23. Remove the alternator drive belts and disconnect the alternator from the engine, positioning it aside.
24. Disconnect the ground cable from the right front corner of the engine.
25. Disconnect the heater hoses.
26. Remove the transmission fluid filler tube attaching bolt from the right side valve cover and position the tube out of the way.
27. Disconnect all vacuum lines at the rear of the intake manifold.
28. Disconnect the speed control cable, if so equipped.
29. Disconnect the accelerator rod and the transmission kickdown rod and secure them out of the way.

30. Disconnect the engine wiring harness at the connector on the fire wall. Disconnect the primary wire at the coil.
31. Remove the upper flywheel housing-to-engine bolts.
32. Raise the vehicle and disconnect the exhaust pipes at the exhaust manifolds.
33. Disconnect the starter cable and remove the starter. Bring the starter forward and rotate the solenoid outward to remove the assembly.
34. Remove the access cover from the converter housing and remove the flywheel-to-converter attaching nuts.
35. Remove the lower the converter housing-to-engine attaching bolts.
36. Remove the engine mount through bolts attaching the rubber insulator to the frame brackets.
37. Lower the vehicle and place a jack under the transmission to support it.
38. Remove the converter housing-to-engine block attaching bolts (left side).
39. Remove the coil and bracket assembly from the intake manifold.
40. Attach an engine lifting device and carefully take up the weight of the engine.
41. Move the engine forward to disengage it from the transmission and slowly lift it from the van.

1968-88 Ford, Mercury and Lincoln Full-Sized Cars

➡ Label all wiring, vacuum hoses, fuel lines, etc. before disconnecting them; thereby making installation much easier.

The following procedure can be used on all years and models. Slight variations may occur due to extra connections, etc., but the basic procedure covers all years and models. Use this as a guide — read the entire service procedure before starting the repair.
1. Disconnect the negative battery cable. Once disconnected, it is recommended that the positive battery cable be disconnected as well.
2. Drain the crankcase and the cooling system into separate containers, and dispose of the fluids properly.

✳✳CAUTION

When draining coolant, keep in mind that cats and dogs are attracted to ethylene glycol antifreeze, and could drink any that is left in an uncovered container or in puddles on the ground. This will prove fatal in sufficient quantity. Always drain the coolant into a sealable container. Coolant should be reused unless it is contaminated or several years old.

3. Relieve the fuel system pressure, if fuel injected, then disconnect the fuel lines. Discharge the air conditioning system into an approved recovery/recycling machine.
4. Mark the position of the hood on the hinges and remove the hood.
5. Unfasten the air cleaner by loosening the wing nut and/or the clips around the cover. On automatic transmission equipped vehicles, disconnect and plug the fluid cooler lines at the radiator.

6. Remove the cooling fan, shroud and radiator, by loosening the upper and lower hose clamps and working the hoses off the radiator. Remove the shroud bolts, then lift the shroud out of the engine compartment. Finally, loosen and remove any remaining hardware securing the radiator, and pull the radiator out of the engine compartment.

7. Remove the air inlet tube. Unclamp the fuel lines from the fuel pump, if carbureted.

8. Tag, then disconnect the accelerator, cruise control cables and the throttle valve cable.

9. Tag any vacuum, breather or wire harnesses on top of or around the engine.

10. Unfasten the alternator harness from the fender apron and junction block. Unbolt the retaining hardware, and remove the alternator from the engine. Unbolt the air conditioning compressor from the engine and place aside. In some cases the compressor lines are not long enough. In this case, you must disconnect the air conditioning hoses from the compressor.

11. Unfasten the Electronic Variable Orifice (EVO) sensor connector from the power steering pump, if equipped. Also disconnect the body ground strap from the firewall.

12. Raise and safely support the vehicle on jackstands.

13. Disconnect the exhaust system from the exhaust manifolds and support the exhaust section with wire hung from the crossmember.

14. Remove the retaining nut from the transmission line bracket and remove the bolts retaining the engine to the transmission braces.

15. Remove the starter and dust seal. Remove the bolts retaining the power steering pump to the engine block and position aside.

16. On cars equipped with manual transmissions, remove the clutch retracting spring. Disconnect the clutch equalizer shaft and arm bracket at the underbody rail and remove the arm bracket and shaft from the vehicle.

17. Remove the plug from the engine block to access the converter retaining nuts. Rotate the crankshaft until each of the nuts is accessible and remove the nuts.

18. Remove the transmission-to-engine retaining bolts, including the flywheel or converter housing upper bolts. Remove the engine mount through-bolts.

19. Lower the vehicle. Support the transmission with a floor jack and remove the bolt retaining the right and left engine mounts to the lower underbody bracket.

20. Install an engine lifting bracket to the left cylinder head on the front and the right cylinder head on the rear. Connect suitable engine lifting equipment to the lifting brackets.

21. Raise the engine slowly, then carefully separate the engine from the transmission.

22. Carefully lift the engine out of the engine compartment and install it on an engine stand. Remove the engine lifting equipment.

1989-94 Ford, Mercury and Lincoln Full-Sized Cars

4.6L Engine

1. Disconnect the negative, then the positive battery cable. Drain the crankcase and the cooling system into suitable containers.

❋❋CAUTION

When draining the coolant, keep in mind that cats and dogs are attracted by the ethylene glycol antifreeze, and are quite likely to drink any that is left in an uncovered container or in puddles on the ground. This will prove fatal in sufficient quantity. Always drain the coolant into a sealable container. Coolant should be reused unless it is contaminated or several years old.

2. Relieve the fuel system pressure and disconnect the fuel lines. Discharge the air conditioning system.

3. Mark the position of the hood on the hinges and remove the hood.

4. Remove the cooling fan, shroud and radiator.

5. Remove the wiper module and support bracket. Remove the air inlet tube.

6. Remove the 42-pin connector from the retaining bracket on the brake vacuum booster. Disconnect the 42-pin connector and transmission harness connector and position aside.

7. Disconnect the accelerator and cruise control cables. Disconnect the throttle valve cable.

8. Disconnect the electrical connector and vacuum hose from the purge solenoid. Disconnect the power supply from the power distribution box and starter relay.

9. Disconnect the vacuum supply hose from the throttle body adapter vacuum port. Disconnect the heater hoses.

10. Disconnect the alternator harness from the fender apron and junction block. Disconnect the air conditioning hoses from the compressor.

11. Disconnect the Electronic Variable Orifice (EVO) sensor connector from the power steering pump and disconnect the body ground strap from the dash panel.

12. Raise and safely support the vehicle.

13. Disconnect the exhaust system from the exhaust manifolds and support with wire hung from the crossmember.

14. Remove the retaining nut from the transmission line bracket and remove the 3 bolts and stud retaining the engine to the transmission knee braces.

15. Remove the starter. Remove the 4 bolts retaining the power steering pump to the engine block and position aside.

16. Remove the plug from the engine block to access the torque converter retaining nuts. Rotate the crankshaft until each of the 4 nuts is accessible and remove the nuts.

17. Remove the 6 transmission-to-engine retaining bolts. Remove the engine mount through bolts, 2 on the left mount and 1 on the right mount.

18. Lower the vehicle. Support the transmission with a floor jack and remove the bolt retaining the right engine mount to the lower engine bracket.

19. Install an engine lifting bracket to the left cylinder head on the front and the right cylinder head on the rear. Connect suitable engine lifting equipment to the lifting brackets.

20. Raise the engine slightly and carefully separate the engine from the transmission.

21. Carefully lift the engine out of the engine compartment and position on a workstand. Remove the engine lifting equipment.

5.0L and 5.8L Engines

1. Disconnect the negative, then the positive battery cable. Drain the crankcase and the cooling system into suitable containers.

✳✳CAUTION

When draining the coolant, keep in mind that cats and dogs are attracted by the ethylene glycol antifreeze, and are quite likely to drink any that is left in an uncovered container or in puddles on the ground. This will prove fatal in sufficient quantity. Always drain the coolant into a sealable container. Coolant should be reused unless it is contaminated or several years old.

2. Relieve the fuel system pressure. Discharge the air conditioning system.

3. Mark the position of the hood on the hinges and remove the hood. Disconnect the battery ground cables from the cylinder block.

4. Remove the air intake duct and the air cleaner, if engine mounted.

5. Disconnect the upper radiator hose from the thermostat housing and the lower hose from the water pump. Disconnect the oil cooler lines from the radiator.

6. Remove the bolts attaching the radiator fan shroud to the radiator. Remove the radiator. Remove the fan, belt pulley and shroud.

7. Remove the alternator bolts and position the alternator aside.

8. Disconnect the oil pressure sending unit wire from the sending unit. Disconnect the fuel lines.

9. Disconnect the accelerator cable from the carburetor or throttle body. Disconnect the throttle valve rod. Disconnect the cruise control cable, if equipped.

10. Disconnect the throttle valve vacuum line from the intake manifold, if equipped. Disconnect the transmission filler tube bracket from the cylinder block.

11. Disconnect the air conditioning lines and electrical connectors at the compressor and remove the compressor. Plug the lines and the compressor fittings to prevent the entrance of dirt and moisture.

12. Disconnect the power steering pump bracket from the cylinder head. Remove the drive belt. Position the power steering pump aside in a position that will prevent the fluid from leaking.

13. Disconnect the power brake vacuum line from the intake manifold.

14. On 5.0L engines, disconnect the heater hoses from the heater tubes. On 5.8L engines, disconnect the heater hoses from the water pump and intake manifold. Disconnect the electrical connector from the coolant temperature sending unit.

15. Remove the transmission-to-engine upper bolts.

16. On 5.8L engines, disconnect the primary wiring connector from the ignition coil. Disconnect the wiring to the solenoid

on the left rocker cover. Remove the wire harness from the left rocker arm cover and position the wires aside. Disconnect the ground strap from the block.

17. On 5.0L engines, disconnect the wiring harness at the two 10-pin connectors.

18. Raise and safely support the vehicle. Disconnect the starter cable from the starter and remove the starter.

19. Disconnect the muffler inlet pipes from the exhaust manifolds. Disconnect the engine mounts from the chassis. Disconnect the downstream thermactor tubing and check valve from the right exhaust manifold stud, if equipped.

20. Disconnect the transmission cooler lines from the retainer and remove the transmission inspection cover. Disconnect the flywheel from the converter and secure the converter assembly in the transmission. Remove the remaining transmission-to-engine bolts.

21. Lower the vehicle and then support the transmission. Attach suitable engine lifting equipment and hoist the engine.

22. Raise the engine slightly and carefully pull it from the transmission. Carefully lift the engine out of the engine compartment. Avoid bending or damaging the rear cover plate or other components. Install the engine on a workstand.

1966-85 Ford and Mercury Mid-Sized Cars, Including Mustang and Cougar

➡**Label all wiring, vacuum hoses, fuel lines, etc. before disconnecting them; thereby making installation much easier.**

The following procedure can be used on all years and models. Slight variations may occur due to extra connections, etc., but the basic procedure covers all years and models. Use this as a guide — read the entire service procedure before starting the repair.

1. Disconnect the negative battery cable. Once disconnected, it is recommended that the positive battery cable be disconnected as well.

2. Drain the crankcase and the cooling system into separate containers, and dispose of the fluids properly.

✳✳CAUTION

When draining coolant, keep in mind that cats and dogs are attracted to ethylene glycol antifreeze, and could drink any that is left in an uncovered container or in puddles on the ground. This will prove fatal in sufficient quantity. Always drain the coolant into a sealable container. Coolant should be reused unless it is contaminated or several years old.

3. Relieve the fuel system pressure, if fuel injected, then disconnect the fuel lines.

4. If the A/C compressor cannot be position out of the way without the compressor lines being removed, then discharge the air conditioning system into an approved recovery/recycling machine.

5. Mark the position of the hood on the hinges and remove the hood.

6. Unfasten the air cleaner by loosening the wing nut and/or the clips around the cover. On automatic transmission

equipped vehicles, disconnect and plug the fluid cooler lines at the radiator.

7. Remove the cooling fan, shroud and radiator, by loosening the upper and lower hose clamps and working the hoses off the radiator. Remove the shroud bolts, then lift the shroud out of the engine compartment. Finally, loosen and remove any remaining hardware securing the radiator, and pull the radiator out of the engine compartment.

8. Remove the air inlet tube. Unclamp the fuel lines from the fuel pump, if carbureted.

9. Tag, then disconnect the accelerator, cruise control cables and the throttle valve cable.

10. Tag any vacuum, breather or wire harnesses on top of or around the engine.

11. Unfasten the alternator harness from the fender apron and junction block. Unbolt the retaining hardware, and remove the alternator from the engine. Unbolt the air conditioning compressor from the engine and place aside. In some cases the compressor lines are not long enough. In this case, you must disconnect the air conditioning hoses from the compressor.

12. Unfasten the Electronic Variable Orifice (EVO) sensor connector from the power steering pump, if equipped. Also disconnect the body ground strap from the firewall.

13. Raise and safely support the vehicle on jackstands.

14. Disconnect the exhaust system from the exhaust manifolds and support the exhaust section with wire hung from the crossmember.

15. Remove the retaining nut from the transmission line bracket and remove the bolts retaining the engine to the transmission braces.

16. Remove the starter and dust seal. Remove the bolts retaining the power steering pump to the engine block and position aside.

17. On cars equipped with manual transmissions, remove the clutch retracting spring. Disconnect the clutch equalizer shaft and arm bracket at the underbody rail and remove the arm bracket and shaft from the vehicle.

18. Remove the plug from the engine block to access the converter retaining nuts. Rotate the crankshaft until each of the nuts is accessible and remove the nuts.

19. Remove the transmission-to-engine retaining bolts, including the flywheel or converter housing upper bolts. Remove the engine mount through-bolts.

20. Lower the vehicle. Support the transmission with a floor jack and remove the bolt retaining the right and left engine mounts to the lower underbody bracket.

21. Install an engine lifting bracket to the left cylinder head on the front and the right cylinder head on the rear. Connect suitable engine lifting equipment to the lifting brackets.

22. Raise the engine slowly, then carefully separate the engine from the transmission.

23. Carefully lift the engine out of the engine compartment and install it on an engine stand. Remove the engine lifting equipment.

1979-88 Mustang and Capri

✳✳WARNING

Disconnect the negative battery cable before beginning any work. Always label all disconnected hoses, vacuum lines and wires, to prevent incorrect reassembly. Do not disconnect any air conditioning lines unless you are thoroughly familiar with A/C systems and the hazards involved; escaping refrigerant (Freon®) will freeze any surface it contacts, including skin and eyes. Have the system discharged professionally before required repairs are started.

1. Scribe the hood hinge outline on the underside of the hood. With the help of an assistant, unbolt the hood and remove it.

2. Drain the entire cooling system and crankcase.

✳✳CAUTION

When draining the coolant, keep in mind that cats and dogs are attracted by the ethylene glycol antifreeze, and are quite likely to drink any that is left in an uncovered container or in puddles on the ground. This will prove fatal in sufficient quantity. Always drain the coolant into a sealable container. Coolant should be reused unless it is contaminated or several years old.

3. Remove the air cleaner and intake duct assembly. Disconnect the battery ground cable from the cylinder block. On automatic transmission equipped cars, disconnect the fluid cooler lines at the radiator.

4. Remove the upper and lower radiator hoses and remove the radiator. If equipped with air conditioning, unbolt the compressor and position it out of the way with refrigerant lines intact. Unbolt and lay the refrigerant condenser forward without disconnecting the refrigerant lines.

➡If there is not enough slack in the refrigerant lines to position the compressor out of the way, the refrigerant in the system must be removed (using proper safety precautions) before the lines can be disconnected from the compressor.

5. Remove the fan, fan belt and upper pulley. On models equipped with an electric cooling fan, disconnect the power lead and remove the fan and shroud as an assembly.

6. On cars with power steering, disconnect the pump and bracket assembly and secure them out of the way in a position which will prevent fluid from leaking out. Do not disconnect the hoses.

7. Disconnect the heater hoses at their engine fittings.

8. Disconnect the alternator wires at the alternator and the positive battery cable at the starter.

9. Disconnect the accelerator cable from the carburetor or throttle body. Disconnect the speed control cable, if so equipped. Disconnect the throttle valve rod on automatic overdrive (AOD) transmissions, if so equipped.

10. Disconnect and plug the fuel line at the fuel pump or, on fuel injected models, at the fuel rail. On fuel injected vehicles, relieve pressure in the fuel lines before disconnecting.

11. Disconnect the coil primary wire at the coil. Disconnect the wires at the oil pressure and coolant temperature sending units. Disconnect the brake booster vacuum line, if so equipped.

12. Remove the starter and dust seal.

13. Remove any additional grounding straps, wiring or vacuum hoses which may interfere with removal of the engine.

14. On cars with a manual transmission, remove the clutch retracting spring. Disconnect the clutch equalizer shaft and arm bracket at the underbody rail and remove the arm bracket and equalizer shaft.

15. Raise the car and safely support on jackstands. Remove the flywheel or converter housing upper attaching bolts.

16. Disconnect the exhaust pipe or pipes at the exhaust manifold(s). Disconnect the right and left motor mount at the underbody bracket. Remove the flywheel or converter housing cover. On models so equipped, disconnect the engine roll damper on the left front of the engine from the frame.

17. On cars with a manual transmission, remove the flywheel housing lower attaching bolts. On models with an automatic transmission, disconnect the throttle valve vacuum line at the intake manifold and disconnect the converter from the flywheel. Remove the converter housing lower attaching bolts.

18. Lower the car. Support the transmission and flywheel or converter housing with a jack.

19. Attach an engine lifting hook. Lift the engine up and out of the compartment and onto a workstand.

1983-96 Thunderbird and Cougar

✳✳CAUTION

When draining the coolant, keep in mind that cats and dogs are attracted by the ethylene glycol antifreeze, and are quite likely to drink any that is left in an uncovered container or in puddles on the ground. This will prove fatal in sufficient quantity. Always drain the coolant into a sealable container. Coolant should be reused unless it is contaminated or several years old.

1. Scribe the hood hinge outline on the under hood, disconnect the hood and remove.

2. Drain the entire cooling system and crankcase.

➡A Chilton environmental tip. Used oil contains heavy metals, and has been determined to be hazardous to the environment. Recycling oil is the best way for disposal. Check local laws and recycle whenever possible.

3. Remove the air cleaner, disconnect the battery ground cable from engine block. On automatic transmission equipped cars, disconnect the fluid cooler lines at the radiator. On the 2.3, remove the exhaust manifold shroud.

4. Remove the upper and lower radiator hoses and remove the radiator. If equipped with A/C, unbolt the compressor and position out of the way with the refrigerant lines still intact.

Unbolt and lay the A/C condenser forward without disconnecting the refrigerant lines.

➡If there is not enough slack in the refrigerant lines to position the compressor out of the way, the refrigerant must be evacuated from the system, using an approved A/C recovery/recycling system, before the lines can be disconnected from the compressor.

5. Remove the fan, fan belt and upper pulley. On models equipped with an electric fan, disconnect the power lead and remove the fan and shroud as an assembly.

6. Disconnect the heater hoses from the engine. On the 2.3, disconnect the heater hose from the water pump and choke fittings.

7. Disconnect the alternator wires at the alternator, the starter cable at the starter, accelerator rod at the carburetor.

8. Disconnect and plug the fuel lines at the fuel pump on models equipped with fuel injection, depressurize the fuel system first.

9. Disconnect the coil primary wire at the coil. Disconnect the wires at the oil pressure and water temperature sending units. On cars equipped with fuel injection disconnect the wires from the throttle body and or multiport injectors. Disconnect the brake booster vacuum hose.

➡On 1989-92 engines the upper intake portion of the fuel injection must be removed. If equipped with supercharger, the intake oil cooler must also be removed.

10. Raise and safely support vehicle on jack stands. Remove the starter and dust seal.

11. On cars with manual transmission, remove the clutch retracting spring. Disconnect the clutch equalizer shaft and arm bracket at the underbody rail and remove the arm bracket and equalizer shaft.

12. Remove the flywheel or converter housing upper retaining bolts.

13. Disconnect the exhaust pipe or pipes at the exhaust manifolds. Disconnect the left and right motor mount at the underbody bracket. Remove the flywheel or converter housing cover. Disconnect the engine roll damper on the left front of engine from the frame, on models so equipped.

14. On cars with manual transmission, remove the lower wheel housing bolts.

15. On cars with automatic transmission, disconnect the throttle valve vacuum line at the intake manifold. Disconnect the converter from the flywheel. Remove the converter housing lower retaining bolts. On models with power steering, disconnect the power steering pump from the cylinder head. remove the drive belt and wire the pump out of the way. Do not disconnect the hoses.

➡At this time it is a good idea to double check all the engine wiring and hoses, to ensure everything is disconnected and or removed to avoid damage and or personal injury

16. Lower the car. Support the transmission and flywheel or converter housing with a jack.

17. Attach an engine lifting hook. Lift the engine up and out of the compartment and onto a workstand.

1989-93 Mustang

1. Disconnect the battery cables. Drain the crankcase and the cooling system.
2. Relieve the fuel system pressure and discharge the air conditioning system.
3. Mark the position of the hood on the hinges and remove the hood. Disconnect the battery ground cables from the cylinder block.
4. Remove the air intake duct and the air cleaner, if engine mounted.
5. Disconnect the upper radiator hose from the thermostat housing and the lower hose from the water pump. If equipped with an automatic transmission, disconnect the oil cooler lines from the radiator.
6. Remove the bolts attaching the radiator fan shroud to the radiator. Remove the radiator. Remove the fan, belt pulley and shroud.
7. Remove the alternator bolts and position the alternator out of the way.
8. Disconnect the oil pressure sending unit wire from the sending unit. Disconnect the flexible fuel line at the fuel tank line. Plug the fuel tank line.
9. Disconnect the accelerator cable from the carburetor or throttle body. Disconnect the TV rod if equipped with an automatic transmission. Disconnect the cruise control cable, if equipped.
10. Disconnect the throttle valve vacuum line from the intake manifold, if equipped. Disconnect the transmission filler tube bracket from the cylinder block.
11. If equipped with air conditioning, disconnect the lines and electrical connectors at the compressor and remove the compressor. Plug the lines and the compressor fittings to prevent the entrance of dirt and moisture.
12. Disconnect the power steering pump bracket from the cylinder head. Remove the drive belt. Position the power steering pump out of the way in a position that will prevent the fluid from leaking.
13. Disconnect the power brake vacuum line from the intake manifold.
14. Disconnect the heater hoses from the heater tubes. Disconnect the electrical connector from the coolant temperature sending unit.
15. Remove the converter housing-to-engine upper bolts.
16. Disconnect the wiring to the solenoid on the left rocker cover. Remove the wire harness from the left rocker arm cover and position the wires out of the way. Disconnect the ground strap from the block.
17. Disconnect the wiring harness at the two 10-pin connectors.
18. Raise and safely support the vehicle. Disconnect the starter cable from the starter and remove the starter.
19. Disconnect the muffler inlet pipes from the exhaust manifolds. Disconnect the engine support insulators from the chassis. Disconnect the downstream thermactor tubing and check valve from the right exhaust manifold stud, if equipped.
20. Disconnect the transmission cooler lines from the retainer and remove the converter housing inspection cover. Disconnect the flywheel from the converter and secure the converter assembly in the housing. Remove the remaining converter housing-to-engine bolts.

21. Lower the vehicle and then support the transmission. Attach engine lifting equipment and hoist the engine.
22. Raise the engine slightly and carefully pull it from the transmission. carefully lift the engine out of the engine compartment. Avoid bending or damaging the rear cover plate or other components. Install the engine on a workstand.

Flywheel/Flex Plate and Ring Gear

You'll have to remove the flywheel before mounting the engine on the stand.

➡ **Flex plate is the term for a flywheel mated with an automatic transmission.**

➡ **The ring gear is replaceable only on engines mated with a manual transmission. Engines with automatic transmissions have ring gears which are welded to the flex plate.**

1. Remove the clutch, if equipped, or torque converter from the flywheel. The flywheel bolts should be loosened a little at a time in a cross pattern to avoid warping the flywheel. On cars with manual transmissions, replace the pilot bearing in the end of the crankshaft.

➡ **You're going to have to hold the crankshaft to keep it from turning. This is best done with a breaker bar and socket on the damper nut.**

2. The flywheel should be checked for cracks and glazing. It can be resurfaced by a machine shop.

The Engine Dolly

1. Roll the crane backwards, CAREFULLY, until the engine is clear of the vehicle.
2. Place the engine dolly under the engine.
3. Carefully lower the engine onto the engine dolly. Make sure that the engine is squarely set on the dolly before removing the crane. Wrap a safety chain around the engine and dolly to avoid an accident.
4. Roll the engine into your garage.
5. Remove the mounting head from the engine stand and bolt it to the back of the engine, aligning the mounting arms with the appropriate bellhousing mating holes.
6. Bring the crane inside and lift the engine off the dolly. Position the engine stand behind the engine, align the tube of the mounting head with the stand upright and slide it into the upright. Tighten the set bolt. Remove the crane.
7. Now you can relax! Take a break! Be proud of yourself!

Cleaning The Engine

Break's over. Whether the engine came from your vehicle or a junkyard, it is pretty dirty. You can't work on a dirty engine. It's not safe, either for you or the parts. There are several ways to clean an engine, but none of them are particularly pleasant.

You don't have to get the engine completely spotless, but you really should remove all heavy surface dirt, grease and oil. This can be done with any number of safe, non-flammable solvents available at any good auto parts store. You can begin by placing a large dropcloth on the floor under the engine.

Then, scrape off the heaviest stuff with a putty knife and wire brush. You'll be surprised at how much you can remove this way.

Once that's done, apply the solvent to specific areas, working from the top down and, with plenty of shop rags, remove as much as you can.

When you're satisfied, dispose of the dropcloth and dirt. Look the engine over at this point for any signs of damage, obvious leaks, etc. Also, just stand back and get familiar with what the engine looks like. The more familiar you are with the general layout, the easier your job will be.

Next, wire-brush all exposed nuts and bolts. Then, take a penetrating solvent, such as Liquid Wrench® or WD-40® and soak all exposed nuts and bolts. Wipe up the mess.

You can now begin disassembly.

Budgeting Your Time

If, as mentioned before, you're working under a deadline, such as getting your car back on the road as soon as possible, you'll be tempted to rush the job. DON'T! If at all possible, take your time. Hurrying leads to mistakes. Mistakes can cause injury, damage and money, and usually, more time. Don't work until you're over-tired. Tired workers make mistakes.

If the job is a hobby or long term project.....no problem. Take your time, take attention to detail and you'll do a great job!

Before Disassembly

By this time, you should have adequate shelf space, at least one work bench, all your tools in order and plenty of places or containers for removed parts, pieces, fasteners, etc.

Before you begin the actual operation, step back, take a deep breath and organize your thoughts. Okay, get your indelible marker ready and begin.

DISASSEMBLY
ALTERNATOR 5-24
CAMSHAFT 5-37
CAMSHAFT BEARINGS 5-37
CORE (FREEZE/OIL GALLERY)
  PLUGS 5-44
CRANKSHAFT AND MAIN
  BEARINGS 5-42
CRANKSHAFT PULLEY (VIBRATION
  DAMPER) 5-34
CYLINDER HEAD 5-28
DISTRIBUTOR 5-24
ENGINE FAN AND FAN
  CLUTCH 5-27
ENGINE OVERHAUL TIPS 5-2
EXHAUST MANIFOLD 5-26
IGNITION COIL 5-24
INTAKE MANIFOLD 5-26
OIL PAN 5-33
OIL PUMP 5-33
PISTONS AND CONNECTING
  RODS 5-38
REAR MAIN OIL SEAL 5-46
ROCKER ARMS AND
  PUSHRODS 5-25
ROCKER COVERS 5-24
THERMOSTAT 5-26
TIMING CHAIN 5-36
TIMING CHAIN FRONT COVER AND
  OIL SEAL 5-35
VALVES 5-29
WATER PUMP 5-28
INSPECTION
CAMSHAFT 5-56
CRANKSHAFT 5-60
CYLINDER HEAD 5-52
MAIN BEARINGS 5-60
PISTONS AND CONNECTING
  RODS 5-56
TIMING CHAIN 5-55
VALVES 5-52
PARTS CLEANING
BLOCK 5-48
COLD SPRAYING 5-47
COLD TANK IMMERSION 5-47
CRANKSHAFT 5-48
CYLINDER HEAD 5-48
HAND CLEANING 5-47
HOT TANK IMMERSION 5-47
MAIN BEARINGS 5-49
PISTON AND ROD 5-48
STEAM CLEANING 5-47
VALVES 5-48
PUTTING IT ALL BACK TOGETHER
ALTERNATOR 5-101
CAMSHAFT AND BEARINGS 5-84
CORE (FREEZE) PLUGS 5-73
CRANKSHAFT AND MAIN
  BEARINGS 5-74
CRANKSHAFT PULLEY (VIBRATION
  DAMPER) 5-89

CYLINDER HEAD 5-92
DISTRIBUTOR 5-98
ENGINE FAN AND FAN
  CLUTCH 5-98
EXHAUST MANIFOLD 5-94
FLYWHEEL/FLEXPLATE 5-101
INTAKE MANIFOLD 5-98
LIFTERS 5-89
OIL PAN 5-85
OIL PUMP 5-84
ONE PIECE REAR MAIN OIL
  SEAL 5-101
PAINTING 5-73
PISTONS AND CONNECTING
  RODS 5-75
ROCKER ARMS AND
  PUSHRODS 5-94
ROCKER COVERS 5-101
THERMOSTAT 5-98
TIMING CHAIN 5-84
TIMING CHAIN FRONT COVER AND
  OIL SEAL 5-88
VALVES 5-91
WATER PUMP 5-94
REPAIR AND REFINISHING
BLOCK 5-71
CYLINDER HEAD 5-65
OIL PUMP 5-71
ROCKER STUDS 5-64
VALVE GUIDES 5-69
VALVES AND SEATS 5-65
SPECIFICATIONS CHARTS
ENGINE MECHANICAL
  SPECIFICATIONS 5-102
TORQUE SPECIFICATIONS 5-102

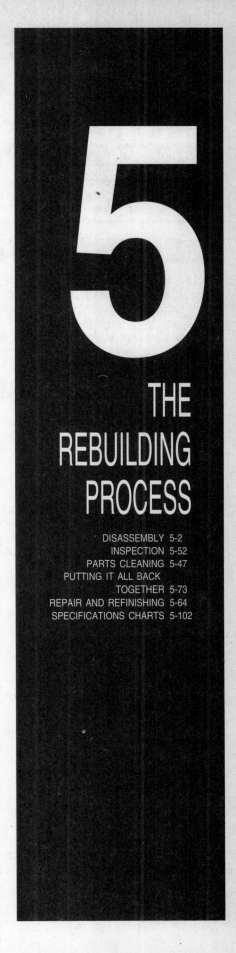

5

THE REBUILDING PROCESS

DISASSEMBLY 5-2
INSPECTION 5-52
PARTS CLEANING 5-47
PUTTING IT ALL BACK
  TOGETHER 5-73
REPAIR AND REFINISHING 5-64
SPECIFICATIONS CHARTS 5-102

DISASSEMBLY

▶ **See Figures 1, 2, 3, 4, 5, 6, 7, 8, 9, 10, 11, 12, 13, 14, 15, 16, 17, 18, 19, 20, 21 and 22**

❋❋CAUTION

Start off slowly and carefully. Don't rush. Take your time. If you get tired, take a break or quit for the day. Tired workers make mistakes.

Engine Overhaul Tips

Most engine overhaul procedures are fairly standard. Examples of standard rebuilding practices are shown and should be used along with specific details concerning your particular engine.

Competent and accurate machine shop services will ensure maximum performance, reliability and engine life. In most instances it is more profitable for the do-it-yourself mechanic to remove, clean and inspect the component, buy the necessary parts and deliver these to a shop for actual machine work.

On the other hand, much of the rebuilding work (crankshaft, block, bearings, piston rods, and other components) is well within the scope of the do-it-yourself mechanic.

TOOLS

The tools required for an engine overhaul or parts replacement will depend on the depth of your involvement. With a few exceptions, they will be the tools found in a mechanic's tool kit. More in-depth work will require any or all of the following:
- a dial indicator (reading in thousandths) mounted on a universal base
  - micrometers and telescope gauges
  - jaw and screw-type pullers
  - scraper
  - valve spring compressor
  - ring groove cleaner
  - piston ring expander and compressor
  - ridge reamer
  - cylinder hone or glaze breaker
  - Plastigage®
  - engine stand

INSPECTION TECHNIQUES

Procedures and specifications are given in this section for inspecting, cleaning and assessing the wear limits of most major components. Other procedures such as Magnaflux® and Zyglo® can be used to locate material flaws and stress cracks. Magnaflux® is a magnetic process applicable only to ferrous materials. The Zyglo® process coats the material with a fluorescent dye penetrant and can be used on any material. Checking for suspected surface cracks can be more readily made using spot check dye. The dye is sprayed onto the suspected area, wiped off and the area sprayed with a developer. Cracks will show up brightly.

OVERHAUL TIPS

Aluminum has become extremely popular for use in engines, due to its low weight. Observe the following precautions when handling aluminum parts:
- Never hot tank aluminum parts (the caustic hot tank solution will eat the aluminum.
- Remove all aluminum parts (identification tag, etc.) from engine parts prior to the tanking.
- Always coat threads lightly with engine oil or anti-seize compounds before installation, to prevent seizure.
- Never overtorque bolts or spark plugs especially in aluminum threads.

Stripped threads in any component can be repaired using any of several commercial repair kits (Heli-Coil®, Microdot®, Keenserts®, etc.).

When assembling the engine, any parts that will be in frictional contact must be prelubed to provide lubrication at initial start-up. Any product specifically formulated for this purpose can be used, but engine oil is not recommended as a prelube.

When semi-permanent (locked, but removable) installation of bolts or nuts is desired, threads should be cleaned and coated with Loctite® or other similar, commercial non-hardening sealant.

87935100

Fig. 1 The engine on a workstand, in the shop

ENGLISH TO METRIC CONVERSION: TORQUE

Torque is now expressed as either foot-pounds (ft./lbs.) or inch-pounds (in./lbs.). The metric measurement unit for torque is the Newton-meter (Nm). This unit—the Nm—will be used for all SI metric torque references, both the present ft./lbs. and in./lbs.

ft lbs	N-m	ft lbs	N-m	ft lbs	N-m	ft lbs	N-m
0.1	0.1	33	44.7	74	100.3	115	155.9
0.2	0.3	34	46.1	75	101.7	116	157.3
0.3	0.4	35	47.4	76	103.0	117	158.6
0.4	0.5	36	48.8	77	104.4	118	160.0
0.5	0.7	37	50.7	78	105.8	119	161.3
0.6	0.8	38	51.5	79	107.1	120	162.7
0.7	1.0	39	52.9	80	108.5	121	164.0
0.8	1.1	40	54.2	81	109.8	122	165.4
0.9	1.2	41	55.6	82	111.2	123	166.8
1	1.3	42	56.9	83	112.5	124	168.1
2	2.7	43	58.3	84	113.9	125	169.5
3	4.1	44	59.7	85	115.2	126	170.8
4	5.4	45	61.0	86	116.6	127	172.2
5	6.8	46	62.4	87	118.0	128	173.5
6	8.1	47	63.7	88	119.3	129	174.9
7	9.5	48	65.1	89	120.7	130	176.2
8	10.8	49	66.4	90	122.0	131	177.6
9	12.2	50	67.8	91	123.4	132	179.0
10	13.6	51	69.2	92	124.7	133	180.3
11	14.9	52	70.5	93	126.1	134	181.7
12	16.3	53	71.9	94	127.4	135	183.0
13	17.6	54	73.2	95	128.8	136	184.4
14	18.9	55	74.6	96	130.2	137	185.7
15	20.3	56	75.9	97	131.5	138	187.1
16	21.7	57	77.3	98	132.9	139	188.5
17	23.0	58	78.6	99	134.2	140	189.8
18	24.4	59	80.0	100	135.6	141	191.2
19	25.8	60	81.4	101	136.9	142	192.5
20	27.1	61	82.7	102	138.3	143	193.9
21	28.5	62	84.1	103	139.6	144	195.2
22	29.8	63	85.4	104	141.0	145	196.6
23	31.2	64	86.8	105	142.4	146	198.0
24	32.5	65	88.1	106	143.7	147	199.3
25	33.9	66	89.5	107	145.1	148	200.7
26	35.2	67	90.8	108	146.4	149	202.0
27	36.6	68	92.2	109	147.8	150	203.4
28	38.0	69	93.6	110	149.1	151	204.7
29	39.3	70	94.9	111	150.5	152	206.1
30	40.7	71	96.3	112	151.8	153	207.4
31	42.0	72	97.6	113	153.2	154	208.8
32	43.4	73	99.0	114	154.6	155	210.2

tccs1c03

Fig. 2 REMEMBER that the proper torque is critical to engine rebuilding

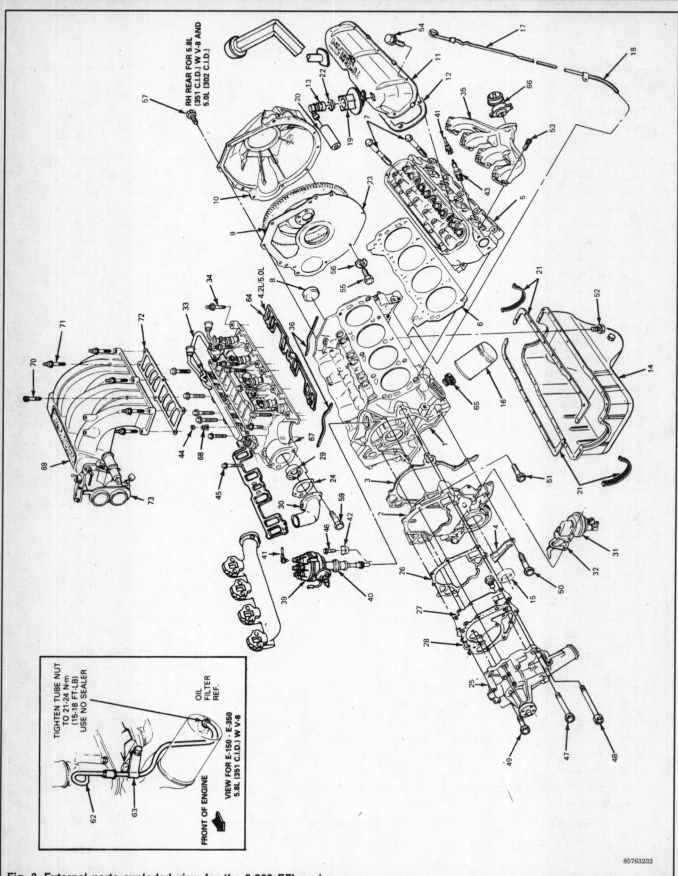

Fig. 3 External parts exploded view for the 8-302 EFI engine

RH REAR FOR 5.8L (351 C.I.D.) W V-8 AND 5.0L (302 C.I.D.)

TIGHTEN TUBE NUT TO 21-24 N·m (15-18 FT-LB) USE NO SEALER

OIL FILTER REF.

VIEW FOR E-150 - E-350 5.8L (351 C.I.D.) W V-8

FRONT OF ENGINE

4.2L/5.0L

85763232

REF. NO.	BASIC PART NO.	DESCRIPTION	REF. NO.	BASIC PART NO.	DESCRIPTION
1	6009	Cylinder Assy. — (Includes internal parts)	48	300958-S	Bolt — 5/16-18 x 5"
2	6019	Cover Assy. — Cylinder Front	49	56128-S	Bolt — 5/16-18 x 2-1/2"
3	6020	Gasket — Cylinder Front cover	50	56126-S	Bolt — 5/16-18 x 2"
4	6023	Pointer — Timing	51	376256-S	Bolt or Screw — 5/16-18 x 1"
5	6049	Head — Cylinder	52	373564-S	Bolt — 5/16-18 x 1-7/8"
6	6051	Gasket — Cylinder Head	53	381731-S	Bolt — 3/8-16 x 1-7/8"
7	6065	Bolt — Cylinder Head	54	356748-S	Bolt — 1/4-20 x 5/8"
8	6266	Plug — Camshaft Rear Bearing	55	20346-S	Bolt — 5/16-18 x 3/4 — 17-24 N·m (12-18 FT-LBS)
9	6375	Flywheel Assy.	56	34806-S	Washer — Lock — 5/16 x 19/32 x 5/64"
10	6392	Housing Assy. — Flywheel	57	20508-S	Bolt — 7/16-14 x 1-3/4"
11	6582	Cover Assy. — Valve Rocker Arm	58	34808-S	Washer — Lock — 7/16"
12	6584	Gasket — Valve Rocker Arm Cover	59		Bolt — 5/16-18
13	383777	Elbows — Positive Crankcase Ventialtion (P.C.V.)	62	6750-BA	Indicator — oil Level
14	6675	Pan Assy. — Oil	63	6754-AC	Tube Assy. — Oil Level Indicator
15	6700	Seal — Cylinder Front Cover			
16	6731	Element Assy. — Oil Filter	64	9441	Gasket Intake Manifold
17	6750	Indicator — Oil Level	65	6890	Insert — Oil Fill Adaptor
18	6784	Tube Assy. — Oil Level Indicator	66	9A427	Valve Assy. — Exhaust Heat Control
19	6766	Cap Assy. — Oil Filler	67	9K461	Lower Intake Manifold Assy.
20	6853	Hose — Positive Crankcase Ventilation	68		Clip
21	6781	Gasket Set — Oil pan	69	9425	Upper Intake Manifold
22	382156	Retainer — Crankcase Ventilation — Grommet	70		Screw
23	7007	Plate Assy. — Engine Rear	71		Stud
24	8255	Gasket — Water Outlet Connection	72		Gasket
25	8501	Pump Assy. — Water	73	9E926	Throttle Body
26	8507	Gasket — Water Pump Housing			
27	8508	Cover — Water Pump			
28	8513	Gasket — Water Pump Cover			
29	8575	Thermostat — Water			
30	8592	Connection — Water Outlet			
31	9350	Pump Assy. — Fuel			
32	9417	Gasket — Fuel Pump Mounting			
33	9D280	Rail Assy. — Fuel			
34		Stud			
35	9430	Manifold — Exhaust			
36	9433	Gasket Set — Manifold			
37		Gasket — Upper to Lower Intake Manifolds			
39	12106	Distributor — Cap			
40	12127	Distributor Assy.			
41	12259	Wire Set — Spark Plug			
42	12270	Clamp — Distributor			
43	12405	Spark Plug Assy.			
44		Nut			
45		Bolt			
46	20386-S	Bolt — 5/16-18 x 1"			
47	383765-S	Bolt — 5/16-18 x 3-5/8"			

87937055

Fig. 4 Key list-external parts exploded view for the 8-302 EFI engine

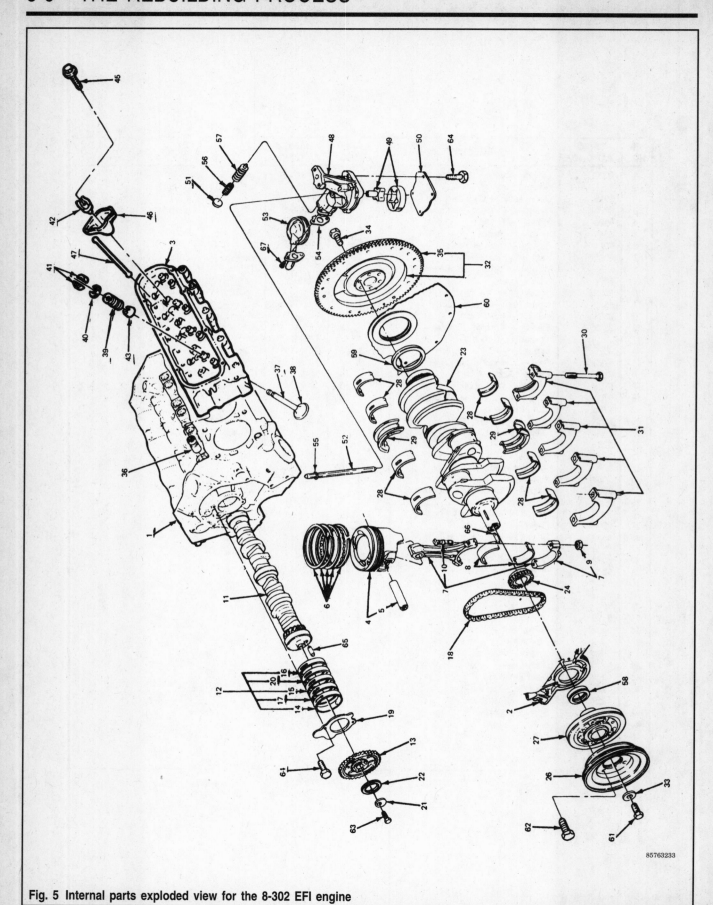

Fig. 5 Internal parts exploded view for the 8-302 EFI engine

85763233

Ref. No.	Basic Part No.	Description	Ref. No.	Basic Part No.	Description	Ref. No.	Basic Part No.	Description
1	6010	Block Assy. (Internal parts not included)	23	6303	Crankshaft Assy.	47	6565	Rod — Valve Push
2	6019	Cover Assy. — Cylinder Front	24		Sprocket — Crankshaft	48	6600	Pump Assy. — Oil
3	6049	Head — Cylinder	26	6A312	Pulley Assy. — Crankshaft Outer	49	6608	Rotor and Shaft Assy. — Oil Pump Drive
4	6108	Piston Assy.	27	6316	Damper Assy. — Crankshaft	50	6616	Plate — Oil Pump Body
5	6135	Pin — Piston	28	6333	Bearing — Crankshaft Main (except center)	51	6A616	Plug — Oil Pump Relief Valve
6	6148	Ring Set — Piston	29	6337	Bearing — Crankshaft Main (center)	52	6A618	Shaft Assy. — Oil Pump Intermediate
7	6200	Rod Assy. — Connecting	30	6345	Bolt — Crankshaft Main Bearing Cap	53	6622	Screen, Tube and Cover Assy. — Oil Pump
8	6211	Bearing — Connecting Rod	31	•	Main Bearing Cap — Supplied in 6010 Block Assy.	54	6626	Gasket — Oil Pump Inlet Tube
9	6212	Nut — Connecting Rod	32	6375	Flywheel Assy.	55	6629	Ring — Oil Pump Intermediate Shaft
10	6214	Bolt — Connecting Rod	33	6378	Washer — Crankshaft Pulley Retaining	56	6670	Spring — Oil Pump Relief Valve
11	6250	Camshaft	34	6379	Bolt — Flywheel to Crankshaft	57	6674	Plunger — Oil Pump Relief Valve
12	6251	Bearing Kit — Camshaft — Standard	35	6384	Gear — Flywheel Ring	58	6700	Seal — Cylinder Front Cover Oil
13		Sprocket — Camshaft	36	6500	Tappet Assy. — Hydraulic	59	6701	Seal — Crankshaft Rear
14	6261	Bearing — Camshaft Front	37	6505	Valve — Exhaust	60	6A372	Plate — Engine Rear
15	6262	Bearing — Camshaft Center	38	6507	Valve — Intake	61	377850-S	Bolt — 5/8-18 x 2"
16	6263	Bearing — Camshaft Rear	39	6513	Spring — Valve	62	42998-S	Bolt — 3/8-16 x 1"
17	6267	Bearing — Camshaft Front Intermediate	40	6514	Retainer — Valve Spring	63	43002-S	Bolt — 3/8-16 x 1-1/2"
18		Chain — Timing	41	6518	Key — Valve Spring Retainer	64	42911-S	Bolt — 1/4-20 x 5/8"
19	6269	Plate — Camshaft Thrust	42	6A528-A	Fulcrum	65	378189-S	Pin — Dowel — 5/16 x 1-3/8"
20	6270	Bearing — Camshaft Rear Intermediate	43	6571	Valve Stem Seal	66	372854-S	Key — Woodruff — 1-3/4 x 7/32 x 3/16"
21	6278	Washer — Camshaft Sprocket	45	6A527-A	Bolt — Rocker Arm Attach	67	357235-S	Bolt — 5/16-18 x 7/8"
22	6287	Ecentric — Camshaft Fuel Pump	46	6564	Arm — Valve Rocker			

87937056

Fig. 6 Key list-internal parts exploded view for the 8-302 EFI engine

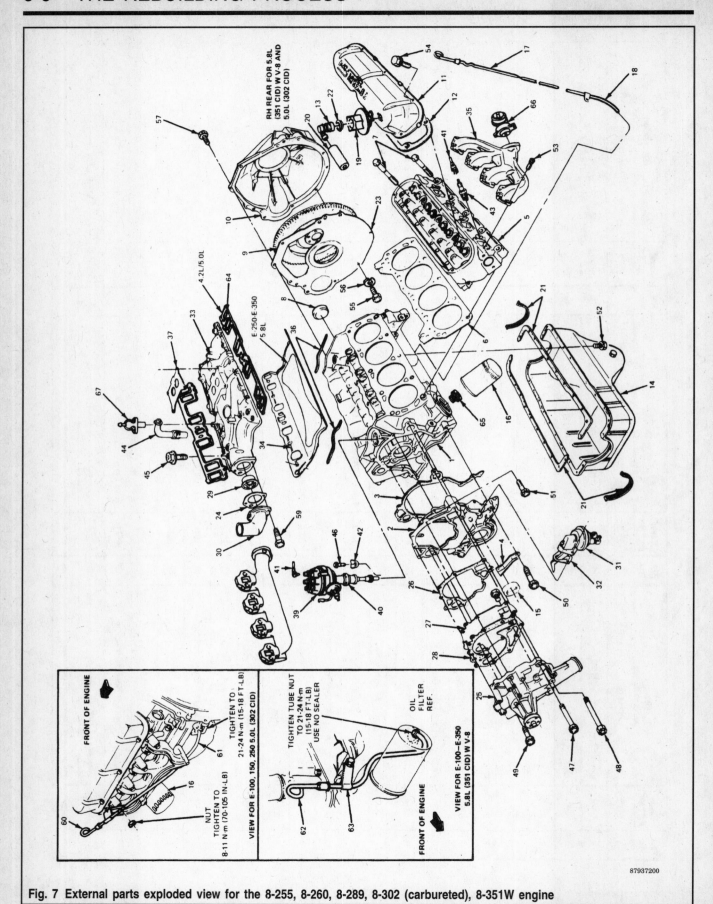

Fig. 7 External parts exploded view for the 8-255, 8-260, 8-289, 8-302 (carbureted), 8-351W engine

87937200

REF. NO.	BASIC PART NO.	DESCRIPTION	REF. NO.	BASIC PART NO.	DESCRIPTION
1	6009	Cylinder Assy. — (Includes internal parts)	39	12106	Distributor — Cap
			40	12127	Distributor Assy.
2	6019	Cover Assy. — Cylinder Front	41	12259	Wire Set — Spark Plug
3	6020	Gasket — Cylinder Front Cover	42	12270	Clamp — Distributor
4	6023	Pointer — Timing	43	12405	Spark Plug Assy.
5	6049	Head — Cylinder	44	18599	Elbow — Hot Water Connection
6	6051	Gasket — Cylinder Head	45	56126-S	Bolt — Washer Head — 5/16-18 x 7/8''
7	6065	Bolt — Cylinder Head			
8	6266	Plug — Camshaft Rear Bearing	46	20386-S	Bolt — 5/16-18 x 1''
9	6375	Flywheel Assy.	47	383765-S	Bolt — 5/16-18 x 3-5/8''
10	6392	Housing Assy. — Flywheel	48	300958-S	Bolt — 5/16-18 x 5''
11	6582	Cover Assy. — Valve Rocker Arm	49	56128-S	Bolt — 5/16-18 x 2-1/2''
12	6584	Gasket — Valve Rocker Arm Cover	50	56126-S	Bolt — 5/16-18 x 2''
13	6B890	Elbow & Valve Assy. — Positive Crankcase Ventilation (P.C.V.)	51	376256-S	Bolt or Screw — 5/16-18 x 1''
			52	373564-S	Bolt — 5/16-18 x 1-7/8''
14	6675	Pan Assy. — Oil	53	381731-S	Bolt — 3/8-16 x 1-7/8''
15	6700	Seal — Cylinder Front Cover	54	356748-S	Bolt — 1/4-20 x 5/8''
16	6731	Element Assy. — Oil Filter	55	20346-S	Bolt – 5/16-18 x 3/4'' - 17-24 N·m (12-18 FT-LBS)
17	6750	Indicator — Oil Level			
18	6754	Tube Assy. — Oil Level Indicator			
19	6766	Cap Assy. — Oil Filler	56	34806-S	Washer — Lock — 5/16 x 19/32 x 5/64''
20	381187	Hose — Positive Crankcase Ventilation			
			57	20508-S	Bolt — 7/16-14 x 1-3/4''
21	6781	Gasket Set — Oil Pan	58	34808-S	Washer — Lock — 7/16''
22	6A892	Retainer — Crankcase Ventilation — Grommet	59		Bolt — 5/16-18
			60	6750-CA	Indicator — Oil Level
23	7007	Plate Assy. — Engine Rear	61	6754-CA	Tube Assy. — Oil Level Indicator
24	8255	Gasket — Water Outlet Connection			
25	8501	Pump Assy. — Water	62	6750-BA	Indicator — Oil Level
26	8507	Gasket — Water Pump Housing	63	6754-AC	Tube Assy. — Oil Level Indicator
27	8508	Cover — Water Pump			
28	8513	Gasket — Water Pump Cover	64	9441	Gasket Intake Manifold
29	8575	Thermostat — Water	65	6890	Insert — Oil Fill Adaptor
30	8592	Connection — Water Outlet			
31	9350	Pump Assy. — Fuel	66	9A427	Valve Assembly — Exhaust Heat Control
32	9417	Gasket — Fuel Pump Mounting			
33	9424	Manifold — Intake	67	9G464	Valve Assembly — Intake Manifold Heat Control (5.0L Unlead Only)
34		Intake Manifold Gasket - Intake Manifold to Cylinder Block			
35	9430	Manifold — Exhaust			
36	9433	Gasket Set — Manifold			
37	9447	Gasket — Carburetor			

87937057

Fig. 8 Key list-external parts exploded view for the 8-255, 8-260, 8-289, 8-302 (carbureted), 8-351W engine

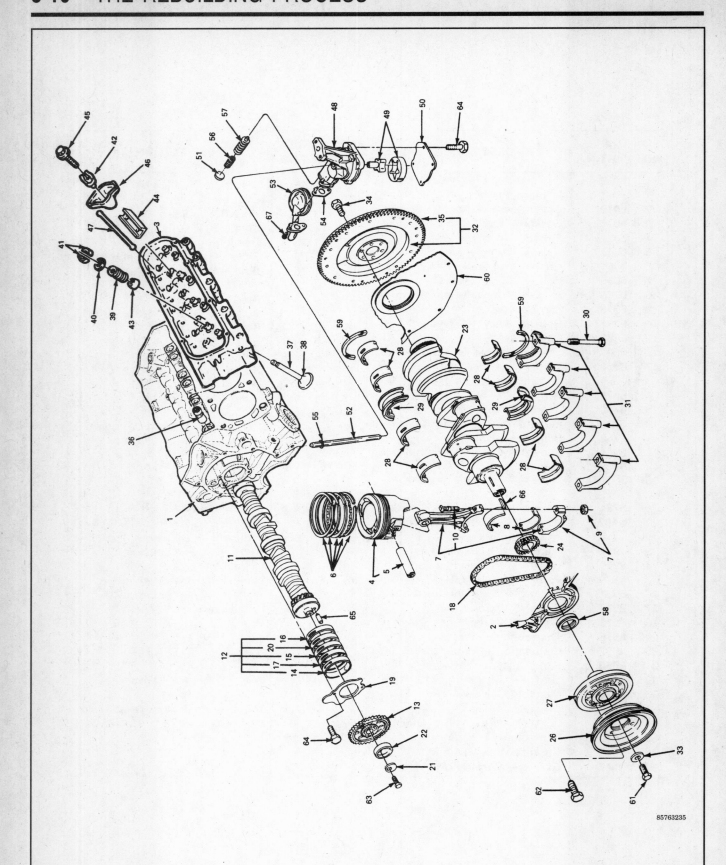

Fig. 9 Internal parts exploded view for the 8-255, 8-260, 8-289, 8-302 (carbureted), 8-351W engine

85763235

Ref. No.	Basic Part No.	Description
1	6010	Block Assy. (Internal parts not included)
2	6019	Cover Assy. — Cylinder Front
3	6049	Head — Cylinder
4	6108	Piston Assy.
5	6135	Pin — Piston
6	6148	Ring Set — Piston
7	6200	Rod Assy. — Connecting
8	6211	Bearing — Connecting Rod
9	6212	Nut — Connecting Rod
10	6214	Bolt — Connecting Rod
11	6250	Camshaft
12	6251	Bearing Kit — Camshaft — Standard
13	6256	Sprocket — Camshaft (Nylon)
14	6261	Bearing — Camshaft Front
15	6262	Bearing — Camshaft Center
16	6263	Bearing — Camshaft Rear
17	6267	Bearing — Camshaft Front Intermediate
18	6268	Chain — Timing
19	6269	Plate — Camshaft Thrust
20	6270	Bearing — Camshaft Rear Intermediate
21	6278	Washer — Camshaft Sprocket
22	6287	Eccentric — Camshaft Fuel Pump
23	6303	Crankshaft Assy.
24	6306	Sprocket — Crankshaft
26	6A312	Pulley Assy. — Crankshaft Outer
27	6316	Damper Assy. — Crankshaft
28	6333	Bearing — Crankshaft Main (except center)
29	6337	Bearing — Crankshaft Main (center)
30	6345	Bolt — Crankshaft Main Bearing Cap
31	*	Main Bearing Cap — Supplied in 6010 Block Assy.
32	6375	Flywheel Assy.
33	6378	Washer — Crankshaft Pulley Retaining
34	6379	Bolt — Flywheel to Crankshaft
35	6384	Gear — Flywheel Ring
36	6500	Tappet Assy. — Hydraulic
37	6505	Valve — Exhaust
38	6507	Valve — Intake
39	6513	Spring — Valve
40	6514	Retainer — Valve Spring
41	6518	Key — Valve Spring Retainer
42	6A528-A	Fulcrum
43	6571	Valve Stem Seal
44	6A53-1	Fulcrum Guide
45	6A527-A	Bolt — Rocker Arm Attach
46	6564	Arm — Valve Rocker
47	6565	Rod — Valve Push
48	6600	Pump Assy. — Oil
49	6608	Rotor and Shaft Assy. — Oil Pump Drive
50	6616	Plate — Oil Pump Body
51	6A616	Plug — Oil Pump Relief Valve
52	6A618	Shaft Assy. — Oil Pump Intermediate
53	6622	Screen, Tube and Cover Assy. — Oil Pump
54	6626	Gasket — Oil Pump Inlet Tube
55	6629	Ring — Oil Pump Intermediate Shaft
56	6670	Spring — Oil Pump Relief Valve
57	6674	Plunger — Oil Pump Relief Valve
58	6700	Seal — Cylinder Front Cover Oil
59	6701	Packing — Crankshaft Rear
60	6A372	Plate — Engine Rear
61	377850-S	Bolt — 5/8-18 x 2"
62	42998-S	Bolt — 3/8-16 x 1"
63	43002-S	Bolt — 3/8-16 x 1-1/2"
64	42911-S	Bolt — 1/4-20 5/8"
65	378189-S	Pin — Dowel — 5/16 x 1-3/8"
66	372854-S	Key — Woodruff — 1-3/4 x 7/32 x 3/16"
67	357235-S	Bolt — 5/16-18 x 7/8"

87937058

Fig. 10 Key list-Internal parts exploded view for the 8-255, 8-260, 8-289, 8-302 (carbureted), 8-351W engine

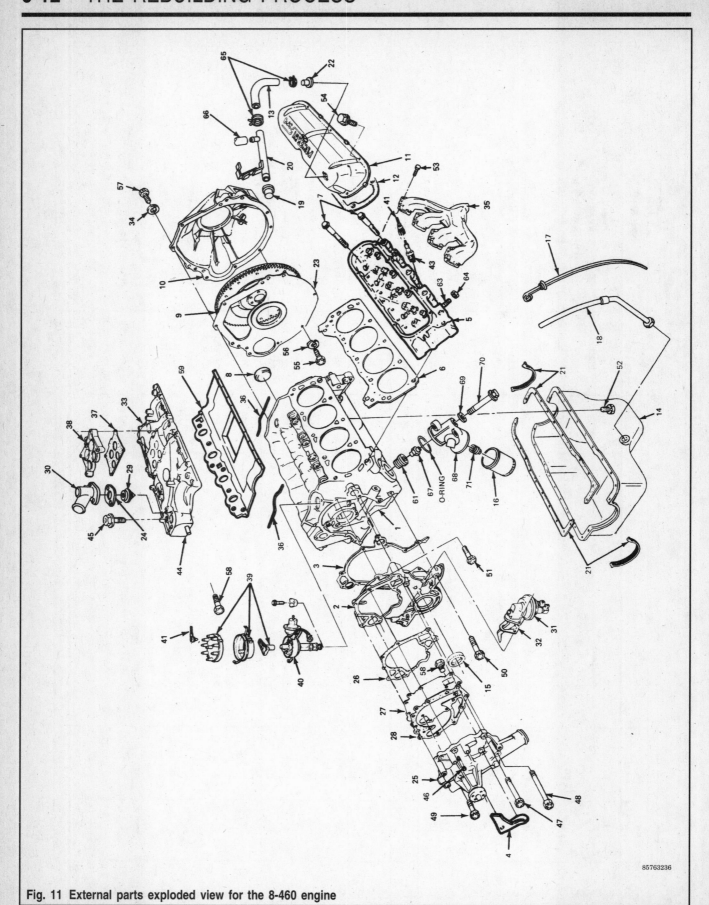

Fig. 11 External parts exploded view for the 8-460 engine

85763236

REF. NO.	BASIC PART NO.	DESCRIPTION	REF. NO.	BASIC PART NO.	DESCRIPTION	REF. NO.	BASIC PART NO.	DESCRIPTION
1	6009	Cylinder Assy. — (Includes internal parts)	26	8507	Gasket — Water Pump Housing	49	56128-S	Bolt — 5/16-18 x 2-1/2"
2	6019	Cover Assy. — Cylinder Front	27	8508	Cover — Water Pump	50	388059-S2	Bolt — 5/16-18 x 2"
3	6020	Gasket — Cylinder Front Cover	28	8513	Gasket — Water Pump Cover	51	376256-S	Bolt or Screw — 5/16-18 x 1"
4	6023	Pointer — Timing	29	8575	Thermostat — Water	52	387549-S	Bolt — 1/4 x 20 x 62
5	6049	Head — Cylinder	30	8A565	Connection — Water Outlet	53	377506-S2	Bolt — 3/8-16 x 1-7/8"
6	6051	Gasket — Cylinder Head	31	9350	Pump Assy. — Fuel	54	387549-S2	Bolt — 1/4-20 x 5/8"
7	6065	Bolt — Cylinder Head	32	9417	Gasket — Fuel Pump Mounting	55	20346-S	Bolt — 5/16-18 x 3/4"
8	6266	Plug — Camshaft Rear Bearing	33	9424	Manifold — Intake	56	34806-S	Washer — Lock — 5/16 x 19/32 x 5/64"
9	6375	Flywheel Assy.	34	34808-S	Washer — Lock — 7/16"	57	20508-S	Bolt — 7/16-14 x 1-3/4"
10	7902	Housing Assy. — Converter	35	9430	Manifold — Exhaust	58	358720-S	Bolt — 5/16-18 x 1.125
11	6582	Cover Assy. — Valve Rocker Arm	36	9433	Gasket Set — Manifold	59	9D440	Gasket — Valley Baffle
12	6584	Gasket — Valve Rocker Arm Cover	37	9447	Gasket — Carburetor	60	OR 9C484	Bolt — 5/16-18
13	6A787	Oil Filler Pipe Hose	38	9A589	Spacer — Carburetor to Intake Manifold	61	6890	Adapter — Oil Filter
14	6675	Pan Assy. — Oil	39	12106	Distributor — Parts	62	10884	Water Temperature Sending Unit
15	6700	Seal — Cylinder Front Cover	40	12127	Distributor Assy.	63	—	Stud
16	6731	Element Assy. — Oil Filter	41	12259	Wire Set — Spark Plug	64	382802-S2	Nut
17	6750	Indicator — Oil Level	42	12270	Clamp — Distributor	65	387061-S35	Hose Clamp
18	6754	Tube Assy. — Oil Level Indicator	43	12405	Spark Plug Assy.	66	6853	Hose — Filler Hose to Carburetor
19	6766	Cap Assy. — Oil Filler	44	8555	Tube — Hot Water Connection	67	6890	Adapter
20	6763	Oil Filler Pipe Assy.	45	56126-S	Bolt — Washer Head — 5/16-18 x 7/8"	68	6881	O-Ring
21	6781	Gasket Set — Oil Pan	46	20386-S	Bolt — 5/16-18 x 1.68"	69	6749	Washer
22	6A873	Oil Filler Adapter Assy.	47	386594-S2	Bolt — 5/16-18 x 3-5/8"	70	6894	Bolt
23	6A373	Plate Assy. — Engine Rear	48	300958-S	Bolt — 5/16-18 x 5"	71	6890	Adapter
24	8255	Gasket — Water Outlet Connection						
25	8501	Pump Assy.— Water						

87937059

Fig. 12 Key list-external parts exploded view for the 8-460 engine

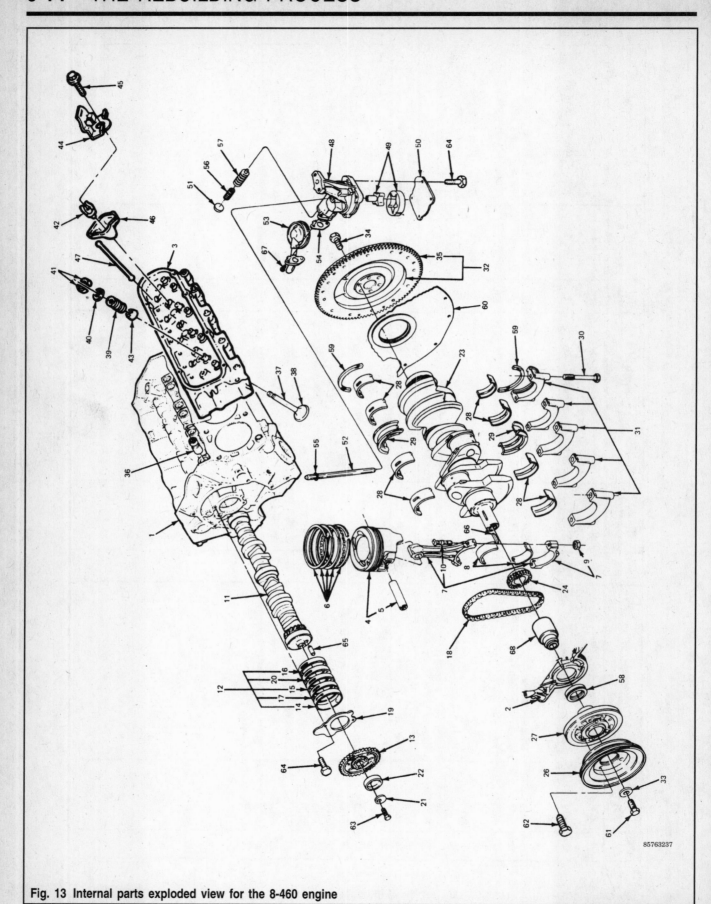

Fig. 13 Internal parts exploded view for the 8-460 engine

85763237

A4942-2D

Ref. No.	Basic Part No.	Description
1	6010	Block Assy. (Internal parts not included)
2	6019	Cover Assy. — Cylinder Front
3	6049	Head — Cylinder
4	6108	Piston Assy.
5	6135	Pin — Piston
6	6148	Ring Set — Piston
7	6200	Rod Assy. — Connecting
8	6211	Bearing — Connecting Rod
9	6212	Nut — Connecting Rod
10	6214	Bolt — Connecting Rod
11	6250	Camshaft
12	6251	Bearing Kit — Camshaft — Standard
13	6256	Sprocket — Camshaft (Nylon)
14	6261	Bearing — Camshaft Front
15	6262	Bearing — Camshaft Center
16	6263	Bearing — Camshaft Rear
17	6267	Bearing — Camshaft Front Intermediate
18	6268	Chain — Timing
19	6269	Plate — Camshaft Thrust
20	6270	Bearing — Camshaft Rear Intermediate
21	6278	Washer — Camshaft Sprocket
22	6287	Eccentric — Camshaft Fuel Pump
23	6303	Crankshaft Assy.
24	6306	Sprocket — Crankshaft
26	6A312	Pulley Assy. — Crankshaft Outer
27	6316	Damper Assy. — Crankshaft
28	6333	Bearing — Crankshaft Main (except center)
29	6337	Bearing — Crankshaft Main (center)
30	6345	Bolt — Crankshaft Main Bearing Cap
31	*	Main Bearing Cap — Supplied in 6010 Block Assy.
32	6380	Flywheel
33	6378	Washer — Crankshaft Pulley Retaining

Ref. No.	Basic Part No.	Description
34	6379	Bolt — Flywheel to Crankshaft
35	6384	Gear — Flywheel Ring
36	6500	Tappet Assy. — Hydraulic
37	6505	Valve — Exhaust
38	6507	Valve — Intake
39	6513	Spring — Valve
40	6514	Retainer — Valve Spring
41	6518	Key — Valve Spring Retainer
42	6A528-A	Fulcrum
43	6571	Valve Stem Seal
44	6A53-1	Oil Deflector
45	6A527-A	Bolt — Rocker Arm Attach
46	6564	Arm — Valve Rocker
47	6565	Rod — Valve Push
48	6600	Pump Assy. — Oil
49	6608	Rotor and Shaft Assy. — Oil Pump Drive
50	6616	Plate — Oil Pump Body
51	6A616	Plug — Oil Pump Relief Valve
52	6A618	Shaft Assy. — Oil Pump Intermediate
53	6622	Screen, Tube and Cover Assy. — Oil Pump
54	6626	Gasket — Oil Pump Inlet Tube
55	6629	Ring — Oil Pump Intermediate Shaft
56	6670	Spring — Oil Pump Relief Valve
57	6674	Plunger — Oil Pump Relief Valve
58	6700	Seal — Cylinder Front Cover Oil
59	6701	Packing — Crankshaft Rear
60	7007	Plate — Engine Rear
61	377850-S	Bolt — 5/8-18 x 2"
62	42998-S	Bolt — 3/8-16 x 1"
63	43002-S	Bolt — 3/8-16 x 1-1/2"
64	42911-S	Bolt — 1/4-20 x 5/8"
65	378189-S	Pin — Dowel — 5/16 x 1-3/8"
66	372854-S	Key — Woodruff — 1-3/4 x 7/32 x 3/16"
67	357235-S	Bolt — 5/16-18 x 7/8"
68	6359	Spacer

87937060

Fig. 14 Key list-internal parts exploded view for the 8-460 engine

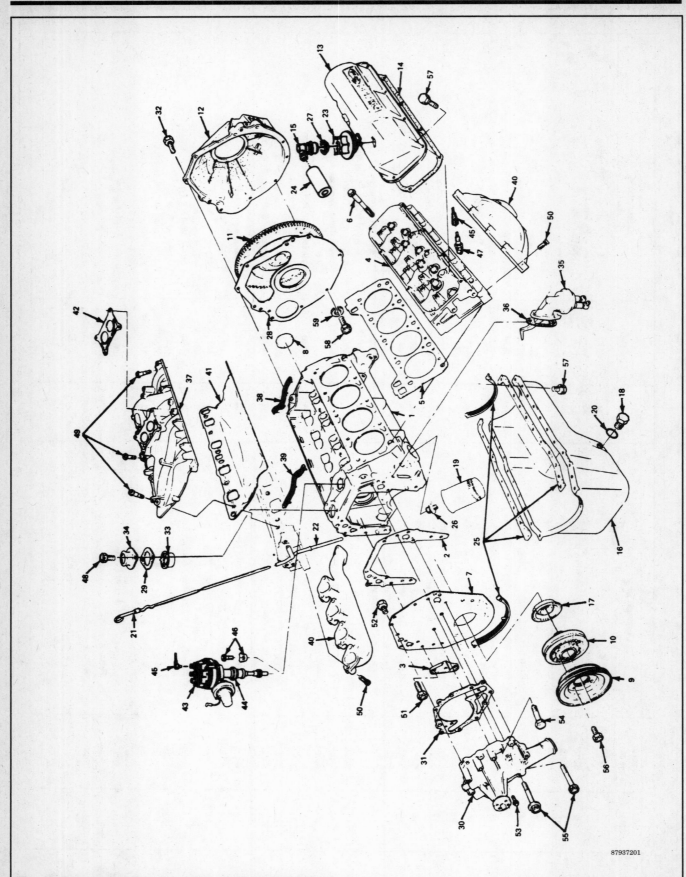

Fig. 15 External parts exploded view for the 8-351M, 8-400

87937201

REF. NO.	BASIC PART NO.	DESCRIPTION
1	6010	Block Assy. (Internal parts not included)
2	6020	Gasket — Cylinder Front Cover Plate
3	6023	Pointer — Timing
4	6049	Head — Cylinder
5	6051	Gasket — Cylinder Head
6	6065	Bolt — Cylinder Head
7	6B070	Plate — Cylinder Front Cover
8	6266	Plug — Camshaft Rear Bearing
9	6312	Pulley Assy. — Crankshaft
10	6316	Damper Assy. — Engine Crankshaft
11	6375	Flywheel Assy.
12	6392	Housing Assy. — Flywheel
13	6582	Cover Assy. — Valve Rocker Arm
14	6584	Gasket — Valve Rocker Arm Cover
15	6A666	Elbow & Valve Assy. — Positive Crankcase
16	6675	Pan Assy. — Oil
17	6700	Seal — Cylinder Front Cover Oil
18	6730	Plug — Oil Pan Drain
19	6731	Element Assy. — Oil Filter
20	6734	Gasket — Oil Pan Drain Plug
21	6750	Indicator — Oil Level
22	6754	Tube Assy. — Oil Level Indicator
23	6766	Cap Assy. — Oil Filler
24	6767	Hose — Crankcase Ventilation
25	6781	Gasket Set — Oil Pan
26	6890	Insert — Oil Filter Mounting Bolt
27	6A892	Retainer — Crankcase Ventilation Grommet
28	7007	Plate Assy. — Engine Rear
29	8255	Gasket — Water Outlet Connection
30	8501	Pump Assy. — Water
31	8507	Gasket — Water Pump Housing
32	376275-S	Bolt — 7/16-14 x 2-9/16"
33	8575	Thermostat — Water
34	8592	Connection — Water Outlet
35	9350	Pump Assy. — Fuel
36	9417	Gasket — Fuel Pump Mounting
37	9424	Manifold — Intake
38	9A424	Seal — Intake Manifold to Cylinder Block (rear)
39	9A425	Seal — Intake Manifold to Cylinder Block (front)
40	9430	Manifold — Exhaust
41	9441	Gasket — Intake Manifold to Cylinder Head
42	9447	Gasket — Carburetor
43	12106	Cap — Distributor
44	12127	Distributor Assy.
45	12259	Wire Set — Spark Plug
46	12270	Clamp — Distributor
47	12405	Spark Plug Assy.
48	57633-S	Screw and Lockwasher — 5/16-18 x 3/4"
49	56126-S	Bolt Hex Washer Head — 5/16-18 x 2"
50	20522-S	Bolt — Washer Head — 3/8-16 x 2"
51	56121-S	Bolt — 5/16-18 x 7/8"
52	382127-S	Screw — Self-Tapping — 5/16-18 x 1-1/4"
53	383965-S	Screw — Self-Tapping — 5/16-18 x 2-7/8"
54	373564-S	Bolt — Washer Head — 5/16-18 x 1-7/8"
55	383963-S	Bolt — Washer Head — 5/16-18 x 2-7/8"
55	42998-S	Bolt — 3/8-16 x 1"
57	373071-S	Bolt — Washer Head — 1/4-20 x 5/8"
58	20346-S	Bolt — 5/16-18 x 3/4"
59	34806-S	Washer — Lock — 5/16 x 19/32 x 5/64"

87937061

Fig. 16 Key list-external parts exploded view for the 8-351M, 8-400

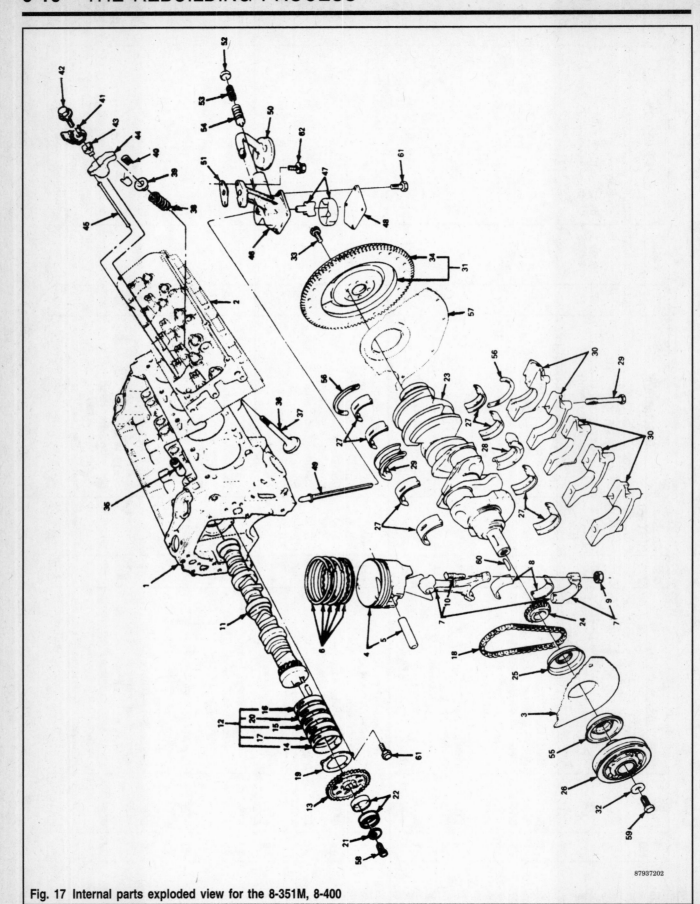

Fig. 17 Internal parts exploded view for the 8-351M, 8-400

87937202

REF. NO.	BASIC PART NO.	DESCRIPTION	REF. NO.	BASIC PART NO.	DESCRIPTION
1	6010	Block Assy.	36	6505	Valve — Exhaust
2	6049	Head — Cylinder	37	6507	Valve — Intake
3	6B070	Plate — Cylinder Front	38	6513	Spring — Valve
4	6108	Piston Assy.	39	6514	Retainer — Valve Spring
5	6135	Pin — Piston	40	6518	Key — Valve Spring Retainer
6	6148	Ring Set — Piston	41	6524	Baffle — Valve Push Rod Valley
7	6200	Rod Assy. — Connecting	42	6A527	Stud — Valve Rocker Arm Support
8	6211	Bearing — Connecting Rod	43	6A528	Seat — Valve Rocker Arm Fulcrum
9	6212	Nut — Connecting Rod			
10	6214	Bolt — Connecting Rod	44	6564	Arm — Valve Rocker
11	6250	Camshaft	45	6565	Rod — Valve Push
12	6251	Bearing Kit — Camshaft — Standard	46	6600	Pump Assy. — Oil
			47	6608	Rotor and Shaft Assy. — Oil Pump Drive
13	6256	Sprocket — Camshaft			
14	6261	Bearing — Camshaft Front	48	6616	Plate — Oil Pump Body
15	6262	Bearing — Camshaft Center	49	6A618	Shaft Assy. — Oil Pump Intermediate
16	6263	Bearing — Camshaft Rear			
17	6267	Bearing — Camshaft Front Intermediate	50	6622	Screen Tube and Cover Assy. — Oil Pump
18	6268	Chain — Timing	51	6659	Gasket — Oil Pump Mounting
19	6269	Plate — Camshaft Thrust	52	6666	Plug — Oil Pump Relief Valve
20	6270	Bearing — Camshaft Rear Intermediate	53	6670	Spring — Oil Pump Relief Valve
			54	6674	Plunger — Oil Pump Relief Valve
21	6287	Washer — Camshaft Sprocket	55	6700	Seal — Cylinder Front
22	6287	Two Piece Fuel Pump Eccentric	56	6701	Packing — Crankshaft Rear
23	6303	Crankshaft Assy.	57	7007	Plate — Engine Rear
24	6306	Sprocket — Crankshaft	58	43002-S	Bolt — Slotted Head — 3/8-16 x 1-1/2''
25	6310	Slinger — Crankshaft Oil			
26	6316	Damper Assy. — Crankshaft	59	377850-S	Bolt — 3/4-16 x 1-25/32''
27	6333	Bearing — Crankshaft Main (except center)	60	372854-S	Key — Woodruff — 1-3/4 x 7/32 x 3/16''
28	6337	Bearing — Crankshaft (center)	61	42911-S	Bolt — 1/4-20 x 5/8''
29	6345	Bolt — Crankshaft Main Bearing Cap	62	359266-S	Bolt — 3/8-16 x 1-1/4''
30	*	Main Bearing Cap — Supplied in 6010 Block Assy.			
31	6375	Flywheel Assy.			
32	6378	Washer — Crankshaft Pulley Retaining			
33	6379	Bolt — Flywheel to Crankshaft			
34	6384	Gear — Flywheel Ring			
35	6500	Tappet Assy. — Hydraulic			

87937062

Fig. 18 Key list-internal parts exploded view for the 8-351M, 8-400

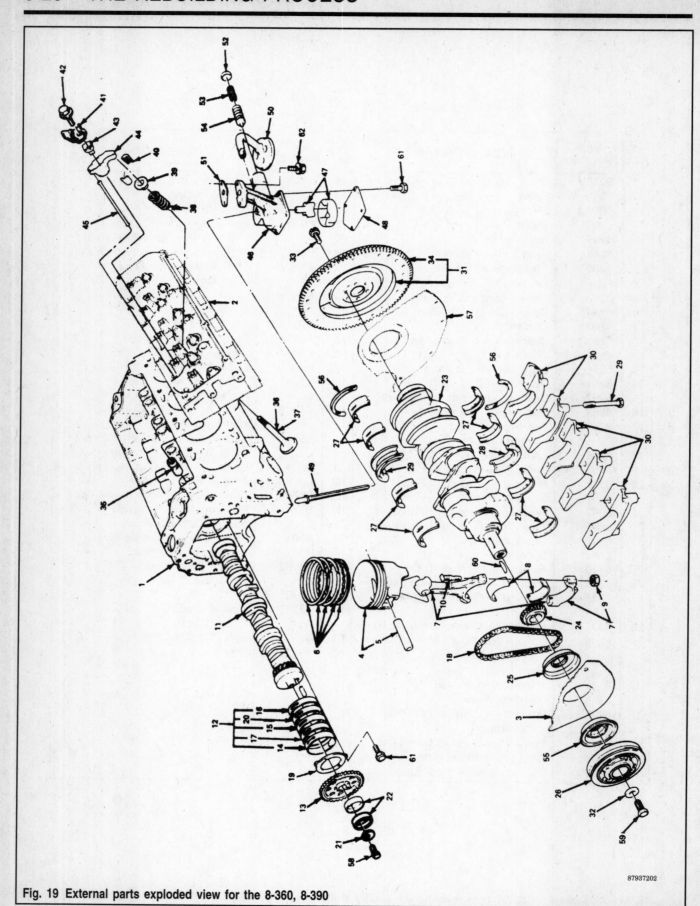

Fig. 19 External parts exploded view for the 8-360, 8-390

87937202

REF. NO.	BASIC PART NO.	DESCRIPTION	REF. NO.	BASIC PART NO.	DESCRIPTION
1	6010	Block Assy. (Internal parts not included)	34	370478-S	Bolt — 3/8-16 x 2-5/8''
			35	20468-S	Bolt — 3/8-16 x 1-1/2''
2	6019	Cover Assy. — Cylinder Front	36	20408-S	Bolt — 3/8-16 x 1-1/8''
3	6020	Gasket — Cylinder Front Cover	37	351385-S	Washer — Flat — 3/8-25/64 x 3/4 x 7/64'' (Steel)
4	6026	Plug — Engine			
5	6049	Head — Cylinder	38	20546-S	Bolt — 7/16-14 x 2-1/2''
6	6051	Gasket — Cylinder Head	39	34808-S	Washer — Lock — 7/16 x 25/32 x 7/64''
7	6065	Bolt — Cylinder Head			
8	6524	Baffle — Valve Spring Oil	40	20310-S	Bolt — 5/16-18 x 1/2''
9	359518-S	Bolt — 3/8-16 x 11/16''	41	34806-S	Washer — Lock — 5/16 x 19/32 x 5/64''
10	6675	Pan Assy. — Oil			
11	6700	Seal — Cylinder Front Cover	42	371065-S	Bolt — 5/16-18 x 5/8''
12	6710	Gasket — Oil Pan	43	9448	Exhaust Manifold Gasket
13	6730	Plug — Oil Pan Drain			
14	6734	Gasket — Oil Pan Drain Plug			
15	6750	Indicator — Oil Level			
16	6754	Tube Assy. — Oil Level Indicator			
17	6766	Cap Assy. — Oil Filler			
18	6763	Pipe — Oil Filler			
19	7505	Housing — Clutch			
20	7522	Trunnion — Clutch Release Lever			
21	7564	Cover — Clutch Housing Dust			
22	9424	Manifold — Intake			
23	9A424	Seal — Intake Manifold to Cylinder Block (Rear)			
24	9A425	Seal — Intake Manifold to Cylinder Block (Front)			
25	9430	Manifold — Exhaust (Right Side)			
26	9431	Manifold — Exhaust (Left Side)			
27	9433	Gasket Set — Manifold			
28	9447	Gasket — Carburetor			
29	9A455	Fitting — Heater Hose Connection			
30	9A589	Spacer — Carburetor to Intake Manifold			
31	10911	Adapter — Water Temperature Indicator Sender			
32	87710-S	Plug — Pipe — 3/8-18 x 15/32'' (Steel)			
33	372226-S	Fitting Connector — Brass — Male Inverted — 5/16 x 1/2''-20-1/2''-20			

87937063

Fig. 20 Key list-external parts exploded view for the 8-360, 8-390

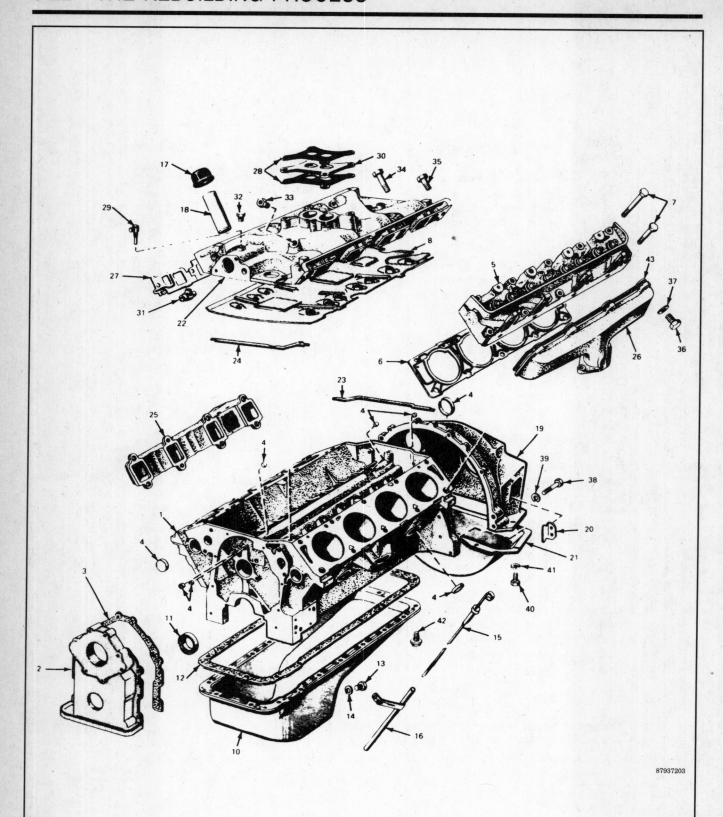

Fig. 21 Internal parts exploded view for the 8-360, 8-390

87937203

REF. NO.	BASIC PART NO.	DESCRIPTION	REF. NO.	BASIC PART NO.	DESCRIPTION	REF. NO.	BASIC PART NO.	DESCRIPTION
1	6010	Block Assy.	35	6384	Gear — Flywheel Ring	66	377850-S	Bolt — 5/8-18 x 2"
2	6049	Head — Cylinder	36	6500	Tappet Assy. — Hydraulic	67	380041-S	Screw — 7/16-14 x 55/64"
3	6108	Piston and Pin Assy.	37	6505	Valve — Exhaust	68	371186-S	Bolt — 3/8-16 x 11/16"
4	6135	Pin — Piston	38	6507	Valve — Intake	69	34847-S	Washer — Lock — 3/8 x 45/64 x 1/8"
5	6140	Retainer — Piston Pin	39	6513	Spring — Valve	70	20346-S	Bolt — 5/16-18 x 3/4"
6	6148	Ring Set — Piston	40	6514	Retainer — Valve Spring	71	34806-S	Washer — Lock — 5/16 x 19/32 x 5/64"
7	6200	Rod Assy. — Connecting	41	6517	Sleeve — Valve Spring Retainer	72	34805-S	Washer — Lock — 1/4 x 1/2 x 1/16"
8	6207	Bushing — Connecting Rod	42	6518	Key — Valve Spring Retainer	73	20324-S	Bolt — 1/4-20 x 5/8"
9	6211	Bearing — Connecting Rod	43	6524	Baffle — Valve Spring Oil	74	378705-S	Key — Woodruff — 3/16 x 1/4 x 1-1/2"
10	6212	Nut — Connecting Rod	44	6A527	Bolt — Valve Rocker Arm Shaft Support	75	378704-S	Key — Woodruff — 1-13/32 x 11/32 x 3/16"
11	6214	Bolt — Connecting Rod	45	6531	Support — Valve Rocker Arm Shaft	76	34807-S	Washer — Lock — 3/8 x 11/16 x 3/32"
12	6250	Camshaft	46	6563	Shaft — Valve Rocker Arm			
13	6251	Bearing Kit — Camshaft — Standard	47	6564	Arm — Valve Rocker			
14	6256	Sprocket — Camshaft	48	6565	Rod — Valve Push			
15	6261	Bearing — Camshaft Front	49	6571	Seal — Valve Stem			
16	6262	Bearing — Camshaft Center	50	6572	Plug — Valve Rocker Arm Shaft			
17	6263	Bearing — Camshaft Rear	51	6587	Spring — Valve Rocker Arm to Shaft			
18	6267	Bearing — Camshaft Front Intermediate	52	6590	Washer — Valve Rocker Arm Shaft			
19	6268	Chain — Timing	53	6600	Pump Assy. — Oil			
20	6269	Plate — Camshaft Thrust	54	6608	Rotor and Shaft Assy. — Oil Pump Drive			
21	6270	Bearing — Camshaft Rear Intermediate	55	6616	Plate — Oil Pump Body			
22	6278	Washer — Camshaft Sprocket	56	6A618	Shaft Assy. — Oil Pump Intermediate			
23	6287	Eccentric — Camshaft Fuel Pump	57	6622	Screen Tube and Cover Assy. — Oil Pump			
24	6303	Crankshaft Assy.	58	6626	Gasket — Oil Pump Inlet Tube			
25	6306	Sprocket — Crankshaft	59	6659	Gasket — Oil Pump to Cylinder Block			
26	6310	Slinger — Crankshaft Oil	60	6666	Plug — Oil Pump Relief Valve			
27	6312	Pulley Assy. — Crankshaft	61	6670	Spring — Oil Pump Relief Valve			
28	6333	Bearing — Crankshaft Main (except center)	62	6674	Plunger — Oil Pump Relief Valve			
29	6337	Bearing — Crankshaft Main (center)	63	6701	Seal — Crankshaft Rear			
30	6345	Bolt — Crankshaft Main Bearing Cap	64	304815-S	Bolt — 7/16-14 x 1-7/8"			
31	*	Main Bearing Cap — Supplied in 6010 Block Assy.	65	34808-S	Washer — Lock — 7/16 x 25/32 x 7/64"			
32	6375	Flywheel Assy.						
33	6378	Washer — Crankshaft Pulley Retaining						
34	6379	Bolt — Flywheel to Crankshaft						

87937064

Fig. 22 Key list-internal parts exploded view for the 8-360, 8-390

Ignition Coil

1. Pull off the plastic wire connector from the coil, or, remove the attaching nuts and the wires. Tag the wires.

2. Remove the bracket bolt and remove the coil and bracket. If you're going to reuse the coil, store it in a safe place on a shelf.

Distributor

▶ See Figures 23, 24 and 25

1. Noting the position of the vacuum line(s) on the distributor diaphragm, disconnect the lines at the diaphragm. Unsnap the two distributor cap retaining clamps and remove the cap.

2. Remove the spark plugs. Rotate the engine so that No.1 piston is at TDC of the compression stroke. If you're not certain of the compression stroke, you can tell by placing your thumb over the No.1 spark plug hole as the damper mark approaches the timing pointer. On the compression stroke, you'll feel air being forced out the spark plug hole.

3. Using an indelible marker, carefully mark the position of the distributor rotor in relation to the distributor housing and mark the position of the distributor housing in relation to the engine block or intake manifold. When this is done, you should have a line on the distributor housing directly in line with the tip of the rotor and another line on the engine block directly in line with the mark on the distributor housing. This is very important because the distributor must be installed in the exact

Fig. 23 Unplug the distributor connectors

Fig. 24 Mark the distributor body for rotor alignment

Fig. 25 Removing the distributor

same location from which it was removed, if correct ignition timing is to be maintained.

4. Remove the distributor hold-down bolt and clamp. Check to see that the distributor rotates.

➡It is very common, in fact expect it, for the distributor to be rusted firmly in place. This is especially common on engines with electronic ignition because the distributor is rarely moved and may not have been moved in many years! If this is the case, soak the area around the base of the distributor with a penetrant such as Liquid Wrench® or WD-40®. Use a lot! Go on to something else for a few hours. DO NOT HAMMER ON THE DISTRIBUTOR BODY OR VACUUM ADVANCE UNIT!!!! If you do, you will break it! Trust me!

5. If the distributor turns (rotates), simply pull it from the engine. The distributor drives the oil pump via a hex-shaped shaft. If this shaft comes out with the distributor, remove it from the distributor, label it and store it in a safe place.

Alternator

1. Remove the adjusting arm bolt.
2. Remove the drive belt from the alternator pulley.
3. Remove the alternator through-bolt.

➡Some engines are equipped with a ribbed, K-section belt and automatic tensioner. A special tool must be made to remove the tension from the tensioner arm. Loosen the idler pulley pivot and adjuster bolts before using the tool. See the accompanying illustration for tool details.

Rocker Covers

1. Remove the crankcase ventilation hose (passenger's side) or oil filler cap and PCV hose (driver's side).
2. Tag and remove any hose or wire left in the way.
3. Remove the hold-down bolts and lift off the valve cover.

➡If the cover(s) will not readily lift off, break it loose by rapping it with a rubber mallet. If that still won't do it, you'll have to carefully pry the cover off, but this will undoubtedly bend the cover lip. Make sure you straighten it before installation

Rocker Arms and Pushrods

▶ **See Figures 26, 27, 28, 29, 30, 31 and 32**

Loosen and remove the rocker arm fulcrum nuts. Remove the fulcrum and rocker arms. KEEP EVERYTHING IN ORDER FOR INSTALLATION!

Remove the pushrods, one at a time, wipe them clean and place them in whatever container that you've chosen for storage and identification. Masking tape can help with identification.

Some engines, notably the 360 and 390 have rocker arms mounted on shafts. To remove these:

On the right side, start at the number 4 cylinder (rearmost) and loosen support bolts in sequence, two turns at a time. Remove the shaft assembly and the baffle plate after all bolts have been loosened.

Fig. 28 Removing a pushrod

Fig. 26 Loosening a rocker arm fulcrum nut

Fig. 29 Removing a fulcrum nut

Fig. 27 Rotating a rocker arm

Fig. 30 Removing a fulcrum seat

Fig. 31 Removing a rocker arm

The same procedure is followed on the left bank, except that the bolt loosening sequence starts with the number 5 cylinder (foremost).

✳✳WARNING

The above bolt loosening procedure must be followed to avoid damage to the rocker arm shaft.

These rocker arms shaft assemblies can be taken apart by driving out the small pin at either end and sliding the parts off. KEEP THE PARTS IN ORDER AND IDENTIFIED FOR STORAGE AND REUSE!

Thermostat

1. Remove the thermostat housing retaining bolts.
2. Remove the gasket and thermostat from the block or intake manifold and clean both mating surfaces.

Intake Manifold

▶ **See Figures 33, 34, 35, 36 and 37**

1. Check the bolt torque illustration for installing the manifold. It's a good idea to reverse the installation sequence for bolt removal. This will avoid warping the manifold. Remove the bolts.
2. Remove the intake manifold. BE CAREFUL! Unless it's aluminum, this thing is heavier than it looks! If possible, get someone to help you. It may be necessary to pry the intake manifold from the cylinder head. There are projections built into the manifold for this purpose. NEVER pry on a gasket surface!
3. Remove the valley pan or gaskets, and the two end seals from the heads and block.

Exhaust Manifold

1. For the left side, remove the oil dipstick tube bracket.

Fig. 33 Removing a front intake manifold bolt

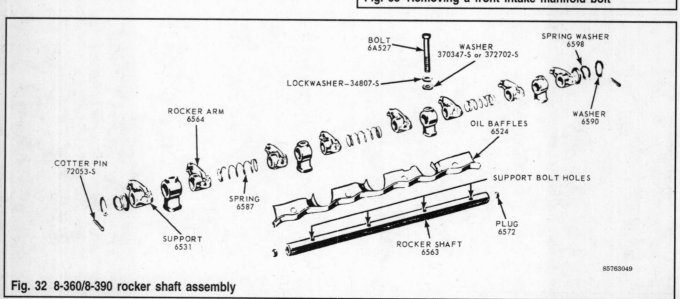

Fig. 32 8-360/8-390 rocker shaft assembly

Fig. 34 Removing a rear intake manifold bolt

Fig. 35 Removing a center intake manifold bolt

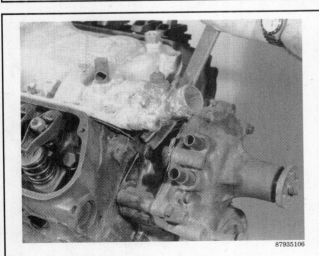

Fig. 36 Breaking loose the intake manifold with a prybar

Fig. 37 Lifting the intake manifold

2. Remove the exhaust manifold attaching bolts and remove the manifold from the cylinder head.

Engine Fan and Fan Clutch

▶ See Figures 38, 39, 40 and 41

Remove the 4 fan clutch-to-water pump hub bolts and lift off the fan/clutch assembly.

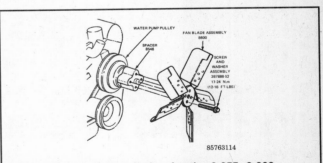

Fig. 38 Fan blade installation for the 8-255, 8-302, 8-351W

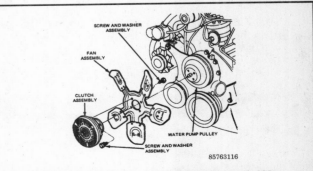

Fig. 39 Fan assembly for the 1984 and later 8-460

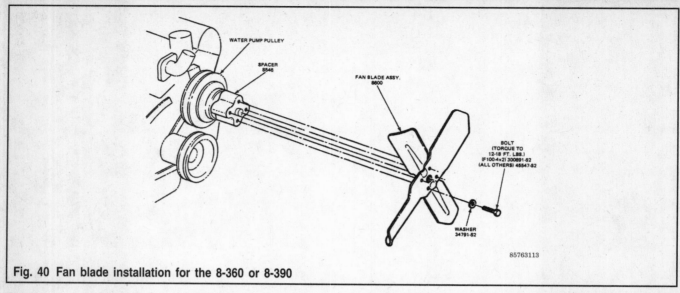

Fig. 40 Fan blade installation for the 8-360 or 8-390

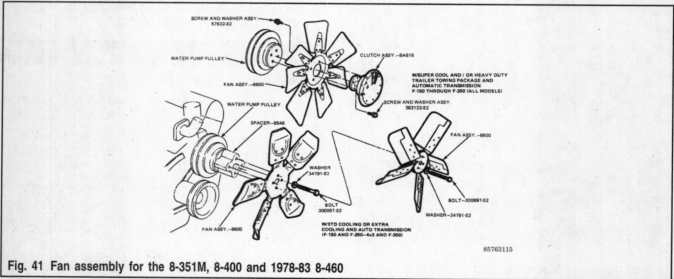

Fig. 41 Fan assembly for the 8-351M, 8-400 and 1978-83 8-460

Water Pump

▶ See Figure 42

1. Remove the water pump pulley.
2. Remove the bolts securing the water pump to the engine and lift off the water pump.

➡The water pump will probably not fall right off. The gasket usually holds it in place. In that case, tap it with a plastic mallet until it breaks loose.

3. Clean all gasket mounting surfaces thoroughly.

Cylinder Head

▶ See Figures 43, 44 and 45

Remove the cylinder head bolts and lift the cylinder head from the block.

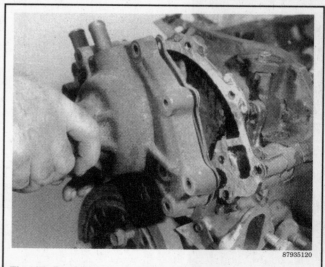

Fig. 42 Removing the water pump

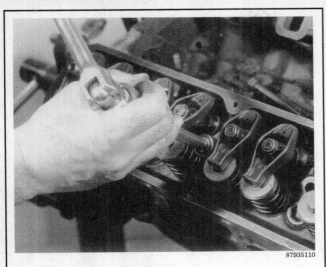

Fig. 43 Removing an upper cylinder head bolt

Fig. 44 Removing a lower cylinder head bolt

Fig. 45 Lifting the cylinder head. Be careful; it's heavy. If you don't think you can do it, get a helper

Valves

▶ See Figures 46, 47, 48, 49, 50, 51, 52, 53 and 54

1. Place the head on its side, on blocks of wood.
2. Use a socket slightly larger than the valve stem and keepers, place the socket over the valve stem and gently hit the socket with a plastic hammer to break loose any varnish buildup.
3. Using a valve spring compressor (the locking C-clamp type is the easiest kind to use) compress a valve.
4. Remove the valve keepers, retainer, spring shield and valve spring.
5. Put the parts in a separate container numbered for the cylinder being worked on; do not mix them with other parts removed.
6. Remove and discard the valve stem oil seals. A new seal will be used at assembly time.

Fig. 46 Place the bottom end of the compressor on the valve face

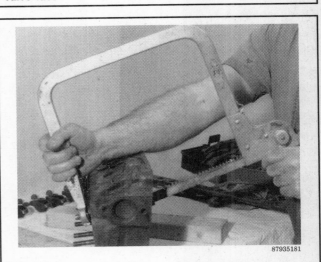

Fig. 47 Position the upper end of the compressor on the valve head

87935600

Fig. 48 Compress the valve, exposing the keepers

7. Remove the valves from the cylinder head and place them, in order, through numbered holes punched in a stiff piece of cardboard or wood valve holding stick.

➡The exhaust valve stems, on some engines, are equipped with small metal caps. Take care not to lose the caps. Make sure to reinstall them at assembly time. Replace any caps that are worn.

Fig. 49 Remove the keepers

Fig. 50 Remove the valve spring

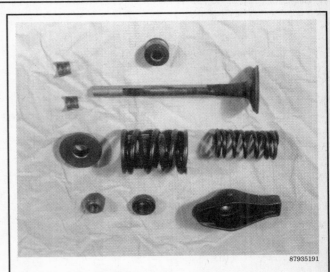

Fig. 51 A disassembled valve

87935602

Fig. 52 If there is one, remove the shim

87935189

Fig. 53 An entire head disassembled

Fig. 54 Remove the seal. This is a positive stop type; some use umbrella types

Oil Pan

▶ See Figures 55, 56 and 57

1. If you haven't already, remove the dipstick and tube.
2. Turn the engine over.
3. Remove the oil pan bolts and remove the pan. The pan may be hard to remove so CAREFULLY break it loose by tapping through the gasket area with a putty knife.

Oil Pump

▶ See Figures 58, 59 and 60

Remove the oil pump attaching bolts and remove the oil pump gasket and intermediate driveshaft.

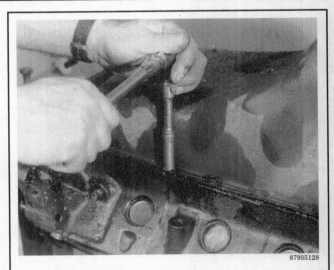

Fig. 55 Removing the oil pan bolts

Fig. 56 Removing the oil pan

Fig. 57 Scraping the oil pan gasket from the block

Fig. 58 Removing the oil pump bolts

Fig. 59 Lifting off the oil pump

Fig. 60 Removing oil pump driveshaft

Crankshaft Pulley (Vibration Damper)

▶ **See Figures 61, 62, 63, 64 and 65**

1. On those engines with a separate pulley, remove the retaining bolts and separate the pulley from the vibration damper.

2. Remove the vibration damper/pulley retaining bolt from the crankshaft end.

➡**To keep the crankshaft from turning, place a couple of flywheel retaining bolts back in their holes in the other end of the crankshaft. Wedge a long breaker bar or prybar in the bolts and against the arms of the engine stand. That should do it. Of course, if you have an impact wrench, you won't need to brace the crankshaft.**

3. Using a puller, remove the damper/pulley from the crankshaft.

Fig. 61 Loosening the damper bolt

Fig. 62 Removing the damper bolt

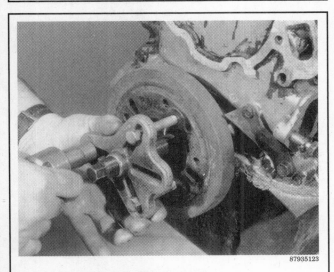

Fig. 63 Installing the damper puller

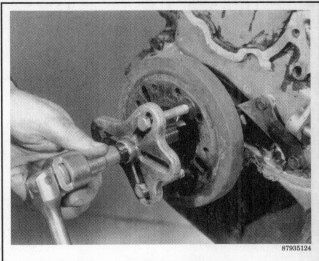

Fig. 64 Tightening the damper puller bolt

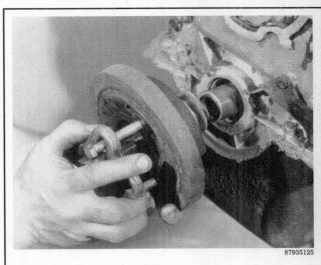

Fig. 65 Removing the damper

Timing Chain Front Cover and Oil Seal

▶ **See Figures 66 and 67**

1. Remove the front cover attaching bolts. Remove the front cover.

➡ **As with most parts, the cover will probably stick, so tap it loose with a plastic mallet. Just be sure you got all the bolts. And take note of the fact that some of the bolts are different lengths.**

2. Discard the front cover gasket.
3. Drive the old seal out, or, place a seal removing tool into the front cover plate and over the front of the seal. Tighten the two through bolts to force the seal puller under the seal flange, then alternately tighten the four puller bolts a half turn at a time to pull the oil seal from the cover.

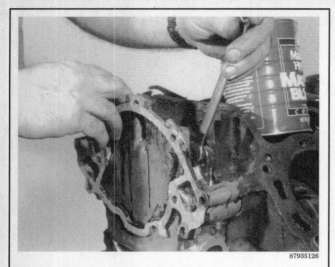

Fig. 66 Removing the timing chain cover bolts

Fig. 68 Removing the camshaft sprocket bolt

Fig. 67 Removing the timing chain cover

Fig. 69 Removing the fuel pump eccentric

Timing Chain

▶ **See Figures 68, 69, 70, 71, 72 and 73**

If you plan to replace the timing chain, skip to Step 5. If you want to check the timing chain for wear, start with Step 1.

1. Rotate the crankshaft counterclockwise to take up the slack on the left side of the chain.

2. Establish a reference point on the cylinder block and measure from this point to the chain.

3. Rotate the crankshaft in the opposite direction to take up the slack on the right side of the chain.

4. Force the left side of the chain out with your fingers and measure the distance between the reference point and the chain. The timing chain deflection is the difference between the two measurements. If the deflection exceeds ½ in. (13mm), replace the timing chain and sprockets.

5. Remove the camshaft sprocket retaining screw and re-move the fuel pump eccentric and washers.

Fig. 70 Removing the oil slinger

Fig. 71 Remove the timing chain by pulling alternately on the camshaft sprocket....

Fig. 72 and the crankshaft sprocket

Fig. 73 Once both sprockets are free, remove the sprockets and chain

6. Alternately slide both of the sprockets and timing chain off the crankshaft and camshaft until free of the engine.

Camshaft

▶ **See Figures 74, 75, 76 and 77**

Remove the camshaft thrust plate attaching screws and carefully slide the camshaft out of its bearing bores. Use extra caution not to scratch the camshaft lobes. If you can't get a good grip on the front end of the camshaft, thread a long bolt into one of the holes and use that to pull the shaft free.

Camshaft Bearings

1. Remove the camshaft rear bearing bore plug. A special tool is needed to replace the bearings. These tools are available for purchase or rent at most auto parts stores. Follow the instructions that come with the tool or:

Fig. 74 Removing the camshaft retainer bolts

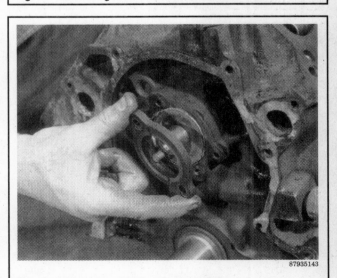

Fig. 75 Removing the camshaft retainer

Fig. 76 Install a long bolt in the nose of the camshaft. It will help you to pull the camshaft out

Fig. 77 Removing the camshaft

2. Select the proper size expanding collet and back-up nut and assemble on the mandrel. With the expanding collet collapsed, install the collet assembly in the camshaft bearing and tighten the back-up nut on the expanding mandrel until the collet fits the camshaft bearing.

3. Assemble the puller screw and extension (if necessary) and install on the expanding mandrel. Wrap a cloth around the threads of the puller screw to protect the front bearing or journal. Tighten the pulling nut against the thrust bearing and pulling plate to remove the camshaft bearing. Be sure to hold a wrench on the end of the puller screw to prevent it from turning.

4. To remove the front bearing, install the puller from the rear of the cylinder block.

Pistons and Connecting Rods

▶ See Figures 78, 79, 80, 81 and 82

1. Turn the crankshaft until the piston to be removed is at the bottom of its travel, then place a cloth on the piston head to collect filings.

2. Remove any ridge or deposits at the end of the piston travel from the upper cylinder bore, using a ridge reaming tool. Do not cut into the piston ring travel area more than $1/32$ in. (0.8mm) when removing the ridge.

3. Turn the engine over.

➡Most manufacturers stamp the rod bearing cap and rod with matching numbers. However, just because the rod and cap are numbered doesn't mean that it's where it should be. If a previous owner had work done, the rod and cap marked, say No.4, might not be in cylinder number 4. Take note of each as you're removing it. Make sure that all of the connecting rod bearing caps can be identified, so they will be reinstalled in their original positions.

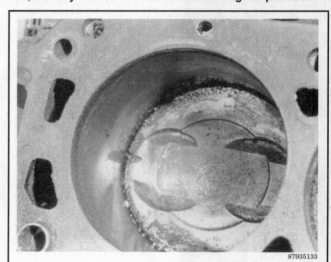

Fig. 78 A view of the cylinder showing the ridge

Fig. 79 Removing the ridge using a ridge reamer

Fig. 80 A view of the cylinder with the ridge removed

Fig. 81 Removing a connecting rod nut. Turn the crank so that the rod being worked on is up

Fig. 82 Removing a connecting rod cap. Note that the bearing lower shell remains with the cap. You'll always replace the rod bearings, so toss the bearing shell

4. Turn the crankshaft until the connecting rod that is to be removed is at the bottom of its stroke and remove the connecting rod nuts and bearing cap.

5. With the bearing caps removed, the connecting rod bearing bolts are potentially damaging to the cylinder walls during removal. To guard against cylinder wall damage, install four or five inch lengths of ³/₈ in. (0.8mm) rubber tubing onto the connecting rod bolts. These will also protect the crankshaft journal from scratches when the connecting rod is installed, and will serve as a guide for the rod.

6. Squirt some clean engine oil into each cylinder before removing the piston assemblies. Using a wooden hammer handle, push the connecting rod and piston assembly out of the top of the cylinder (pushing from the bottom of the rod). Be careful to avoid damaging both the crank journal and the cylinder wall when removing the rod and piston assembly.

7. Remove the bearing inserts from the connecting rod and cap if the bearings are to be replaced, and place the cap onto the piston/rod assembly from which it was removed.

➡The connecting rod and bearing caps are numbered from 1 to 4 in the right bank and from 5 to 8 in in the left bank, beginning at the front of the engine. The numbers on the rod and cap must be on the same side when they are installed in the cylinder bore. Also, the largest chamfer at the bearing end of the rod should be positioned toward the crank pin thrust face of the crankshaft and the notch in the head of the piston faces toward the front of the engine.

PISTON AND ROD DISASSEMBLY

▶ See Figures 83, 84, 85, 86, 87 and 88

All Ford gasoline engines utilize pressed-in wrist pins, which can only be removed by a press. If you don't have one, the piston/connecting rod assemblies should be taken to an engine specialist or qualified machinist for piston removal and installation.

A piston ring expander is necessary for removing the piston rings without damaging them; any other method (screwdriver blades, pliers, etc.) usually results in the rings being bent, scratched or distorted, or the piston itself being damaged. When the rings are removed, clean the ring grooves using an appropriate ring groove cleaning tool, using care not to cut too deeply.

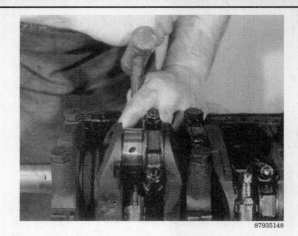

Fig. 83 Removing a piston/rod assembly. Once the ridge is removed, the piston should be easy to drive out of the cylinder. Use a hammer handle and your fist

Fig. 84 Catch the piston as it exits the cylinder

Fig. 85 Removing the oil control rings

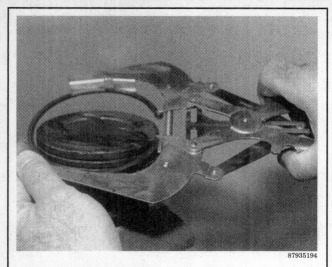

Fig. 86 Removing the compression rings

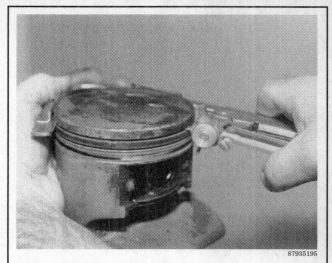

Fig. 87 Installing a groove cleaner

Fig. 88 Cleaning the grooves. Don't cut too deeply!

Crankshaft and Main Bearings

▶ See Figures 89, 90, 91, 92, 93, 94, 95 and 96

Fig. 89 Removing the rear main bearing cap bolts

Fig. 90 Break loose the cap using a soft mallet

Fig. 91 Lifting off the rear main cap

Fig. 92 Removing the rest of the main bearing caps

Fig. 93 The crankshaft is heavier than it looks. Get a good grip before lifting

Fig. 94 The crankshaft removed

Fig. 95 All the parts that you've removed from the bottom end. Not bad! Take a break

Fig. 96 Remove and discard the upper bearing shells. Note the difference between the thrust bearing, left, and the other bearings

1. Make sure all bearing caps (main and connecting rod) are marked so that they can be installed in their original locations.

2. Remove the main bearings cap bolts. Tap each bearing cap with a plastic mallet to loosen it and lift it off.

3. Carefully lift the crankshaft out of the block so that the thrust bearing surfaces are not damaged. Handle the crankshaft with care to avoid possible fracture to the finished surfaces.

4. Using a pick, remove the rear journal seal from the block and rear main bearing cap.

5. Remove the main bearing inserts from the block and bearing caps.

Core (Freeze/Oil Gallery) Plugs

▶ See Figures 97, 98, 99, 100, 101, 102, 103, 104, 105 and 106

Fig. 98 Once it is cocked and loosened, it can be removed

Fig. 97 Some freeze plugs may be removed using a punch

Fig. 99 The preferred method to remove a non-threaded oil gallery plug is by drilling a pilot hole . . .

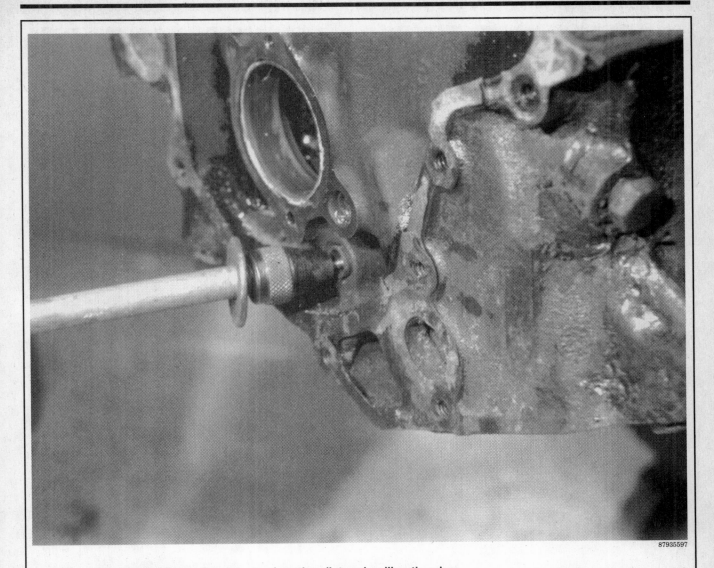

87935597

Fig. 100 . . . then threading a slide hammer into the pilot and pulling the plug

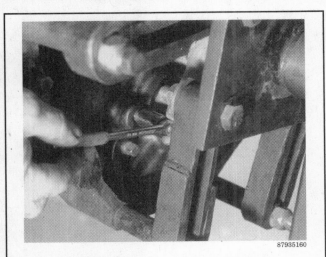

87935160

Fig. 101 Some oil gallery plugs are threaded, and should be removed like this

87935159

Fig. 102 Removing a block drain plug

Fig. 103 A leaking block core plug

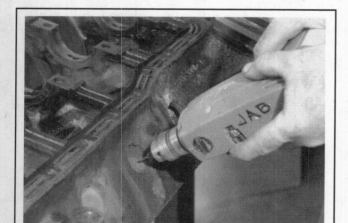

Fig. 104 Drilling the core plug

Fig. 105 Yanking the core plug with a slidehammer

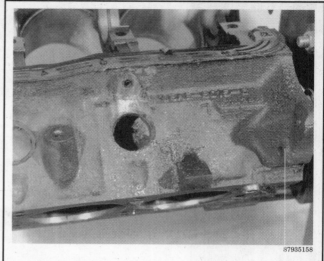

Fig. 106 The core plug bore

1. Drill or center-punch a hole in the plug. For large plugs, drill a ½ in. hole; for small plugs, drill a ¼ in. hole.
2. For large plugs, using a slide-hammer, thread a machine screw adapter or insert 2-jawed puller adapter into the hole in the plug. Pull the plug from the block; for small plugs, pry the plug out with a pin punch.

Rear Main Oil Seal

TWO PIECE SEAL

▶ See Figures 107 and 108

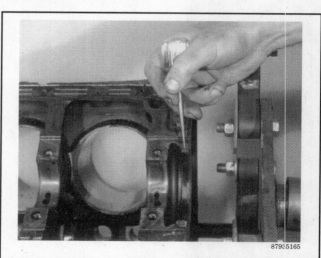

Fig. 107 Removing the upper rear main seal half using a pick

Fig. 108 Pull the upper seal half from its bore

1. Remove the rear main bearing cap, and remove the oil seal from the bearing cap and cylinder block. On the block half of the seal use a seal removal tool, or install a small metal screw in one end of the seal, and pull on the screw to remove the seal. Exercise caution to prevent scratching or damaging the crankshaft seal surfaces.

2. Remove the oil seal retaining pin from the bearing cap if so equipped. The pin is not used with the split-lip seal.

PARTS CLEANING

➡You really don't have to have the engine parts professionally cleaned. You can do the job adequately yourself if you have the time, patience and plenty of rags.

Don't worry about absolute cleanliness at this time because machine work still has to be done. After that has been completed, the time for that extra special cleaning job will be at hand. If the block is to be hot tanked, take the head(s) along. Hot tanking will remove grease, corrosion, and scale from the surfaces and water passages. Heads that are to be hot tanked should have the freeze plugs removed so the solution can reach as many places in the water passages as possible.

Some machine shops offer glass bead cleaning. This does a good job, and the part comes back looking like new.

Parts cleaning can be handled in several different ways, depending on the part and the cleaning equipment available. The basic methods of cleaning parts are:
1. Hand scrubbing and scraping
2. Cold spraying
3. Hot tank immersion
4. Cold tank immersion
5. Steam cleaning
6. Glass bead cleaning

Hand Cleaning

Many parts of the engine block and cylinder head are cleaned best by hand. Carbon deposits are usually scraped by hand scrapers or with a wire brush. Soft metal parts, such as bearings, should be washed in a cleaning solvent. Aluminum should be cleaned by hand with a safe solvent.

As each part and fastener is removed you should a least wipe it off with a shop rag before storing it. Once the engine is completely disassembled you'll be ready for mass cleaning.

All parts should be cleaned in a safe, non-flammable solvent. NEVER USE GASOLINE!! Inhaling gasoline vapors is harmful; gasoline wrecks your skin; gasoline vapors are extremely flammable!

Some of the major components that require special attention are:

Cold Spraying

In this method, a cleaning solvent is sprayed over the part to be cleaned. The chemical softens the dirt and helps loosen the bond. The grime and grease are flushed off with water. If the grime and grease are stubborn, a heavier application of spray and some working in with a cleaning brush and strong water pressure will help remove it. Several coats of spray and some soaking time also help to remove stubborn deposits.

Hot Tank Immersion

A hot tank immersion is one of the most efficient and economical means of cleaning parts. The work is placed in the hot solution and agitation takes place making cleaning more efficient. The parts are rinsed off with a high-pressure water hose after cleaning. Remember, never have aluminum parts hot tanked. Cam bearings immersed in a hot tank will have to be replaced.

Cold Tank Immersion

Cold tanks are generally used for cleaning small parts; however, they are usually big enough to take a cylinder head or a disassembled engine block. Some cold tanks have a sliding tray near the top to put parts on and a pump that circulates the cleaning solvent through an adjustable nozzle to help clean and wash the parts.

Steam Cleaning

Steam cleaners get their name from the fact that steam is used to generate pressure and is also the by-product of heating the cleaning solution. The steam itself has little cleaning power. However, the cleaning solution, when heated and under pressure, does a reasonable job of cleaning.

Valves

▶ See Figure 109

1. Use an electric drill and rotary wire brush to clean the intake and exhaust valve ports, combustion chamber and valve seats. In some cases, the carbon will need to be chipped away. Use a blunt pointed drift for carbon chipping. Be careful around the valve seat areas.

2. Use a wire valve guide cleaning brush and safe solvent to clean the valve guides.

3. Clean the valves with a revolving wire brush. Heavy carbon deposits may be removed with the blunt drift.

➡When using a wire brush to clean carbon on the valve ports, valves etc., be sure that the deposits are actually removed, rather than burnished.

4. Wash and clean all valve springs, keepers, retaining caps etc., in safe solvent.

Cylinder Head

▶ See Figure 110

1. With the valves installed to protect the valve seats, remove deposits from the combustion chambers and valve heads with a scraper and a wire brush. Be careful not to damage the cylinder head gasket surface. After the valves are removed, clean the valve guide bores with a valve guide cleaning tool. Using cleaning solvent to remove dirt, grease and other deposits, clean all bolts holes; be sure the oil passage is clean.

2. Remove all deposits from the valves with a fine wire brush or buffing wheel.

Piston And Rod

▶ See Figure 111

Thoroughly clean all carbon and varnish from the piston with solvent.

✳✳WARNING

Do not use a wire brush or caustic solvent (acids, etc.) on aluminum pistons.

Block

▶ See Figures 112, 113, 114 and 115

Clean the oil gallery a water jacket. If you are a gun owner, you can use both a shotgun cleaning rod and brush and a .30 cal. cleaning rod and brush. If you aren't a gun owner. Buy the cleaning rods wherever they sell firearms equipment.

Crankshaft

➡Handle the crankshaft carefully to avoid damage to the finish surfaces.

1. Clean the crankshaft with solvent, and blow out all oil passages with compressed air. Clean the oil seal contact surface at the rear of the crankshaft with solvent to remove any corrosion, sludge or varnish deposits.

2. Use crocus cloth to remove any sharp edges, burrs or other imperfections which might damage the oil seal during installation or cause premature seal wear.

➡Do not polish the seal surfaces. A finely polished surface may produce poor sealing or cause premature seal wear.

Fig. 109 Cleaning a valve with a rotary brush

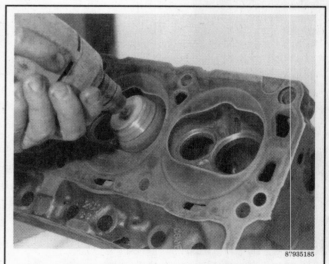

Fig. 110 Cleaning the combustion chambers

Fig. 111 Cleaning the upper ring groove

Main Bearings

Clean the bearing inserts and caps thoroughly in solvent, and dry them with compressed air.

➡ **Do not scrape varnish or gum deposits from the bearing shells.**

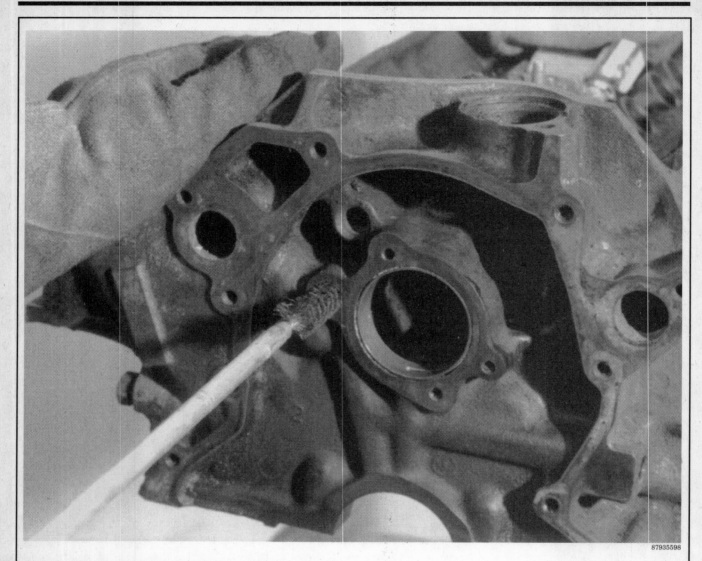

Fig. 112 Cleaning the lifter gallery with a shotgun cleaning rod

Fig. 113 Cleaning the upper gallery with the plug removed

Fig. 114 Cleaning block/head mating surface

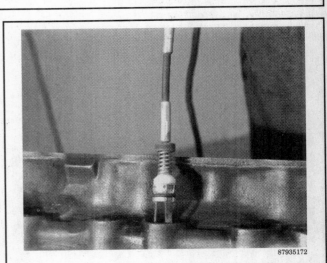

Fig. 115 Cleaning the lifter bores with a wheel cylinder hone

INSPECTION

Once everything is cleaned and sorted, inspect each part. Fasteners should be inspected of cracks, bad or stripped threads, rounded corners, rust, etc. Anything that appears at all suspect should be replaced. When replacing bolts, make sure that they are of equal grade. That's the markings on the bolt head.

Parts that require special attention are:

Cylinder Head

▶ **See Figures 116, 117, 118 and 119**

1. Check the head for cracks. Cracks in the cylinder head usually start around an exhaust valve seat because it is the hottest part of the combustion chamber. If a crack is suspected but cannot be detected visually have the area checked with dye penetrant or similar method, have check performed by the machine shop.

Fig. 116 Clean the combustion chambers, prior to disassembly, with a wire brush

Fig. 117 A cleaned cylinder head

Fig. 118 Placing a straightedge on the head

2. Inspect the cylinder heads for cracks or excessively burned areas in the exhaust outlet ports.

3. On cylinder heads that incorporate valve seat inserts, check the inserts for excessive wear, cracks, or looseness.

Valves

▶ **See Figure 120**

After all cylinder head parts are reasonably clean, check the valve stem-to-guide clearance. If a dial indicator is not on hand, a visual inspection can give you a fairly good idea if the guide, valve stem or both are worn.

Insert the valve into the guide until slight away from the valve seat. Wiggle the valve sideways. A small amount of wobble is normal, excessive wobble means a worn guide or valve stem. If a dial indicator is on hand, mount the indicator so that the stem of the valve is at 90 degrees to the valve stem, as close to the valve guide as possible. Move the valve off the seat, and measure the valve guide-to-stem clearance by rocking the stem back and forth to actuate the dial indicator. Measure the valve stem using a micrometer and compare to specifications to determine whether stem or guide wear is causing excessive clearance.

Check the valve stems using a 0-1 in. micrometer. Check the unworn part of the stem (below or above the valve guide travel) against the worn part. A 0.001 in. wear is usually all right, but up to 0.002 in. is borderline. New 'standard' valves should be used if the stem wear is greater than 0.002 in.

Next inspect the cleaned valve faces. Deeply grooved faces may not clean enough, or if they do, will not have enough existing metal for good heat control. Burnt valves (usually exhaust) must be replaced. Some light burning might be cleaned up by refacing.

Check the valve stem tips and keeper grooves. If the tip has been hammered by the rocker arm and worn to within 1/16 in. of the keeper retainer, replace the valve.

The valve guide, if worn, must be repaired before the valve seats can be resurfaced. Ford supplies valves with oversize

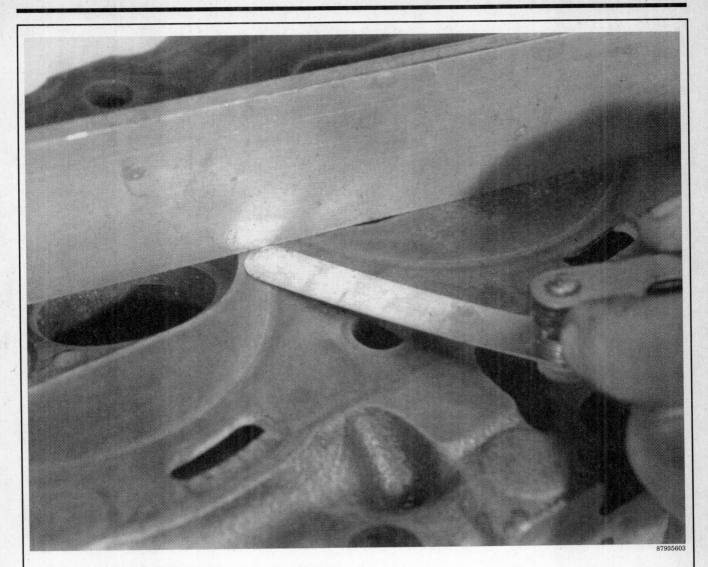

Fig. 119 Checking the head for flatness

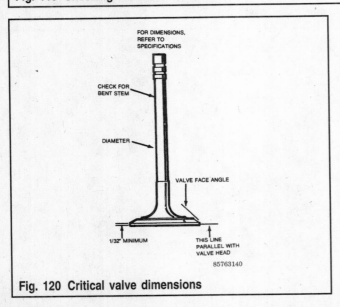

Fig. 120 Critical valve dimensions

stems to fit valve guides that are reamed to oversize for repair. The machine shop will be able to handle the guide reaming for you. In some cases, if the guide is not too badly worn, knurling may be all that is required.

VALVE SPRINGS

▶ **See Figures 121 and 122**

Place the valve spring on a flat surface next to a carpenter's square. Measure the height of the spring, and rotate the spring against the edge of the square to measure distortion. If the spring height varies (by comparison) by more than 1/16 in. (1.6mm) or if the distortion exceeds 1/16 in. (1.6mm), replace the spring.

Have the valve springs tested for spring pressure at the installed and compressed (installed height minus valve lift) height using a valve spring tester. Springs should be within one pound, plus or minus each other. Replace springs as necessary.

85763148

Fig. 121 Have the valve spring pressure checked at a machine shop. Make sure the readings are within specifications

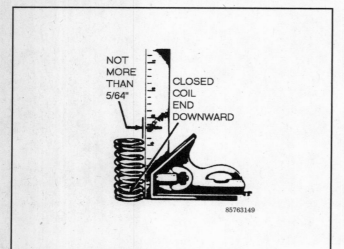

NOT MORE THAN 5/64"

CLOSED COIL END DOWNWARD

85763149

Fig. 122 Check the valve spring free length and squareness

VALVE SPRING INSTALLED HEIGHT

After installing the valve spring, measure the distance between the spring mounting pad and the lower edge of the spring retainer. Compare the measurement to specifications. If the installed height is incorrect, add shim washers between the spring mounting pad and the spring. Use only washers designed for valve springs, available at most parts houses.

VALVE STEM-TO-GUIDE CLEARANCE

Valve stem-to-guide clearance should be checked upon assembling the cylinder head, and is especially necessary if the valve guides have been reamed or knurled, or if oversized valves have been installed. Excessive oil consumption often is

a result of too much clearance between the valve guide and valve stem.

1. Clean the valve stem with lacquer thinner or a similar solvent to remove all gum and varnish. Clean the valve guides using solvent and an expanding wire-type valve guide cleaner (a rifle cleaning brush works well here).

2. Mount a dial indicator so that the stem is 90 degrees to the valve stem and as close to the valve guide as possible.

3. Move the valve off its seat, and measure the valve guide-to-stem clearance by rocking the stem back and forth to actuate the dial indicator. Measure the valve stems using a micrometer and compare to specifications, to determine whether stem or guide wear is responsible for excessive clearance.

HYDRAULIC VALVE LIFTER

◗ See Figures 123, 124 and 125

Remove the lifters from their bores and remove any gum and varnish with safe solvent. Check the lifters for concave wear. If the bottom of the lifter is worn concave or flat, replace the lifter. Lifters are built with a convex bottom, flatness indicates wear. If a worn lifter is detected, carefully check the camshaft for wear.

To test lifter leak down, submerge the lifter in a container of kerosene. Chuck a used pushrod or its equivalent into a drill press. Position the container of kerosene so the pushrod acts on the lifter plunger. Pump the lifter with the drill press until resistance increases. Pump several more times to bleed any air from the lifter. Apply very firm, constant pressure to the lifter and observe the rate which fluid bleeds out of the lifter. If the lifter bleeds down very quickly (less than 15 seconds), the lifter should be replaced. If the time exceeds 60 seconds, the lifter is sticking and should be cleaned or replaced. If the lifter is operating properly (leak down time 15-60 seconds) and not worn, lubricate and reinstall in engine.

➡Always inspect the valve pushrods for wear, straightness and oil blockage. Damaged pushrods will cause erratic valve operation.

87935118

Fig. 123 Removing a lifter using a lifter puller

87935594

Fig. 124 Sometimes, this is about as far as you can get the lifter, using a puller. If a lot of resistance is encountered, stop using the puller; you'll only break the jaws. Wait until the crankshaft is out and drive the lifter(s) out of their bores using a hammer and brass drift

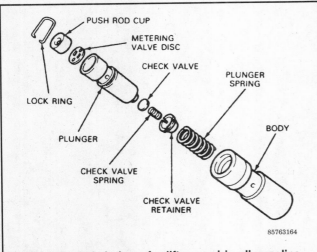

85763164

Fig. 125 Exploded view of a lifter used in all gasoline engines

Timing Chain

CHECKING TIMING CHAIN DEFLECTION

To measure timing chain deflection, rotate the crankshaft clockwise to take up slack on the left side of chain. Choose a reference point and measure the distance from this point and the chain. Rotate the crankshaft in the opposite direction to take up slack on the right side of the chain. Force the left (slack) side of the chain out and measure the distance to the reference point chosen earlier. The difference between the two measurements is the deflection.

The deflection measurement should not exceed 1/2 in. (13mm). The timing chain should be replaced if the deflection measurement exceeded the specified limit.

Camshaft

CHECKING CAMSHAFT

▶ See Figure 126

Check each camshaft journal with a micrometer. Check the readings against the figure in the chart at the end of this section.

Pistons and Connecting Rods

▶ See Figure 127

Inspect the pistons for scuffing, scoring, cracks, pitting, or excessive ring groove wear. If these are evident, the piston must be replaced.

The piston should also be checked in relation to the cylinder diameter. Using a telescoping gauge and micrometer, or a dial gauge, measure the cylinder bore diameter perpendicular (90 degrees) to the piston pin, 2½ in. (64mm) below the cylinder block deck (surface where the block mates with the heads). Then, with the micrometer, measure the piston, perpendicular to its wrist pin on the skirt. the difference between the two measurements is the piston clearance. If the clearance is within specifications or slightly below (after the cylinders have been bored or hones), finish honing is all that is necessary. If the clearance is excessive, try to obtain a slightly larger piston to bring clearance to within specifications. If this is not possible, obtain the first oversize piston and hone (or if necessary, bore) the cylinder to size. Generally, if the cylinder bore is tapered 0.005 in. (0.127mm) or more or is out-of-round 0.003 in. (0.076mm) or more, it is advisable to rebore for the smallest possible oversize piston and rings.

After measuring, mark pistons with a felt tip pen for reference and for assembly.

➡**Cylinder boring should be performed by a reputable, professional mechanic with the proper equipment.**

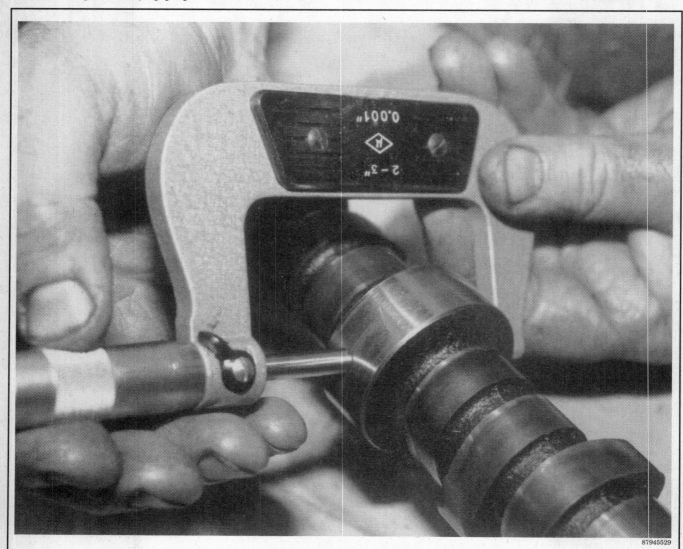

Fig. 126 Checking the camshaft journals with a micrometer

Fig. 127 A piston with damaged lands

PISTON RING END-GAP

▶ **See Figures 128, 129 and 130**

Piston ring end-gap should be checked while the rings are removed from the pistons. Incorrect end-gap indicates that the wrong size rings are being used; ring breakage could occur.

Compress the piston rings to be used in a cylinder, one at a time, into that cylinder. Squirt clean oil into the cylinder, so that the rings and the top 2 in. (51mm) of cylinder wall are coated. Using an inverted piston, press the rings approximately 1 in. (25mm) below the deck of the block (on diesels, measure ring gap clearance with the ring positioned at the bottom of ring travel in the bore). Measure the ring end-gap with the feeler gauge, and compare it to the specifications chart. Carefully pull the ring out of the cylinder and file the ends squarely with a fine file to obtain the proper clearance.

Fig. 128 Placing a ring in a cylinder bore

87935591

Fig. 129 Pushing the ring into the bore with a clean piston

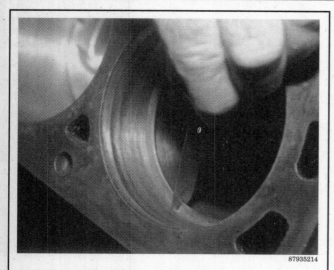

87935214

Fig. 130 Measuring the ring end-gap

PISTON RING SIDE CLEARANCE CHECK

Check the pistons to see that the ring grooves and oil return holes have been properly cleaned. Slide a piston ring into its groove, and check the side clearance with a feeler gauge. Make sure you insert the gauge between the ring and its lower land (lower edge of the groove), because any wear that occurs forms a step at the inner portion of the lower land. If the piston grooves have worn to the extent that relatively high steps exist on the lower land, the piston should be replaced, because these will interfere with the operation of the new rings and ring clearance will be excessive. Piston rings are not furnished in oversize widths to compensate for ring groove wear.

MEASURING THE OLD PISTONS

▶ **See Figure 131**

Check used piston-to-cylinder bore clearance as follows:

1. Measure the cylinder bore diameter with a telescope gauge.

2. Measure the piston diameter. When measuring the pistons for size or taper, measurements must be made with the piston pin removed.

3. Subtract the piston diameter from the cylinder bore diameter to determine piston-to-bore clearance.

4. Compare the piston-to-bore clearances obtained with those clearances recommended. Determine if the piston-to-bore clearance is in the acceptable range.

5. When measuring taper, the largest reading must be at the bottom of the skirt.

SELECTING NEW PISTONS

1. If the used piston is not acceptable, check the service piston size and determine if a new piston can be selected. Service pistons are available in standard, high limit and standard oversize.

2. If the cylinder bore must be reconditioned, measure the new piston diameter, then hone the cylinder bore to obtain the preferred clearance.

3. Select a new piston and mark the piston to identify the cylinder for which it was fitted. Oversize pistons may be found. These pistons will be 0.010 in. (0.254mm) oversize).

CONNECTING ROD BEARING INSPECTION

➡ **Make sure connecting rods and their caps are kept together, so that the caps are installed in the proper direction.**

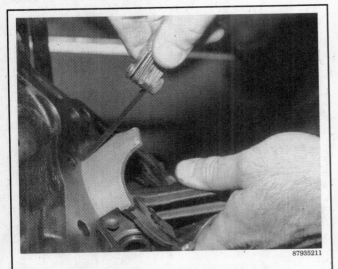

Fig. 131 Measuring piston-to-bore clearance

87935211

Connecting rod bearings for the engines covered in this guide consist of two halves or shells which are interchangeable in the rod and cap. When the shells are placed in position, the ends extend slightly beyond the rod and cap surfaces so that with the rod bolts torqued the shells will be clamped tightly in place to insure positive seating and to prevent turning. A tang holds the shells in place.

➡ **The ends of the bearing shells must never be filed flush with the mating surfaces of the rod and cap.**

If a rod bearing becomes noisy or is worn so that its clearance on the crank journal is sloppy, a new bearing of the correct undersize must be selected and installed since there is no provision for adjustment.

✳✳WARNING

Under no circumstances should the rod end or cap be filed to adjust the bearing clearance, nor should shims of any kind be used.

Inspect the rod bearings while the rod assemblies are out of the engine. If the shells are scored or show flaking, they should be replaced. If they are in good shape, check for proper clearance on the crank journal (see below). Any scoring or ridges on the crank journal means the crankshaft must be reground and fitted with undersized bearings, or replaced.

Replacement bearings are available in standard size, and in undersizes for reground crankshaft. Connecting rod-to-crankshaft bearing clearance is checked using Plastigage® at either the top or bottom of each crank journal. Plastigage® has a range of 0 to 0.003 in. (0.076mm).

1. Remove the rod cap with the bearing shell. Completely clean the bearing shell and the crank journal, and blow any oil from the oil hole in the crankshaft.

➡ **The journal surfaces and bearing shells must be completely free of oil, because Plastigage® is soluble in oil.**

2. Place a strip of Plastigage® lengthwise along the bottom center of the lower bearing shell, then install the cap with shell and torque the bolt or nuts to specification. DO NOT TURN the crankshaft with the Plastigage® installed in the bearing.

3. Remove the bearing cap with the shell. The flattened Plastigage® will be found sticking to either the bearing shell or crank journal. Do not remove it yet.

4. Use the printed scale on the Plastigage® envelope to measure the flattened material at its widest point. The number within the scale which most closely corresponds to the width of the Plastigage® indicated bearing clearance in thousandths of an inch.

5. Check the specifications chart at the back of this book for the desired clearance. It is advisable to install a new bearing if clearance exceeds 0.003 in. (0.076mm); however, if the bearing is in good condition and is not being checked because of bearing noise, bearing replacement is not necessary.

6. If you are installing new bearings, try a standard size, then each undersize in order until one is found that is within the specified limits when checked for clearance with Plastigage®. Each under size has its size stamped on it.

Crankshaft

▶ See Figure 132

1. Inspect the main and connecting rod journals for cracks, scratches, grooves or scores.

2. Measure the diameter of each journal at least four places to determine out-of-round, taper or undersize condition.

3. On an engine with a manual transmission, check the fit of the clutch pilot bearing in the bore of the crankshaft. A needle roller bearing and adapter assembly is used as a clutch pilot bearing. It is inserted directly into the engine crank shaft. The bearing and adapter assembly cannot be serviced separately. A new bearing must be installed whenever a bearing is removed.

4. Inspect the pilot bearing, when used, for roughness, evidence of overheating or loss of lubricant. Replace if any of these conditions are found.

5. Inspect the rear oil seal surface of the crankshaft for deep grooves, nicks, burrs, porosity, or scratches which could damage the oil seal lip during installation. Remove all nicks and burrs with crocus cloth.

If the crankshaft is in bad shape, it's probably best to purchase what is called a crank kit. A crank kit is a new or remanufactured crankshaft with a complete set of matched main bearings. You can't go wrong with a crank kit. It will save money and time.

Main Bearings

▶ See Figure 133

1. Inspect each bearing carefully. Bearings that have a scored, chipped, or worn surface should be replaced.

2. The copper-lead bearing base may be visible through the bearing overlay in small localized areas. This may not mean that the bearing is excessively worn. It is not necessary to replace the bearing if the bearing clearance is within recommended specifications.

3. Check the clearance of bearings that appear to be satisfactory with Plastigage® or its equivalent. Fit the new bearings

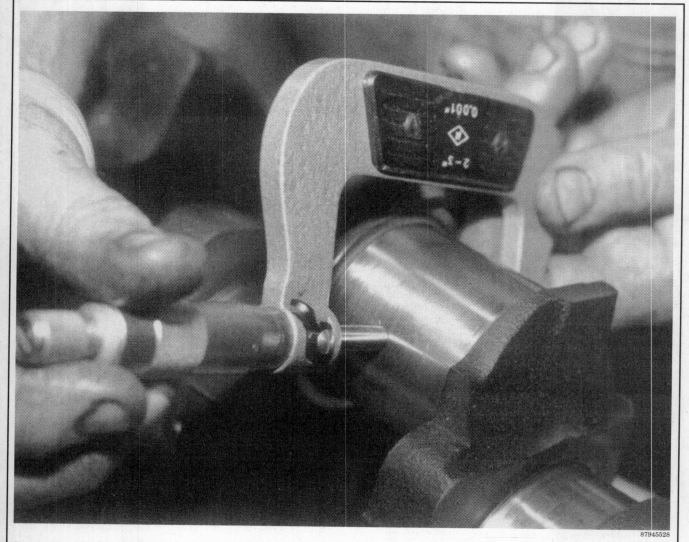

Fig. 132 Checking the rod journals with a micrometer

87945528

following the procedure Crankshaft and Main Bearings removal and installation, they should be reground to size for the next undersize bearing.

4. Regrind the journals to give the proper clearance with the next undersize bearing. If the journal will not clean up to maximum undersize bearing available, replace the crankshaft.

5. Always reproduce the same journal shoulder radius that existed originally. Too small a radius will result in fatigue failure of the crankshaft. Too large a radius will result in bearing failure due to radius ride of the bearing.

6. After regrinding the journals, chamfer the oil holes, then polish the journals with a #320 grit polishing cloth and engine oil. Crocus cloth may also be used as a polishing agent.

CHECKING MAIN BEARING CLEARANCES

▶ **See Figures 134, 135 and 136**

1. Check the clearance of each main bearing by using the following procedure:

a. Place a piece of Plastigage® or its equivalent, on bearing surface across full width of bearing cap and about ¼ in. (6mm) off center.

b. Install cap and tighten bolts to specifications. Do not turn crankshaft while Plastigage® is in place.

c. Remove the cap. Using Plastigage® scale, check width of Plastigage® at widest point to get the minimum clearance. Check at narrowest point to get maximum clearance. Difference between readings is taper of journal.

d. If clearance exceeds specified limits, try a 0.001 in. (0.0254mm) or 0.002 in. (0.051mm) undersize bearing in combination with the standard bearing. Bearing clearance must be within specified limits. If undersize bearings do not bring clearance within desired limits, refinish crankshaft journal, then install undersize bearings.

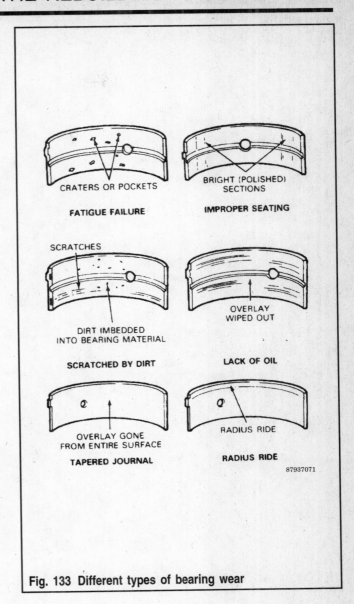

Fig. 133 Different types of bearing wear

Fig. 134 Plastigage in place before crushing it

Fig. 135 Tightening the main bearing cap

Fig. 136 Measuring the flattened Plastigage

REPAIR AND REFINISHING

Many parts can be reused when repaired or refinished. Most of these jobs are best left to a qualified machine shop since the tools and machinery needed are very expensive and not practical for the do-it-yourselfer. Among them are:

Rocker Studs

▶ **See Figures 137, 138 and 139**

Rocker arm studs which are broken or have damaged threads may be replaced with standard studs. Studs which are loose in the cylinder head must be replaced with oversize

studs which are available for service. The amount of oversize and diameter of the studs are as follows:

- 0.006 in. (0.152mm) oversize: 0.3774-0.3781 in. (9.586-9.604mm)
- 0.010 in. (0.254mm) oversize: 0.3814-0.3821 in. (9.688-9.705mm)
- 0.015 in. (0.381mm) oversize: 0.3864-0.3871 in. (9.815-9.832mm)

Tool kits for replacing the rocker studs are available and contain a stud remover and two or three oversize reamers: 0.006 in., 0.010 in., and 0.015 in., oversize studs. To press the replacement studs into the cylinder head, use the stud replacer tool. Use the smaller reamer tool first when boring the hole for oversize studs.

1. Position the sleeve of the rocker arm stud remover over the stud with the bearing end down. When working on a 289/302, cut the threaded part of the stud off with a hacksaw. Thread the puller into the sleeve and over the stud until it is fully bottomed. Hold the sleeve with a wrench and rotate the puller clockwise to remove the stud.

An alternate method of removing the rocker studs without the special tool is to put spacers over the stud until just enough threads are left showing at the top, so a nut can be screwed onto the top of the rocker arm stud and get a full bite. Turn the nut clockwise until the stud is removed, adding spacers under the nut as necessary.

➡**If the rocker stud was broken off flush with the stud boss, use a screw extractor to remove the broken-off part of the stud from the cylinder head.**

2. If a loose rocker arm stud is being replaced, rearn the stud bore for the selected oversize stud.

➡**Keep all metal particles away from the valves.**

3. Coat the end of the stud with Lubriplate® or equivalent. Align the stud and installer with the stud bore and top the sliding driver until it bottoms. When the installer contacts the stud boss, the stud is installed to its correct height.

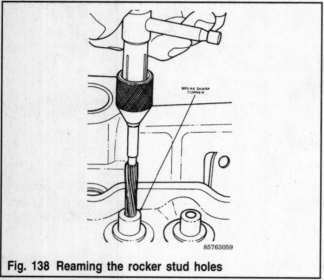

Fig. 138 Reaming the rocker stud holes

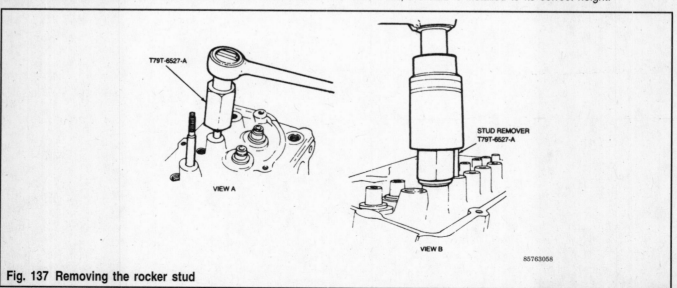

Fig. 137 Removing the rocker stud

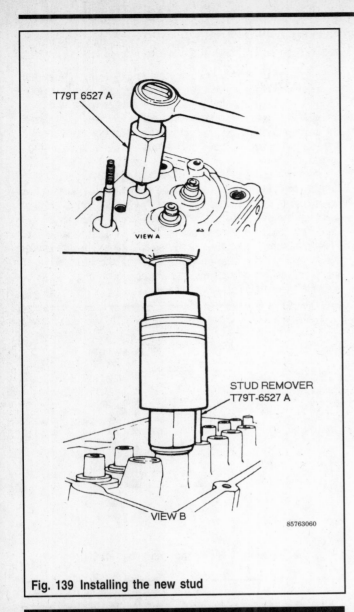

T79T 6527 A

VIEW A

STUD REMOVER
T79T-6527 A

VIEW B

85763060

Fig. 139 Installing the new stud

Valves and Seats

After the valve faces and stems are cleaned, the next step is to resurface the valve face. If the valve guides have been machined to accept an oversize valve stem, new valves will be used.

The valves are refaced in a specialized piece of equipment called a valve grinder. It consists of a motor-driven chuck used to hold and rotate the valve face against a rotating grinding wheel. The chuck is adjustable to the correct angle required by the valve face. A cooling fluid is fed over the wheel and valve face while the valve is being ground. The wheel grinds the face of the valve, removing all burned spots and pits.

Always check the angle specifications before grinding the valves. The face angle is not always identical to the valve seat angle. A minimum margin of $1/32$ in. should remain at the edge of the valve after grinding. The valve stem top should always be dressed. This is done by placing the stem in the V-block of the grinder and rotating the valve stem while pressing lightly against the grinding wheel.

Sodium-filled exhaust valves must not be refaced on a machine. If the face is not too badly worn or burnt, the valve should be hand lapped. Valves that are in bad shape should be replaced.

1. If you you have access to head reconditioning machines and will do the job yourself, read on. The valve seats should be a true 45° angle. Remove only enough material to clean up any pits or grooves. Be sure the valve seat is not too wide or narrow. Use a 60° grinding wheel to remove material from the bottom of the seat for raising and a 30° grinding wheel to remove material from the top of the seat to narrow.

2. After the valves are refaced by machine, hand lap them to the valve seat. Clean the grinding compound off and check the position of face-to-seat contact. Contact should be close to the center of the valve face. If contact is close to the top edge of the valve, narrow the seat; if too close to the bottom edge, raise the seat. Valves should be refaced to a true angle of 44°. Remove only enough metal to clean up the valve face or to correct runout. If the edge of a valve head, after machining, is $1/32$ inch; (0.8mm) or less, replace the valve. The tip of the valve stem should also be dressed on the valve grinding machine, however, do not remove more than 0.010 inch.

4. After all valve and valve seats have been machined, check the remaining valve train parts (springs, retainers, keepers, etc.) for wear. Check the valve springs for straightness and tension.

CYLINDER HEAD

CRACK REPAIR

Cracks in a cylinder head or block can usually be repaired, although it usually is less expensive, in the long run, to pick up a good used head or block and recondition it. A crack under a valve seat can be repaired by inserting a series of tapered threaded pins all along the crack and across the valve seat. The valve seat area is then machined to receive a valve seat insert.

If a crack is to be repaired on a cast iron head, the tapered threaded pin repair is not possible because of the fine thread line left. However, a repair is possible using tapered drive-in plugs that can be ground smooth. Check with your local machine shop and ask their advice.

If a crack is repaired in either the head or the engine block, always add a can of heavy-duty ceramic sealer to the cooling system.

HEAD RESURFACING

▶ **See Figures 140 and 141**

Check the flatness of the cylinder head gasket surfaces.

1. Place a straightedge across the gasket surface of the cylinder head. Using feeler gauges, determine the clearance at the center of the straightedge.

2. If warpage exceeds 0.003 inch in a 6 inch span, or 0.006 inch over the total length, the cylinder head must be resurfaced.

Fig. 140 Rebuilt cylinder heads stacked in the machine shop

Fig. 141 A cylinder head being resurfaced at a machine shop

3. If necessary to refinish the cylinder head gasket surface, do not plane or grind off more than 0.010 inch from the original gasket surface.

➡When milling the cylinder heads, the intake manifold mounting position is altered, and must be corrected by milling the manifold flange a proportionate amount. Consult an experienced machinist about this.

VALVE SEATS

Valve seats may be resurfaced either by reaming or by grinding. Valve seats in cast iron heads may be reamed, while hardened valve seat inserts must be ground. A reamed seat must be lapped with valve grinding compound and the refaced or new valve that will be installed. It is not a bad idea to hand lap any valve when installing it in a newly machined seat.

Reaming the Valve Seat
◗ **See Figures 142, 143 and 144**

Select a reamer of the correct seat angle, slightly larger than the diameter of the valve seat, and assemble it with the pilot of the correct size. Install the pilot in the valve guide and using steady pressure, turn the reamer clockwise (never turn the reamer counterclockwise, the cutters and the valve seat can be damaged). Remove only enough material to clean the seat.

Check the concentricity (roundness) of the valve seat. This can be done by using Prussian blue dye. Coat the face of the valve that is to be installed with the dye. Install and rotate the valve on the valve seat. Using the dye marked area as a centering guide, center and narrow the valve seat to specifications with correction cutters. If the specifications are not available, minimum seat width for exhaust valves should be $5/64$ in.; intake valves $1/16$ in. After making any correction cuts, recheck with the seats and valves with the dye.

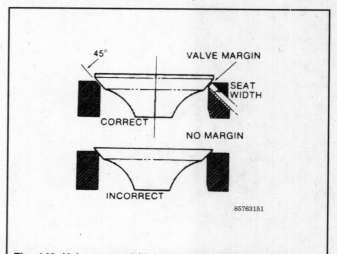

Fig. 142 Valve seat width and centering after proper reaming

Fig. 143 Checking valve seat concentricity with a dial gauge

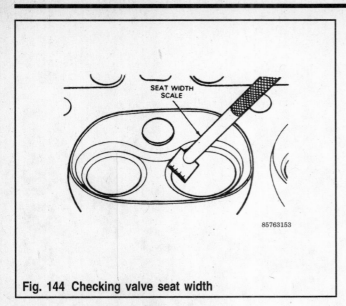

Fig. 144 Checking valve seat width

Refacing Valve Seats with a Grinder

▶ **See Figure 145**

A high-speed grinder, driving a grinding stone mounted on a holder and riding on a valve-guide-mounted pilot probably is used more than any other method to reface valve seats.

The finish on the valve seat depends on what grinding stone is used. By the correct use of various angle stones, the seat may be narrowed, stepped, or centered.

Checking Valve Seat Concentricity

Always check the concentricity of the valve seat after grinding either by the Prussian dye method (see Reaming the Valve Seat) or by using a dial indicator. Install the dial indicator pilot into the valve guide, rest the arm on the valve seat, and zero the gauge. Rotate the arm around the center of the seat. The run-out should not exceed. 0.002 in. Refinish the seat if the run-out is over 0.002. in.

Stepped Valve Seat Angles

▶ **See Figure 146**

Many miles on an automobile engine can cause 'sunken' valve seats; that is, seats that are very wide after grinding. To prevent too large a diameter seat or one that is too deep in the head, the top and bottom of the seat are cut at different angles, and then the center. For example, a normal 45 percent seat would have the top portion at 30 percent, the center at 45 percent and the bottom at 60 percent. Not only does this method of grinding center the valve contact point, it also prevents the restriction of air flow.

If the stepped method of valve seat grinding is used, the width of the seat must be measured.If measurement is impossible, check the valve contact width by using the Prussian dye method. If the contact point is too wide or too narrow, a correction to the valve seat must be made or valve burning and face recession can occur.

VALVE LAPPING

▶ **See Figures 147, 148, 149, 150 and 151**

The valve must be lapped into their seats after resurfacing, to ensure proper sealing. Even if the valves have not been refaced, they should be lapped into the head before they are installed.

Set the cylinder head on the workbench, combustion chamber side up. Rest the head on wooden blocks on either end, so there is 2-3 inches between the tops of the valve guides and the bench.

1. Lightly lube the valve stem with clean engine oil. Coat the valve seat completely with valve grinding compound. Use just enough compound so that the full width and circumference of the seat are covered.

2. Install the valve in its proper location in the head. Attach the suction cup end of the valve lapping tool to the valve head. It usually helps to put a small amount of saliva into the suction cup to aid it sticking to the valve.

3. Rotate the tool between the palms, changing position and lifting the tool often to prevent grooving. Lap the valve in

Fig. 145 A valve ready to be refaced at a machine shop

Fig. 146 Valve seats being reground. This machine cuts compound angles

Fig. 147 Applying lapping compound to the valve seat

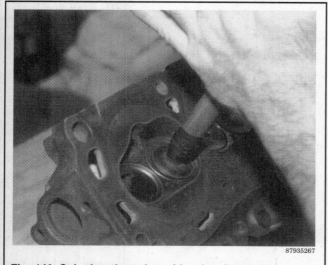

Fig. 148 Spinning the valve with a lapping tool

Fig. 149 Removing the valve

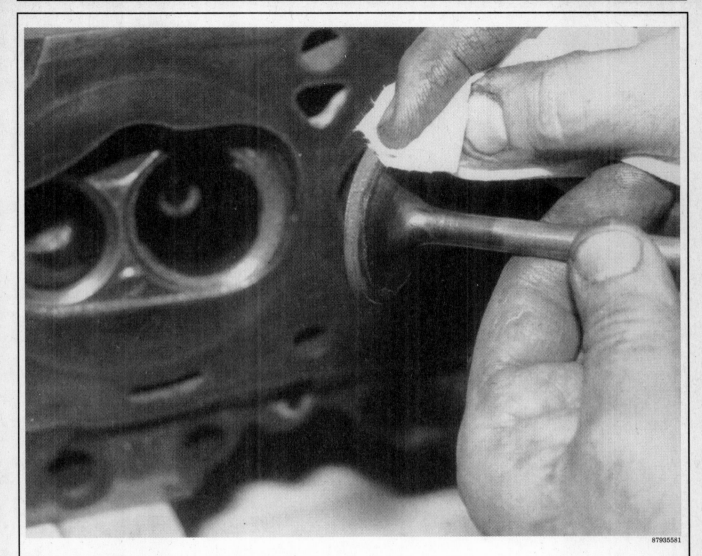

Fig. 150 Wiping the valve and seat contact surfaces

until a smooth, evenly polished seat and valve face are evident.

4. Remove the valve from the head. Wipe away all traces of grinding compound from the valve face and seat. Wipe out the port with a solvent soaked rag, and swab out the valve guide with a piece of solvent soaked rag to make sure there are no traces of compound grit inside the guide. This cleaning is very important, as engine scoring and damage will result if any grit is remaining when started.

5. Proceed through the remaining valves, one at a time. Make sure the valve faces, sets, cylinder ports and valve guides are clean before reassembling the valve train.

Valve Guides

Worn valve guides can, in most cases, be reamed to accept a valve with an oversized stem. Valve guides that are not excessively worn or distorted may, in some cases, be knurled rather than reamed. However, if the valve stem is worn, ream-ing for an oversized valve stem is the answer since a new valve would be required anyway.

Knurling is a process in which metal is displaced and raised, thereby reducing clearance. Knurling also produces excellent oil control. The possibility of knurling instead of reaming the valve guides should be discussed with a machinist.

REAMING THE GUIDES

▶ **See Figure 152**

If it becomes necessary to ream a valve guide to install a valve with an oversized stem, a reaming kit is available which contains an oversize reamers and pilot tools.

When replacing a standard size valve with an oversized valve always use the reamer in sequence (smallest oversize first, then next smallest, etc.) so as not to overload the ream-ers. Always reface the valve seat after the valve guide has been reamed, and use a suitable scraper to brake the sharp corner at the top of the valve guide.

87935580

Fig. 151 Checking the contact patterns on the valve and seat

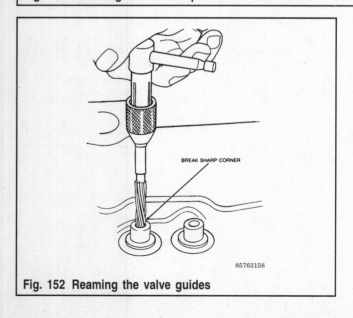

BREAK SHARP CORNER

85763158

Fig. 152 Reaming the valve guides

KNURLING

▶ **See Figures 153 and 154**

Valve guides which are not excessively worn or distorted may, in some cases, be knurled rather than reamed. Knurling is a process in which metal inside the valve guide bore is displaced and raised (forming a very fine cross-hatch pattern), thereby reducing clearance. Knurling also provides for excellent oil control. The possibility of knurling rather than reaming the guides should be discussed with a machinist.

VALVE GUIDE INSERTS

▶ **See Figure 155**

A coil insert can be installed in the valve guide. The guide is tapped and a bronze insert installed. The insert is then reamed to size.

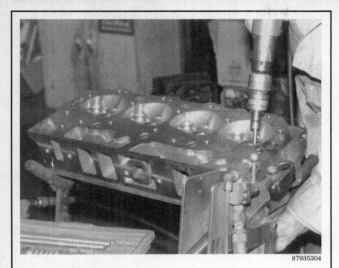

Fig. 153 Knurling a guide

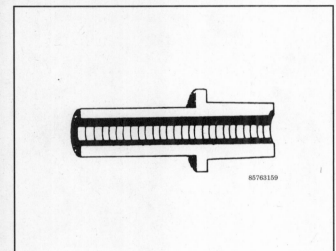

Fig. 154 Cross-section of a knurled valve guide

Fig. 155 Compound seat refacer in position

A second type of guide insert, and probably the best way of repairing the cast valve guide is the thin-walled bronze insert. The guide is reamed slightly oversize and a split-sleeve thin-walled insert is installed. A special tool is run through the guide bore which expands the insert into the cast guide. The guide is reamed to standard size.

REPLACEMENT GUIDES

It is possible to have the old cast guide bored oversize and a replacement guide pressed into the enlarged hole. This is not a bad idea, but the thin-walled bronze insert is a better method.

Oil Pump

1. Wash all parts in solvent and dry them thoroughly with compressed air. Use a brush to clean the inside of the pump housing and the pressure relief valve chamber. Be sure all dirt and metal particles are removed.
2. Check the inside of the pump housing and the outer race and rotor for damage or excessive wear or scoring.
3. Check the mating surface of the pump cover for wear. If the cover mating surface is worn, scored, or grooved, replace the pump.
4. Measure the inner rotor tip clearance.
5. With the rotor assembly installed in the housing, place a straight edge over the rotor assembly and the housing. Measure the clearance (rotor end play) between the straight edge and the rotor and the outer race.
6. Check the drive shaft to housing bearing clearance by measuring the OD of the shaft and the ID of the housing bearing.
7. Inspect the relief valve spring to see if it is collapsed or worn.
8. Check the relief valve piston for scores and free operation in the bore.
9. Components of the oil pump are not serviceable. If any part of the pump requires replacement, replace the complete pump assembly.

Block

CYLINDER HONING

▶ **See Figures 156, 157, 158, 159, 160, 161 and 162**

1. When cylinders are being honed, follow the manufacturer's recommendations for the use of the hone.
2. Occasionally, during the honing operation, the cylinder bore should be thoroughly cleaned and checked for correct fit with the selected piston.
3. When finish-honing a cylinder bore, the hone should be moved up and down at a sufficient speed to obtain a very fine uniform surface finish in a cross-hatch pattern of approximately 45-65 degrees included angle. The finish marks should be

Fig. 156 A cylinder block being bored oversize at a machine shop

Fig. 159 Chuck the hone into a drill and break the glaze with a constant up and down motion

Fig. 157 A cylinder block ready to be resurfaced at a machine shop

Fig. 160 Crankshaft journals being reground at the machine shop

Fig. 158 Place the hone in the cylinder, spray it with WD-40

Fig. 161 Crankshafts refinished ready to go at the machine shop

clean but not sharp, free from imbedded particles and torn or folded metal.

✳✳WARNING

Handle the pistons with care. Do not attempt to force the pistons through the cylinders until the cylinders have been honed to the correct size. Pistons can be distorted through careless handling.

4. Thoroughly clean the bores with hot water and detergent. Scrub them well with a stiff bristle brush and rinse thoroughly with hot water. It is extremely essential that a good cleaning operation be performed. If any of the abrasive material is allowed to remain in the cylinder bores, it will rapidly wear the new rings and cylinder bores. The bores should be swabbed several times with light engine oil and a clean cloth and then wiped with a clean dry cloth. CYLINDERS SHOULD NOT BE CLEANED WITH KEROSENE OR GASOLINE! Clean the remainder of the cylinder block to remove the excess material that got spread around during the honing operation.

Fig. 162 Clean the bores thoroughly with hot, soapy water

PUTTING IT ALL BACK TOGETHER

By now, you should be pretty sure of yourself. After all, you've disassembled, cleaned and inspected an entire V8 engine! Putting it back together should be no problem. Right? Right! If you thought cleanliness, care and attention to detail were important before, they are of supreme importance now! Let's get started.

Painting

At this point you can do the fun part and paint the engine. It's up to you to decide what color or colors you'd like. Traditionalists would paint the engine Ford Blue. That's fine. But, it's your engine now! You can paint it whatever you'd like! There are a lot of different colors of engine enamel on the market. Just make sure that you use a good quality, high-temperature engine paint. Also, remember that paint doesn't adhere to oily or greasy surfaces. That includes nice, clean oily surfaces. So, if you've applied oil or grease to any part, you'll have to thorough clean it before painting.

➡Be careful! Don't get paint on gasket mating surfaces!

Core (Freeze) Plugs

◗ See Figures 163, 164 and 165

Thoroughly clean the opening in the block, using steel wool or emery paper to polish the hole rim.

Coat the outer diameter of the new plug with RTV silicone sealer and place it in the hole.

For cup-type core plugs: these plugs are installed with the flanged end outward. The maximum diameter of this type of plug is located at the outer edge of the flange. Carefully and evenly, drive the new plug into place.

Fig. 163 Cleaning the core plug bore

For expansion-type plugs: these plugs are installed with the flanged end inward. The maximum diameter of this type of plug is located at the base of the flange. It is imperative that the correct type of installation tool is used with this type of plug. Under no circumstances is this type of plug to be driven in using a tool that contacts the crowned portion of the plug. Driving in this plug incorrectly will cause the plug to expand prior to installation. When installed, the trailing (maximum) diameter of the plug MUST be below the chamfered edge of the bore to create an effective seal. If the core plug replacing tool has a depth seating surface, do not seat the tool against a non-machined (casting) surface.

For both type plugs, when you're satisfied with the installation, wipe a coating of sealer around the outside edge of the plug.

Fig. 164 Coat the bore with RTV silicone sealant

Fig. 165 Hammering in the new plug

Crankshaft and Main Bearings

▶ See Figures 166, 167, 168, 169, 170, 171 and 172

➡During the following procedure, we describe the installation of the 2-piece type rear main seal. For engine with a 1-piece real main seal, we'll describe that installation just before Flywheel Installation a little later.

❋❋WARNING

Make sure that all bearing and journal surfaces are absolutely clean and stay that way during assembly!

Before assembly, coat the bearing halves and crankshaft journals with assembly lube or an equivalent oil. The idea is to have a lubricant in place that is compatible with engine oil and will stay on the metal surfaces during engine assembly.

1. If the crankshaft main bearing journals have been refinished to a definite undersize, install the correct undersize bearings. Be sure the bearing inserts and bearing bores are clean.

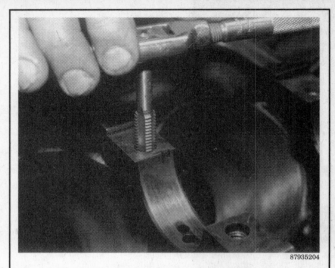

Fig. 166 Chasing the main cap bolt hole threads

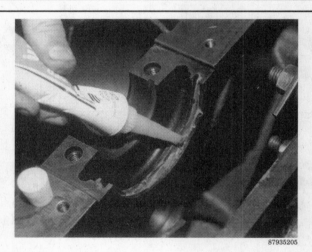

Fig. 167 Applying RTV sealant to the main seal upper saddle

Fig. 168 Installing the main seal upper half. If there is a retaining spike in the upper saddle, remove it when the new seal is made of neoprene

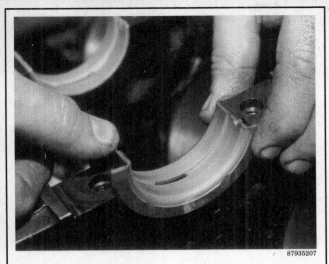

Fig. 169 Installing the thrust bearing upper bearing half

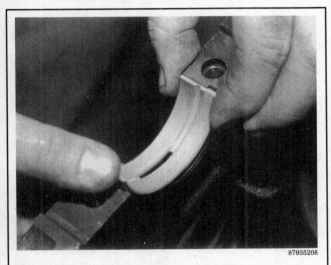

Fig. 170 Installing the rest of the upper bearing halves

Fig. 171 Applying assembly lube to a bearing half

Fig. 172 Installing the crankshaft

Dirt, grit or metal particles under the inserts will distort the bearing and cause a failure.

2. Place the upper main bearing inserts in position in the bores with the tang fitting in the slot. Be sure the oil holes in the bearing inserts are aligned with the oil holes in the cylinder block.

3. Install the lower main bearing inserts in the bearing caps.

4. Clean the rear journal oil seal groove and the mating surfaces of the block and rear main bearing cap.

5. Dip the lip-type seal halves in clean engine oil. Install the seals in the bearing cap and block with the undercut side of the seal toward the front of the engine.

➡This procedure applies only to engines with two piece rear main bearing oil seals. Those having one piece seals will be installed after the crankshaft is in place.

6. Carefully lower the crankshaft into place. Be careful not to damage the bearing surfaces.

Pistons and Connecting Rods

▶ See Figures 173, 174, 175, 176, 177, 178, 179 and 180

Install the rings on the piston, lowest ring first, using a piston ring expander. There is a high risk of breaking or distorting the rings, or scratching the piston, if the rings are installed by hand or other means. The envelopes that the rings come in have illustrations and instructions showing proper installation techniques.

Position the rings on the piston; spacing of the various piston ring gaps is crucial to proper oil retention and even cylinder wear. When installing new rings, refer to the installation diagram furnished with the new parts.

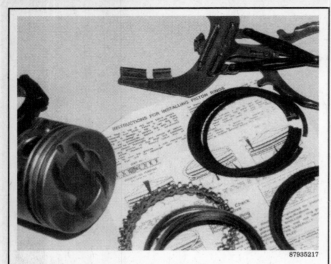

Fig. 173 Everything you need to install new rings

Fig. 174 Mark the top of the piston (3 times at 120 degrees apart) as a reference to position the ring gaps once the rings are installed

Fig. 175 Installing the oil control ring

87935588

Fig. 176 Installing the oil control ring lower rail

Fig. 177 Installing the oil control ring upper rail

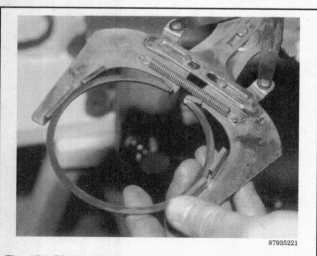

Fig. 178 Placing the lower compression ring on the expander

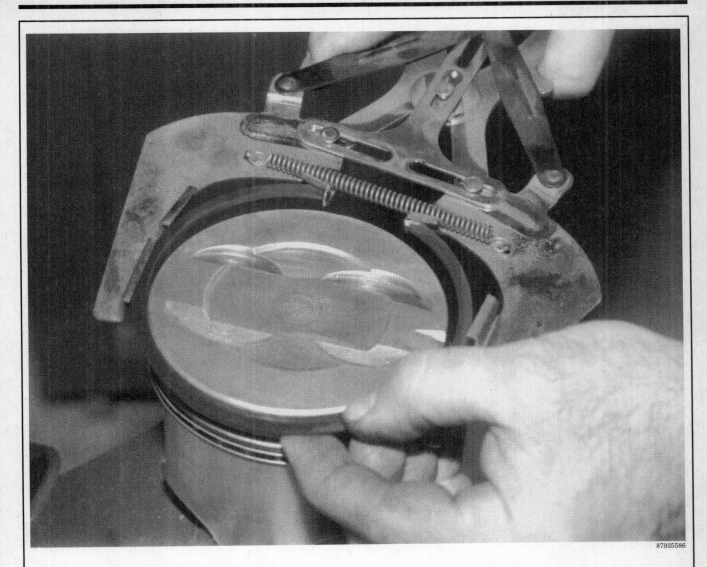

Fig. 179 Installing the lower compression ring

Fig. 180 Installing the upper compression ring

PISTON AND CONNECTING ROD ASSEMBLY AND INSTALLATION

▶ **See Figures 181, 182, 183, 184, 185, 186, 187, 188, 189, 190, 191, 192 and 193**

If you have purchased matched pistons and rod, skip this paragraph. If rods and pistons were purchased separately, attach the connecting rod to the piston making sure piston installation notches and any marks on the rod are in proper relation to one another. Lubricate the wrist pin with clean engine oil and install the pin into the rod and piston assembly by using an arbor press as required. Install the wrist pin snaprings if equipped, and rotate them in their grooves to make sure they are seated. To install the piston and rod assemblies:

1. Fit pieces of rubber hose over the connecting rod bolt to protect the crankshaft journals.

2. Using a ring compressor, insert the piston assembly in the cylinder so the piston notch (in the top) faces the front of

the engine on all but the 360/390. On these engines, the V-shaped indentation faces in towards the center of the engine. This assumes the dimple(s) or other markings on the con rods are correct relation to the piston notch(s).

3. Turn the engine over, then coat each crank journal with clean oil. Pull the connecting rod, with the new bearing shell in place, into position against the crank journal. See Connecting Rod Bearing Replacement, below.

4. Remove the rubber hoses. Install the bearing cap and cap nuts and torque to specification.

➡ **When more than one piston is being installed, the rod cap nuts should be tightened only enough to keep each rod in position until all have been installed. This will ease installation of the remaining pistons.**

5. Check the clearance between the sides of the connecting rods and the crankshaft using a feeler gauge. Spread the rods slightly with a screwdriver to insert the gauge. If clearance is below the minimum tolerance, the rod may be machined to provide adequate clearance.

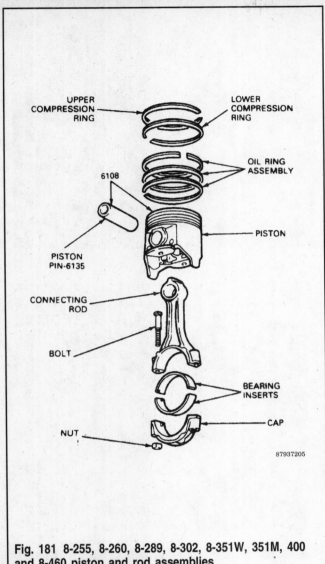

Fig. 181 8-255, 8-260, 8-289, 8-302, 8-351W, 351M, 400 and 8-460 piston and rod assemblies

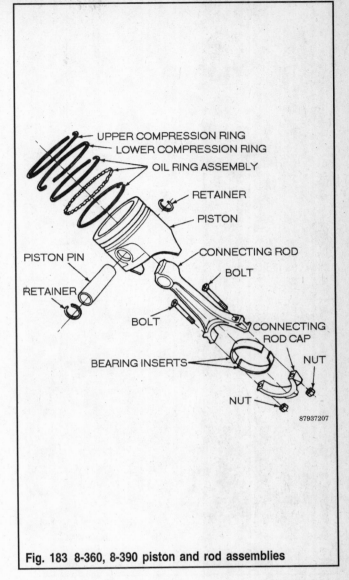

Fig. 183 8-360, 8-390 piston and rod assemblies

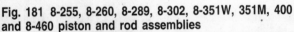

Fig. 182 8-255, 8-260, 8-289, 8-302, 8-351W piston installation orientation

Fig. 184 Place pieces of hose on the rod studs

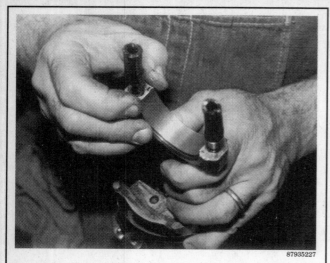

Fig. 185 Installing the upper bearing shell

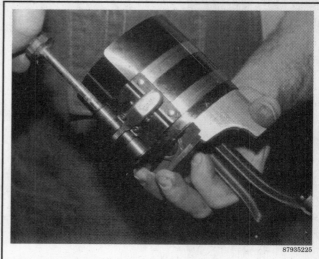

Fig. 187 Compressing the rings

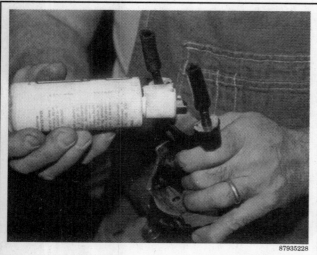

Fig. 186 Applying assembly lube to the upper shell

Fig. 188 Pushing the piston in with a hammer handle. It should slide right in. If not, recompress the rings

Fig. 189 The piston/rod assembly installed on a journal

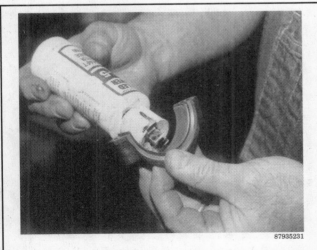

Fig. 190 Applying assembly lube to a lower rod bearing shell

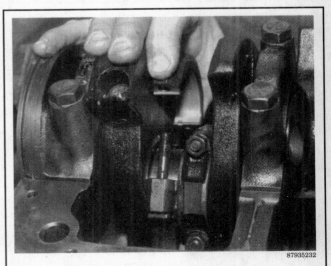

Fig. 191 Installing the a lower rod bearing shell

Fig. 192 Torquing the rod bearing cap nuts

Fig. 193 Paired rods installed on a journal

Camshaft and Bearings

1. Position the new bearings at the bearing bores, and press them in place with the tool. Be sure to center the pulling plate and puller screw to avoid damage to the bearing. Failure to use the correct expanding collet can cause severe bearing damage. Align the oil holes in the bearings with the oil holes in the cylinder block before pressing bearings into place.

➡**Be sure the front bearing is installed 0.005-0.020 inch below the front face of the cylinder block.**

2. Install the camshaft rear bearing bore plug.
3. Coat the camshaft with engine oil liberally before installing it. Slide the camshaft into the engine very carefully so as not to scratch the bearing bores with the camshaft lobes. Install the camshaft thrust plate and tighten the attaching screws to 9-12 ft. lbs. Measure the camshaft end-play. If the end-play is more than 0.009 inch, replace the thrust plate.

Oil Pump

◗ **See Figures 194, 195, 196, 197 and 198**

1. Before installing the oil pump, prime it by filling the inlet and outlet port with engine oil and rotating the shaft of the pump to distribute it.
2. Position the new gasket on the pump body and insert the intermediate driveshaft into the pump body.
3. Install the pump and intermediate driveshaft as an assembly. Do not force the pump if it does not seat readily.
4. Install the oil pump attaching bolts and torque them to 20-25 ft. lbs.

Timing Chain

◗ **See Figure 199**

1. Position the timing chain on the sprockets so that the timing marks on the sprockets are aligned vertically. Alternately

Fig. 194 Assembling the pickup on the oil pump

Fig. 195 Installing the pickup bolts

Fig. 196 Tightening the pickup bolts

Fig. 197 Positioning the oil pump on the block

Fig. 198 Installing the oil pump bolts

Fig. 199 Align the timing marks on the sprockets

slide the sprockets and chain onto the crankshaft and camshaft sprockets.

2. Install the fuel pump eccentric washers and attaching bolt on the camshaft sprocket. Tighten to 40-45 ft. lbs.

Oil Pan

◆ **See Figures 200, 201, 202, 203, 204, 205, 206, 207 and 208**

1. Clean the oil pan, inlet tube and gasket surfaces. Inspect the gasket sealing surface for damages and distortion due to overtightening of the bolts. Repair and straighten as required.

2. Position new oil pan gaskets on the pan using a high-tack gasket sealer. Place new seals in the front and rear of the block. Coat the seals with RTV gasket sealer. Coat the block gasket surfaces with non-hardening gasket sealer such as Permatex No.2®

3. Position the pan onto the block and install 2 bolts on each side, finger tight.

4. Install the remaining bolts and torque them to 11-13 ft. lbs. for the 5/16 bolts and 7-9 ft. lbs. for the 1/4 bolts in a criss-cross pattern.

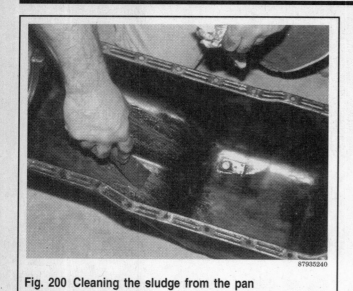
Fig. 200 Cleaning the sludge from the pan

Fig. 203 Installing the oil pan right side gasket

Fig. 201 Cleaning the oil pan gasket rail

Fig. 204 Installing the oil pan left side gasket

Fig. 202 Applying RTV to the oil pan front seal groove

Fig. 205 Indexing the gasket tab with the slot in the seal

Fig. 206 Installing the oil pan

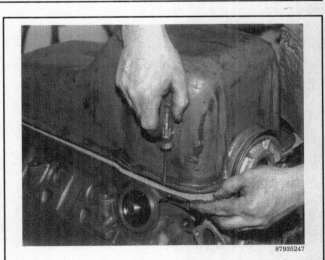

Fig. 207 Use an awl to line up the holes in the gasket with the bolt holes in the pan and block

Fig. 208 Installing the front pan bolts

Timing Chain Front Cover and Oil Seal

▶ See Figures 209, 210, 211, 212, 213, 214, 215 and 216

1. Coat a new front cover oil seal with Lubriplate® or equivalent and drive it into place with a seal driver.
2. Coat the gasket surface of the oil pan with sealer. Cut and position the required sections of a new seal on the oil pan. Apply sealer to the corners.
3. Coat the gasket surfaces of the cylinder block and cover with sealer and position the new gasket on the block.
4. Position the front cover on the cylinder block. Use care not to damage the seal and gasket or lose them.
5. Coat the front cover attaching screws with sealer and install them.

➡️It may be necessary to force the front cover downward to compress the oil pan seal in order to install the front cover attaching bolts. Use a screwdriver or drift to engage the cover screw holes through the cover and pry downward.

6. Apply Lubriplate® or equivalent to the oil seal rubbing surface of the vibration damper inner hub to prevent damage to the seal. Coat the front of the crankshaft with engine oil for damper installation.

Fig. 209 Driving out the front seal

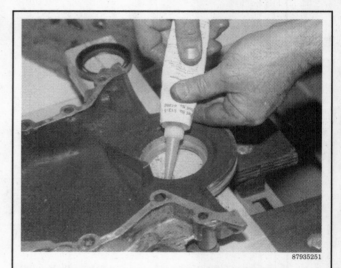
Fig. 210 Applying RTV sealer to the front seal bore

Fig. 211 Positioning the front seal in the bore

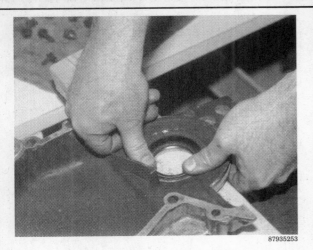

Fig. 212 Pushing the front seal into place. You might have to drive it in until it seats fully

Fig. 213 Applying gasket sealer to the front cover-to-block mating surface

Fig. 214 Installing the front cover

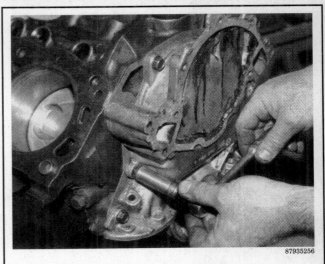

Fig. 215 Installing the front cover bolts

Fig. 216 Torquing the front cover bolts

Crankshaft Pulley (Vibration Damper)

▶ See Figures 217, 218, 219 and 220

Coat the nose of the crankshaft with engine oil. Coat the front seal lip with chassis lube. Slide the damper onto the crankshaft, aligning the crank key and slot in the damper. Install the washer and bolt and torque the bolt to specification. The damper may be tight and require force to install. You can hammer it lightly with a rubber dead blow hammer but don't use too much force. Torque the retaining bolt to the specifications found in the Torque Specifications Chart.

Lifters

▶ See Figures 221 and 222

If you're installing the old lifters, coat them with engine oil and drop them into their original bores. If you're installing new lifters, coat them with clean engine oil and drop them into any

Fig. 217 Applying anti-sieze compound to the nose of the crankshaft

Fig. 218 Applying assembly lube to the damper

Fig. 219 Installing the damper

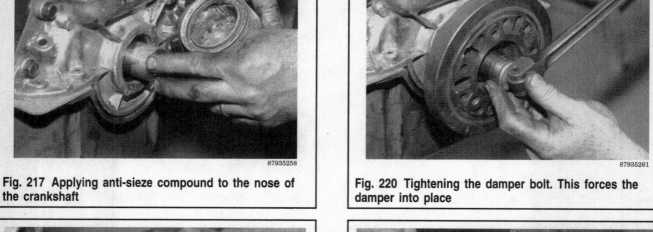

Fig. 220 Tightening the damper bolt. This forces the damper into place

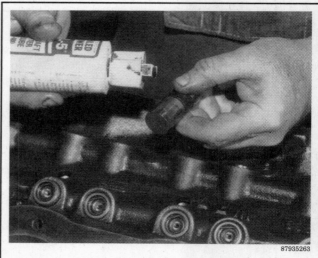

Fig. 221 Applying assembly lube to the lifters

Fig. 222 Installing the lifters

of the bores. In either case, don't fill them with oil prior to installation.

Valves

▶ **See Figures 223, 224, 225 and 226**

1. Install the valves in the cylinder head.
2. Install new valve stem oil seals (and install exhaust metal caps if so equipped).

➡**When installing valve stem oil seals, ensure that a small amount of oil is able to pass the seal to lubricate the valve stems and guide walls, otherwise, excessive wear will occur.**

3. Using a valve spring compressor (the locking C-clamp type is the easiest kind to use), install the valve keepers, retainer, spring shield and valve spring .

Fig. 224 Installing the valve springs

Fig. 223 Installing a valve stem seal. These are the positive stop type. Some engines use umbrella type seals

Fig. 225 Installing the keepers. This can be tricky. Count on dropping a few of them

Fig. 226 Tap the assembled valves with a plastic or rubber mallet. This will reveal any keepers that aren't secure

Cylinder Head

▶ **See Figures 227, 228, 229, 230, 231, 232 and 233**

1. Clean the cylinder head gasket surfaces.
2. Follow the gasket manufacturer's recommendation for using sealer. Position the new gasket over the locating dowels on the cylinder block. Then, position the cylinder head on the block and install the attaching bolts.
3. The cylinder head bolts are tightened in 3 progressive steps. Tighten all the bolts in the proper sequence as specified.
4. Apply Lubriplate® to the ends of the pushrods and install them in their original positions.

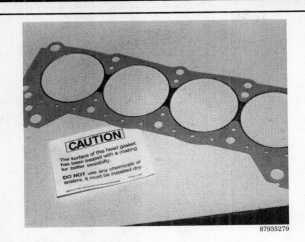

Fig. 227 The head gaskets and warning label. Depending on the gasket maker, you may or may not use sealer. Usually not

Fig. 228 Chasing the bolt hole threads

Fig. 229 These dowels will help you line up the head properly

Fig. 230 Positioning the head gasket on the block. The gasket will usually say 'front' or 'up'

Fig. 231 Installing the right cylinder head

Fig. 232 Installing the left cylinder head

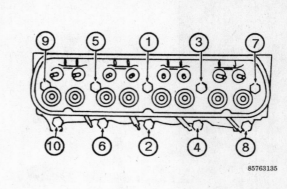

Fig. 233 Cylinder head bolt torque sequence

Exhaust Manifold

Not all engines are originally assembled with an exhaust manifold gasket. The idea is the expansion of the manifold metal and heads creates an exhaust proof seal.

All replacement gasket sets have exhaust manifold gaskets. Use them. It's better!

Clean the manifold and head mating surfaces and wire-brush the studs. It's a good idea to chase the threads with your tap and die set.

Place the gasket over the suds and install the manifold. Tighten the nuts and/or bolts. DON'T USE SEALER! Tighten the fasteners, starting from the center and working to both ends alternately.

Water Pump

▶ See Figure 234

Make sure that the mating surfaces of the pump and engine are clean. Check the bolts that you removed. Not all of them are the same size or length. You should have marked them for installation.

Coat the gasket surfaces with the high-tack gasket sealer and place the gasket on the water pump. Place the water pump on the engine and loosely install the bolts. When everything is lined up and look okay, tighten the bolts. Use the torque figure in the charts. Don't over-tighten them!

Rocker Arms and Pushrods

▶ See Figures 235, 236, 237, 238, 239, 240, 241 and 242

1. Coat each end of each pushrod with multi-purpose grease and install them.

2. Coat the top of the valve stems, the rocker arms and the fulcrum seats with multi-purpose grease.

3. Rotate the crankshaft by hand until No. 1 piston is at TDC of compression. The firing order marks on the damper will be aligned at TDC with the timing pointer.

Fig. 234 Installing the water pump

Fig. 237 Installing the pivot fulcrum

Fig. 235 Installing the pushrods

Fig. 238 Installing the rocker arm nut

Fig. 236 Installing the rocker arm

Fig. 239 Tightening the rocker arm nut

Fig. 240 You might have to back off the nut to pivot the rocker arm over the pushrod

Fig. 241 Rotating the rocker arm over the pushrod

Fig. 242 Tightening the rocker arm nut until the pushrod just stops turning

4. Install the rocker arms, seats, deflectors and bolts on the following valves:
- No. 1 intake and exhaust
- No. 3 intake
- No. 8 exhaust
- No. 7 intake
- No. 5 exhaust
- No. 8 intake
- No. 4 exhaust

Engage the rocker arms with the pushrods and tighten the rocker arm fulcrum bolts to 18-25 ft. lbs.

5. Rotate the crankshaft one full turn — 360° — and re-align the TDC mark and pointer. Install the parts and tighten the bolts on the following valves:
- No. 2 intake and exhaust
- No. 4 intake
- No. 3 exhaust
- No. 5 intake
- No. 6 exhaust
- No. 6 intake
- No. 7 exhaust

6. Check the valve clearance as described below.

CLEARANCE ADJUSTMENT

Adjustable Rocker Arms

▶ **See Figure 243**

Some early models are equipped with adjustable rockers whereas the later models are equipped with positive stop type rocker mounting studs. Positive stop equipped rockers are adjusted by turning the adjusting nut down until it stops. You can identify a positive stop mounting stud by determining whether or not the shank portion of the stud that is exposed just above the cylinder head is the same diameter as the threaded portion at the top of the stud, to which the rocker arm retaining nut attaches. If the shank portion is larger than the threaded area, it is a positive stop mounting stud. Use the procedure given

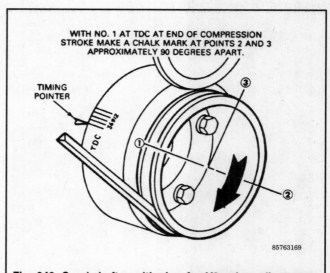

Fig. 243 Crankshaft positioning for V8 valve adjustment

below for adjusting the valve lash on positive stop type mounting stud equipped vehicles.

1. Position the piston(s) on TDC of the compression stroke, using the timing mark on the crankshaft pulley as a reference for starting with the No. 1 cylinder. You can tell if a piston is coming up on its compression stroke by removing the spark plug of the cylinder you are working on and placing your thumb over the hole while the engine is cranked over. Air will try to force its way past your thumb when the piston comes upon the compression stroke. Make sure that the high tension coil wire leading to the distributor is removed before cranking the engine. Remove the valve covers.

2. Starting with No. 1 cylinder, and the piston in the position as mentioned above, apply pressure to slowly bleed down the valve lifter until the plunger is completely bottomed.

3. While holding the valve lifter in the fully collapsed position, check the available clearance between the rocker arm and the valve stem tip. Use a feeler gauge.

4. If the clearance is not within the specified amount, rotate the rocker arm stud nut clockwise to decrease the clearance and counterclockwise to increase the clearance. Normally, one turn of the rocker arm stud nut will vary the clearance by 0.066 in. (1.676mm). Check the break-away torque of each stud nut with a torque wrench, turning it counterclockwise. It should be anywhere from 4.5 to 15 ft. lbs. Replace the nut and/or the stud as necessary.

5. When both valves for the No. 1 cylinder have been adjusted, proceed on to the other valves, following the firing order sequence.

6. Replace the valve covers and gaskets.

ALTERNATE PROCEDURE

Follow Step 1 of the preferred procedure given above, but instead of collapsing the lifter as in Step 2, loosen the rocker retaining nut until there is endplay present in the pushrod; then tighten the nut to remove all pushrod-to-rocker arm clearance. When the pushrod-to-rocker arm clearance has been eliminated, tighten the stud nut an additional ¾ turn to place the lifter plunger in the desired operating range.

Repeat this procedure for all of the cylinders, using the firing order sequence as a guide. It takes ¼ turn of the crankshaft to bring the next piston in the firing order sequence up to TDC at the end of its compression stroke. Collapsed Tappet Gap Clearance:
- Allowable: 0.071-0.193 in. (1.8-4.9mm)
- Desired: 0.096-0.165 in. (2.4-4.2mm)

Positive Stop Rocker arms

EXCEPT 351M AND 400

▶ See Figure 244

1. Rotate the crankshaft by hand so that No. 1 piston is at TDC of the compression stroke. Make a chalk mark on the damper at that point, then, make 2 more chalk marks about 90 degrees apart in a clockwise direction. See the accompanying illustration.

2. With No. 1 at TDC, slowly apply pressure, using Lifter Bleed-down wrench T70P-6513-A, or equivalent, to completely bottom the lifter, on the following valves:
- No. 1 intake and exhaust
- No. 7 intake
- No. 5 exhaust
- No. 8 intake
- No. 4 exhaust

Take care to avoid excessive pressure that might bend the pushrod. Hold the lifter in this position and check the clearance between the rocker arm and the valve stem tip. Allowable clearance is 1.9-4.4mm (0.075-0.175 in.) with a desired clearance of 2.5-3.8mm (0.100-0.150 in.).

3. If the clearance is less than specified, install a shorter pushrod. If the clearance is greater than specified, install a longer pushrod.

4. Rotate the crankshaft clockwise — viewed from the front — 180 degrees, until the next chalk mark is aligned with the timing pointer. Repeat the procedure for:
- No. 5 intake
- No. 2 exhaust
- No. 4 intake
- No. 6 exhaust

5. Rotate the crankshaft to the next chalk mark — 90 degrees — and repeat the procedure for:
- No. 2 intake
- No. 7 exhaust
- No. 3 intake and exhaust
- No. 6 intake
- No. 8 exhaust

351M and 400

1. Rotate the crankshaft by hand so that No. 1 piston is at TDC of the compression stroke. Make a chalk mark on the damper at that point, then, make 2 more chalk marks about 90 degrees apart in a clockwise direction.

2. With No. 1 at TDC, slowly apply pressure, using Lifter Bleed-down wrench T70P-6513-A, or equivalent, to completely bottom the lifter, on the following valves:
- No. 1 intake and exhaust
- No. 4 intake
- No. 3 exhaust
- No. 8 intake
- No. 7 exhaust

Take care to avoid excessive pressure that might bend the pushrod. Hold the lifter in this position and check the clearance between the rocker arm and the valve stem tip. Allowable clearance is 2.5-5.0mm (0.098-0.198 in.) with a desired clearance of 3.1-4.4mm (0.123-0.173 in.).

3. If the clearance is less than specified, install a shorter pushrod. If the clearance is greater than specified, install a longer pushrod.

4. Rotate the crankshaft clockwise — viewed from the front — 180 degrees, until the next chalk mark is aligned with the timing pointer. Repeat the procedure for:
- No. 3 intake
- No. 2 exhaust
- No. 7 intake
- No. 6 exhaust

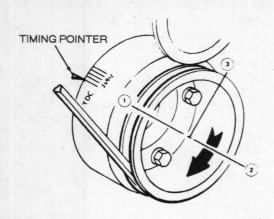

TIMING POINTER

WITH NO 1 AT TDC AT END OF COMPRESSION STROKE MAKE A CHALK MARK AT POINTS 2 AND 3 APPROXIMATELY 90 DEGREES

POSITION 1 - NO. 1 AT TDC AT END OF COMPRESSION STROKE
POSITION 2 - ROTATE THE CRANKSHAFT 180 DEGREES (1/2 REVOLUTION) CLOCKWISE FROM POSITION 1
POSITION 3 - ROTATE THE CRANKSHAFT 270 DEGREES (THREE QUARTER REVOLUTION CLOCK WISE FROM POSITION 2

85763170

Fig. 244 V8 positive stop valve clearance crankshaft positioning

5. Rotate the crankshaft to the next chalk mark — 90 degrees — and repeat the procedure for:
- No. 2 intake
- No. 4 exhaust
- No. 5 intake and exhaust
- No. 6 intake
- No. 8 exhaust

Intake Manifold

▶ See Figures 245, 246, 247, 248, 249, 250, 251 and 252

1. Clean the mating surfaces of the intake manifold, cylinder heads, and block with lacquer thinner or similar solvent. Apply a ⅛ in. (3mm) bead of silicone-rubber RTV sealant at the points shown in the accompanying diagram.

❋❋WARNING

Do not apply sealer to the waffle portions of the seals as the sealer will rupture the end seal material.

2. Position new seals on the block and press the seal locating extensions into the holes in the mating surfaces.
3. Apply a ¹/₁₆ in. (1.6mm) bead of sealer to the outer end of each manifold seal for the full length of the seal (4 places). Do not apply sealer to the waffle portion of the end seals.

➡**This sealer sets in about 15 minutes, depending on brand, so work quickly but carefully. DO NOT DROP ANY SEALER INTO THE MANIFOLD CAVITY. IT WILL FORM, SET AND PLUG THE OIL GALLERY.**

4. Your new valley pan gasket will have an instruction sheet showing a change in the sealer application for the pan-to-heads contact. RTV silicone sealer is to be used around the water passages, while non-hardening gasket sealer is to be used everywhere else.
5. Position the valley pan onto the block and heads with the alignment notches and ridge engaged. Be sure gasket holes align with head holes.

6. Carefully lower the manifold into position. Run your finger around the front and rear seals to make sure they are in position. If not, remove the manifold and reposition them.
7. Install the manifold nuts and bolts. Following the tightening sequence, tighten all fasteners.

Thermostat

1. Position a new thermostat in its recess with the spring side down.
2. Coat a new gasket with water resistant sealer and position it on the outlet over the thermostat.
3. Position the thermostat housing onto the mounting surface of the outlet. Torque the bolts.

Distributor

1. Rotate the engine so that No.1 piston is at TDC of the compression stroke.
2. Align the timing marks to the correct ignition timing.
3. Install the distributor with the alignment marks that you made, all lined up, or, with the rotor in the No.1 firing position and any armature pole aligned with a stator pole.

➡**Make sure that the oil pump intermediate shaft properly engages the distributor shaft. It may be necessary to rotate the engine after the distributor gear is partially engaged in order to engage the oil pump intermediate shaft and fully seat the distributor in the block.**

4. If it was necessary to rotate the engine to align the oil pump, repeat Steps 1, 2 and 3.
5. Install the hold-down bolt finger tight.

Engine Fan and Fan Clutch

Position the pulley and fan assembly on the water pump hub. Install the bolts and torque them to the figure shown in the torque chart.

Fig. 245 Indexing the intake manifold gasket with the tabs on the head gasket; 289/302 shown

Fig. 246 Intake manifold gaskets installed

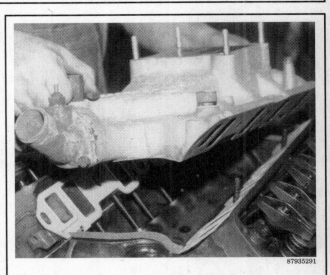

Fig. 247 Lowering the manifold into position

Fig. 248 Installing the manifold bolts

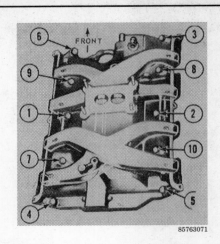

Fig. 250 Intake manifold bolt torque sequence for the 8-360 and 8-390

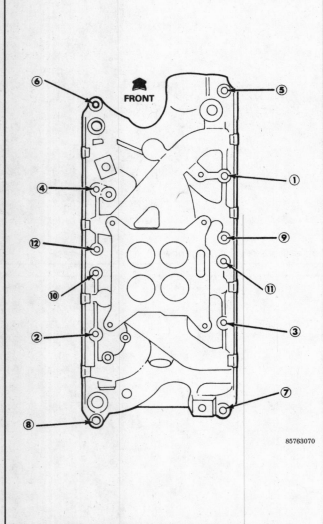

Fig. 249 Intake manifold bolt torque sequence for the 8-255, 8-260, 8-289, 8-302 and 8-351W

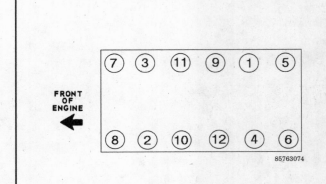

Fig. 251 Intake manifold bolt torque sequence for the 8-351M and 8-400

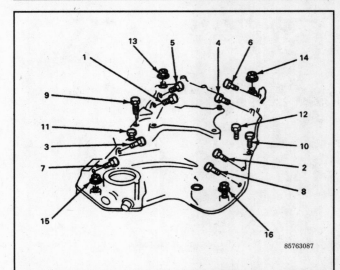

Fig. 252 8-460 intake manifold bolt tightening sequence

Alternator

1. If you haven't installed the adjusting arm, do so now.
2. Hold the alternator in position and install the through-bolt and spacer.
3. Install the adjusting bolt. Keep everything loose until the belts are installed.

BELT TENSION ADJUSTMENT

The fan belt drives the alternator and water pump. If the belt is too loose, it will slip and the alternator will not be able to produce it rated current. Also, the water pump will not operate efficiently and the engine could overheat.

1. Loosen the alternator mounting bolt and the adjusting arm bolts.
2. Apply pressure on the alternator front housing only, moving the alternator away from the engine to tighten the belt. Do not apply pressure to the rear of the cast aluminum housing of an alternator; damage to the housing could result.

Check the tension of the belt by pushing your thumb down on the longest span of the belt, midway between the pulleys. Belt deflection should be approximately ½ in. (13mm).

3. Tighten the alternator mounting bolt and the adjusting arm bolts when the correct tension is reached.

Rocker Covers

▶ **See Figures 253 and 254**

1. Thoroughly clean the mating surfaces of both the cover and head. Make sure the cover flanges are straight.

2. Coat both mating surfaces with gasket sealer and place the new gasket on the head.
3. Place the cover on the head making sure the gasket is evenly seated. Install the bolts and torque them to the figure shown in the torque charts.

One Piece Rear Main Oil Seal

1. Clean the oil seal recess in the cylinder block and main bearing cap.
2. Coat the new oil seal and the crankshaft with a light film of engine oil. Start the seal in the recess with the seal lip facing forward and install it with a seal driver. Keep the tool straight with the centerline of the crankshaft and install the seal until the tool contacts the cylinder block surface. Remove the tool and inspect the seal to be sure it was not damaged during installation.
3. Install the engine rear cover plate.

Flywheel/Flexplate

This job can't be done with the engine on the stand, so you'll have to wait until the engine is on the dolly.

Position the flywheel on the crankshaft flange. You'll notice that the bolt holes are not evenly spaced, so the flywheel goes on in only one position. Coat the threads of the flywheel attaching bolts with oil-resistant sealer and install the bolts. Tighten the bolts in a star-shaped sequence, a little at a time, to the specifications listed in the Torque chart.

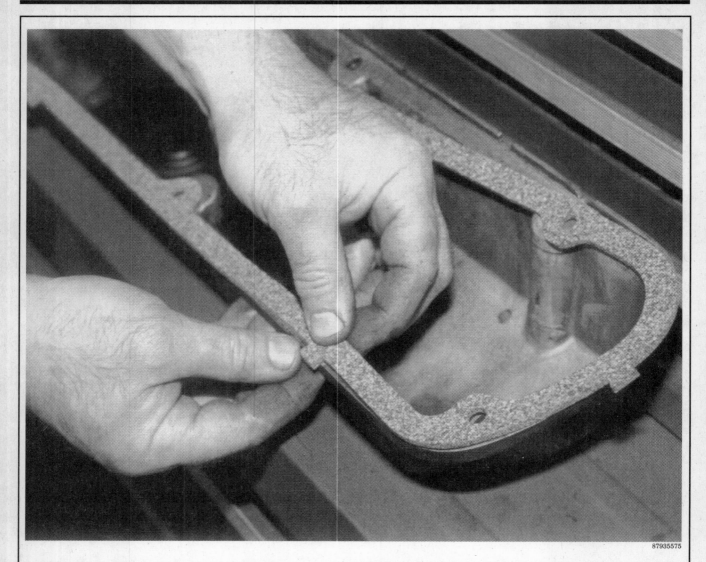

87935575

Fig. 253 Installing the rocker cover gaskets. Make sure that the tabs on the gasket lock into the notches in the cover

87935294

Fig. 254 Installing the rocker covers

Engine Mechanical Specifications

COMPONENT	U.S.	METRIC
Bore x Stroke		
255	3.6800 in. x 3.0000 in.	93.5mm x 76.2mm
289	4.0000 in. x 2.8700 in.	101.6mm x 72.9mm
302	4.0000 in. x 3.0000 in.	101.6mm x 76.2mm
351W	4.0000 in. x 3.5000 in.	101.6mm x 88.9mm
351M	4.0000 in. x 3.5000 in.	101.6mm x 88.9mm
352	4.0000 in. x 3.5000 in.	101.6mm x 88.9mm
360	4.0500 in. x 3.5000 in.	102.9mm x 88.9mm
390	4.0500 in. x 3.7800 in.	102.9mm x 96.0mm
400	4.0000 in. x 4.0000 in.	101.6mm x 101.6mm
460	4.3600 in. x 3.8500 in.	110.7mm x 97.8mm
Actual Displacement		
255	255.3 cu. in.	4183cc (4.2L)
289	288.5 cu. in.	4728cc (4.7L)
302	301.6 cu. in.	4942cc (5.0L)
351W	351.8 cu. in.	5766cc (5.8L)
351M	351.8 cu. in.	5766cc (5.8L)
352	351.9 cu. in.	5767cc (5.8L)
360	360.7 cu. in.	5911cc (5.9L)
390	389.5 cu. in.	6384cc (6.4L)
400	402.1 cu. in.	6590cc (6.6L)
460	464.1 cu. in.	7605cc (7.6L)
Camshaft Bearing ID		
255/289/302/351W		
No. 1	2.0825 - 2.0835 in.	52.8955 - 52.9209mm
No. 2	2.0675 - 2.0685 in.	52.5145 - 52.5399mm
No. 3	2.0525 - 2.0535 in.	52.1335 - 52.1589mm
No. 4	2.0375 - 2.0385 in.	51.7525 - 51.7779mm
No. 5	2.0225 - 2.0235 in.	51.3715 - 51.3969mm
351M/400		
No. 1	2.1258 - 2.1268 in.	53.9953 - 54.0207mm
No. 2	2.0675 - 2.0685 in.	52.5145 - 52.5399mm
No. 3	2.0525 - 2.0535 in.	52.1335 - 52.1589mm
No. 4	2.0375 - 2.0385 in.	51.7525 - 51.7779mm
No. 5	2.0225 - 2.0235 in.	51.3715 - 51.3969mm
352/360/390/ All	2.1258 - 1.1268 in.	53.9953 - 54.0207mm
460 All	2.1258 - 2.1268 in.	53.9953 - 54.0207mm
Camshaft End-Play		
255/289/302/351W/352	0.0010 - 0.0070 in.	0.0254 - 0.1778mm
351M/400	0.0010 - 0.0060 in.	0.0254 - 0.1524mm
360/390	0.0010 - 0.0050 in.	0.0254 - 0.1270mm
460		
1976-85	0.0010 - 0.0070 in.	0.0254 - 0.1778mm
1986 and later	0.0010 - 0.0060 in.	0.0254 - 0.1524mm

87935c01

Engine Mechanical Specifications

COMPONENT	U.S.	METRIC
Camshaft Front Bearing Location		
255/289/302/351W/352/360/390	0.0050 - 0.0200 in.	0.1270 - 0.5080mm
351M/400/460	0.0400 - 0.0600 in.	1.0160 - 1.5240mm
Camshaft Journal-to-Bearing Clearance		
All	0.0010 - 0.0030 in.	0.0254 - 0.0762mm
Camshaft Journal Diameter		
255/289/302/351W		
No. 1	2.0805 - 2.0815 in.	52.8447 - 52.8701mm
No. 2	2.0655 - 2.0665 in.	52.4637 - 52.4891mm
No. 3	2.0505 - 2.0515 in.	52.8027 - 52.1081mm
No. 4	2.0355 - 2.0365 in.	51.7017 - 51.7271mm
No. 5	2.0205 - 2.0215 in.	51.3207 - 51.3461mm
351M/400		
No. 1	2.1248 - 2.1328 in.	53.9699 - 54.1731mm
No. 2	2.0655 - 2.0665 in.	52.4637 - 52.4891mm
No. 3	2.0505 - 2.0515 in.	52.0827 - 52.1081mm
No. 4	2.0355 - 2.0365 in.	51.7017 - 51.7271mm
No. 5	2.0205 - 2.0215 in.	51.3207 - 51.3461mm
352/360/390/460/ All	2.1238 - 2.1248 in.	53.9445 - 54.9699mm
Camshaft Lobe Lift		
255		
Intake	0.2375 in.	6.0325mm
Exhaust	0.2375 in.	6.0325mm
289/302		
1966-77		
Intake	0.2303 in.	5.8496mm
Exhaust	0.2375 in.	6.0325mm
1978 and later		
Intake	0.2375 in.	6.0325mm
Exhaust	0.2474 in.	6.2840mm
351W		
1976-77		
Intake	0.2303 in.	5.8496mm
Exhaust	0.2375 in.	6.0325mm
1978 and later		
Intake	0.2600 in.	6.6040mm
Exhaust	0.2600 in.	6.6040mm
351M		
Intake	0.2350 in.	5.9690mm
Exhaust	0.2350 in.	5.9690mm
352		
Intake	0.2320 in.	5.8928mm
Exhaust	0.2320 in.	5.8928mm

Engine Mechanical Specifications

COMPONENT	U.S.	METRIC
360/390		
Intake	0.2470 in.	6.2738mm
Exhaust	0.2490 in.	6.3246mm
400		
Intake	0.2472 in.	6.2788mm
Exhaust	0.2500 in.	6.3500mm
460		
1976-79		
Intake	0.2530 in.	6.4262mm
Exhaust	0.2780 in.	7.0612mm
1980 and later		
Intake	0.2520 in.	6.4008mm
Exhaust	0.2780 in.	7.0612mm
Connecting Rod Bearing Bore ID		
255/289/302	2.2390 - 2.2398 in.	56.8706 - 56.8909mm
351W		
1976-77	2.2390 - 2.2398 in.	56.8706 - 56.8909mm
1978 and later	2.4265 - 2.4273 in.	61.6331 - 61.6534mm
351M/400	2.4361 - 2.4369 in.	61.8769 - 61.8973mm
352		
Coded Red	2.5907 - 2.5911 in.	65.8038 - 65.8139mm
Coded Blue	2.5911 - 2.5915 in.	65.8139 - 65.8241mm
360/390	2.5907 - 2.5915 in.	65.8038 - 65.8241mm
460	2.6522 - 2.6530 in.	67.3659 - 67.3862mm
Connecting Rod Bend (max.)		
All, except 352	0.0120 in.	0.0406mm
352	0.0040 in.	0.1016mm
Connecting Rod Lower End Bearing Clearance		
All, except 352	0.0008 - 0.0015 in.	0.0020 - 0.0381mm
352	0.0007 - 0.0028 in.	0.0178 - 0.0711mm
Connecting Rod-to-Crankshaft Side Clearance		
255/289/302/351W/351M/400/460	0.0100 - 0.0200 in	0.2540 - 0.5080mm
352	0.0060 - 0.0160 in	0.1524 - 0.4064mm
360/390	0.0080 - 0.0250 in	0.2032 - 0.6350mm
Connecting Rod Journal Diameter		
255/289/302	2.1228 - 2.1236 in.	53.9191 - 53.9394mm
351W/351M/400	2.3103 - 2.3111 in.	58.6816 - 58.7019mm
352		
Coded Red	2.4384 - 2.4388 in.	61.9354 - 61.9455mm
Coded Blue	2.4380 - 2.4384 in.	61.9252 - 61.9455mm
360/390	2.4380 - 2.4388 in.	61.9252 - 61.9455mm
460	2.4992 - 2.5000 in.	63.4797 - 63.5000mm

87935c03

Engine Mechanical Specifications

COMPONENT	U.S.	METRIC
Connecting Rod Journal Taper (max.)		
All, except 352	0.0006 in.	0.0152mm
352	0.0003 in.	0.0076mm
Connecting Rod Length (center-to-center)		
289	5.1535 - 5.1565 in.	130.8989 - 130.9751mm
255/302	5.0885 - 5.0915 in.	129.2479 - 129.3241mm
351W	5.9545 - 5.9575 in.	151.2443 - 151.3205mm
351M/400	6.5785 - 6.5815 in.	167.0939 - 167.1701mm
352/360	6.5380 - 6.5420 in.	166.0652 - 166.1668mm
390	6.4860 - 6.4900 in.	164.7444 - 164.8460mm
460	6.6035 - 6.6065 in.	167.7289 - 167.8051mm
Connecting Rod Piston Pin Bore ID		
255	0.9096 - 0.9112 in.	23.1038 - 23.1445mm
289/302/351W		
1966-77	0.9104 - 0.9112 in.	23.1242 - 23.1445mm
1978 and later	0.9096 - 0.9112 in.	23.1038 - 23.1445mm
351M/400	0.9726 - 0.9742 in.	24.7040 - 24.7447mm
352/360/390	0.9752 - 0.9755 in.	24.7701 - 24.7777mm
460	1.0386 - 1.0393 in.	26.3804 - 26.3982mm
Connecting Rod Twist (max.)		
All, except 352	0.0240 in.	0.6096mm
352	0.0120 in.	0.3048mm
Crankshaft End-play		
All, except 352	0.0040 - 0.0080 in.	0.1016 - 0.2032mm
352	0.0040 - 0.0100 in.	0.1016 - 0.2540mm
Crankshaft Thrust Bearing Journal Length		
255/289/302/351W/400	1.1370 - 1.1390 in.	28.8798 - 28.9306mm
352/360/390/460	1.1240 - 1.1260 in.	28.5496 - 28.6004mm
Cylinder Block Head Gasket Surface Flatness (in any 6 inch/152mm span)		
All	0.0030 in.	0.0762mm
Cylinder Bore Diameter		
255	3.6800 - 3.6835 in.	93.4720 - 93.5609mm
289/302	4.0004 - 4.0052 in.	101.6102 - 101.7321mm
351W/351M/400	4.0000 - 4.0048 in.	101.6000 - 101.7219mm
352	4.0000 - 4.0024 in.	101.6000 - 101.6610mm
360/390	4.0500 - 4.0536 in.	102.8700 - 102.9614mm
460	4.3600 - 4.3636 in.	110.7440 - 101.6381mm
Cylinder Bore Maximum Taper		
All	0.0010 in.	0.0254mm
Cylinder Bore Out-of-Round (max.)		
All, except 352	0.0015 in.	0.0381mm
352	0.0010 in.	0.0254mm
Cylinder Head Gasket Surface Flatness (in any 6 inch/152m		
All	0.0030 in.	0.0762mm

87935c04

Engine Mechanical Specifications

COMPONENT	U.S.	METRIC
Flywheel Ring Gear Lateral Runout		
255/289/302/351W/351M/400/460		
Automatic Transmission	0.0600 in.	1.5240mm
Manual Transmission	0.0300 in.	0.7620mm
352 All	0.0200 in.	0.5080mm
360/390		
Automatic Transmission	0.0750 in.	1.9050mm
Manual Transmission	0.0400 in.	1.0160mm
Flywheel Clutch Face Runout		
All	0.0100 in.	0.2540mm
Lifter-to-Bore Clearance		
All, except 352	0.0007 - 0.0027 in.	0.0178 - 0.0686mm
352	0.0005 - 0.0020 in.	0.0127 - 0.0508mm
Lifter Bore Diameter		
All, except 352	0.8752 - 0.8767 in.	22.2301 - 22.2682mm
352	0.8745 - 0.8765 in.	22.2123 - 22.2631mm
Lifter Collapsed Gap		
255	0.0980 - 0.1980 in.	2.4892 - 5.0292mm
289/302		
1966-77	0.0900 - 0.1900 in.	2.2860 - 4.8260mm
1978 and later	0.0960 - 0.1650 in.	2.4384 - 4.1910mm
351W		
1976-77	0.1060 - 0.2060 in.	2.6924 - 5.2324mm
1978 and later	0.1230 - 0.1730 in.	3.1242 - 4.3942mm
351M/400/460	0.0750 - 0.1750 in.	1.9050 - 4.4450mm
352	0.0500 - 0.1500 in.	1.2700 - 3.8100mm
360/390	0.0800 - 0.1800 in.	2.3020 - 4.5720mm
Lifter Diameter		
All	0.8740 - 0.8745 in.	22.1996 - 22.2123mm
Lifter Leakdown Rate (seconds @ inch/mm)		
All, except 352	5-50 @ 0.0625/1.586	
352	10-15 @ 0.0625/1.586	
Main Bearing Bore Diameter		
255		
No. 1	2.2483 - 2.2505 in	57.1068 - 57.1627mm
Nos. 2, 3, 4, 5	2.2487 - 2.2505 in	57.1170 - 57.1627mm
289	2.4412 - 2.4420 in.	62.0065 - 62.0268mm
302		
1969-71	2.4412 - 2.4420 in.	62.0065 - 62.0268mm
1972-77 All	2.2490 - 2.2505 in	57.1246 - 57.1627mm
1978 and later		
No. 1	2.2483 - 2.2505 in	57.1068 - 57.1627mm
Nos. 2, 3, 4, 5	2.2487 - 2.2505 in	57.1170 - 57.1627mm
351W/351M/400	3.0002 - 3.0017 in.	76.2051 - 76.2432mm

87935c05

Engine Mechanical Specifications

COMPONENT	U.S.	METRIC
352		
Code Red	2.9412 - 2.9416 in.	74.7065 - 74.7166mm
Code Blue	2.9416 - 2.9420 in.	74.7166 - 74.7268mm
360/390	2.7489 - 2.7507 in.	69.8221 - 69.8678mm
460		
1976-77		
No. 1	3.0002 - 3.0017 in.	76.2051 - 76.2432mm
Nos. 2, 3, 4, 5	3.0002 - 3.0028 in.	76.2051 - 76.2711mm
1978 and later	3.0002 - 3.0017 in.	76.2051 - 76.2432mm
Main Bearing Clearance		
255		
No. 1	0.0001 - 0.0015 in.	0.0025 - 0.0381mm
Nos. 2, 3, 4, 5	0.0005 - 0.0015 in.	0.0127 - 0.0381mm
289/302		
1966-71	0.0005 - 0.0015 in.	0.0127 - 0.0381mm
1972-77 All	0.0008 - 0.0015 in.	0.0127 - 0.0381mm
1978 and later	0.0021 - 0.0033 in.	0.0540 - 0.0840mm
No. 1	0.0001 - 0.0015 in.	0.0025 - 0.0381mm
Nos. 2, 3, 4, 5	0.0005 - 0.0015 in.	0.0127 - 0.0381mm
351W/351M/400	0.0008 - 0.0015 in.	0.0127 - 0.0381mm
352		
Nos. 1 & 3	0.0007 - 0.0031 in.	0.0178 - 0.0787mm
Nos. 2, 4, 5	0.0005 - 0.0028 in.	0.0127 - 0.0381mm
360/390	0.0005 - 0.0015 in.	0.0127 - 0.0381mm
460		
1976-77		
No. 1	0.0008 - 0.0015 in.	0.0127 - 0.0381mm
Nos. 2, 3, 4, 5	0.0008 - 0.0026 in.	0.0127 - 0.0660mm
Main Bearing Journal Diameter		
255/289/302	2.2482 - 2.2490 in.	57.1043 - 57.1246mm
351W/351M/400/460	2.9994 - 3.0002 in.	76.1848 - 76.2051mm
352		
Code Red	2.7488 - 2.7492 in.	69.8195 - 69.8297mm
Code Blue	2.7484 - 2.7488 in.	69.8094 - 69-8195mm
360/390	2.7484 - 2.7492 in.	69.8094 - 69.8297mm
Main Bearing Journal Runout (max.)		
All	0.0020 in.	0.0508mm
Main Bearing Journal Taper (max.)		
255/351W/351M/360/390/400	0.0005 in.	0.0127mm
302/460	0.0006 in.	0.0152mm
289/352	0.0003 in.	0.0076mm
Main Bearing Thrust Face Runout		
All	0.0010 in.	0.0254mm

Engine Mechanical Specifications

COMPONENT	U.S.	METRIC
Oil Pump Driveshaft-to-Housing Clearance		
All	0.0015 - 0.0029 in.	0.0381 - 0.0737mm
Oil Pump Gear Backlash		
All	0	
Oil Pump Outer Race-to-Housing Clearance		
All, except 352	0.0010 - 0.0130 in.	0.0254 - 0.3302mm
352	0.0060 - 0.0120 in.	0.1524 - 0.3048mm
Oil Pump Relief Valve-to-Housing Clearance		
All	0.0015 - 0.0029 in.	0.0381 - 0.0737mm
Oil Pump Relief Valve Spring Pressure		
289/302		
1966-71	11.2 - 11.8 lbs. @ 1.70 in.	5.1 - 5.4kg @ 43.2mm
255/302		
1972 and later	10.6 - 12.2 lbs. @ 1.70 in.	4.8 - 5.5kg @ 43.2mm
351W	18.2 - 20.2 lbs. @ 2.49 in.	8.3 - 9.2kg @ 63.2mm
351M/400/460	20.6 - 22.6 lbs. @ 2.49 in.	9.3 - 10.25kg @ 63.2mm
352	9.0 - 9.6 lbs. @ 1.53 in.	4.0 - 4.4kg @ 38.9mm
360/390	8.7 - 9.5 lbs. @ 1.56 in.	3.9 - 4.3kg @ 39.6mm
Oil Pump Rotor End Clearance		
All	0.0010 - 0.0040 in.	0.0254 - 0.1016mm
Piston Diameter (centerline)		
255		
Code Red	3.6784 - 3.6790 in.	93.4314 - 93.4466mm
Code Blue	3.6798 - 3.6804 in.	93.4669 - 93.4823mm
0.003 OS	3.6812 - 3.6818 in.	93.5025 - 93.5177mm
289/302		
Code Red	3.9984 - 3.9990 in.	101.5594 - 101.5746mm
Code Blue	3.9996 - 4.0002 in.	101.5898 - 101.6051mm
0.003 OS	4.0008 - 4.0014 in.	101.6203 - 101.6356mm
Code Yellow	4.0020 - 4.0026 in.	101.6508 - 101.6660mm
351W		
Code Red	3.9978 - 3.9984 in.	101.5441 - 101.5594mm
Code Blue	3.9990 - 3.9996 in.	101.5746 - 101.5898mm
0.003 OS	4.0002 - 4.0008 in.	101.6051 - 101.6203mm
Code Yellow	4.0020 - 4.0026 in.	101:6508 - 101.6660mm
351M/352/400		
Code Red	3.9982 - 3.9988 in.	101.5543 - 101.5695mm
Code Blue	3.9994 - 4.0000 in.	101.5848 - 101.6000mm
0.003 OS	4.0006 - 4.0012 in.	101.6152 - 101.6305mm
360/390		
Code Red	4.0484 - 4.0490 in.	102.8294 - 102.8446mm
Code Blue	4.0496 - 4.0502 in.	102.8598 - 102.8751mm
0.003 OS	4.0508 - 4.0514 in.	102.8903 - 102.9056mm

Engine Mechanical Specifications

COMPONENT	U.S.	METRIC
460		
Code Red	4.3585 - 4.3591 in.	110.7059 - 110.7211mm
Code Blue	4.3597 - 4.3603 in.	110.7364 - 110.7516mm
0.003 OS	4.3609 - 4.3615 in.	110.7669 - 110.7821mm
Piston-to-Bore Clearance		
255/289/302/351W	0.0018 - 0.0026 in.	0.0457 - 0.0660mm
351M/400	0.0014 - 0.0022 in.	0.0356 - 0.0559mm
352/360/390	0.0015 - 0.0023 in.	0.0381 - 0.0584mm
460	0.0022 - 0.0030 in.	0.0559 - 0.0762mm
Piston Pin Bore Diameter in Piston		
255/289/302	0.9122 - 0.9126 in.	23.1724 - 23.1800mm
351W	0.9124 - 0.9127 in.	23.1750 - 23.1826mm
351M/352/400	0.9754 - 0.9757 in.	24.7752 - 24.7828mm
360/390	0.9752 - 0.9755 in.	24.7701 - 24.7777mm
460	1.0402 - 1.0405 in.	26.4211 - 26.4287mm
Piston Pin Diameter		
255/289/302/351W	0.9120 - 0.9123 in.	23.1648 - 23.1724mm
351M/400	0.9745 - 0.9754 in.	24.7523 - 24.7752mm
352/360/390	0.9749 - 0.9754 in.	24.7627 - 24.7752mm
460	1.0410 - 1.0413 in.	26.4109 - 26.4236mm
5.0L	0.9270 - 0.9273 in.	23.5458 - 23.5534mm
Piston Pin Length		
255/289/302/351W	3.0100 - 3.0400 in.	76.4540 - 77.2160mm
351M/352/360/390/400	3.1500 - 3.1700 in.	80.0100 - 80.5180mm
460	3.2900 - 3.3200 in.	83.5660 - 84.3280mm
Piston Pin-to-Piston Bore Clearance		
255/289/302	0.0002 - 0.0004 in.	0.0051 - 0.0102mm
351W/351M/400	0.0003 - 0.0005 in.	0.0076 - 0.0127mm
352/360/390	0.0001 - 0.0003 in.	0.0025 - 0.0076mm
460	0.0002 - 0.0004 in.	0.0051 - 0.0102mm
Piston Pin-to-Rod Clearance		
255/289/302/351W/351M/400/460	Press Fit	
352	0.0001 - 0.0005 in.	0.0025 - 0.0127mm
360/390	0.0002 - 0.0005 in.	0.0051 - 0.0127mm
Piston Ring End Gap		
255		
Top	0.0100 - 0.0200 in.	0.2540 - 0.5080mm
Middle	0.0100 - 0.0200 in.	0.2540 - 0.5080mm
Oil	0.0100 - 0.0350 in.	0.2540 - 0.8890mm
289/302		
1966-71		
Top	0.0100 - 0.0200 in.	0.2540 - 0.5080mm
Middle	0.0100 - 0.0200 in.	0.2540 - 0.5080mm
Oil	0.0150 - 0.0690 in.	0.3810 - 1.7526mm

Engine Mechanical Specifications

COMPONENT	U.S.	METRIC
302/351W		
1972 and later		
Top	0.0100 - 0.0200 in.	0.2540 - 0.5080mm
Middle	0.0100 - 0.0200 in.	0.2540 - 0.5080mm
Oil	0.0100 - 0.0550 in.	0.2540 - 1.3970mm
351M/400		
Top	0.0100 - 0.0200 in.	0.2540 - 0.5080mm
Middle	0.0100 - 0.0200 in.	0.2540 - 0.5080mm
Oil	0.0150 - 0.0550 in.	0.3810 - 1.3970mm
352		
Top	0.0100 - 0.0200 in.	0.2540 - 0.5080mm
Middle	0.0100 - 0.0200 in.	0.2540 - 0.5080mm
Oil	0.0150 - 0.0660 in.	0.3810 - 1.6764mm
360/390		
Top	0.0150 - 0.0230 in.	0.3810 - 0.5842mm
Middle	0.0100 - 0.0200 in.	0.2540 - 0.5080mm
Oil	0.0150 - 0.0550 in.	0.3810 - 1.3970mm
460		
Top	0.0100 - 0.0200 in.	0.2540 - 0.5080mm
Middle	0.0100 - 0.0200 in.	0.2540 - 0.5080mm
Oil		
1976-77	0.0150 - 0.0550 in.	0.3810 - 1.3970mm
1978	0.0100 - 0.0300 in.	0.2540 - 0.7620mm
1979 and later	0.0100 - 0.0350 in.	0.2540 - 0.8890mm
Piston Ring Grove Width		
255/289/302/351W/351M		
Top	0.0800 - 0.0810 in	2.0320 - 2.0574mm
Middle	0.0800 - 0.0810 in	2.0320 - 2.0574mm
Oil	0.1880 - 0.1890 in	4.7752 - 4.8006mm
360/390		
Top	0.0800 - 0.0810 in.	2.0320 - 2.0574mm
Middle	0.0960 - 0.0970 in.	2.4384 - 2.4638mm
Oil	0.1880 - 0.1890 in.	4.7752 - 4.8006mm
460		
Top	0.0805 - 0.0815 in.	2.0447 - 2.0701mm
Middle	0.0805 - 0.0815 in.	2.0447 - 2.0701mm
Oil	0.1880 - 0.1890 in.	4.7752 - 4.8006mm
Piston Ring Side Clearance		
255		
Top	0.0019 - 0.0036 in.	0.0483 - 0.0914mm
Middle	0.0020 - 0.0040 in.	0.0508 - 0.1016mm
Oil	Snug	

87935c09

Engine Mechanical Specifications

COMPONENT	U.S.	METRIC
289/302/351W		
Top		
1966-71	0.0019 - 0.0036 in.	0.0483 - 0.0914mm
1972-77	0.0020 - 0.0040 in.	0.0508 - 0.1016mm
1978 and later	0.0019 - 0.0036 in.	0.0483 - 0.0914mm
Middle	0.0020 - 0.0040 in.	0.0508 - 0.1016mm
Oil	Snug	
351M/400		
Top	0.0019 - 0.0036 in.	0.0483 - 0.0914mm
Middle	0.0020 - 0.0040 in.	0.0508 - 0.1016mm
Oil	Snug	
352		
Top	0.0024 - 0.0041 in.	0.0610 - 0.1041mm
Middle	0.0020 - 0.0040 in.	0.0508 - 0.1016mm
Oil	Snug	
360/390/460		
Top	0.0020 - 0.0040 in.	0.0508 - 0.1016mm
Middle	0.0020 - 0.0040 in.	0.0508 - 0.1016mm
Oil	Snug	
Piston Ring Width		
All		
Top	0.0770 - 0.0780 in.	1.9885 - 1.9812mm
2nd	0.0770 - 0.0780 in.	1.9885 - 1.9812mm
Pushrod Runout (max.)		
255/289/302/351W/351M/400/460	0.0150 in.	0.3810mm
352	0.0250 in.	0.6350mm
360/390	0.0200 in.	0.5080mm
Rocker Arm Bore Diameter		
352	0.8340 - 0.8440 in.	21.1836 - 21.4376mm
360/390	0.8425 - 0.8440 in.	21.3995 - 21.4376mm
Rocker Arm Lift Ratio		
255/289/302/351W	1.61:1	
351M/360/390/400/460	1.73:1	
Rocker Arm-to-Shaft Clearance		
352	0.0035 - 0.0055 in.	0.0889 - 0.1397mm
360/390	0.0020 - 0.0050 in.	0.0508 - 0.1270mm
Rocker Shaft OD		
352	0.8385 - 0.8395 in.	21.2979 - 21.3233mm
360/390	0.8390 - 0.8400 in.	21.3106 - 21.3360mm
Timing Chain Deflection (max.)		
All	0.5000 in.	12.7000mm
Timing Sprockets (gears) Assembled Face Runout (max.)		
All, except 352	0.0500 in.	0.1270mm
352	0.0060 in.	0.1524mm

Engine Mechanical Specifications

COMPONENT	U.S.	METRIC
Valve Face Angle		
All	44 Degrees	
Valve Face Minimum Margin		
All	0.0625 in.	1.5875mm
Valve Face Runout (max.)		
All	0.0020 in.	0.0508mm
Valve Guide Bore		
255/289/302/351W/351M/400/460	0.3433 - 0.3443 in.	8.7198 - 8.7452mm
352	0.3735 - 0.3827 in.	9.4869 - 9.7206mm
360/390	0.3728 - 0.3738 in.	9.4691 - 9.4945mm
Valve Head Diameter		
255		
Intake	1.6900 - 1.6940 in.	42.9260 - 43.0276mm
Exhaust	1.4390 - 1.4630 in.	36.5506 - 37.1602mm
289/302		
1966-71		
Intake	1.7730 - 1.7830 in.	45.0342 - 45.2882mm
Exhaust	1.4420 - 1.4570 in.	36.6268 - 37.0078mm
1972-77		
Intake	1.7730 - 1.7910 in.	45.0342 - 45.4914mm
Exhaust	1.4530 - 1.4680 in.	36.9062 - 37.2872mm
1978-80		
Intake	1.7700 - 1.7940 in.	44.9580 - 45.5676mm
Exhaust	1.4390 - 1.4630 in.	36.5506 - 37.1602mm
1981 and later		
Intake	1.6900 - 1.6940 in.	42.9260 - 43.0276mm
Exhaust	1.4390 - 1.4630 in.	36.9062 - 37.1602mm
351W		
1976-77		
Intake	1.7730 - 1.7910 in.	45.0342 - 45.4914mm
Exhaust	1.4530 - 1.4680 in.	36.9062 - 37.2872mm
1978 and later		
Intake	1.7700 - 1.7940 in.	44.9580 - 45.5676mm
Exhaust	1.4390 - 1.4630 in.	36.5506 - 37.1602mm
351M/400		
Intake	2.0320 - 2.0500 in.	51.6128 - 52.0700mm
Exhaust	1.6495 - 1.6595 in.	41.8973 - 42.1513mm
352/360/390		
Intake	2.0220 - 2.0370 in.	51.3588 - 51.7398mm
Exhaust	1.5510 - 1.5665 in.	39.3954 - 39.7764mm
460		
Intake	2.0750 - 2.0900 in.	52.7050 - 53.0860mm
Exhaust	1.6460 - 1.6610 in.	41.8084 - 42.1894mm

87935c11

Engine Mechanical Specifications

COMPONENT	U.S.	METRIC
Valve Seat Angle		
All	45 Degrees	
Valve Seat Runout (max.)		
255/351W/351M/352/400	0.0020 in.	0.0500mm
289/302/360/390/460	0.0015 in.	0.0381mm
Valve Seat Width		
255/289/302/351W/460		
Intake	0.0600 - 0.0800 in.	1.5240 - 2.0320mm
Exhaust	0.0600 - 0.0800 in.	1.5240 - 2.0320mm
351M/352/360/390/400		
Intake	0.0600 - 0.0800 in.	1.5240 - 2.0320mm
Exhaust	0.0700 - 0.0900 in.	1.7780 - 2.2860mm
Valve Spring Compression Pressure		
255		
Intake	190-212 lbs. @ 1.360 in.	86-96 kg @ 34.5mm
Exhaust	190-212 lbs. @ 1.360 in.	86-96 kg @ 34.5mm
289/302		
1976-77		
Intake	171-189 lbs. @ 1.660 in.	78-86 kg @ 42.2mm
Exhaust	171-189 lbs. @ 1.660 in.	78-86 kg @ 42.2mm
302		
1972-78		
Intake	190-210 lbs. @ 1.310 in.	86-95 kg @ 33.3mm
Exhaust	190-210 lbs. @ 1.340 in.	86-95 kg @ 34.0mm
1979		
Intake	192-212 lbs. @ 1.360 in.	87-96 kg @ 34.5mm
Exhaust	190-210 lbs. @ 1.200 in.	86-95 kg @ 30.0mm
1980 and later		
Intake	196-212 lbs. @ 1.360 in.	86-96 kg @ 34.5mm
Exhaust	190-210 lbs. @ 1.200 in.	86-95 kg @ 30.5mm
351W		
1976-77		
Intake	190-210 lbs. @ 1.310 in.	86-95 kg @ 33.3mm
Exhaust	190-210 lbs. @ 1.340 in.	86-95 kg @ 34.0mm
1978		
Intake	190-210 lbs. @ 1.340 in.	86-95 kg @ 34.0mm
Exhaust	190-210 lbs. @ 1.200 in.	86-95 kg @ 30.5mm
1979-83		
Intake	190-210 lbs. @ 1.360 in.	86-95 kg @ 34.5mm
Exhaust	190-210 lbs. @ 1.200 in.	86-95 kg @ 30.5mm
1984 and later		
Intake	190-210 lbs. @ 1.200 in.	86-95 kg @ 30.5mm
Exhaust	190-210 lbs. @ 1.200 in.	86-95 kg @ 30.5mm

87935c12

Engine Mechanical Specifications

COMPONENT	U.S.	METRIC
351M/400		
Intake	215-237 lbs. @ 1.390 in.	98-108 kg @ 35.3mm
Exhaust	215-237 lbs. @ 1.250 in.	98-108 kg @ 31.8mm
352		
Intake & Exhaust	175-194 lbs. @ 1.240 in.	79-88 kg @ 31.5.mm
360/390		
F-100 Exhaust	175-194 lbs. @ 1.240 in.	79-88 kg @ 31.5.mm
All others, Intake & Exhaust	209-231 lbs. @ 1.318 in.	95-105 kg @ 33.5mm
460		
1976-77		
Intake	240-265 lbs. @ 1.33 in.	109-120 kg @ 33.8mm
Exhaust	240-265 lbs. @ 1.33 in.	109-120 kg @ 33.8mm
1978 and later		
Intake	218-240 lbs. @ 1.33 in.	99-109 kg @ 33.8mm
Exhaust	218-240 lbs. @ 1.33 in.	99-109 kg @ 33.8mm

Valve Spring Free Length (approx.)

	U.S.	METRIC
255		
Intake	2.0400 in.	51.8160mm
Exhaust	1.8500 in.	46.9900mm
289/302		
1966-71 Intake & Exhaust	1.9700 in.	50.0380mm
302		
1972-77		
Intake	1.9400 in.	49.2760mm
Exhaust	1.8500 in.	46.9900mm
1978		
Intake	1.9400 in.	49.2760mm
Exhaust	1.8700 in.	47.4980mm
1979 and later		
Intake	2.0400 in.	51.8160mm
Exhaust	1.8500 in.	46.9900mm
351W		
1976-77		
Intake	2.0600 in.	52.3240mm
Exhaust	2.1200 in.	53.8480mm
1978		
Intake	2.0600 in.	52.3240mm
Exhaust	1.8700 in.	47.4980mm
1979 and later		
Intake	2.0400 in.	51.8160mm
Exhaust	1.8500 in.	46.9900mm
351M/400		
Intake	2.0600 in.	52.3240mm
Exhaust	2.0600 in.	52.3240mm

Engine Mechanical Specifications

COMPONENT	U.S.	METRIC
352 Intake & Exhaust	2.2600 in.	57.4040mm
360/390		
F-100 Exhaust	2.0000 in.	50.8000mm
All others, Intake & Exhaust	2.1200 in.	53.8480mm
460		
1966-71 Intake & Exhaust	2.0300 in.	51.5620mm
1978 Intake & Exhaust	2.0680 in.	52.5272mm
1979 and later Intake & Exhaust	2.0600 in.	52.3240mm
Valve Spring Installed Height (3)		
255		
Intake	1.6719 - 1.7031 in.	42.4656 - 43.2594mm
Exhaust	1.5781 - 1.6094 in.	40.0844 - 40.8781mm
289/302		
1966-71	1.6250 - 1.6875 in.	41.2750 - 42.8625mm
302		
1972-78		
Intake	1.6719 - 1.7031 in.	42.4656 - 43.2594mm
Exhaust	1.5938 - 1.6094 in.	40.4813 - 40.8781mm
1979 and later		
Intake	1.6719 - 1.7031 in.	42.4656 - 43.2594mm
Exhaust	1.5781 - 1.6094 in.	40.0844 - 40.8781mm
351W		
1976-78		
Intake	1.7656 - 1.8125 in.	44.8469 - 46.0375mm
Exhaust	1.8125 - 1.8438 in.	46.0375 - 46.8313mm
1979 and later		
Intake	1.7656 - 1.7969 in.	44.8469 - 45.6406mm
Exhaust	1.5781 - 1.6094 in.	40.0844 - 40.8781mm
351M/352/400 Intake & Exhaust	1.8125 - 1.8438 in.	46.0375 - 46.8313mm
360/390		
F-100 Exhaust	1.6563 - 1.6875 in.	42.0688 - 42.8625mm
All others, Intake & Exhaust	1.8125 - 1.8438 in.	46.0375 - 46.8313mm
460 Intake & Exhaust	1.7989 - 1.8283 in.	45.6406 - 46.4344mm
Valve Spring Out-of-Square (max.)		
All, except 352	0.0783 in.	1.9844mm
352	0.0720 in.	1.8288mm
Valve Stem Diameter		
255/289/302/351W/351M/400		
1966-71 Intake & Exhaust	0.3416 - 0.3423 in.	8.6766 - 8.6944mm
1972 and later		
Intake	0.3416 - 0.3423 in.	8.6766 - 8.6944mm
Exhaust	0.3411 - 0.3418 in.	8.6639 - 8.6817mm

87935c14

Engine Mechanical Specifications

COMPONENT	U.S.	METRIC
360/390		
Intake	0.3711 - 0.3718 in.	9.4259 - 9.4437mm
Exhaust	0.3703 - 0.3706 in.	9.4056 - 9.4132mm
352		
Intake	0.3711 - 0.3718 in.	9.4259 - 9.4437mm
Exhaust	0.3701 - 0.3708 in.	9.4005 - 9.4183mm
460 Intake & Exhaust	0.3416 - 0.3423 in.	8.6766 - 8.6944mm
Valve Stem-to-Guide Clearance		
255/289/351M/360/390/400		
1966-71 Intake & Exhaust	0.0010 - 0.0027 in.	0.0254 - 0.0686mm
1972 and later		
Intake	0.0010 - 0.0027 in.	0.0254 - 0.0686mm
Exhaust	0.0015 - 0.0032 in.	0.0381 - 0.0813mm
302/351W		
Intake	0.0010 - 0.0027 in.	0.0254 - 0.0686mm
Exhaust		
1976-77	0.0010 - 0.0027 in.	0.0254 - 0.0686mm
1978 and later	0.0015 - 0.0032 in.	0.0381 - 0.0813mm
352		
Intake	0.0010 - 0.0024 in.	0.0254 - 0.0610mm
Exhaust	0.0020 - 0.0034 in.	0.0508 - 0.0864mm
460 Intake & Exhaust	0.0010 - 0.0027 in.	0.0254 - 0.0686mm

1 Distance from the front face of the block to the front edge of the bearing
2 per inch
3 Pad to retainer

87935c15

TORQUE SPECIFICATIONS

COMPONENT	U.S.	METRIC
Alternator Adjusting Bolt		
All	24 - 40 ft. lbs.	33 - 54 Nm
Alternator Pivot Bolt		
All	45 - 57 ft. lbs.	61 - 76 Nm
Camshaft Sprocket-to-Camshaft		
255/289/302/351W/351M/352/400/460	40 - 45 ft. lbs.	54 - 61 Nm
360/390	45 - 57 ft. lbs.	61 - 76 Nm
Camshaft Thrust Plate Bolts		
255/351W/351M/360/390/400/460	9 - 12 ft. lbs.	13 - 17 Nm
289	72 - 108 inch lbs.	8 - 12 Nm
302		
1968-70	72 - 108 inch lbs.	8 - 12 Nm
1971 and later	9 - 12 ft. lbs.	13 - 17 Nm
352	12 - 15 ft. lbs.	16 - 20 Nm
Carburetor Mounting Nuts		
All	12 - 15 ft. lbs.	17 - 20 Nm
Connecting Rod Nuts		
255/289/302	19 - 24 ft. lbs	26 - 33 Nm
351W		
1976-77	19 - 24 ft. lbs	26 - 33 Nm
1978 and later	40 - 45 ft. lbs.	54 - 61 Nm
351M/352/400	40 - 45 ft. lbs.	54 - 61 Nm
360/390	40 - 45 ft. lbs.	54 - 61 Nm
460		
1976-82	40 - 45 ft. lbs.	54 - 61 Nm
1983 and later	45 - 50 ft. lbs.	61 - 67 Nm
Crankshaft Pulley-to-Damper		
All	35 - 50 ft. lbs.	48 - 68 Nm
Cylinder Head Bolts		
255		
Step 1	55 - 65 ft. lbs.	75 - 88 Nm
Step 2	65 - 72 ft. lbs.	88 - 97 Nm
289/302		
1967-77		
Step 1	50 ft. lbs.	67 Nm
Step 2	60 ft. lbs.	82 Nm
Step 3	65 - 70 ft. lbs.	88 - 95 Nm
1978 and later		
Step 1	55 - 65 ft. lbs.	75 - 88 Nm
Step 2	65 - 72 ft. lbs.	88 - 97Nm

87935c16

TORQUE SPECIFICATIONS

COMPONENT	U.S.	METRIC
351W		
1967-77		
Step 1	50 ft. lbs.	67 Nm
Step 2	60 ft. lbs.	82 Nm
Step 3	65 - 70 ft. lbs.	88 - 95 Nm
1978 and later		
Step 1	85 ft. lbs.	115 Nm
Step 2	95 ft. lbs.	129 Nm
Step 3	105 - 112 ft. lbs.	143 - 151 Nm
351M/400		
Step 1	75 ft. lbs.	102 Nm
Step 2	95 ft. lbs.	129 Nm
Step 3	105 ft. lbs.	143 Nm
352/360/390		
Step 1	70 ft. lbs.	95 Nm
Step 2	80 ft. lbs.	110 Nm
Step 3	90 ft. lbs.	122 Nm
460		
Step 1	80 ft. lbs	110 Nm
Step 2	110 ft. lbs.	149 Nm
Step 3	130 - 140 ft. lbs.	177 - 189 Nm
Damper-to-Crankshaft		
255/289/302/351W/351M/352/400/460	70 - 90 ft. lbs.	94 - 122 Nm
360/390	130 - 150 ft. lbs.	177 - 203 Nm
Distrtibutor Clamp Bolt		
All	22 ft. lbs.	30 Nm
Engine Fan Clutch-to-Water Pump Hub		
All	18 ft. lbs.	24 Nm
Engine Front Cover		
255/289/302/351W/351M/352/360/390/400	12 - 18 ft. lbs.	17 - 24 Nm
460		
1976-77	15 - 20 ft. lbs.	20 - 27 Nm
1978	12 - 18 ft. lbs.	17 - 24 Nm
1979	15 - 20 ft. lbs.	20 - 27 Nm
1980-81		
5/16 in. bolts	12 - 18 ft. lbs.	17 - 24 Nm
7/16 in. bolts	45 - 55 ft. lbs.	61 - 75 Nm
1982 and later	15 - 20 ft. lbs.	20 - 27 Nm
Exhaust Manifold-to-Cylinder Head		
255/351W/351M/400	18 - 24 ft. lbs.	24 - 32 Nm
289	15 - 20 ft. lbs.	20 - 27 Nm
302		
1968-70	12 - 20 ft. lbs	20 - 27 Nm

TORQUE SPECIFICATIONS

COMPONENT	U.S.	METRIC
1971 and later	18 - 24 ft. lbs.	24 - 32 Nm
352/360/390	12 - 18 ft. lbs.	17 - 24 Nm
460	28 - 33 ft. lbs.	38 - 45 Nm
Exhaust Pipe-to-Manifold		
255/302/351W/351M/360/390/400	25 - 30 ft. lbs.	35 - 41 Nm
352/460	25 - 35 ft. lbs.	35 - 48 Nm
Flywheel-to-Crankshaft		
All	75 - 85 ft. lbs.	102 - 115 Nm
Fuel Pump Mounting Bolts		
255/289/302/351W/360/390/460	19 - 27 ft. lbs.	26 - 36 Nm
351M/400		
Nut	14 - 20 ft. lbs.	17 - 26 Nm
Bolt	10 - 15 ft. lbs.	13 - 20 Nm
352	20 - 25 ft. lbs.	26 - 35 Nm
Intake Manifold-to-Cylinder Heads		
255/351W	23 - 25 ft. lbs.	31 - 34 Nm
289	20 - 22 ft. lbs.	26 - 30 Nm
302		
1968-70	20 - 22 ft. lbs.	26 - 30 Nm
1971 and later	23 - 25 ft. lbs.	31 - 34 Nm
351M/400		
3/8 in.	22 - 32 ft. lbs.	30 - 43 Nm
5/16 in.	17 - 25 ft. lbs.	23 - 34 Nm
360/390	40 - 45 ft. lbs.	54 - 61 Nm
352	32 - 35 ft. lbs.	43 - 47 Nm
460		
1976-77	28 - 33 ft. lbs.	38 - 45 Nm
1978 and later	22 - 32 ft. lbs.	30 - 43 Nm
Main Bearing Cap Bolts		
255/289/302	60 - 70 ft. lbs.	82 - 95 Nm
351W		
1976-77	60 - 70 ft. lbs.	82 - 95 Nm
1978 and later	95 - 105 ft. lbs.	129 - 143 Nm
351M/352/360/390/400/460	95 - 105 ft. lbs.	129 - 143 Nm
Oil Filter Adapter-to-Block Cover		
255/289/302/351W/351M/400	20 - 30 ft. lbs.	27 - 41 Nm
360/390	17 - 25 ft. lbs.	23 - 34 Nm
352	12 - 15 ft. lbs.	16 - 20 Nm
460		
1976-79	20 - 30 ft. lbs.	27 - 41 Nm
1980-81	40 - 60 ft. lbs.	54 - 82 Nm
1982 and later	40 - 50 ft. lbs.	54 - 68 Nm

TORQUE SPECIFICATIONS

COMPONENT	U.S.	METRIC
Oil Pan Bolts		
255	9 - 11 ft. lbs.	12 - 15 Nm
302/351W		
1967-80		
1/4 in. bolts	84 - 96 inch lbs.	10 - 12 Nm
5/16 in. bolts	9 - 11 ft. lbs.	11 - 15 Nm
1981 and later	9 - 11 ft. lbs.	12 - 15 Nm
351M/400		
1/4 in. bolts	84 - 96 inch lbs.	10 - 12 Nm
5/16 in. bolts	11 - 13 ft. lbs.	15 - 18 Nm
352	10 - 12 ft. lbs.	14 - 16 Nm
360/390	8 - 10 ft. lbs.	11 - 14 Nm
460		
1/4 in. bolts	84 - 96 inch lbs.	10 - 12 Nm
5/16 in. bolts	9 - 11 ft. lbs.	11 - 15 Nm
Oil Pan Drain Plug		
All	15 - 25 ft. lbs.	20 - 34 Nm
Oil Pickup Tube-to-Pump		
255/289/302/351W	10 - 15 ft. lbs	13 - 20 Nm
352	12 - 15 ft. lbs.	16 - 20 Nm
460		
1976-79	Press Fit	
1980 and later	12 - 18 ft. lbs.	17 - 24 Nm
Oil Pump Cover		
All	10 ft, lbs,	14 Nm
Oil Pump-to-Block		
255/289/302/351W/351M/400/460	22 - 32 ft. lbs.	30 - 43 Nm
352	20 - 25 ft. lbs.	27 - 34 Nm
360/390	17 - 27 ft. lbs.	23 - 37 Nm
Rocker Arm Cover		
255/289/302/351W/351M/400	36 - 60 inch lbs.	4 - 7 Nm
352	10 - 12 ft. lbs.	13 - 16 Nm
360/390	48 - 84 inch lbs	5 - 9 Nm
460	60 - 72 inch lbs.	7 - 8 Nm
Rocker Arm Stud Nut		
255	18 - 25 ft. lbs	24 - 34 Nm
302/351W		
1976-78	17 - 23 ft. lbs	23 - 31 Nm
1979 and later	18 - 25 ft. lbs	24 - 34 Nm
351M/400/460	18 - 25 ft. lbs	24 - 34 Nm
Rocker Shaft Support-to-Head		
352/360/390	40 45 ft. lbs.	54 - 61 Nm

TORQUE SPECIFICATIONS

COMPONENT	U.S.	METRIC
Spark Plugs		
255/302/351W/351M/352/360/390/400	10 - 15 ft. lbs.	13 - 20 Nm
460		
1976-78	10 - 15 ft. lbs.	13 - 20 Nm
1979 and later	5 - 10 ft. lbs.	7 - 14 Nm
Starter Mounting Bolts		
All	15 - 20 ft. lbs.	20 - 26 Nm
Thermostat Housing Bolts		
255	9 - 12 ft. lbs.	12 - 16 Nm
289	12 - 15 ft. lbs.	16 - 20 Nm
302		
1968-79	12 - 15 ft. lbs.	16 - 20 Nm
1980 and later	9 - 12 ft. lbs.	12 - 16 Nm
351W		
1976-79	23 - 28 ft. lbs.	32 - 38 Nm
1980 and later	9 - 12 ft. lbs.	12 - 16 Nm
351M/360/390/400	23 - 28 ft. lbs.	32 - 38 Nm
352	12 - 15 ft. lbs.	16 - 20 Nm
460		
1976-78	23 - 28 ft. lbs.	32 - 38 Nm
1979-81	10 - 15 ft. lbs.	13 - 20 Nm
1982-83	12 - 18 ft. lbs.	17 - 24 Nm
1984 and later	10 - 15 ft. lbs.	13 - 20 Nm
Water Pump Mounting Bolts		
255/289/302/351W/351M/400	12 - 18 ft. lbs.	17 - 24 Nm
352/360/390	20 - 25 ft.lbs.	26 - 35 Nm
460		
1976-78	12 - 18 ft. lbs.	17 - 24 Nm
1979-81	15 - 21 ft. lbs.	20 - 28 Nm
1982-83	12 - 18 ft. lbs.	17 - 24 Nm
1984 and later	15 - 21 ft. lbs.	20 - 28 Nm

87935c20

ENGINE INSTALLATION
1964-85 FORD AND MERCURY MID-
SIZED CARS, INCLUDING 1964-78
MUSTANG AND COUGAR 6-7
1966-86 PICKUPS AND BRONCO 6-2
1968-88 FORD, MERCURY AND
LINCOLN FULL-SIZED CARS 6-5
1971-96 FULL-SIZED VANS 6-4
1979-88 MUSTANG AND CAPRI 6-7
1986-96 THUNDERBIRD AND
COUGAR 6-8
1987-96 PICKUPS AND BRONCO 6-3
1989-93 MUSTANG 6-8
1989-95 FORD, MERCURY AND
LINCOLN FULL-SIZED CARS 6-6
BREAK-IN PROCEDURE 6-9
SPECIFICATIONS CHARTS
1961-71 TRUCK TUNE-UP
SPECIFICATIONS 6-32
1964-71 COMET, COUGAR,
FAIRLANE, FALCON, MAVERICK,
MONTEGO, MUSTANG AND
TORINO TUNE-UP
SPECIFICATIONS 6-19
1964-71 FULL-SIZED FORD,
MERCURY, LINCOLN AND
THUNDERBIRD TUNE-UP
SPECIFICATIONS 6-21
1971-79 TRUCK TUNE-UP
SPECIFICATIONS 6-33
1972-76 THUNDERBIRD TUNE-UP
SPECIFICATIONS 6-31
1972-79 COMET, FAIRMONT,
GRANADA, MAVERICK, MONARCH
AND 1979 MUSTANG AND CAPRI
TUNE-UP SPECIFICATIONS 6-23
1972-79 COUGAR, ELITE, LTD II,
MONTEGO, MUSTANG THROUGH
1973, TORINO AND 19776-79
THUNDERBIRD TUNE-UP
SPECIFICATIONS 6-25
1972-79 FORD FULL-SIZE CAR
TUNE-UP SPECIFICATIONS 6-27
1972-79 MERCURY AND LINCOLN
FULL-SIZE CAR TUNE-UP
SPECIFICATIONS 6-29
1980-86 TUNE-UP SPECIFICATIONS
— ALL CAR AND TRUCK
MODELS 6-34
1987-93 TUNE-UP SPECIFICATIONS
— ALL CAR AND TRUCK
MODELS 6-36
TUNE-UP PROCEDURES
BREAKER POINTS AND
CONDENSER 6-10
DWELL ANGLE 6-13
IDLE SPEED AND MIXTURE
ADJUSTMENTS 6-14
IGNITION TIMING 6-13
SPARK PLUG WIRES 6-10
SPARK PLUGS 6-9

VALVE LASH 6-17

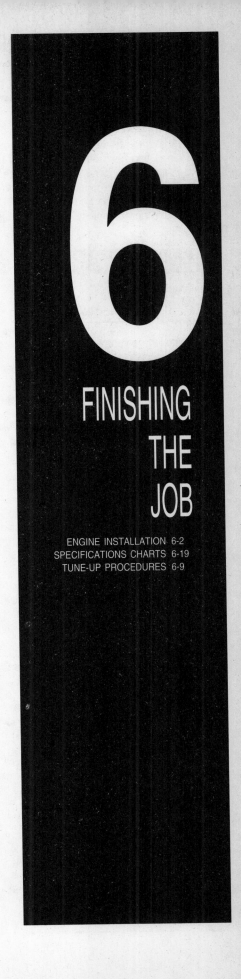

6

FINISHING
THE
JOB

ENGINE INSTALLATION 6-2
SPECIFICATIONS CHARTS 6-19
TUNE-UP PROCEDURES 6-9

ENGINE INSTALLATION

▶ **See Figure 1**

Attach the crane to the engine and remove it from the stand with the mounting head attached. Lower it onto the dolly and remove the mounting head. Roll the engine out of the garage and up to a convenient point in front of the vehicle. Attach the crane and lift the engine from the dolly.

Now, using the appropriate procedure found below, install the engine.

1966-86 Pickups and Bronco

Except 460

1. Lower the engine carefully into the engine compartment and slide it back into the transmission. Make sure that the dowel in the engine block engage the holes in the bellhousing through the rear cover plate. If the engine hangs up after the transmission input shaft enters the clutch disc (manual transmission only), turn the crankshaft with the transmission in gear until the input shaft splines mesh with the clutch disc splines.

2. Install the engine mount nuts and washers. Torque the nuts to 80 ft. lbs.

3. Remove the engine lifting device.

4. Install the lower bellhousing-to-engine attaching bolts. Torque the bolts to 50 ft. lbs.

5. Remove the transmission support jack.

6. On vehicles with automatic transmissions, install the torque converter-to-flywheel attaching bolts. Torque the bolts to 30 ft. lbs.

7. Install the converter inspection plate. Torque the bolts to 60 inch lbs.

8. Install the starter. Torque the mounting bolts to 20 ft. lbs.

9. Connect the starter cable to the starter.

Fig. 1 Lowering the engine onto the dolly

87935295

10. Connect the exhaust pipe to the exhaust manifolds. Tighten the exhaust pipe-to-exhaust manifold nuts to 25-35 ft. lbs.

11. Lower the vehicle.

12. Install the upper bellhousing-to-engine attaching bolts. Torque the bolts to 50 ft. lbs.

13. Connect the wiring harness at the left rocker arm cover.

14. Connect the ground strap to the cylinder block.

15. Connect the air conditioning compressor clutch wire.

16. Connect the heater hoses at the water pump and intake manifold or tee (EFI).

17. Connect the temperature sending unit wire at the sending unit.

18. Connect the accelerator linkage and speed control linkage at the carburetor or throttle body.

19. Connect the automatic transmission kick-down rod and install the return spring, if so equipped.

20. Connect the power brake booster vacuum hose.

21. On EFI models, connect the throttle bracket to the upper intake manifold.

22. Connect the fuel tank-to-pump fuel line at the fuel pump. On 5.0L EFI, connect the chassis fuel line at the fuel rails.

23. Connect the oil pressure sending unit lead to the sending unit.

24. Install the alternator.

25. Connect the refrigerant lines to the compressor.

26. Install the radiator and fan, shroud, fan, spacer, pulley and belt.

27. Connect the upper and lower radiator hoses, and, if so equipped, the automatic transmission oil cooler lines.

28. On carbureted engines, install the air cleaner and intake duct assembly, plus the crankcase ventilation hose. On EFI engines, install the air intake hoses, PCV tube and carbon canister hose.

29. Connect the battery and alternator cables.

30. Fill the cooling system and crankcase.

31. Charge the air conditioning system.

32. Install the hood.

If the torque for a particular fastener was not mentioned above, use the following torque values as a guide:

- $1/4''$-20: 6-9 ft. lbs.
- $5/16''$-18: 12-18 ft. lbs.
- $3/8''$-16: 22-32 ft. lbs.
- $7/16''$-14: 45-57 ft. lbs.
- $1/2''$-13: 55-80 ft. lbs.
- $9/16''$: 85-120 ft. lbs.

➡**All fasteners are assumed to be at least grade 5.**

w/460

1. Lower the engine slowly into the vehicle.

2. Slide the engine rearward to engage it with the transmission and slowly lower it onto the supports.

3. Install the engine support nuts and torque them to 74 ft. lbs.

4. Remove the engine lifting device.

5. Install the converter housing-to-engine block upper and left side attaching bolts. Torque the bolts to 50 ft. lbs.

6. Install the coil and bracket assembly on the intake manifold.

7. Remove the jack from under the transmission.

8. Raise the vehicle.

9. Install the lower converter housing-to-engine attaching bolts. Torque the bolts to 50 ft. lbs.

10. Install the flywheel-to-converter attaching nuts. Torque the nuts to 34 ft. lbs.

11. Install the access cover on the converter housing. Torque the bolts to 60-90 inch lbs.

12. Install the starter.

13. Connect the starter cable.

14. Connect the exhaust pipes at the exhaust manifolds and lower the vehicle.

15. Connect the engine wiring harness at the connector on the fire wall.

16. Connect the primary wire at the coil.

17. Connect the accelerator rod and the transmission kickdown rod.

18. Connect the speed control cable.

19. Connect all vacuum lines at the rear of the intake manifold.

20. Install the transmission fluid filler tube attaching bolt from the right side valve cover and position the tube out of the way.

21. Connect the heater hoses.

22. Connect the ground cable at the right front corner of the engine.

23. Install the alternator and drive belts.

24. Connect the oil pressure sending unit wire at the sending unit.

25. Connect the fuel pump inlet line at the pump and plug the line.

26. Install the power steering pump and belt.

27. Install air conditioning compressor. Connect the refrigerant lines.

28. Install the fan, belts and pulley on the water pump.

29. Position the fan shroud over the fan.

30. Install the radiator.

31. Attach the fan shroud.

32. Install the condenser.

33. Connect the refrigerant lines at the condenser.

34. Charge the air conditioning system.

35. Connect the engine oil cooler lines at the oil filter adapter.

36. Connect the transmission oil cooler lines at the radiator.

37. Connect the upper and lower radiator hoses.

38. Connect the canister hose.

39. Connect the crankcase ventilation hose.

40. Connect the negative battery cable from the block.

41. Fill the cooling system.

42. Install the air cleaner assembly.

43. Install the hood.

If the torque for a particular fastener was not mentioned above, use the following torque values as a guide:

- $1/4''$-20: 6-9 ft. lbs.
- $5/16''$-18: 12-18 ft. lbs.
- $3/8''$-16: 22-32 ft. lbs.
- $7/16''$-14: 45-57 ft. lbs.
- $1/2''$-13: 55-80 ft. lbs.
- $9/16''$: 85-120 ft. lbs.

➡It is assumed that all fasteners are at least grade 5.

1987-96 Pickups and Bronco

8-5.0L, 8-5.8L

1. Lower the engine carefully into the transmission. Make sure that the dowel in the engine block engage the holes in the bellhousing through the rear cover plate. If the engine hangs up after the transmission input shaft enters the clutch disc (manual transmission only), turn the crankshaft with the transmission in gear until the input shaft splines mesh with the clutch disc splines.

2. Install the engine mount nuts and washers. Torque the nuts to 80 ft. lbs.

3. Remove the engine lifting device.

4. Install the lower bellhousing-to-engine attaching bolts. Torque the bolts to 50 ft. lbs.

5. Remove the transmission support jack.

6. On trucks with automatic transmissions, install the torque converter-to-flywheel attaching bolts. Torque the bolts to 30 ft. lbs.

7. Install the converter inspection plate. Torque the bolts to 60 inch lbs.

8. Connect the exhaust pipe to the exhaust manifolds. Tighten the exhaust pipe-to-exhaust manifold nuts to 25-35 ft. lbs.

9. Install the starter. Torque the mounting bolts to 20 ft. lbs.

10. Connect the starter cable to the starter.

11. Lower the truck.

12. Install the upper bellhousing-to-engine attaching bolts. Torque the bolts to 50 ft. lbs.

13. Connect the wiring harness at the left rocker arm cover.

14. Connect the ground strap to the cylinder block.

15. Connect the air conditioning compressor clutch wire.

16. Connect the heater hoses at the water pump and intake manifold or tee (EFI).

17. Connect the temperature sending unit wire at the sending unit.

18. Connect the accelerator linkage and speed control linkage at the carburetor or throttle body.

19. Connect the automatic transmission kick-down rod and install the return spring, if so equipped.

20. Connect the power brake booster vacuum hose.

21. On EFI models, connect the throttle bracket to the upper intake manifold.

22. Connect the fuel tank-to-pump fuel line at the fuel pump. On trucks with EFI, disconnect the chassis fuel line at the fuel rails.

23. Connect the oil pressure sending unit lead to the sending unit.

24. Install the alternator.

25. Connect the refrigerant lines to the compressor.

26. Install the radiator and fan, shroud, fan, spacer, pulley and belt.

27. Connect the upper and lower radiator hoses, and, if so equipped, the automatic transmission oil cooler lines.

28. On carbureted engines, install the air cleaner and intake duct assembly, plus the crankcase ventilation hose.

29. On fuel injected engines, install the air intake hoses, PCV tube and carbon canister hose.
30. Connect the battery and alternator cables.
31. Fill the cooling system and crankcase.
32. Charge the air conditioning system. Install the hood.

7.5L

1. Lower the engine slowly into the truck.
2. Slide the engine rearward to engage it with the transmission and slowly lower it onto the supports.
3. Install the engine support nuts and torque them to 74 ft. lbs.
4. Remove the engine lifting device.
5. Install the converter housing-to-engine block upper and left side attaching bolts. Torque the bolts to 50 ft. lbs.
6. Install the coil and bracket assembly on the intake manifold.
7. Remove the jack from under the transmission.
8. Lower the truck.
9. Install the upper converter housing-to-engine attaching bolts. Torque the bolts to 50 ft. lbs.
10. Install the flywheel-to-converter attaching nuts. Torque the nuts to 34 ft. lbs.
11. Install the access cover on the converter housing. Torque the bolts to 60-90 inch lbs.
12. Install the starter.
13. Connect the starter cable.
14. Raise the vehicle and connect the exhaust pipes at the exhaust manifolds.
15. Connect the engine wiring harness at the connector on the fire wall.
16. Connect the primary wire at the coil.
17. Connect the accelerator rod and the transmission kickdown rod.
18. Connect the speed control cable.
19. Connect all vacuum lines at the rear of the intake manifold.
20. Install the transmission fluid filler tube attaching bolt from the right side valve cover and position the tube out of the way.
21. Connect the heater hoses.
22. Connect the ground cable at the right front corner of the engine.
23. Install the alternator and drive belts.
24. Connect the oil pressure sending unit wire at the sending unit.
25. Connect the fuel pump inlet line at the pump and plug the line.
26. Install the power steering pump and belt.
27. Install air conditioning compressor. Connect the refrigerant lines.
28. Install the fan, belts and pulley on the water pump.
29. Position the fan shroud over the fan.
30. Install the radiator.
31. Attach the fan shroud.
32. Install the condenser.
33. Connect the refrigerant lines at the condenser.
34. Charge the air conditioning system.
35. Connect the engine oil cooler lines at the oil filter adapter.
36. Connect the transmission oil cooler lines at the radiator.

37. Connect the upper and lower radiator hoses.
38. Connect the canister hose.
39. Connect the crankcase ventilation hose.
40. Connect the negative battery cable from the block.
41. Fill the cooling system.
42. Install the air cleaner assembly.
43. Install the hood.

1971-96 Full-Sized Vans

5.0L, 5.7L

1. Lower the engine carefully into the transmission. Make sure that the dowel in the engine block engage the holes in the bellhousing through the rear cover plate. If the engine hangs up after the transmission input shaft enters the clutch disc (manual transmission only), turn the crankshaft with the transmission in gear until the input shaft splines mesh with the clutch disc splines.
2. Install the engine mount nuts and washers. Torque the nuts to 80 ft. lbs.
3. Remove the engine lifting device.
4. Install the lower bellhousing-to-engine attaching bolts. Torque the bolts to 50 ft. lbs.
5. Remove the transmission support jack.
6. On vans with automatic transmissions, install the torque converter-to-flywheel attaching bolts. Torque the bolts to 30 ft. lbs.
7. Install the converter inspection plate. Torque the bolts to 60 inch lbs.
8. Connect the exhaust pipe to the exhaust manifolds. Tighten the exhaust pipe-to-exhaust manifold nuts to 25-35 ft. lbs.
9. Install the starter. Torque the mounting bolts to 20 ft. lbs.
10. Connect the starter cable to the starter.
11. Lower the van.
12. Install the upper bellhousing-to-engine attaching bolts. Torque the bolts to 50 ft. lbs.
13. Connect the wiring harness at the left rocker arm cover.
14. Connect the ground strap to the cylinder block.
15. Connect the air conditioning compressor clutch wire.
16. Connect the heater hoses at the water pump and intake manifold or tee.
17. Connect the temperature sending unit wire at the sending unit.
18. Connect the accelerator linkage and speed control linkage at the throttle body.
19. Connect the automatic transmission kick-down rod and install the return spring, if so equipped.
20. Connect the power brake booster vacuum hose.
21. Connect the throttle bracket to the upper intake manifold.
22. Connect the fuel tank-to-pump fuel line at the fuel pump. Disconnect the chassis fuel line at the fuel rails.
23. Connect the oil pressure sending unit lead to the sending unit.
24. Install the alternator.
25. Connect the refrigerant lines to the compressor.
26. Install the hood lock support.
27. Install the upper grille support bracket.

28. Install the bumper.
29. Install the gravel deflector.
30. Install the grille.
31. Install the radiator and fan, shroud, fan, spacer, pulley and belt.
32. Connect the upper and lower radiator hoses, and, if so equipped, the automatic transmission oil cooler lines.
33. Install the air intake hoses, PCV tube and carbon canister hose.
34. Connect the battery and alternator cables.
35. Fill the cooling system and crankcase.
36. Charge the air conditioning system.
37. Install the engine cover.

7.5L

1. Lower the engine slowly into the van.
2. Slide the engine rearward to engage it with the transmission and slowly lower it onto the supports.
3. Install the engine support nuts and torque them to 74 ft. lbs.
4. Remove the engine lifting device.
5. Install the converter housing-to-engine block upper and left side attaching bolts. Torque the bolts to 50 ft. lbs.
6. Install the coil and bracket assembly on the intake manifold.
7. Remove the jack from under the transmission.
8. Lower the van.
9. Install the upper converter housing-to-engine attaching bolts. Torque the bolts to 50 ft. lbs.
10. Install the flywheel-to-converter attaching nuts. Torque the nuts to 34 ft. lbs.
11. Install the access cover on the converter housing. Torque the bolts to 60-90 inch lbs.
12. Install the starter.
13. Connect the starter cable.
14. Raise the vehicle and connect the exhaust pipes at the exhaust manifolds.
15. Connect the engine wiring harness at the connector on the fire wall.
16. Connect the primary wire at the coil.
17. Connect the accelerator rod and the transmission kickdown rod.
18. Connect the speed control cable.
19. Connect all vacuum lines at the rear of the intake manifold.
20. Install the transmission fluid filler tube attaching bolt from the right side valve cover and position the tube out of the way.
21. Connect the heater hoses.
22. Connect the ground cable at the right front corner of the engine.
23. Install the alternator and drive belts.
24. Connect the oil pressure sending unit wire at the sending unit.
25. Connect the fuel pump inlet line at the pump and plug the line.
26. Install the power steering pump and belt.
27. Install air conditioning compressor. Connect the refrigerant lines.
28. Install the fan, belts and pulley on the water pump.

29. Position the fan shroud over the fan.
30. Install the radiator.
31. Attach the fan shroud.
32. Install the condenser.
33. Connect the refrigerant lines at the condenser.
34. Charge the air conditioning system.
35. Connect the engine oil cooler lines at the oil filter adapter.
36. Connect the transmission oil cooler lines at the radiator.
37. Connect the upper and lower radiator hoses.
38. Connect the canister hose.
39. Install the grille and bumper.
40. Connect the crankcase ventilation hose.
41. Connect the negative battery cable from the block.
42. Fill the cooling system.
43. Install the air cleaner assembly.
44. Install the hood and engine cover.

1968-88 Ford, Mercury and Lincoln Full-Sized Cars

1. Install the engine lifting brackets to the cylinder head. Connect the engine lifting equipment to the brackets and remove the engine from the stand.
2. Carefully lower the engine into the engine compartment. Make sure the studs on the converter align with the holes in the flexplate on automatic transmissions.
3. Fully engage the engine to the transmission and slowly lower the engine onto the left and right engine mounts. Remove the engine lifting equipment and brackets. Install the bolts securing the left and right engine mounts to the frame.
4. Raise and safely support the vehicle. Install the 6 engine-to-transmission bolts and tighten to 30-44 ft. lbs. (40-60 Nm).
5. Install the engine mount through-bolts and tighten to 15-22 ft. lbs. (20-30 Nm). Install the converter retaining nuts and tighten to 22-25 ft. lbs. (20-30 Nm). Install the plug into the access hole in the engine block.
6. Position the power steering pump on the engine block and install the retaining nuts. Tighten to 15-22 ft. lbs. (20-30 Nm). Install the starter.
7. Position the engine-to-transmission braces and install the bolt. Tighten the bolts to 18-31 ft. lbs. (25-43 Nm).
8. Position the transmission line bracket to the brace stud and install the retaining nut. Tighten to 15-22 ft. lbs. (20-30 Nm).
9. Cut the wire securing the exhaust, and position the exhaust system to the manifolds. Use a new gasket. Install the nuts and tighten to 20-30 ft. lbs. (27-41 Nm).

➡**Make sure the exhaust system does not interfere with the crossmember. Adjust as necessary.**

10. Lower the vehicle and connect the EVO sensor, if equipped.
11. Connect the air conditioner lines to the compressor. Have the A/C system charged by a certified professional. Connect the alternator harness from the fender apron and junction block.
12. Connect the heater hoses and fasten the vacuum supply hose to the throttle body adapter vacuum port.

13. Connect the power supply to the power distribution box and starter relay. Plug in and secure the remaining electrical connectors and vacuum hoses to their respective connections.

14. Connect and if necessary, adjust the throttle valve, accelerator and cruise control cables.

15. Install the wiper module and support bracket. Secure the fuel lines, including the connection to the fuel pump, if carbureted.

16. Install the radiator, cooling fan and shroud. Install the air inlet tube.

17. Fill the crankcase with the proper type and quantity of engine oil. Fill the cooling system.

18. Install the hood, aligning the marks that were made during removal. Connect the battery cables.

19. Start the engine and adjust the timing and idle, if necessary. Check the levels of the coolant oil and transmission fluids. Check for leaks

20. Road test the vehicle.

1989-95 Ford, Mercury and Lincoln Full-Sized Cars

4.6L

1. Install the engine lifting brackets as in Step 19. Connect the engine lifting equipment to the brackets and remove the engine from the workstand.

2. Carefully lower the engine into the engine compartment. Start the converter pilot into the flexplate and align the paint marks on the flexplate and torque converter. Make sure the studs on the torque converter align with the holes in the flexplate.

3. Fully engage the engine to the transmission and lower onto the mounts. Remove the engine lifting equipment and brackets. Install the bolt retaining the right engine mount to the frame.

4. Raise and safely support the vehicle. Install the 6 engine-to-transmission bolts and tighten to 30-44 ft. lbs. (40-60 Nm).

5. Install the engine mount through bolts and tighten to 15-22 ft. lbs. (20-30 Nm). Install the 4 torque converter retaining nuts and tighten to 22-25 ft. lbs. (20-30 Nm). Install the plug into the access hole in the engine block.

6. Position the power steering pump on the engine block and install the 4 retaining nuts. Tighten to 15-22 ft. lbs. (20-30 Nm). Install the starter.

7. Position the engine to transmission braces and install the 3 bolts and 1 stud. Tighten the bolts and stud to 18-31 ft. lbs. (25-43 Nm).

8. Position the transmission line bracket to the knee brace stud and install the retaining nut. Tighten to 15-22 ft. lbs. (20-30 Nm).

9. Cut the wire and position the exhaust system to the manifolds. Install the 4 nuts and tighten to 20-30 ft. lbs. (27-41 Nm).

➡**Make sure the exhaust system clears the No. 3 crossmember. Adjust as necessary.**

10. Lower the vehicle and connect the EVO sensor.

11. Connect the air conditioner lines to the compressor. Connect the alternator harness from the fender apron and junction block.

12. Connect the heater hoses and connect the vacuum supply hose to the throttle body adapter vacuum port.

13. Connect the power supply to the power distribution box and starter relay. Connect the electrical connector and vacuum hose to the purge solenoid.

14. Connect and if necessary, adjust the throttle valve cable. Connect the accelerator and cruise control cables.

15. Connect the 42-pin engine harness connector and transmission harness connector. Install the 42-pin connector to the retaining bracket on the brake vacuum booster.

16. Install the wiper module and support bracket. Connect the fuel lines.

17. Install the radiator, cooling fan and shroud. Install the air inlet tube.

18. Fill the crankcase with the proper type and quantity of engine oil. Fill the cooling system.

19. Install the hood, aligning the marks that were made during removal. Connect the battery cables.

20. Start the engine and bring to operating temperature. Check for leaks. Check all fluid levels. Evacuate and charge the air conditioning system.

21. Road test the vehicle.

5.0L, 5.8L

1. Attach the engine lifting equipment and remove the engine from the workstand.

2. Lower the engine carefully into the engine compartment. Make sure the exhaust manifolds are properly aligned with the muffler inlet pipes.

3. Start the converter pilot into the crankshaft. Align the paint mark on the flywheel to the paint mark on the torque converter.

4. Install the transmission upper bolts, making sure the dowels in the cylinder block engage the transmission.

5. Install the engine mount-to-chassis attaching fasteners and remove the engine lifting equipment.

6. Raise and safely support the vehicle. Connect both muffler inlet pipes to the exhaust manifolds. Install the starter and connect the starter cable.

7. Remove the retainer holding the torque converter in the transmission. Attach the converter to the flywheel. Install the converter housing inspection cover and install the remaining transmission attaching bolts.

8. Remove the support from the transmission and lower the vehicle.

9. On 5.8L engines, connect the wiring harness to the left rocker arm cover and connect the coil wiring connector. On 5.0L engines, connect the wiring harness at the two 10-pin connectors.

10. Connect the coolant temperature sending unit wire and connect the heater hoses. Connect the wiring to the metal heater tubes and the engine coolant temperature, air charge temperature and oxygen sensors.

11. Connect the transmission filler tube bracket. Connect the manual shift rod and the retracting spring. Connect the throttle valve vacuum line, if equipped.

12. Connect the accelerator cable and throttle valve cable. Connect the cruise control cable, if equipped.

13. Connect the fuel lines and the oil pressure sending unit wire.

14. Install the pulley, water pump belt and fan/clutch assembly.

15. Position the alternator bracket and install the alternator bolts. Connect the alternator and ground cables. Adjust the drive belt tension.

16. Install the air conditioning compressor. Unplug and connect the refrigerant lines and connect the electrical connector to the compressor.

17. Install the power steering drive belt and power steering pump bracket. Connect the power brake vacuum line.

18. Place the shroud over the fan and install the radiator. Connect the radiator hoses and the transmission oil cooler lines. Position the shroud and install the bolts.

19. Connect the heater hoses to the heater tubes. Fill the cooling system. Fill the crankcase with the proper type and quantity of engine oil. Adjust the transmission throttle linkage.

20. Connect the negative battery cable. Start the engine and bring to normal operating temperature. Check for leaks. Check all fluid levels.

21. Install the air intake duct assembly. Install the hood, aligning the marks that were made during removal.

22. Evacuate and charge the air conditioning system. Road test the vehicle.

1964-85 Ford and Mercury Mid-Sized Cars, Including 1964-78 Mustang and Cougar

1. Install the engine lifting brackets to the cylinder head. Connect the engine lifting equipment to the brackets and remove the engine from the stand.

2. Carefully lower the engine into the engine compartment. Make sure the studs on the converter align with the holes in the flexplate on automatic transmissions.

3. Fully engage the engine to the transmission and slowly lower the engine onto the left and right engine mounts. Remove the engine lifting equipment and brackets. Install the bolts securing the left and right engine mounts to the frame.

4. Raise and safely support the vehicle. Install the 6 engine-to-transmission bolts and tighten to 30-44 ft. lbs. (40-60 Nm).

5. Install the engine mount through-bolts and tighten to 15-22 ft. lbs. (20-30 Nm). Install the converter retaining nuts and tighten to 22-25 ft. lbs. (20-30 Nm). Install the plug into the access hole in the engine block.

6. Position the power steering pump on the engine block and install the retaining nuts. Tighten to 15-22 ft. lbs. (20-30 Nm). Install the starter.

7. Position the engine-to-transmission braces and install the bolt. Tighten the bolts to 18-31 ft. lbs. (25-43 Nm).

8. Position the transmission line bracket to the brace stud and install the retaining nut. Tighten to 15-22 ft. lbs. (20-30 Nm).

9. Cut the wire securing the exhaust, and position the exhaust system to the manifolds. Use a new gasket. Install the nuts and tighten to 20-30 ft. lbs. (27-41 Nm).

➡**Make sure the exhaust system does not interfere with the crossmember. Adjust as necessary.**

10. Lower the vehicle and connect the EVO sensor, if equipped.

11. Connect the heater hoses and fasten the vacuum supply hose to the throttle body adapter vacuum port.

12. Connect the power supply to the power distribution box and starter relay. Plug in and secure the remaining electrical connectors and vacuum hoses to their respective connections.

13. Connect the alternator harness from the fender apron and junction block.

14. Connect and if necessary, adjust the throttle valve, accelerator and cruise control cables.

15. Install the wiper module and support bracket. Secure the fuel lines, including the connection to the fuel pump. if carbureted.

16. Install the radiator, cooling fan and shroud. Install the air inlet tube.

17. Fill the crankcase with the proper type and quantity of engine oil. Fill the cooling system.

18. If the A/C lines were unfastened, connect the these lines to the compressor.

19. Install the hood, aligning the marks that were made during removal. Connect the battery cables.

20. Start the engine and adjust the timing and idle, if necessary. Check the levels of the coolant oil and transmission fluids. Check for leaks

21. Road test the vehicle.

22. Have the A/C system charged by a certified professional using an approved recovery/recycling machine.

1979-88 Mustang and Capri

1. Place a new gasket on the exhaust pipe flange.

2. Attach an engine sling and lifting device. Lift the engine from the workstand.

3. Lower the engine into the engine compartment. Be sure the exhaust manifold(s) is (are) in proper alignment with the muffler inlet pipe(s), and the dowels in the block engage the holes in the flywheel housing. -On cars with an automatic transmission, start the converter pilot into the crankshaft, making sure that the converter studs align with the flexplate holes. On cars with a manual transmission, start the transmission main drive gear into the clutch disc. If the engine hangs up after the shaft enters, rotate the crankshaft slowly (with transmission in gear) until the shaft and clutch disc splines mesh.

4. Install the flywheel or converter housing upper bolts.

5. Install the engine support insulator to bracket retaining nuts. Disconnect the engine lifting sling and remove the lifting brackets.

6. Raise the front of the car. Connect the exhaust line(s) and tighten the attachments.

7. Install the starter.

8. On cars with a manual transmission, install the remaining flywheel housing-to-engine bolts. Connect the clutch release rod. Position the clutch equalizer bar and bracket, and

install the retaining bolts. Install the clutch pedal retracting spring.

9. On cars with an automatic transmission, remove the retainer holding the converter in the housing. Attach the converter to the flywheel. Install the converter housing inspection cover and the remaining converter housing retaining bolts.

10. Remove the support from the transmission and lower the car.

11. Connect the engine ground strap and coil primary wire.

12. Connect the heater hoses to the coolant outlet housing and the water pump. Connect the water temperature sending unit wire.

13. Connect the accelerator cable to the carburetor or throttle body. Connect the speed control cable, if so equipped. Connect the throttle valve rod on automatic overdrive (AOD) transmissions, if so equipped.

14. On cars with an automatic transmission, connect the transmission filler tube bracket, if applicable. Connect the throttle valve vacuum line.

15. On cars with power steering, install the drive belt and power steering pump bracket. Install the bracket retaining bolts. Adjust the drive belt to proper tension.

16. Remove the plug from the fuel tank line. Connect the flexible fuel line and the oil pressure sending unit wire.

17. Install the pulley, belt, spacer, and fan. Adjust the belt tension.

18. Tighten the alternator adjusting bolts. Connect the wires and the battery ground cable.

19. Reconnect any other grounding straps, wiring or vacuum hoses which had been removed.

20. Install the radiator. Connect the radiator hoses. On air conditioned cars, install the compressor and condenser.

21. On cars with an automatic transmission, connect the fluid cooler lines. On cars with power brakes, connect the brake booster line.

22. Install an oil filter and fill the crankcase with the correct grade of oil. Run the engine at fast idle and check for leaks.

23. Install the air cleaner and make the final engine adjustments.

24. Install and adjust the hood.

1989-93 Mustang

1. Attach the engine lifting equipment and remove the engine from the workstand.

2. Lower the engine carefully into the engine compartment. Make sure the exhaust manifolds are properly aligned with the muffler inlet pipes.

3. Start the converter pilot into the crankshaft. Align the paint mark on the flywheel to the paint mark on the torque converter.

4. Install the converter housing upper bolts, making sure the dowels in the cylinder block engage the converter housing.

5. Install the engine support insulator-to-chassis attaching fasteners and remove the engine lifting equipment.

6. Raise and safely support the vehicle. Connect both muffler inlet pipes to the exhaust manifolds. Install the starter and connect the starter cable.

7. Remove the retainer holding the converter in the housing. Attach the converter to the flywheel. Install the converter

housing inspection cover and install the remaining converter housing attaching bolts.

8. Remove the support from the transmission and lower the vehicle.

9. Connect the wiring harness at the two 10-pin connectors.

10. Connect the coolant temperature sending unit wire and connect the heater hoses. Connect the wiring to the metal heater tubes, engine coolant temperature, air charge temperature and oxygen sensors.

11. Connect the transmission filler tube bracket. Connect the manual shift rod and the retracting spring. Connect the throttle valve vacuum line, if equipped.

12. Connect the accelerator cable and TV cable. Connect the cruise control cable, if equipped.

13. Remove the plug from the fuel tank line and connect the fuel line and the oil pressure sending unit wire.

14. Install the pulley, water pump belt and fan clutch assembly.

15. Position the alternator bracket and install the alternator bolts. Connect the alternator and ground cables. Adjust the drive belt tension.

16. Install the air conditioning compressor. Unplug and connect the refrigerant lines and connect the electrical connector to the compressor.

17. Install the power steering drive belt and power steering pump bracket. Connect the power brake vacuum line.

18. Install the fan on the water pump pulley. Place the shroud over the fan and install the radiator. Connect the radiator hoses and the transmission oil cooler lines. Position the shroud and install the bolts.

19. Connect the heater hoses to the heater tubes. Fill and bleed the cooling system. Fill the crankcase with the proper type and quantity of engine oil. Adjust the transmission throttle linkage.

20. Connect the negative battery cable. Start the engine and bring to normal operating temperature. Check for leaks. Check all fluid levels.

21. Install the air intake duct assembly. Install the hood, aligning the marks that were made during removal.

22. Leak test, evacuate and charge the air conditioning system according to the proper procedure. Observe all safety precautions.

1986-96 Thunderbird and Cougar

1. Place a new gasket on the exhaust pipe flange.

2. Attach an engine sling and lifting device. Lift the engine from the workstand.

3. Lower the engine into the engine compartment. Be sure the exhaust manifold(s) is in proper alignment with the muffler inlet pipe(s), and the dowels in the block engage the holes in the flywheel housing.

➡**On cars with automatic transmission, start the converter pilot into the crankshaft, making sure that the converter studs align with the flexplate holes. On cars with manual transmission, start the transmission main drive gear into the clutch disc. If the engine hangs up after the shaft enters, rotate the crankshaft slowly (with transmission in gear) until the shaft and clutch disc splines mesh.**

4. Install the flywheel or converter housing upper bolts.

5. Install the engine support insulator to bracket retaining nuts. Disconnect the engine lifting sling and remove the lifting brackets.

6. Raise the front of the car. Connect the exhaust line(s) and tighten the attachments.

7. Install the starter.

8. On cars with manual transmission, install the remaining flywheel housing-to-engine bolts. Connect the clutch release rod. Position the clutch equalizer bar and bracket, and install the retaining bolts. Install the clutch pedal retracting spring.

9. On cars with automatic transmission, remove the retainer holding the converter in the housing. Attach the converter to the flywheel. Install the converter housing inspection cover and the remaining converter housing retaining bolts.

10. Remove the support from the transmission and lower the car.

11. Connect the engine ground strap and coil primary wire.

➡**On models equipped with EFI it is important to make sure that all ground wires are reconnected to rear of engine block to avoid no start, hard start, or poor performance.**

12. Connect the water temperature gauge wire and the heater hose at the coolant outlet housing. Connect the accelerator rod at the bellcrank.

13. On cars with automatic transmission, connect the transmission filler tube bracket. Connect the throttle valve vacuum line.

14. On cars with power steering, install the drive belt and power steering pump bracket. Install the bracket retaining bolts. Adjust the drive belt to proper tension.

15. Remove the plug from the fuel tank line. Connect the flexible fuel line and the oil pressure sending unit wire.

16. Install the pulley, belt, spacer, and fan. Adjust the belt tension.

17. Tighten the alternator adjusting bolts. Connect the wires and the battery ground cable.

18. Install the radiator. Connect the radiator hoses. On air conditioned cars, install the compressor and condenser.

19. On cars with automatic transmission, connect the fluid cooler lines. On cars with power brakes, connect the brake booster line.

20. Install the oil filter. Connect the heater hose at the water pump and carburetor choke.

21. Bring the crankcase to the full level with the correct grade of oil. Run the engine at fast idle and check for leaks. Install the air cleaner and make the final engine adjustments.

22. Install and adjust the hood.

BREAK-IN PROCEDURE

Start the engine, and allow it to run at low speed for a few minutes, while checking for leaks. Stop the engine, check the oil level, and fill as necessary. Restart the engine, and fill the cooling system to capacity. Check and adjust the ignition timing. Run the engine at low to medium speed (800-2,500 rpm) for approximately ½ hour, and retorque the cylinder head bolts. Road test the truck, and check again for leaks.

➡**Some gasket manufacturers recommend not retorquing the cylinder head(s) due to the composition of the head gasket. Follow the directions in the gasket set.**

TUNE-UP PROCEDURES

Spark Plugs

INSTALLATION

1. Inspect the spark plugs and clean or replace, as necessary. Inspect the spark plug boot for tears or damage. If a damaged boot is found, the spark plug wire must be replaced.

2. Using a feeler gauge, check and adjust the spark plug gap to specification. When using a gauge, the proper size should pass between the electrodes with a slight drag. The next larger size should not be able to pass while the next smaller size should pass freely.

✳✳CAUTION

Do not use the spark plug socket to thread the plugs. Always thread the plug by hand to prevent the possibility of cross-threading and damaging the cylinder head bore.

3. Lubricate the spark plug threads with a drop of clean engine oil, then carefully start the spark plugs by hand and tighten a few turns until a socket is needed to continue tightening the spark plug. Do not apply the same amount of force you would use for a bolt; just snug them in. If a torque wrench is available, tighten the plugs to 11-15 ft. lbs. (15-20 Nm).

➡**A spark plug threading tool may be made using the end of an old spark plug wire. Cut the wire a few inches from the top of the spark plug boot. The boot may be used to hold the plug while the wire is turned to thread it. Because the wire is so flexible, it may be turned to bend around difficult angles and, should the plug begin to crossthread, the resistance should be sufficient to bend the wire instead of forcing the plug into the cylinder head, preventing serious thread damage.**

4. Apply a small amount of silicone dielectric compound to the end of the spark plug lead or inside the spark plug boot to prevent sticking, then install the boot to the spark plug and push until it clicks into place. The click may be felt or heard, then gently pull back on the boot to assure proper contact.

5. Connect the negative battery cable.

Spark Plug Wires

CHECKING AND REPLACING SPARK PLUG CABLES

▶ See Figures 2 and 3

Visually inspect the spark plug cables for burns, cuts, or breaks in the insulation. Check the spark plug boots and the nipples on the distributor cap and coil. Replace any damaged wiring. If no physical damage is obvious, the wires can be checked with an ohmmeter for excessive resistance.

When installing a new set of spark plug cables, replace the cables on at a time so there will be no mix-up. Start by replacing the longest cable first. Install the boot firmly over the spark plug. Route the wire exactly the same as the original. Insert the nipple firmly into the tower on the distributor cap. Repeat the process for each cable.

Breaker Points and Condenser

▶ See Figures 4 and 5

All engines through 1973, and some 1974 engines use a breaker point type ignition system.

The points function as a circuit breaker for the primary circuit of the ignition system. The ignition coil must boost the 12 volts of electrical current supplied by the battery to as much as 25,000 volts in order to properly fire the spark plugs. To do this, the coil depends on the points and the condenser to make a clean break in the primary circuit.

The coil has both primary and secondary circuits. When the ignition is turned **ON**, the battery supplies voltage through the coil to the points. The points are connected to ground, completing the primary circuit. As the current passes through the coil, a magnetic field is created in the iron center core of the coil. As the cam in the distributor turns, the points open and the primary circuit collapses. The magnetic field in the primary circuit of the coil cuts through the secondary circuit winding

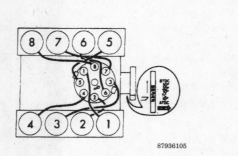

Fig. 2 255, 260, 289, 302 exc. HO, 360, 390, 429, 460 engines
Firing order: 1-5-4-2-6-3-7-8
Distributor rotation: Counterclockwise

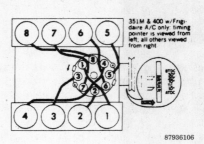

Fig. 3 302HO, 351W and M, 400 engines
Firing order: 1-3-7-2-6-5-4-8
Distributor rotation: Counterclockwise

around the iron core. Because of the scientific phenomenon called 'electromagnetic induction," the battery voltage is increased to a level sufficient to fire the spark plugs.

When the points open, the electrical charge in the primary circuit jumps the gap created between the two open contacts of the points. If this electrical charge is not transferred elsewhere, the metal contacts of the points would melt and the gap would start to change rapidly. Without the proper gap, the points will be unable to break the primary circuit, and the end result will be the secondary circuit will not have enough voltage to fire the spark plugs.

The function of the condenser is to absorb excessive voltage from the points when they open and prevent the points from becoming pitted or burned.

It is interesting to note that the cycle must be completed by the ignition system every time a spark plug fires. In a V8 engine, all of the spark plugs fire once for every two revolutions of the crankshaft. That means that in one revolution, four spark plugs fire. So when the engine is at an idle speed of 800 rpm, the points are opening and closing 3,200 times a minute.

There are two ways to inspect the breaker point gap: it can be checked with a feeler gauge, or a dwell meter. In either way, when you set the points, you are basically adjusting the amount of time that the points remain open. The time is measured in degrees of distributor rotation. When you measure the gap between the breaker points with a feeler gauge, you are setting the maximum level at which the points will open when the rubbing block on the points is on a high point of the distributor cam. When you adjust the points with a dwell meter, you are adjusting the number of degrees that the points will remain closed as a high point of the distributor cam approaches the rubbing block of the points.

➡**When you replace a set of points, ALWAYS replace the condenser at the same time.**

When you change the point gap or dwell, you will also have to check the ignition timing. If the point gap or dwell is changed, the ignition timing must be checked and adjusted as needed.

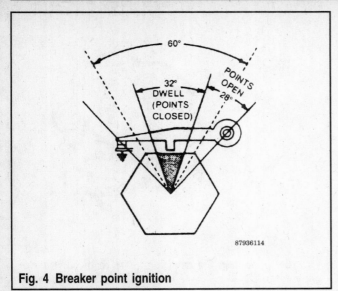

Fig. 4 Breaker point ignition

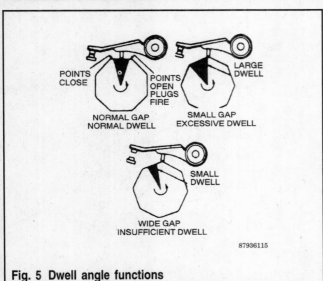

Fig. 5 Dwell angle functions

INSPECTION

▶ **See Figure 6**

1. Disconnect the negative battery cable.

2. Disconnect the high tension wire from the top of the distributor and the coil.

3. Remove the distributor cap by prying off the spring clips on the sides of the cap.

4. Remove the rotor from the distributor shaft by pulling it straight up. Examine the condition of the rotor. If it is cracked or the metal tip is excessively worn, it should be replaced.

5. Pry open the contacts of the points with a small prytool and check the condition of the contacts. If they are excessively worn, burned or pitted, they should be replaced.

6. Inspect the condition of the condenser. If the wire insulation is cracked or burnt, replace the unit.

7. If the points and condenser are in good condition, adjust them, and install the rotor and the distributor cap. If the points need to be replaced, follow the replacement procedure given below.

REPLACEMENT

▶ **See Figures 7, 8, 9, 10, 11, 12 and 13**

1. Disconnect the negative battery cable.

2. Remove the coil high tension wire from the top of the distributor cap. Remove the cap from the distributor and place it out of the way. Remove the rotor from the distributor shaft.

3. Loosen the screw that holds the condenser lead to the body of the breaker points, then disconnect the lead.

4. Remove the screw that holds and grounds the condenser to the distributor body. Remove the condenser from the distributor and discard it.

5. Unfasten the points assembly attaching screws and adjustment lockscrews. A screwdriver with a magnetic tip will come in handy here so you don't drop a screw into the distributor and have to remove the entire assembly to retrieve it.

6. Remove the points. Wipe off the cam and apply new cam lubricant. Discard the old point set.

   To install:

7. Position the new set of points with the locating peg in the hole on the breaker plate, and install the screws that hold the assembly onto the plate. Do not tighten them all the way.

8. Attach the new condenser to the plate with the ground screw.

9. Attach the condenser lead to the points.

10. Apply a small amount of cam lubricant to the shaft where the rubbing block of the points touches.

11. Attach the negative battery cable.

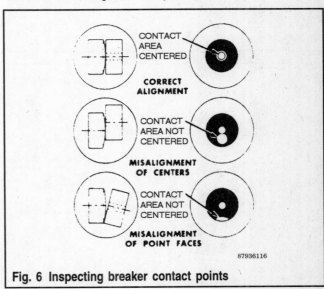

Fig. 6 Inspecting breaker contact points

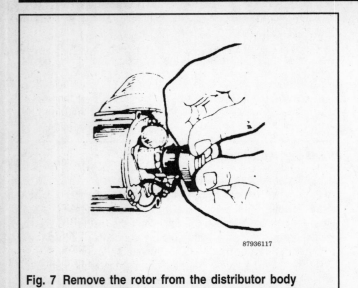

Fig. 7 Remove the rotor from the distributor body

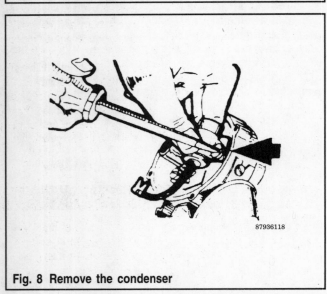

Fig. 8 Remove the condenser

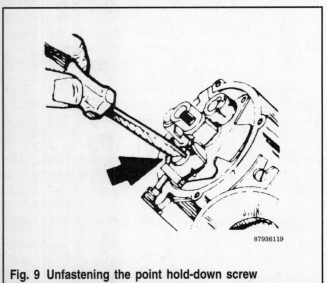

Fig. 9 Unfastening the point hold-down screw

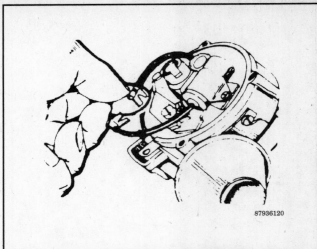

Fig. 10 Connecting the new point wire to the distributor body

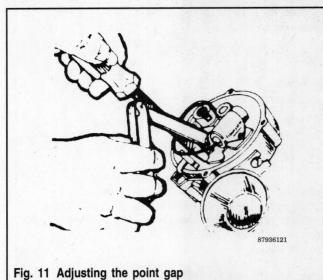

Fig. 11 Adjusting the point gap

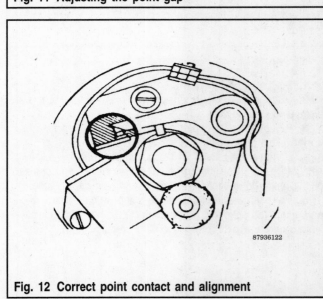

Fig. 12 Correct point contact and alignment

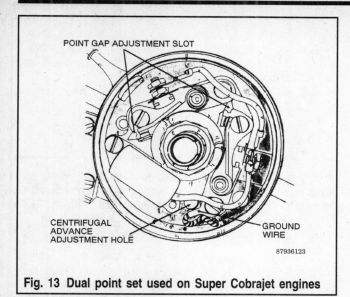

POINT GAP ADJUSTMENT SLOT

CENTRIFUGAL
ADVANCE
ADJUSTMENT HOLE

GROUND
WIRE

87936123

Fig. 13 Dual point set used on Super Cobrajet engines

Dwell Angle

ADJUSTMENT

Using a Feeler Gauge

1. If the contact points of the assembly are not parallel, bend the stationary contact so they make contact across the entire surface of the contacts. Bend only the stationary bracket part of the point assembly, not the movable contact.

2. Turn the engine until the rubbing block of the point is on one of the high points of the distributor cam. You can do this by either turning the ignition switch to the **START** position and releasing it quickly (bumping the engine) or by using a wrench on the crankshaft pulley bolt and rotating the crankshaft. Be sure to remove the wrench before starting the engine!

3. Place the correct size feeler gauge between the contacts. Make sure the feeler gauge is parallel with the contact surfaces. Refer to the Tune-Up Specifications Chart in this section.

4. With your free hand, insert a small screwdriver into the notch provided for adjustment or into the eccentric adjusting screw, then twist the screwdriver to either increase or decrease the gap to the proper setting.

5. Tighten the adjustment lockscrew and recheck the contact gap to make sure that it did not change when the lockscrew was tightened.

6. Install the rotor and distributor cap, along with the high tension wire that connects the top of the distributor and the coil. Make sure that the rotor is firmly seated all the way onto the distributor shaft. Align the tab in the base of the distributor cap with the notch in the distributor body. Make sure that the cap is firmly seated on the distributor and that the retainer springs are in place. Make sure that the end of the high tension wire is firmly placed in the top of the distributor and the coil.

Using a Dwell Meter
▶ **See Figure 14**

1. Adjust the points with a feeler gauge as described earlier.

2. Connect the dwell meter to the ignition circuit according to the tool manufacturer's instructions. One lead of the meter should be connected to a ground, and the other lead is to be connected to the distributor post (-) on the coil. An adapter is usually provided for this purpose.

3. If the dwell meter has a set line on it, adjust the meter to zero the indicator.

4. Start the engine.

➡**Be careful when working on any vehicle while the engine is running. Make sure that the transmission is in PARK or NEUTRAL depending on type of transmission, and that the parking brake is applied. Keep hands, clothing, tools, and the wires of the test instruments clear of the rotating fan blades.**

5. Observe the reading on the dwell meter. If the reading is within the specified range, turn **OFF** the engine and remove the dwell meter. Refer to the Tune-Up Specifications Chart in this section.

6. If the reading is above the specified range, the breaker point gap is too small. If the reading is below the specified range, the gap is too large. In either case, the engine must be stopped and the gap adjusted in the manner previously covered. After making the adjustment, start the engine and check the reading on the dwell meter. When the correct reading is obtained, disconnect the dwell meter.

7. Check the ignition timing and adjust if necessary.

Ignition Timing

Ignition timing is the measurement, in degrees of crankshaft rotation, of the point at which the spark plugs fire in each of the cylinders. It is measured in degrees before or after Top Dead Center (TDC) of the compression stroke.

Ideally, the air/fuel mixture in the cylinder will be ignited by the spark plug just as the piston passes TDC of the compression stroke. If this happens, the piston will be beginning the power stroke just as the compressed and ignited air/fuel mixture starts to expand. The expansion of the air/fuel mixture then forces the piston down on the power stroke and turns the crankshaft.

Because it takes a fraction of a second for the spark plug to ignite the mixture in the cylinder, the spark plug must fire a little before the piston reaches TDC. Otherwise, the mixture will not be completely ignited as the piston passes TDC and the full power of the explosion will not be used by the engine.

The timing measurement is given in degrees of crankshaft rotation before the piston reaches TDC (BTDC, or Before Top Dead Center). If the setting for the ignition timing is 5 degrees BTDC, each spark plug must fire 5 degrees before each piston reaches TDC. This only holds true, however, when the engine is at idle speed.

As the engine speed increases, the pistons go faster. The spark plugs have to ignite the fuel even sooner if it is to be completely ignited when the piston reaches TDC.

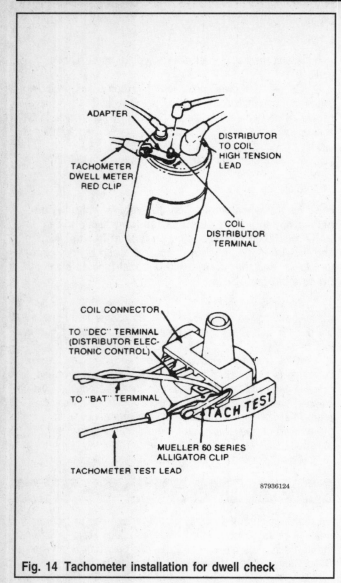

Fig. 14 Tachometer installation for dwell check

With the Dura Spark II system, the distributor has a means to advance the timing of the spark as the engine speed increases. This is accomplished by centrifugal weights within the distributor and a vacuum diaphragm mounted on the side of the distributor. It is necessary to disconnect the vacuum lines from the diaphragm when the ignition timing is being set.

With the TFI-IV system, ignition timing is calculated at all phases of vehicle operation by the TFI module. Therefore, no provision for adjustment is provided.

If the ignition is set too far advanced (BTDC), the ignition and expansion of the fuel in the cylinder will occur too soon and tend to force the piston down while it is still traveling up. This causes engine ping. If the ignition spark is set too far retarded after TDC (ATDC), the piston will have already passed TDC and started on its way down when the fuel is ignited. This will cause the piston to be forced down for only a portion of its travel. This will result in poor engine performance and lack of power.

The timing is best checked with a timing light. This device is connected in series with the No. 1 spark plug. The current that fires the spark plug also causes the timing light to flash.

A scale of degrees of crankshaft rotation is attached to the engine block in such a position that the notch will pass close by the scale. On the V8 engines, the scale is located on the crankshaft pulley and a pointer is attached to the engine block so that the scale will pass close by. When the engine is running, the timing light is aimed at the mark on the crankshaft pulley and the scale.

Ignition Timing Adjustment

➡**With the Dura Spark II system, only an initial timing adjustment is possible. Ignition timing is not considered to be a part of tune-up or routine maintenance. With the TFI-IV system no ignition timing adjustment is possible and none should be attempted.**

1. Locate the timing marks on the crankshaft pulley and the front of the engine.
2. Clean the timing marks so that you can see them.
3. Mark the timing marks with a piece of chalk or with paint. Color the mark on the scale that will indicate the correct timing when it is aligned with the mark on the pulley or the pointer. It is also helpful to mark the notch in the pulley or the tip of the pointer with a small dab of color.
4. Attach a tachometer to the engine.
5. Attach a timing light according to the manufacturer's instructions. If the timing light has three wires, one is attached to the No. 1 spark plug with an adapter. The other wires are connected to the battery. The red wire goes to the positive side of the battery and the black wire is connected to the negative terminal of the battery.
6. Disconnect the vacuum line to the distributor at the distributor and plug the vacuum line. A golf tee does a fine job.
7. Check to make sure that all of the wires clear the fan and then start the engine.
8. Adjust the idle to the correct setting.
9. Aim the timing light at the timing marks. if the marks that you put on the flywheel or pulley and the engine are aligned with the light flashes, the timing is correct. Turn off the engine and remove the tachometer and the timing light. If the mark are not in alignment, loosen the distributor holddown bolt and rotate the distributor until the marks align. Tighten the bolt.

Idle Speed and Mixture Adjustments

CARBURETED ENGINES

◆ **See Figures 15, 16, 17, 18 and 19**

IDLE SPEED ADJUSTMENT

1966-76

1. Remove the air cleaner and plug the vacuum lines.
2. Set the parking brake and block the wheels.
3. Connect a tachometer according to the manufacturer's instructions.
4. Run the engine to normalize underhood temperatures.
5. Check, and if necessary, reset the ignition timing.
6. Make certain that the choke plate is fully open.

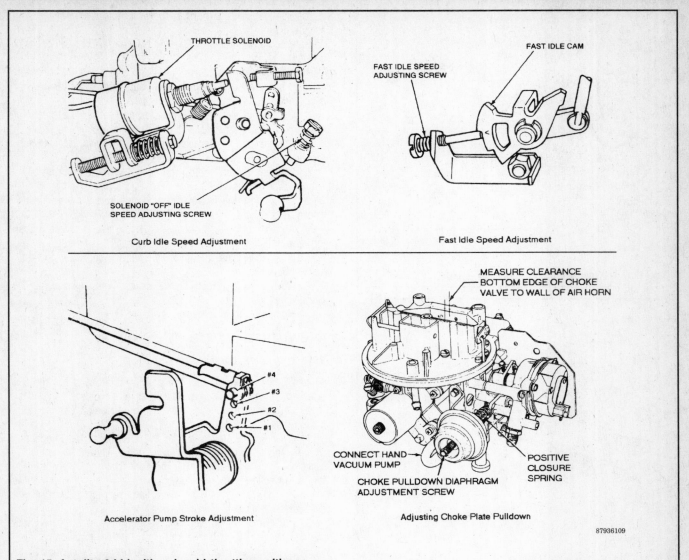

THROTTLE SOLENOID

SOLENOID "OFF" IDLE
SPEED ADJUSTING SCREW

Curb Idle Speed Adjustment

FAST IDLE CAM

FAST IDLE SPEED
ADJUSTING SCREW

Fast Idle Speed Adjustment

#4
#3
#2
#1

Accelerator Pump Stroke Adjustment

MEASURE CLEARANCE
BOTTOM EDGE OF CHOKE
VALVE TO WALL OF AIR HORN

CONNECT HAND
VACUUM PUMP

CHOKE PULLDOWN DIAPHRAGM
ADJUSTMENT SCREW

POSITIVE
CLOSURE
SPRING

Adjusting Choke Plate Pulldown

87936109

Fig. 15 Autolite 2-bbl with solenoid throttle positioner

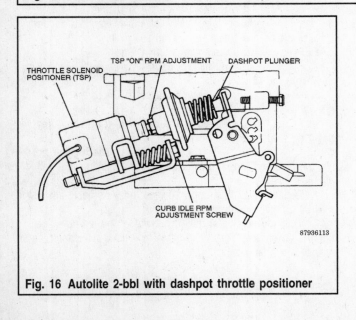

THROTTLE SOLENOID
POSITIONER (TSP)

TSP "ON" RPM ADJUSTMENT

DASHPOT PLUNGER

CURB IDLE RPM
ADJUSTMENT SCREW

87936113

Fig. 16 Autolite 2-bbl with dashpot throttle positioner

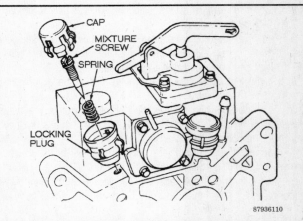

CAP

MIXTURE
SCREW

SPRING

LOCKING
PLUG

87936110

Fig. 17 Some 1980 and later 2150 2-bbls have metal plugs and caps in place of the plastic limiter caps on the idle mixture adjusting screws. They should be carefully removed before attempting any adjustments.

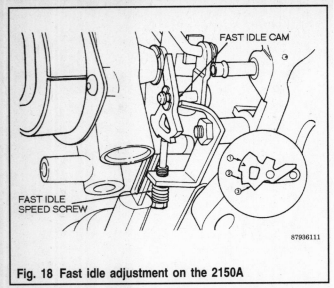

Fig. 18 Fast idle adjustment on the 2150A

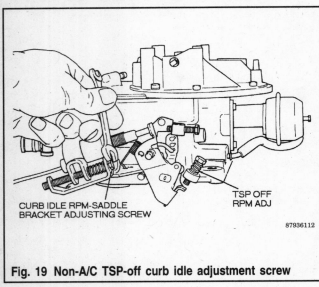

Fig. 19 Non-A/C TSP-off curb idle adjustment screw

7. Place the manual transmission in neutral; the automatic in Drive. Block the wheels.

8. Turn the solenoid adjusting screw in or out to obtain the specified idle speed. The idle speed is the higher of the two rpm figures on the underhood specification sticker.

9. Disconnect the solenoid lead wire. Place the automatic transmission in neutral.

10. Turn the solenoid off adjusting screw to obtain the solenoid off rpm. This is the lower of the two rpm figures on the underhood specifications sticker.

11. Connect the solenoid lead wire and open the throttle slightly to allow the solenoid plunger to extend.

12. Stop the engine, replace the air cleaner and connect the vacuum lines. Check the idle speed. Readjust if necessary with the air cleaner installed.

1977-86

1. Block the wheels and apply parking brake.

2. Run engine until normal operating temperature is reached.

3. Place the vehicle in Park or Neutral, A/C in Off position, and set parking brake.

4. Remove air cleaner.

5. Disconnect and plug decel throttle control kicker diaphragm vacuum hose.

6. Connect a slave vacuum hose from an engine manifold vacuum source to the decel throttle control kicker.

7. Run engine at approximately 2,500 rpm for 15 seconds, then release the throttle.

8. If decel throttle control rpm is not within ± 50 rpm of specification, adjust the kicker.

9. Disconnect the slave vacuum hose and allow engine to return to curb idle.

10. Adjust curb idle, if necessary, using the curb idle adjusting screw.

11. Rev the engine momentarily, recheck curb idle and adjust if necessary.

12. Reconnect the decel throttle control vacuum hose to the diaphragm.

13. Reinstall the air cleaner.

IDLE MIXTURE ADJUSTMENT

1966 and Later

1. Block the wheels, set the parking brake and run the engine to bring it to normal operating temperature.

2. Disconnect the hose between the emission canister and the air cleaner.

3. On engines equipped with the Thermactor air injection system, the routing of the vacuum lines connected to the dump valve will have to be temporarily changed. Mark them for reconnection before switching them.

4. For dump valves with one or two vacuum lines at the side, disconnect and plug the lines.

5. For dump valves with one vacuum line at the top, check the line to see if it is connected to the intake manifold or an intake manifold source such as the carburetor or distributor vacuum line. If not, remove and plug the line at the dump valve and connect a temporary length of vacuum hose from the dump valve fitting to a source of intake manifold vacuum.

6. Remove the limiter caps from the mixture screws by CAREFULLY cutting them with a sharp knife.

7. Place the transmission in neutral and run the engine at 2500 rpm for 15 seconds.

8. Place the automatic transmission in Drive; the manual in neutral.

9. Adjust the idle speed to the higher of the two figures given on the underhood sticker.

10. Turn the idle mixture screws to obtain the highest possible rpm, leaving the screws in the leanest position that will maintain this rpm.

11. Repeat steps 7 through 10 until further adjustment of the mixture screws does not increase the rpm.

12. Turn the screws in until the lower of the two idle speed figures is reached. Turn the screws in ¼ turn increments each to insure a balance.

13. Turn the engine off and remove the tachometer. Reinstall all equipment.

➡ **Rough idle, that cannot be corrected by normal service procedures on 1977 and later models, may be cause by leakage between the EGR valve body and diaphragm. To determine if this is the cause:**

14. Tighten the EGR bolts to 15 ft.lb. Connect a vacuum gauge to the intake manifold.

15. Lift to exert a sideways pressure on the diaphragm housing. If the idle changes or the reading on the vacuum gauge varies, replace the EGR valve.

FUEL INJECTED ENGINES

These engines have idle speed controlled by the TFI-IV/EEC-IV system and no adjustment is possible.

Valve Lash

Valve adjustment determines how far the valves enter the cylinder and how long they stay open and closed.

If the valve clearance is too large, part of the lift of the camshaft will be used in removing the excessive clearance. Consequently, the valve will not be opening as far as it should. This condition has two effects: the valve train components will emit a tapping sound as they take up the excessive clearance and the engine will perform poorly because the valves don't open fully and allow the proper amount of gases to flow into and out of the engine.

If the valve clearance is too small, the intake valve and the exhaust valves will open too far and they will not fully seal on the cylinder head when they close. When a valve seats itself on the cylinder head, it does two things: it seals the combustion chamber so that none of the gases in the cylinder escape and it cools itself by transferring some of the heat it absorbs from the combustion in the cylinder to the cylinder head and to the engine's cooling system. If the valve clearance is too small, the engine will run poorly because of the gases escaping from the combustion chamber. The valves will also become overheated and will warp, since they cannot transfer heat unless they are touching the valve seat in the cylinder head.

➡ **While all valve adjustments must be made as accurately as possible, it is better to have the valve adjustment slightly loose than slightly tight as a burned valve may result from overly tight adjustments.**

Hydraulic valve lifters operate with zero clearance in the valve train, and because of this the rocker arms are nonadjustable. The only means by which valve system clearances can be altered is by installing over or undersize pushrods; but, because of the hydraulic lifter's natural ability to compensate for slack in the valve train, all components of all the valve system should be checked for wear if there is excessive play in the system.

ADJUSTMENT

Adjustable Rocker Arms
▶ **See Figures 20 and 21**

1. Crank the engine until the No. 1 cylinder is at TDC of the compression stroke and the timing pointer is aligned with the mark on the crankshaft damper.

2. Scribe a mark on the damper at this point.

3. Scribe two additional marks on the damper (see illustration).

4. With the timing pointer aligned with mark 1 on the damper, back off the rocker arm adjusting nut on the following valves until there is end-play in the pushrod. Tighten the adjusting nut until all clearance is removed, then tighten the adjusting nut one additional turn. To determine when all clearance is removed from the rocker arm, turn the pushrod with

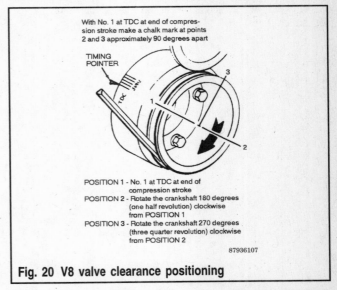

With No. 1 at TDC at end of compression stroke make a chalk mark at points 2 and 3 approximately 90 degrees apart

TIMING POINTER

POSITION 1 - No. 1 at TDC at end of compression stroke
POSITION 2 - Rotate the crankshaft 180 degrees (one half revolution) clockwise from POSITION 1
POSITION 3 - Rotate the crankshaft 270 degrees (three quarter revolution) clockwise from POSITION 2

87936107

Fig. 20 V8 valve clearance positioning

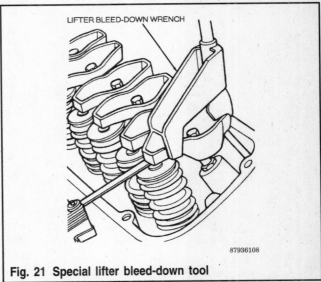

LIFTER BLEED-DOWN WRENCH

87936108

Fig. 21 Special lifter bleed-down tool

the fingers. When the pushrod can no longer be turned, all clearance has been removed.

- Nos. 1, 7 and 8 Intake
- Nos. 1, 5 and 4 Exhaust

5. Rotate the crankshaft 180 degrees to point 2 and adjust the following valves:

- Nos. 5 and 4 Intake
- Nos. 2 and 6 Exhaust

6. Rotate the crankshaft 270 degrees to point 3 and adjust the following valves:

- Nos. 2, 3 and 6 Intake
- Nos. 7, 3 and 8 Exhaust

Non-adjustable Rocker Arms

1. Crank the engine until the No. 1 cylinder is at TDC of the compression stroke and the timing pointer is aligned with the mark on the crankshaft damper.

2. Scribe a mark on the damper at this point.

3. Scribe two additional marks on the damper (see illustration).

4. With the timing pointer aligned with mark 1 on the damper, tighten the following valves on the specified torque:

- 255, 302, 360, 390 and 460: Nos. 1, 7 and 8 Intake; Nos. 1, 5 and 4 Exhaust
- 351, 400: Nos. 1, 4 and 8 Intake; Nos. 1,3 and 7 Exhaust

5. Rotate the crankshaft 180 degrees to point 2 and tighten the following valves:

- 255, 302, 360, 390 and 460: Nos. 5 and 4 Intake; Nos. 2 and 6 Exhaust
- 351, 400: Nos. 3 and 7 Intake; Nos. 6 and 6 Exhaust

6. Rotate the crankshaft 270 degrees to point 3 and tighten the following valves:

- 255, 302, 360, 390 and 460: Nos. 2, 3 and 6 Intake; Nos. 7, 3 and 8 Exhaust
- 351, 400: Nos. 2, 5 and 6 Intake; Nos. 4, 5 and 8 Exhaust

7. Rocker arm tightening specifications are:

- Except 460: tighten the nut until it contacts the rocker shoulder, then torque to 18-20 ft. lbs.
- 460: tighten the nut until it contacts the rocker shoulder, then torque to 18-22 ft. lbs.

TUNE-UP SPECIFICATIONS
Comet, Cougar, Fairlane, Falcon, Maverick, Montego, Mustang and Torino

| YEAR | MODEL | SPARK PLUGS | | DISTRIBUTOR | | IGNITION TIMING (Deg.) ▲ | CRANKING COMP. PRESSURE (Psi) | VALVES | | | FUEL PUMP PRESSURE (Psi) | IDLE SPEED (Rpm) * |
		Type	Gap (In.)	Point Dwell (Deg.)	Point Gap (In.)			Tappet (Hot) Clearance (In.) Intake	Exhaust	Intake Opens (Deg.)		
1964–65	6 Cyl.—Exc. 200	BF82	.034	37.5°	.025	8B	170	Hyd.	Hyd.	13B	4½	500
	6 Cyl.—Exc. 200 Auto.	BF82	.034	37.5°	.025	12B	170	Hyd.	Hyd.	13B	4½	485
	6 Cyl.—200 Auto. Trans.	BF82	.034	37.5°	.025	12B	150	Hyd.	Hyd.	6B	4½	485
	V8—260 Std. Trans.	BF42	.034	27.0°	.015	6B①	150	Hyd.	Hyd.	21B	5	575
	V8—260 Auto. Trans.	BF42	.034	27.0°	.015	10B①	150	Hyd.	Hyd.	21B	5	500
	V8—289 Std. Trans.	BF42	.034	27.0°	.015	6B②	150	Hyd.	Hyd.	20B	5	575
	V8—289 Auto. Trans.	BF42	.034	27.0°	.015	8B	150	Hyd.	Hyd.	20B	5	500
	V8—289 Hi Perf.	BF32	.034	27.0°	.020	10B	200	.018	.018	46B	5	750
1966	6 Cyl. 170, 200 M.T.	BF82	.034	39.0°	.025	6B⊙	170	Hyd.	Hyd.	13B	4½	500
	6 Cyl. 170, 200 A.T.	BF82	.034	39.0°	.025	12B⊙	170	Hyd.	Hyd.	13B	4½	500
	V8—289 M.T.	BF42	.034	27.0°	.017	6B⊙	150	Hyd.	Hyd.	20B	5	600
	V-8, 289 A.T.	BF42	.034	27.0°	.017	6B⊙	150	Hyd.	Hyd.	20B	5	500
	V-8, 289 Hi Perf.	BF32	.030	31.0°	.020	12B	200	.018	.018	46B	5	750
	V-8, 390 M.T.	BF42	.034	27.0°	.017	10B⊙	180	Hyd.	Hyd.	26B	5	600
	V-8, 390 A.T.	BF42	.034	28.0°	.017	10B⊙	180	Hyd.	Hyd.	26B	5	500
1967	6 Cyl.—170, 200 M.T.	BF82	.034	37.0°	.025	6B⊙	170	Hyd.	Hyd.	9B	4½	600
	6 Cyl.—170, 200 A.T.	BF82	.034	37.0°	.025	12B⊙	170	Hyd.	Hyd.	9B	4½	525
	V8—289, 2-BBL.	BF42	.034	27.0°	.017	6B⊙	150	Hyd.	Hyd.	16B	5	600
	V8—289, 4-BBL.	BF42	.034	27.0°	.017	6B⊙	150	Hyd.	Hyd.	16B	5	600
	V8—289 Hi-Perf.	BF32	.034	31.0°	.020	12B⊙	200	.019	.021	46B	5	750
	V8—390, 2-BBL. M.T.	BF42	.034	26.0°	.017	10B⊙	180	Hyd.	Hyd.	16B	5	600
	V8—390, 2-BBL. A.T	BF42	.034	26.0°	.017	10B⊙	180	Hyd.	Hyd.	16B	5	500
	V8—390, 4-BBL. M.T	BF32	.034	26.0°	.017	12B⊙	180	Hyd.	Hyd.	20B	5	575
	V8—390, 4-BBL. A.T	BF32	.034	26.0°	.017	12B⊙	180	Hyd.	Hyd.	20B	5	500
	V8—427, Transistor—All	BF32	.030	23.0°	.020	8B	180	.025	.025	48B	5	800
1968	6 Cyl. 170, 200	BF82	.034	37.0°	.027	6B	170	Hyd.	Hyd.	9B	4½	600
	V8—289 M.T.	BF42	.034	27.0°	.017	6B	150	Hyd.④	Hyd.④	9B	5	625
	V8—289 A.T	BF42	.034	27.0°	.017	6B	150	Hyd.	Hyd.	9B	5	525
	V8—302	BF42	.034	27.0°	.017	6B	150	Hyd.	Hyd.	15B	5	650③
	V8—390 2-BBL	BF32	.034	27.0°	.020	6B	180	Hyd.	Hyd.	13B	5	650
	V8—390 4-BBL	BF32	.034	27.0°	.020	6B	180	Hyd.	Hyd.	18B	5	650
	V8—427	BF32	.034	27.0°	.020	6B	180	Hyd.	Hyd.	18B	5	650
1969	6 Cyl. 170, 200	BF82	.034	37.0°	.027	6B	170	Hyd.	Hyd.	9B	4½	⑪
	6 Cyl. 250	BF82	.034	40.0°	.025	6B	170	Hyd.	Hyd.	10B	5	⑤ ⑯
	V8—302, 2-BBL. A.T.	BF42	.034	29.0°	.017	6B	150	Hyd.	Hyd.	16B	5	550
	V8—302, 2-BBL. M.T	BF42	.034	27.0°	.021	6B	150	Hyd.	Hyd.	16B	5	650
	V8—351, 2-BBL.	BF42	.034	29.0°	.017	6B	170	Hyd.	Hyd.	11B	5	⑰
	V8—351, 4-BBL.	BF32	.034	29.0°	.017	6B	170	Hyd.	Hyd.	11B	5	⑱
	V8—390, 4-BBL. A.T.	BF32	.034	29.0°	.017	6B	170	Hyd.	Hyd.	16B	5	550
	V8—390, 4-BBL. M.T.	BF42	.034	29.0°	.017	6B	170	Hyd.	Hyd.	16B	5	650–700
	V8—428, 4-BBL. A.T CJ	BF32	.034	29.0°	.017	6B	180	Hyd.	Hyd.	18B	5	650
	V8—428, 4-BBL. M.T CJ	BF32	.034	29.0°	.017	6B	180	Hyd.	Hyd.	18B	5	700

87936c01

TUNE-UP SPECIFICATIONS
Comet, Cougar, Fairlane, Falcon, Maverick, Montego, Mustang and Torino (Cont.)

YEAR	MODEL	SPARK PLUGS		DISTRIBUTOR		IGNITION TIMING (Deg.) ▲	CRANKING COMP. PRESSURE (Psi)	VALVES			FUEL PUMP PRESSURE (Psi)	IDLE SPEED (Rpm) ★
		Type	Gap (In.)	Point Dwell (Deg.)	Point Gap (In.)			Tappet (Hot) Clearance (In.) Intake	Exhaust	Intake Opens (Deg.)		
1970-71	6 Cyl. 170, 200	BF82	.035	37.0°	.027	6B	170	Hyd.	Hyd.	9B	4½	(11)
	6 Cyl. 250	BF82	.035	40.0°	.025	6B	170	Hyd.	Hyd.	10B	5	(12)
	V8—302, 2-BBL. A.T.	BF42	.035	(9)	(9)	6B	150	Hyd.	Hyd.	16B	5	600/500 (3)(8)
	V8—302, 2-BBL. M.T.	BF42	.035	27.0° (9)	(9)	6B	150	Hyd.	Hyd.	16B	5	800/500 (5)
	V8—302 Boss	AF32	.035	30-33°	.020 (10)	16B	180	.025	.025	40B	5-6	800/500 (5)
	V8—351, 2-BBL. A.T. (6)	BF42	.035	(9)	(9)	10B	170	Hyd.	Hyd.	11B	5	600/500 (3)(8)
	V8—351, 2-BBL. M.T. (6)	BF42	.034	(9)	(9)	10B	170	Hyd.	Hyd.	11B	5	700/500 (3)
	V8—351, 2-BBL. A.T (7)	AF42	.035	(9)	(9)	6B	170	Hyd.	Hyd.	12B	5	600/500 (3)(8)
	V8—351, 2-BBL. M.T.(7)	AF42	.035	(9)	(9)	6B	170	Hyd.	Hyd.	12B	5	700/500 (3)
	V8—351, 4-BBL. A.T.(7)	AF32	.035	(9)	(9)	6B	170	Hyd.	Hyd.	14B	5	600/500 (3)(8)
	V8—351, 4-BBL. M.T.(7)	AF32	.035	(9)	(9)	6B	170	Hyd.	Hyd.	14B	5	700/500 (5)
	V8—428, 4-BBL. A.T. CJ	BF32	.035	(9)	(9)	6B	180	Hyd.	Hyd.	18B	5	(14)(5)
	V8—428, 4-BBL. M.T. CJ	BF32	.035	(9)	(9)	6B	180	Hyd.	Hyd.	18B	5	(14)(5)
	V8—429 Boss	AF32	.035	30-33°	.020 (10)	10B	180	.013C	.013C	40B	6-8	700/500 (5)
	V8—429, 4-BBL. CJ	AF32	.035	(9)	(9)	10B	180	Hyd.	Hyd.	32B	6-8	850/500(3)(13)
	V8—429, 4-BBL. SCJ	AF32	.035	(9)	(9)	10B	180	.019	.019	40½B	6-8	(13)(5)

★—With manual transmission in N and automatic in D. Add 50 rpm if air conditioned.

▲—With vacuum advance disconnected and plugged. NOTE: These settings are only approximate. Engine design, altitude, temperature, fuel octane rating and the condition of the individual engine are all factors which can influence timing. The limiting advance factor must, therefore, be the "knock point" of the individual engine.

B—Before top dead center.

CJ—Cobra Jet.

A.T.—Automatic transmission.

M.T.—Manual transmission.

(1)—Mustang—4B.

(2)—Mustang—8B.

(3)—550 rpm with automatic.

(4)—High perf. engine—Intake = .019 in.; Exhaust = .021 in.

(5)—Higher idle speed with solenoid throttle positioner energized, lower with it disconnected.

(6)—Windsor-built engine.

(7)—Cleveland-built engine.

(8)—575 rpm (600 for 351C) with no solenoid throttle positioner installed.

(9)—Dual diaphragm unit—one set of points = 24-29° dwell, .021 point gap. Single diaphragm unit—one set of points = 26-31° dwell, .017 point gap.

(10)—Dual points.

(11)—M.T.—750
A.T.—550

(12)—M.T.—750/500
A.T.—600/500

(13)—A.T.—600

(14)—M.T.—725/500 } 725 w/o A/C.
A.T.—675/500 } 675 w/o A/C.

(15)—M.T.—650/500
A.T.—700/500

(16)—M.T.—700 w/o A/C
700/500 with A/C
A.T.—550 w/o A/C
550/450 with A/C

(17)—M.T.—650
A.T.—550

(18)—M.T.—675
A.T.—575

(19)—1966 with Thermactor system:
Timing—170,200,289 = TDC
390 = 6B
Idle speed—M.T. = 625 rpm
A.T. = 550-575 for 170 & 200
475-500 for 289 & 390

(20)—1967 with Thermactor system:
Timing—170 = TDC
200 = 5B
289 = TDC
289 High perf. & 390 = 6B

87936c02

TUNE-UP SPECIFICATIONS
1964 - 71 Full-Sized Ford, Mercury, Lincoln and Thunderbird

| YEAR | MODEL | SPARK PLUGS | | DISTRIBUTOR | | IGNITION TIMING (Deg.) ▲ | CRANKING COMP. PRESSURE (Psi) | VALVES | | Intake Opens (Deg.) | FUEL PUMP PRESSURE (Psi) | IDLE SPEED (Rpm) * |
| | | Type | Gap (In.) | Point Dwell (Deg.) | Point Gap (In.) | | | Tappet (Hot) Clearance (In.) | | | | |
								Intake	Exhaust			
1964-65	6 Cyl.—223 Cu. In., M.T.	BTFG	.034	37	.025	4B	150	Zero	Zero	23B	4.5	475
	6 Cyl.—223 Cu. In., A.T.	BTFG	.034	37	.025	10B	150	Zero	Zero	23B	4.5	475
	6 Cyl.—240 Cu. In., M.T.	BF42	.034	37	.025	6B	150	Zero	Zero	23B	4.5	475
	6 Cyl.—240 Cu. In., A.T.	BF42	.034	37	.025	8B	150	Zero	Zero	23B	4.5	475
	V8—289 Cu. In., M.T.	BF42	.034	27	.015	6B	150	Zero	Zero	20B	5.0	575
	V8—289 Cu. In.; A.T	BF42	.034	27	.015	10B	150	Zero	Zero	20B	5.0	500
	V8—352 Cu. In.; M.T	BF42	.034	27	.015	6B	180	Zero	Zero	22B	5.0	500
	V8—352 Cu. In., A.T.	BF42	.034	27	.015	10B	180	Zero	Zero	22B	5.0	475
	V8—390 Cu. In.; M.T.	BF42	.034	27	.015	4B	180	Zero	Zero	26B	5.0	500
	V8—390 Cu. In.; A T	BF42	.034	27	.015	6B	180	Zero	Zero	26B	5.0	500
	V8—427 Cu. In.; M.T.	BF32	.030	35	.020	8B	180	.025H	.025H	5A	6.0	700
1966	6 Cyl.—240 Cu. In., M.T	BTF42	.034	39	.025	6B⊙	150	Zero	Zero	23B	5.0	525⊙
	6 Cyl.—240 Cu. In. A.T	BTF42	.034	39	.025	12B⊙	150	Zero	Zero	23B	5.0	525
	V8—289 Cu. In.	BF42	.034	28	.017	6B⊙	150	Zero	Zero	20B	5.0	*
	V8—352 Cu. In.	BF42	.034	28	.017	10B	180	Zero	Zero	22B	6.0	550⊙
	V8—390 Cu. In.	BF42	.034	28	.017	10B⊙	180	Zero	Zero	26B	6.0	600⊙
	V8—427 Cu. In.	BF32	.034	23	.020	8B	180	.025H	.025H	5A	6.0	800
	V8—428 Cu. In.	BF42	.030	28	.017	10B⊙	180	Zero	Zero	16B	6.0	*
1967	6 Cyl.—240, M.T.	BF42	.034	39	.025	6B⊙	150	Zero	Zero	12B	5	525⊙
	6 Cyl.—240, A.T.	BF42	.034	39	.025	10B⊙	150	Zero	Zero	12B	5	525⊙
	V8—289, All	BF42	.034	28	.015	6B⊙	150	Zero	Zero	16B	5	525⊙
	V8—390, 2-BBL., A.T	BF42	.034	28	.015	10B⊙	150	Zero	Zero	16B	5	500⊙
	V8—390, 4-BBL., M.T	BF42	.034	28	.015	10B	150	Zero	Zero	16B	5	575
	V8—390, 4-BBL., A T	BF42	.034	28	.015	10B	150	Zero	Zero	16B	5	500
	V8—427 All	BF32	.030	23	.020	8B	180	.025H	.025H	48B	6	800
	V8—428 All	BF42	.034	28	.017	10B⊙	180	Zero	Zero	16B	6	600
1968	6 Cyl. 240	BF42	.034	39	.025	6B	150	Zero	Zero	12B	5	*
	V8—302	BF32	.034	27	.021	6B	150	Zero	Zero	15B	5	625●●
	V8—390 2-BBL.	BF32	.034	27	.021	6B	150	Zero	Zero	13B	6	625●●
	V8—390, 4-BBL.	BF32	.034	27	.021	6B	150	Zero	Zero	16B	6	625●●
	V8—390, G.T.	BF32	.034	27	.021	6B	150	Zero	Zero	16B	6	700●●
	V8—428	BF32	.034	27	.021	6B	150	Zero	Zero	16B	6	625●●
	V8—428 Interceptor	BF32	.034	27	.021	6B	150	Zero	Zero	18B	6	N.A.
	V8—429	BF42	.034	27	.021	6B	150	Zero	Zero	16B	6	550
1969	6 Cyl.—240	BF42	.034	39	.027	6B	150	Zero	Zero	6B	5	*
	V8—302, 2-BBL.	BF42	.034	27	.021	6B	150	Zero	Zero	6B	5	625●●
	V8—390, 2-BBL.	BF42	.034	27	.021	6B	150	Zero	Zero	6B	5	625●●
	V8—428, 4-BBL.	BF32	.034	29	.021	6B	180	Zero	Zero	6B	6	550
	V8—429, 2-BBL.	BF42	.034	29	.021	6B	180	Zero	Zero	6B	6	550
	V8—429, 4-BBL.	BF42	.034	29	.021	6B	180	Zero	Zero	6B	6	550
1970	6 Cyl.—240	BF42	.034	39	.027	6B	150	Zero	Zero	6B	4-6	*
	V8—302, 2-BBL.	BF42	.034	27	.021	6B	150	Zero	Zero	6B	4-6	625●●
	V8—351, 2-BBL	BF42	.034	27	.017	6B	170	Zero	Zero	11B	4-6	600
	V8—390, 2-BBL.	BF42	.034	27	.021	6B	170	Zero	Zero	18B	5-6	650
	V8—428, 4-BBL.	BF32	.035	24-29	.021	6B	190	Zero	Zero	18B	5-6	600
	V8—429, 2-BBL.	BF42	.034	27	.021	6B	180	Zero	Zero	6B	5.5-6.5	550
	V8—429, 4-BBL.	BF42	.034	27	.021	6B	180	Zero	Zero	6B	5.5-6.5	550

87936c03

TUNE-UP SPECIFICATIONS
1964 - 71 Full-Sized Ford, Mercury,
Lincoln and Thunderbird (Cont.)

YEAR	MODEL	SPARK PLUGS		DISTRIBUTOR		IGNITION TIMING (Deg.) ▲	CRANKING COMP PRESSURE (Psi)	VALVES		Intake Opens (Deg.)	FUEL PUMP PRESSURE (Psi)	IDLE SPEED (Rpm) *
		Type	Gap (In.)	Point Dwell (Deg.)	Point Gap (In.)			Tappet (Hot) Clearance (In.)				
								Intake	Exhaust			
1971	6 Cyl.—240	BF42	.034	38	.027	6B	150	Zero	Zero	12B	4-6	500 ①
	V8—302, 2-BBL.	BF42	.034	27	.021	6B	150	Zero	Zero	16B	4-6	575 ②
	V8—351, 2-BBL.	BF42	.034	27	.021	6B	170	Zero	Zero	11B	4-6	575 ②
	V8—390, 2-BBL.	BF42	.034	27	.021	6B	180	Zero	Zero	13B	5.5-6.5	575 ③
	V8—400, 2-BBL.	BF42	.034	27	.021	6B	180	Zero	Zero	18B	5.5-6.5	575 ③
	V8—429, 2-BBL.	BF42	.034	27	.021	6B	180	Zero	Zero	16B	5.5-6.5	600
	V8—429, 4-BBL.	BF42	.034	27	.021	6B	180	Zero	Zero	16B	5.5-6.5	600
	V8—429, 4-BBL. ④	BF42	.034	30	.017	6B	180	Zero	Zero	16B	5.5-6.5	600

B—Before top dead center.
TDC—Top dead center.
●—With mechanical, zero lash rocker arms, see text
*—With manual transmission in N and automatic in D. Add 50 rpm if equipped with air conditioning.
▲—With vacuum advance disconnected and plugged. NOTE: These settings are only approximate. Engine design, altitude, temperature, fuel octane rating and the condition of the individual engine are all factors which can influence timing. The limiting advance factor must, therefore, be the "knock point" of the individual engine.

*—M.T.—600
  A.T.—500
●●—A.T. 550 RPM
⊙—1966 with thermactor system:
  timing: 6 Cyl. & V8 289—TDC
  idle speed: 6 Cyl. M.T.—650 rpm
  V8 352—635, 289—600
  V8 390 A.T.—500

⊙—1967 with thermactor system:
  6 Cyl. M.T.—TDC A.T.—4B
  V8—289 exc. Hi Per.—TDC
  V8—289—Hi Per.—12B
  V8—390, 428—6B
①—M.T.—775
②—M.T.—700
③—M.T. 725
④—Thunderbird

87936c04

TUNE-UP SPECIFICATIONS
1972 - 79 Comet, Fairmont, Granada, Maverick, Monarch
1979 Mustang and Capri

When analyzing compression test results, look for uniformity among cylinders rather than specific pressures.

Year	ENGINE No. Cyl Displacement (cu in.)	hp	SPARK PLUGS Orig. Type	● Gap (in.)	DISTRIBUTOR Point Dwell* (deg)	Point Gap (in.)	IGNITION TIMING (deg)▲ Man Trans	Auto Trans	VALVES Intake Opens ■(deg)	Fuel Pump Pressure (psi)	IDLE SPEED (rpm)▲ Man Trans	● Auto Trans
'72	6-170	82	BRF-82	.034	37	.027/	6B	—	9	4-6	750	—
	6-200	91	BRF-82	.034	37	.027	6B	6B	9	4-6	800/500	600/500
	6-250	98	BRF-82	.034	37	.027	6B	6B	10	4-6	750/500	600/500
	8-302	143	BRF-42	.034	28	.017	6B	6B	16	4-6	800/500	600/500
'73	6-200	91	BRF-82	.034	37	.027/ .025	6B	6B	9	4-6	800/500	600/500
	6-250	98	BRF-82	.034	37	.027/ .025	—	6B	10	4-6	—	600/500
	8-302	143	BRF-42	.034	28	.017	6B	6B	16	4-6	800/500	600/500
'74	6-200	84	BRF-82	.034⑥	37⑤	.024/ .030	6B	6B	28	4½-5½	750/500	550/500
	6-250	91	BRF-82	.034⑥	37⑤	.024/ .030	6B	6B	26	4½-5½	750/500	600/500
	8-302	140	BRF-42	.034⑥	27⑤	.014/ .020	6B	6B	②	5½-6½	800/500	650/500①
'75	6-200	All	BRF-82	.044	Electronic		6B	6B	20	4½-5½	750/500	600/500
	6-250	All	BRF-82	.044	Electronic		6B	6B	26	4½-5½	850/500	600/500
	8-302	All	ARF-42	.044	Electronic		6B	6B	20	5½-6½	900/500	650/500
	8-302	115	ARF-42	.044	Electronic		6B	8B	20	5½-6½	900/500	650/500
	8-351 W	143	ARF-42	.044	Electronic		—	4B	15	5½-6½	—	700/500
	8-351 W④	153	ARF-42	.044	Electronic		—	6B	15	5½-6½	—	650/500
'76	6-200	All	BRF-82	.044	Electronic		③	③	20	4½-5½	800	650
	6-250	All	BRF-82	.044	Electronic		③	③	26	4½-5½	850	600
	8-302	All	ARF-42/52③	.044	Electronic		③	③	20	5½-6½	750	650(700)
	8-351W	All	ARF-52	.044	Electronic		—	8(10B) @ 625(650)	15	5½-6½	—	625(650)
'77	6-200	All	BRF-82	.050	Electronic		6B	6B	20	5½-6½	800	650
	6-250	All	BRF-82	.050	Electronic		4B	68(8B)	18	5½-6½	850	600
	8-302	All	ARF-52 (ARF-52-6)	.050 (.060)	Electronic		6B	4B(12B)	16	5½-6½	750	650(700)
	8-351W	All	ARF-52 (ARF-52-6)	.050 (.060)	Electronic		—	4B	23	5½-6½	—	625

87936c08

TUNE-UP SPECIFICATIONS
1972 - 79 Comet, Fairmont, Granada, Maverick, Monarch
1979 Mustang and Capri (Cont.)

When analyzing compression test results, look for uniformity among cylinders rather than specific pressures.

Year	ENGINE No. Cyl Displacement (cu in.)	hp	SPARK PLUGS Orig. Type	Gap (in.)	DISTRIBUTOR Point Dwell* (deg)	Point Gap (in.)	IGNITION TIMING (deg)▲ Man Trans	Auto Trans	VALVES Intake Opens ■(deg)	Fuel Pump Pressure (psi)	IDLE SPEED (rpm)▲ Man Trans	Auto Trans
'78	4-140	All	AWRF-42	.034	Electronic		6B	20B	22	5½-6½	850	800
	6-200	All	BRF-82	.050 (.060)	Electronic		10B	10B(6B)	20	5½-6½	800	650
	6-250	All	BRF-82	.050	Electronic		4B	14B(6B)	18	5½-6½	800	600
	8-302	All	ARF-52 (ARF-52-6)	.050 (.060)	Electronic		10B	6B(12B⑦)	16	5½-6½	500	650
'79		All			See Underhood Specifications Sticker							

* Where two dwell or point gap figures are separated by a slash, the first figure is for engines equipped with dual diaphragm distributors and the second figure is for engines equipped with single diaphragm distributors
▲ See text for procedure
■ All figures Before Top Dead Center
● Where two idle speed figures are separated by a slash, the first figure is for idle speed with solenoid energized and automatic transmission in Drive, while the second is for idle speed with solenoid disconnected and automatic transmission in Neutral. Figures in parentheses are for California
B Before Top Dead Center
— Not applicable

① 600/500 with air conditioning
② 16° B—manual transmission
20° B—automatic transmission
③ Depends on emission equipment; check underhood specifications sticker
④ Granada/Monarch
⑤ Electronic ignition used on all engines assembled after May, 1974
⑥ .044 in. with electronic ignition
⑦ 14B for high altitude
NOTE: The underhood specifications sticker often reflects tune-up specification changes made in production. Sticker figures must be used if they disagree with those in this chart.

87936c09

TUNE-UP SPECIFICATIONS
1972 - 79 Cougar, Elite, LTD II, Montego, Mustang
Through 1973, Torino, and 1977 - 79 Thunderbird

When analyzing compression test results, look for uniformity among cylinders rather than specific pressures.

Year	ENGINE No. Cyl Displacement (cu in.)	hp	SPARK PLUGS Orig. Type	Gap (in.)	DISTRIBUTOR Point Dwell* (deg)	Point Gap (in.)	IGNITION TIMING (deg)▲ Man Trans	Auto Trans	VALVES Intake Opens ■(deg)	Fuel Pump Pressure (psi)	IDLE SPEED (rpm)▲ Man Trans	Auto Trans
'72	6-250	95	BRF-82	.034	37	.027	6B	6B	10(16)	4½-6½	750/500	600/500
	8-302	140	BRF-42	.034	28	.017	6B	6B	16	5½-6½	800/500	575 600/500
	8-351C	165	ARF-42	.034	28	.017	6B	6B	12	5½-6½		575/500 (625/500)
	8-351W	165	BRF-42	.034	28	.017	—	6B	12	5½-6½	—	575 600/500
	8-351CJ	266	ARF-42	.034	28	.017/.020	16B	16B④	14	5½-6½		700/500④ (800/500)
	8-351HO	N.A.	ARF-42	.034	28	.020	10B	—	17½	5½-6½	1000/500	—
	8-400	168	ARF-42	.034	28	.017	—	6B	17	4½-5½	—	625/500
	8-429	205	ARF-42	.034	28	.017	—	10B	8	5½-6½	—	600/500
'73	6-250	95	BRF-82	.034	37	.027/.025	6B	6B	16	4½-6½	750/500	600/500
	8-302	140	BRF-42	.034	28	.017	6B	6B	16	5½-6½	800/500	575 600/500
	8-351C	165	ARF-42	.034	28	.017		6B	12	5½-6½	—	625/500
	8-351W	165	BRF-42	.034	28	.017	—	6B	12	5½-6½	—	575 600/500
	8-351CJ	266	ARF-42	.034	28⑤	.017③	16B	16B④	14	5½-6½	1000/500	800/500④
	8-400	168	ARF-42	.034	28	.017	—	6B	17	5½-6½	—	625/500
	8-429	205	ARF-42	.034	28	.017	—	10B	8	5½-6½	—	600/500
	8-460PI	269	ARF-42	.035	28	.017	—	10B	18	5½-7½	—	600
'74	6-250	91	BRF-82	.034①	37⑩	.027	6B	6B	26	5½-6½	800/500	625/500
	8-302	140	BRF-42	.034①	28⑩	.017	10B	6B	16⑦	5½-6½	800/500	625/500
	8-351W	162	BRF-42	.034①	28⑩	.017	—	6B	15	5½-6½	—	600/500
	8-351C	163	ARF-42	.034①	28⑩	.017	—	14B	11.5	5½-6½	—	600/500
	8-351CJ	255	ARF-42	.034①	28⑩	.017	—	20B⑥	14	5½-6½	—	800/500
	8-400	170	ARF-42	.044	Electronic		—	12B⑥	17	5½-6½	—	625/500
	8-460	195, 220, 260	ARF-42	.054	Electronic		—	14B	8	5½-6½	—	650/500
'75	8-351W	153, 154	ARF-42	.044	Electronic		—	6B	15	5½-6½	—	600/500
	8-351M	148, 150	ARF-42	.044	Electronic		—	6B	19½	5½-6½	—	700/500
	8-400	144, 158	ARF-42	.044	Electronic		—	6B	17	5½-6½	—	625/500
	8-460	216, 217	ARF-52	.044	Electronic		—	14B	8	5½-6½	—	650/500
	8-460PI	226	ARF-52	.044	Electronic		—	14B	18	5½-7	—	700/500
'76	8-351W	All	ARF-42/52⑧	.054	Electronic		—	⑧	15	5½-6½	—	650
	8-351M	All	ARF-42/52⑧	.044	Electronic		—	⑧	19½	5½-6½	—	650 (650/675⑧)
	8-400	All	ARF-42/52⑧	.044	Electronic		—	⑧	17	5½-6½	—	650(625)
	8-460	All	ARF-52	.044	Electronic		—	8/14B⑧⑨	8	5½-6½	—	650
	8-460PI	226	ARF-52	.044	Electronic		—	14B⑨	18	5½-7	—	650

87936c05

TUNE-UP SPECIFICATIONS
1972 - 79 Cougar, Elite, LTD II, Montego, Mustang
Through 1973, Torino, and 1977 - 79 Thunderbird (Cont.)
When analyzing compression test results, look for uniformity among cylinders rather than specific pressures.

Year	ENGINE No. Cyl Displacement (cu in.)	hp	SPARK PLUGS Orig. Type	● Gap (in.)	DISTRIBUTOR Point Dwell* (deg)	Point Gap (in.)	IGNITION TIMING (deg)▲ Man Trans	●	Auto Trans	VALVES Intake Opens ■(deg)	Fuel Pump Pressure (psi)	IDLE SPEED (rpm)▲ Man Trans	●	Auto Trans
'77	8-302	All	ARF-52 (ARF-52-6)	.050(.060)	Electronic		—		8B	16	5½-6½	—		650
	8-351W	All	ARF-52 (ARF-52-6)	.050(.060)	Electronic		—		4B	23	4-6	—		650
	8-351M	All	ARF-52 (ARF-52-6)	.050(.060)	Electronic		—		8B(9B)	19½	6½-7½	—		650
	8-400	All	ARF-52 (ARF-52-6)	.050(.060)	Electronic		—		8B	17	7-8	—		650
'78	8-302	All	ARF-52 (ARF-52-6)	.050(.060)	Electronic				14B	16	5½-6½	—		650
	8-351W	All	ARF-52 (ARF-52-6)	.050(.060)	Electronic				14B	23	4-6	—		650
	8-351M	All	ARF-52 (ARF-52-6)	.050(.060)	Electronic				14B(16B)	19½	6½-7½	—		650
	8-400	All	ARF-52 (ARF-52-6)	.050(.060)	Electronic				13B(16B)	17	6½-7½	—		650
'79		All					See Underhood Specifications Sticker							

NOTE: The underhood specifications sticker often reflects tune-up specification changes made in production. Sticker figures must be used if they disagree with those in this chart.

* Where two dwell or point gap figures are separated by a slash, the first figure is for engines equipped with dual diaphragm distributors and the second figure is for engines equipped with single diaphragm distributors

▲ See text for procedure

● In all cases where two idle speed figures are separated by a slash, the first is for idle speed with solenoid energized and automatic transmission in Drive, while the second is for idle speed with solenoid disconnected and automatic transmission in Neutral. Figures in parentheses are for California.

■ All figures are in degrees Before Top Dead Center

① .044 with electronic ignition
② Not used

③ Figure is .020 for manual transmission with dual point distributor
④ On Cougars with automatic transmission, set ignition timing to 6B and set idle speed to 650 rpm
⑤ Figure is 32°-35° on manual transmission model with dual point distributor with both point sets combined
⑥ At 500 rpm
⑦ 20° BTC for 302 automatic
⑧ Depends on emission equipment; check underhood specifications sticker
⑨ In Drive
⑩ Electronic ignition used on all engines assembled after May, 1974
B Before Top Dead Center
C Cleveland
M Modified Cleveland
CJ Cobra Jet
HO High Output
W Windsor
— Not applicable

MECHANICAL VALVE LIFTER CLEARANCE

Year	Engine	Intake (Hot) In.	Exhaust (Hot) In.
1972	351 HO	.025	.025
1979	170 V6	.014 (cold)	.016 (cold)

87936c06

TUNE-UP SPECIFICATIONS
1972 - 79 Full-Sized Ford

Year	ENGINE No. Cyl. Displacement (cu. In.)	hp	SPARK PLUGS Orig. Type	SPARK PLUGS Gap (in.)	DISTRIBUTOR Point Dwell (deg)	DISTRIBUTOR Point Gap (in.)	IGNITION TIMING (deg) ▲ Man Trans	IGNITION TIMING (deg) ▲ Auto Trans	VALVES Intake Opens ■ (deg)	Fuel Pump Pressure (psi)	IDLE SPEED (rpm) ▲ Man Trans	IDLE SPEED (rpm) ▲ Auto Trans
'72	6-240	103	BRF-42	.034	35-39	.027	—	6B	18	4-6	—	500
	8-302	140	BRF-42	.034	26-30	.017	—	6B	16	5-7	—	575 600/500
	8-351W	153	BRF-42	.034	26-30	.017	—	6B	11	5-7	—	575 600/500
	8-351C	163	ARF-42	.034	26-30	.017	—	6B	12	5-7	—	600/500
	8-400	172	ARF-42	.034	26-30	.017	—	6B	17	5-7	—	625/500
	8-429	208	BRF-42	.034	26-30	.017	—	10B	8	5-7	—	600/500
	8-429PI	N.A.	ARF-42	.034	26-30	.017	—	10B	32	4½-6½	—	650/500
'73	8-351W	153	BRF-42	.034	26-30	.017	—	6B	11	5-7	—	575 600/500
	8-351C	163	ARF-42	.034	26-30	.017	—	6B	12	5-7	—	600/500
	8-400	172	ARF-42	.034	26-30	.017	—	6B	17	5-7	—	625/500
	8-429	208	BRF-42	.034	26-30	.017	—	10B	8	5-7	—	600/500
	8-460PI	267, 274	ARF-42	.034	26-30	.017	—	10B	32	4½-6½	—	650/500
'74	8-351W	162	BRF-42	.034②	26-30③	.014-.020③	—	6B	15	4-6		600/500
	8-351C	163	ARF-42	.044	26-30③	.014-.020③	—	14B	19½	5½-6½	—	700/500
	8-400	170	ARF-42	.044 (.054)	Electronic		—	12B	17	5½-6½	—	625/500
	8-460	195	ARF-52	.054 (.044)	Electronic		—	14B	8	5½-6½	—	650(675) 500
	8-460PI	275	ARF-52	.054	Electronic		—	10B	18	Electric	—	700/500
'75	8-351M	148, 150	ARF-42	.044	Electronic		—	8B	19½	5½-6½	—	700
	8-400	144, 158	ARF-42	.044	Electronic		—	6B④	17	5½-6½	—	625
	8-460	218	ARF-52	.044	Electronic		—	14B	8	6.2-7.2	—	650
	8-460PI	226	ARF-52	.044	Electronic		—	14B	18	6.2-7.2	—	650
'76	8-351M	2 bbl	ARF-52	.044	Electronic		—	8B	19½	5½-6½	—	650
	8-351M	4 bbl	ARF-42	.044	Electronic		—	8B	19½	5½-6½	—	650
	8-400	2 bbl	ARF-52	.044	Electronic		—	10B	17	5½-6½	—	650
	8-400	4 bbl	ARF-42	.044	Electronic		—	10B	17	5½-6½	—	650
	8-460	All	ARF-52	.044	Electronic		—	8B(14B)	8	5-7	—	650
	8-460	PI	ARF-52	.044	Electronic		—	14B	18	6-7	—	650
'77	8-351M	All	ARF-52	.050	Electronic		—	8B	19½	6½-7½	—	650
	8-400	All	ARF-52	.050	Electronic		—	8B	17	6½-7½	—	650(625)
	8-460	All	ARF-52-6	.060	Electronic		—	16B	8	7-8	—	650
	8-460	PI	ARF-52-6	.060	Electronic		—	16B	8	7-8	—	650

87936c10

TUNE-UP SPECIFICATIONS
1972 - 79 Full-Sized Ford (Cont.)

Year	ENGINE No. Cyl. Displacement (cu. In.)	hp	SPARK PLUGS Orig. Type	• Gap (in.)	DISTRIBUTOR Point Dwell (deg)	Point Gap (in.)	IGNITION TIMING (deg) ▲ Man Trans •	Auto Trans	VALVES Intake Opens ■ (deg)	Fuel Pump Pressure (psi)	IDLE SPEED (rpm) ▲ Man Trans *	• Auto Trans
'78	8-302	All	ARF-52 (ARF-52-6)	.050 (.060)	Electronic		—	14B	16	5½-6½	—	650
	8-351W	All	ARF-52 (ARF-52-6)	.050 (.060)	Electronic		—	4B	23	4-6	—	650
	8-351M	All	ARF-52 (ARF-52-6)	.050 (.060)	Electronic		—	12B(16B)	19½	6½-7½	—	650
	8-400	All	ARF-52 (ARF-52-6)	.050 (.060)	Electronic		—	13B(16B)	17	6½-7½	—	650
	8-460	All	ARF-52 (ARF-52-6)	.050 (.060)	Electronic		—	10B	8	7¼-8¼	—	580
	8-460	PI	ARF-52-6	.060	Electronic		—	16B	18	7¼-8¼	—	580
'79	8-302	All	ARF-52	.050	Electronic		—	14B	16	5½-6½	—	650
	8-351 W	All	ARF-52	.050	Electronic		—	4B (EECII)①	23	4-6	—	650

NOTE: The underhood specifications sticker often reflects tune-up specification changes made in production. Sticker figures must be used if they disagree with those in this chart.
▲ See text for procedure
● Figure in parentheses indicates California engine
■ All figures Before Top Dead Center
* In all cases where two idle speed figures are separated by a slash, the first is for idle speed with solenoid energized and the automatic transmission in Drive, while the second is for idle speed with solenoid disconnected and automatic transsion in Neutral.
① California engines have variable EEC II timing; see text for description.

② .044 on California models and all cars using Solid State Ignition
③ Solid State Ignition used on all engines nationwide on cars assembled after May, 1974.
④ 8B with 3.25:1 rear axle, Code 9 or R on Certification label, except in California
B Before Top Dead Center
C Cleveland
M Modified Cleveland
PI Police Interceptor
TDC Top Dead Center
W Windsor
— Not applicable

87936c11

TUNE-UP SPECIFICATIONS
1972 - 79 Full-Sized Mercury and Lincoln
When analyzing compression test results, look for uniformity among cylinders rather than specific pressures.

Year	ENGINE No. Cyl. Displacement (cu. In.)	hp	SPARK PLUGS Orig. Type ●	Gap (in.)	DISTRIBUTOR Point Dwell (deg)	Point Gap (in.)	IGNITION TIMING (deg) ▲ Man Trans ●	Auto Trans	VALVES Intake Opens ■ (deg)	Fuel Pump Pressure (psi)	IDLE SPEED (rpm) ▲ Man Trans *	Auto Trans ●
'72	8-351C	163	ARF-42	.034	28	.017	—	6B	12	5½-6½	—	575/500 (625/500)
	8-400	172	ARF-42	.034	28	.017	—	8B(6B)	17	5½-6½	—	625/500
	8-429	208	BRF-42	.034	28	.017	—	10B	8	5½-6½	—	650/500
	8-429PI	N.A.	ARF-42	.034	28	.020	—	10B	32	5½-6½	—	650/500
	8-460	200	BRF-42	.034	28	.017	—	10B(6B)②	8	5½-6½	—	625/500
'73	8-351C	163	ARF-42	.034	28	.017	—	6B	12	5½-6½	—	650/500
	8-400	172	ARF-42	.034	28	.017	—	6B	17	5½-6½	—	650/500
	8-429	208	BRF-42	.034	28	.017	—	10B	8	5½-6½	—	650/500
	8-429PI	N.A.	ARF-42	.034	28	.020	—	10B	32	5½-6½	—	650/500
	8-460	200	BRF-42	.034	28	.017	—	6B	8	5½-6½	—	(625/500)
'74	8-351C	163	ARF-42	.044	28③	.017③	—	14B	19½	5½-6½	—	600/500
	8-400	170	ARF-42	.044 (.054)	Electronic		—	12B	17	5½-6½	—	625/500
	8-460	195	ARF-52	.054	Electronic		—	10B	8	5½-6½	—	625/500
'75	8-400	144, 158	ARF-42	.044	Electronic		—	12B	17	5.5-6.5	—	625
	8-460	218	ARF-52	.044	Electronic		—	14B	8	6.2-7.2	—	650
	8-460PI	226	ARF-52	.044	Electronic		—	14B	18	6.2-7.2	—	650
'76	8-400	2 bbl	ARF-52	.044	Electronic		—	10B	17	5½-6½	—	650
	8-400	4 bbl	ARF-42	.044	Electronic		—	10B	17	5½-6½	—	650
	8-460	All	ARF-52	.044	Electronic		—	8B(14B)	8	5-7	—	650
	8-460	PI	ARF-52	.044	Electronic		—	14B	18	6-7	—	650
'77	8-400	All	ARF-52	.050	Electronic		—	8B	17	6½-7½	—	650(625)
	8-460	All	ARF-52-6	.060	Electronic		—	16B	8	7-8	—	650
	8-460	PI	ARF-52-6	.060	Electronic		—	16B	8	7-8	—	650

87936c12

TUNE-UP SPECIFICATIONS
1972 - 79 Full-Sized Mercury and Lincoln (Cont.)

When analyzing compression test results, look for uniformity among cylinders rather than specific pressures.

Year	ENGINE No. Cyl. Displacement (cu. In.)	hp	SPARK PLUGS Orig. Type •	Gap (in.)	DISTRIBUTOR Point Dwell (deg)	Point Gap (in.)	IGNITION TIMING (deg) ▲ Man Trans •	Auto Trans	VALVES Intake Opens ■ (deg)	Fuel Pump Pressure (psi)	IDLE SPEED (rpm) ▲ Man Trans *	Auto Trans •
'78	8-351M	All	ARF-52 (ARF-52-6)	.050 (.060)	Electronic		—	12B	19½	6½-7½	—	650(625)
	8-400	All	ARF-52 (ARF-52-6)	.050 (.060)	Electronic		—	13B(16B)	17	6½-7½	—	650(625)
	8-460	All	ARF-52 (ARF-52-6)	.050 (.060)	Electronic		—	16B	8	7¼-8¼	—	580
	8-460 PI	All	ARF-52 (ARF-52-6)	.050 (.060)	Electronic		—	16B	18	7¼-8¼	—	580
'79	8-302	All	ARF-52	.050	Electronic		—	14B	16	5½-6½	—	650
	8-351W	All	ARF-52	.050	Electronic		—	EEC II①	23	4-6	—	650

NOTE: The underhood specifications sticker often reflects tune-up specification changes made in production. Sticker figures must be used if they disagree with those in this chart.
▲ See text for procedure
● Figure in parentheses indicates California engine
■ All figures Before Top Dead Center
* In all cases where two figures are separated by a slash, the first figure is for idle speed with solenoid energized and automatic transmission in Drive, while the second is for idle speed with solenoid disconnected and automatic transmission in Neutral.

① All 351W engines have variable EEC II timing; see text for description.
② For all vehicles with 3.00 axles, Code 6 or 0 on certification label, figure is 6B
③ Solid State Ignition used on all engines nationwide on cars assembled after May 1974.
 B Before Top Dead Center
 C Cleveland
 PI Police Interceptor
 W Windsor
 — Not applicable

87936c13

TUNE-UP SPECIFICATIONS
1972 - 76 Thunderbird
When analyzing compression test results, look for uniformity among cylinders rather than specific pressures.

Year	ENGINE No. Cyl Displacement (cu in.)	hp	SPARK PLUGS Orig. Type	Gap (in.)	DISTRIBUTOR Point Dwell (deg)	Point Gap (in.)	IGNITION TIMING (deg) ▲ Man Trans ●	Auto Trans	VALVES Intake Opens ■ (deg)	Fuel Pump Pressure (psi)	IDLE SPEED (rpm) ▲ Man Trans *	Auto Trans
'72	8-429	208, 212	BRF-42	.034	26-30	.020	—	10B	8	5½-6½	—	650/500
	8-460	200, 212	BRF-42	.034	26-30	.020	—	10B(6B)	8	5½-6½	—	650/500
'73	8-429	208, 212	BRF-42	.034	26-30	.020	—	10B	8	5½-6½	—	650/500
	8-460	200, 212	BRF-42	.034	26-30	.020	—	6B	8	5½-6½	—	650/500
'74	8-460	195	ARF-52	.044	Electronic		—	14B	8	5½-6½		675/500
'75	8-460	All	ARF-52	.044	Electronic		—	14B	8	6½-7½		650
'76	8-460	All	ARF-52	.044	Electronic		—	8B(14B)	8	6-7	—	650

NOTE: The underhood specifications sticker often reflects tune-up specification changes made in production. Sticker figures must be used if they disagree with those in this chart.
▲ See text for procedure
● Figure in parentheses indicates California engine
■ All figures Before Top Dead Center
— Not applicable

* First figure is for idle speed with solenoid energized and automatic transmission in Drive, while the second figure is for idle speed with solenoid disconnected and automatic transmission in Neutral

B Before Top Dead Center

87936c14

TUNE-UP SPECIFICATIONS
1961 - 71 Truck

CU. IN. DISPLACEMENT	YEAR	SPARK PLUG GAP	DISTRIBUTOR POINT DWELL	POINT GAP	IGNITION TIMING DEGREES	CRANKING COMP. PRESSURE	VALVE CLEARANCE INLET	EXHAUST	GOV. R.P.M. NO LOAD	FUEL PUMP PRESS.	IDLE SPEED STD.	AUTO.
289	1966	.034	26-31	.017	6[2]	150	Zero		——	4-6	—	—
	1967	.034	26-31	.017	6	150	Zero		——	4-6	—	—
	1968	.034	24-29	.021	6	150	Zero		——	4-6	625	500
292	1961	.030	26-31	.017	6	150	.019	.019	3800	3½-5½	500	500D
	1962	.030	26-31	.017	8	150	.019	.019	3800	3½-5½	500	500D
2 Bbl.	1963	.030	26-31	.017	6	150	.019	.019	3800	4-6	500	500D
4 Bbl.	1963	.030	26-31	.017	8	150	.019	.019	3600	4-6	500	500D
	1964	.030	26-31	.017	6	150	.019	.019	3900	4-6	500	500D
302	1961-63	.030	26-31	.017	8	150	.020	.020	3600	3½-6½	500	500D
	1968-71	.030	24-29	.021	6	150	Zero		——	5	625	550D
330	1964-71	.030	26-31[4]	.017[5]	12[6]	140	Zero		3900	4½-6½	525	500D
332	1961	.030	26-31	.017	8	140	.020	.020	3600	3½-6½	500	500D
2 Bbl.	1962-63	.030	26-31	.017	2	150	.020	.020	3600	4-6	500	500D
4 Bbl.	1962-63	.030	26-31	.017	8	150	.020	.020	3600	4-6	500	500D
352	1965-67	.034	26-31	.017	6[2]	140	Zero		——	5-6	550	475D
360	1968-71	.034	26-31	.017	6[7]	140	Zero		——	4½-6½	625	550
w/Exh. Em.	1968-71	.034	24-29	.021	6	140	Zero		——	4½-6½	625	550
361	1964	.030	26-31[4]	.017[5]	10	140	Zero		3800	4½-6½	525	500D
	1965	.030	26-31[4]	.017[5]	12	140	Zero		3800	4½-6½	525	500D
	1966-68	.030	26-31[4]	.017[5]	10	140	Zero		3800	4½-6½	525	500
	1969-71	.030	26-31[4]	.017[5]	6	140	Zero		3800	4½-6½	550	500
390	1968-71	.034	26-31	.017	10	140	Zero		3800	4½-6½	625	550
w/Exh. Em.	1968-71	.034	24-29	.021	6	140	Zero		3800	4½-6½	625	550
391	1964	.030	26-31[4]	.017[5]	8	140	Zero		3800	4½-6½	525	500D
	1965	.030	26-31[4]	.017[5]	10	140	Zero		3800	4½-6½	525	500D
	1966-68	.030	26-31[4]	.017[5]	8	140	Zero		3800	4½-6½	525	500
	1969-71	.030	26-31[4]	.017[5]	6	140	Zero		3800	4½-6½	550	500
401	1961	.030	26-31	.017	8	150	.020	.020	3400	8	525	500D
	1962-71	.030	26-31[4]	.017[5]	8	150	.020	.020	3400	8	525	500D
477	1961-71	.030	26-31[4]	.017[5]	8	150	.020	.020	3200	8	525	500D
534	1961-68	.030	26-31[4]	.017[5]	8	150	.020	.020	3200	8	525	500D
	1969-71	.030	22-24	.020	8	150	.020	.020	3000	8	550	500

1—1967, With Exhaust Emission, Std. Trans. 3B, Auto. Trans. 5B.
2—With Exhaust Emission TDC.
3—With Exhaust Emission 68.
4—Transistor Ignition 22-24.

5—Transistor Ignition .020.
6—Heavy Duty—1964-68. 10, 1969-70 6.
7—Auto. Trans. Without Exhaust Emission 10.
8—Electric.

87936c17

TUNE-UP SPECIFICATIONS
1972 - 79 Truck

CU. IN. DISPLACEMENT	YEAR	SPARK PLUG GAP	DISTRIBUTOR POINT DWELL	POINT GAP	IGNITION TIMING DEGREES	CRANKING COMP. PRESSURE	VALVE CLEARANCE INLET	EXHAUST	GOV. R.P.M. NO LOAD	FUEL PUMP PRESS.	IDLE SPEED STD.	AUTO.
302	1971-72	.034	24-29	.017[8]	6B	150	Zero		—	5	500	500
	1973	.034	24-30	.017	[1]	150	Zero		—	5	[1]	[1]
	1974-78	[1]	[1]	[1]	[1]	[12]	Zero		—	5	[1]	[1]
330	1971-73	.030	24-30[2]	.017[3]	[1]	140	Zero		3900	4½-6½	[1]	[1]
	1974-78	[1]	[1]	[1]	[1]	[12]	Zero		3900	4½-6½	[1]	[1]
351W	1976-78	[1]	[11]	[11]	[1]	[12]	Zero		—	4½-6½	[1]	[1]
351M	1977-78	[1]	[11]	[11]	[1]	[12]	Zero		—	4½-6½	[1]	[1]
360/359	1971-72	.034	24-29[9]	.021[10]	6B	140	Zero		—	4½-6½	650	550
	1973	.034	24-30	.017	[1]	[12]	Zero		—	4½-6½	[1]	[1]
	1974-78	[1]	[1]	[1]	[1]	[12]	Zero		—	4½-6½	[1]	[1]
361	1974-78	[1]	[1]		[1]	[12]	Zero		3800	4½-6½	[1]	[1]
390	1971-72	.034	24-39[9]	.021	6	140	Zero		3800	4½-6½	650	550
	1973	.034	24-30	.017	[1]	[12]	Zero		3800	4½-6½	[1]	[1]
	1974-78	[1]	[1]	[1]	[1]	[12]	Zero		3800	4½-6½	[1]	[1]
391/389	1971-73	.030	26-31[2]	.017[3]	[1]	140	Zero		3800	4½-6½	550[1]	500[1]
	1974-78	[1]	[1]	[1]	[1]	[12]	Zero		3800	4½-6½	[1]	[1]
400	1977-78	[1]	[11]	[11]	[1]	[12]	Zero		—	4½-6½	[1]	[1]
401	1971-74	.030	26-31[2]	.017[3]	8[1]	150	.020	.020	3600	[4]	525[1]	500D[1]
	1975-78	[1]	[1]	[1]	[1]	[12]	.020	.020	[1]	[8]	[1]	[1]
460	1973-78	[1]	[1]	[1]	[1]	[12]	Zero		—	4½-6½	[1]	[1]
475	1977-78	[1]	[1]	[1]	[1]	[12]	.020	.020	[1]	[8]	[1]	[1]
477	1971-74	.030	26-31[2]	.017[3]	8[1]	150	.020	.020	3400	[4]	525[1]	500D[1]
	1975-78	[1]	[1]	[1]	[1]	[12]	.020	.020	[1]	[8]	[1]	[1]
534	1971-74	.030	22-24	.020	8[1]	150	.020	.020	3200	[4]	550[1]	500[1]
	1975-78	[1]	[1]	[1]	[1]	[12]	.020	.020	[1]	[8]	[1]	[1]

[1] Set to specifications shown on engine decal.
[2] Transistor Ignition 22-24.
[3] Transistor Ignition .020.
[4] Electric.
[5] F-250 and 1972 Models—34-40.
[6] 1971 F-250—.025.
[7] Over 6000 GVW California—550.
[8] .021 w/Dual Diaphragm Distributor.
[9] 26-31 on F-250 and 1972 Models.
[10] .017 on F-250 and 1972 Models.
[11] Electronic ignition.
[12] Take the highest reading and compare it to the lowest reading. The lower reading must be within 75% of the highest.

87936c19

TUNE-UP SPECIFICATIONS
1980 - 86 All Car and Truck Models
When analyzing compression test results, look for uniformity among cylinders rather than specific pressures

Year	Eng. V.I.N. Code	No. Cyl. Displacement (cu. in.)	Eng. Mfg.	Orig. Type	Gap (in.)	Distributor	Man. Trans.	Auto. Trans.	Valves Intake Opens (deg)	Fuel Pump Pressure (psi)	Man. Trans.	Auto. Trans.
'80	A	4-140	Ford	AWSF-42	.035	Electronic	6B	20B(12B)	22	5½–6½	850	750
	T	4-140T	Ford	AWSF-32	.050	Electronic	6B(2B)	8B(2B)	22	6½–7½	900	800①
	B	6-200	Ford	BRF-82	.050	Electronic	10B	12B	20	5½–6½	900	700
	C	6-250	Ford	BSF-82	.050	Electronic	8B	10B	18	5½–6½	700	550
	D	8-255	Ford	ASF-42	.050	Electronic	8B	8B(6B)④	16	4–6	500	550(500)④
	F	8-302	Ford	ASF-52	.050	Electronic	—	8B④	16	5½–6½	—	550④
	G	8-351	Ford	ASF-52	.050	Electronic	—	①④	23	6½–8	—	600④
'81	A	4-140	Ford	AWSF-42	.034	Electronic	6B	6B	22	5½–6½	700	700
	T	4-140T	Ford	AWSF-32	.034	Electronic	6B	8B	22	5½–6½	850	750(650)
	B	6-200	Ford	BSF-92	.050	Electronic	10B	10B	20	5½–6½	900	700①
	D	8-255	Ford	ASF-52	.050	Electronic	10B	10B	16	5½–6½	900	700①
	F	8-302	Ford	ASF-52	.050	Electronic	8B	8B	16	5½–6½	800	800
	G	8-351	Ford	ASF-52	.050	Electronic	—	①④	23	6½–8	—	600④
'82	A	4-140	Ford	AWSF-42	.034	Electronic	①	①	22	5½–6½	850	750
	B	6-200	Ford	BSF-92	.050	Electronic	①	①	20	6–8	700①	600(700)①
	3	6-232	Ford	AGSP-52	.044	Electronic	①	①	13	6–8	①	①
	F	8-302	Ford	ASF-52	.050	Electronic	—	①④	16	6–8⑧	①④	①④
	G	8-351	Ford	ASF-52	.050	Electronic	—	①④	23	6½–8	—	600④
'83	A	4-140	Ford	AWSF-44	.044	Electronic	①	①	16	5½–6½	850	800
	X	6-200	Ford	BSF-92	.050	Electronic	①	①	20	6–8	600	600
	3	V-6-232	Ford	AWSF-52	.044	Electronic	①	①	13	39	550	550
	F	8-302	Ford	ASF-52②	.050	Electronic	①	①	16	6–8③	—	550
	G	8-351	Ford	ASF-42	.044	Electronic	①	①	23	6–8	—	700/600
'84	A	4-140	Ford	AWSF-44	.044	Electronic	①	①	16	5–7	850	750
	W	4-140-T	Ford	AWSF-32	.034	Electronic	①	①	—	39	①④	①④
	T	4-140-T⑤	Ford	AWSF-32	.034	Electronic	①	①	—	39	①④	①④
	3	V6-232	Ford	AWSF-54	.044	Electronic	①	①	13	39	—	550
	F	8-302	Ford	ASF-52	.050	Electronic	①	①	16	39	550	550
	M	8-302HO	Ford	ASF-42	.044	Electronic	①	①	—	6–8	700	700
	G	8-351	Ford	ASF-42	.044	Electronic	①	①	23	6–8	—	600⑥

87936c15

TUNE-UP SPECIFICATIONS
1980 - 86 All Car and Truck Models (Cont.)

When analyzing compression test results, look for uniformity among cylinders rather than specific pressures

Year	Eng. V.I.N. Code	No. Cyl. Displacement (cu. in.)	Eng. Mfg.	Spark Plugs Orig. Type	Gap (in.)	Distributor	Ignition Timing (deg) Man. Trans.	Auto. Trans.	Valves Intake Opens (deg)	Fuel Pump Pressure (psi)	Idle Speed (rpm) Man. Trans.	Auto. Trans.
'85	A	4-140	Ford	AWSF-44	.044	Electronic	①	①	16	6–8	850	750
	W	4-140T	Ford	AWSF-32	.034	Electronic	①	①	—	39	750	750
	T	4-140T ⑤	Ford	AWSF-32	.034	Electronic	①	①	—	39	①④	①④
	R	4-140-HSC	Ford	AWSF-52	.044	Electronic	①	①	—	39	800	700
	3	V6-232	Ford	AGSP-52	.044	Electronic	①	①	13	6–8	600	600
	F	8-302	Ford	ASF-52	.050	Electronic	①	①	13	39	—	550
	M	8-302HO	Ford	ASF-42	.044	Electronic	①	①	—	6–8	700	700
	G	8-351	Ford	ASF-42	.044	Electronic	①	①	—	6–8	—	600⑥
'86	A	4-140	Ford	AWSF-44C	.044	Electronic	①	①	16	6–8	750	750
	T	4-140T	Ford	AWSF-32C	.034	Electronic	①	①	—	39	825/975	825/975
	W	4-140T	Ford	AWSF-32C	.034	Electronic	①	①	—	39	825/975	825/975
	3	V6-232	Ford	AWSF-54	.044	Electronic	①	①	13	39	—	550
	F	8-302	Ford	ASF-32C	.044	Electronic	①	①	—	39	①④	①④
	M	8-302HO	Ford	ASF-42	.044	Electronic	①	①	—	6–8	700	700
	G	8-351	Ford	ASF-32C	.044	Electronic	①	①	—	6–8	650	650

NOTE: The underhood specifications sticker often reflects tune-up specification changes made in production. Sticker figures must be used if they disagree with those in this chart.

T Turbocharger
B Before Top Dead Center
HO High Output
— Not applicable
HSC High Swirl Combustion

① Calibrations vary depending upon the model; refer to the underhood calibration sticker.
② The carbureted models use spark plug ASF-42 (.044) and the idle speed rpm is 700 rpm.

③ On fuel injected models the pressure is 39 psi.
④ Electronic engine control models the ignition timing, idle speed and idle mixture is not adjustable.
⑤ SVO Mustang
⑥ 700 rpm with the VOTM on.

87936c16

TUNE-UP SPECIFICATIONS
1987 - 93 All Car and Truck Models

Year	Engine ID/VIN	Engine Displacement Liters	Spark Plugs Gap (in.)	Ignition Timing (deg.) MT	AT	Fuel Pump (psi) ②	Idle Speed (rpm) MT	AT	Valve Clearance In.	Ex.
1987	B	4.9	0.044	①	①	33	①	①	Hyd.	Hyd.
	G	5.0	0.044	①	①	7–9	①	①	Hyd.	Hyd.
	H	5.8	0.044	①	①	7–9	①	①	Hyd.	Hyd.
	L	7.5	0.044	①	①	7–9	①	①	Hyd.	Hyd.
1988	Y	4.9	0.044	①	①	33	①	①	Hyd.	Hyd.
	N	5.0	0.044	①	①	33	①	①	Hyd.	Hyd.
	H	5.8	0.044	①	①	33	①	①	Hyd.	Hyd.
	G	7.5	0.044	①	①	33	①	①	Hyd.	Hyd.
1989	Y	4.9	0.044	①	①	33	①	①	Hyd.	Hyd.
	N	5.0	0.044	①	①	33	①	①	Hyd.	Hyd.
	H	5.8	0.044	①	①	33	①	①	Hyd.	Hyd.
	G	7.5	0.044	①	①	33	①	①	Hyd.	Hyd.
1990	Y	4.9	0.044	①	①	33	①	①	Hyd.	Hyd.
	N	5.0	0.044	①	①	33	①	①	Hyd.	Hyd.
	H	5.8	0.044	①	①	33	①	①	Hyd.	Hyd.
	G	7.5	0.044	①	①	33	①	①	Hyd.	Hyd.
1991	Y	4.9	0.044	①	①	45–60	①	①	Hyd.	Hyd.
	N	5.0	0.044	①	①	30–45	①	①	Hyd.	Hyd.
	H	5.8	0.044	①	①	30–45	①	①	Hyd.	Hyd.
	G	7.5	0.044	①	①	30–45	①	①	Hyd.	Hyd.
1992	Y	4.9	0.044	①	①	45–60	①	①	Hyd.	Hyd.
	N	5.0	0.044	①	①	30–45	①	①	Hyd.	Hyd.
	H	5.8	0.044	①	①	30–45	①	①	Hyd.	Hyd.
	G	7.5	0.044	①	①	30–45	①	①	Hyd.	Hyd.
1993	Y	4.9	0.044	①	①	45–60	①	①	Hyd.	Hyd.
	N	5.0	0.044	①	①	30–45	①	①	Hyd.	Hyd.
	H	5.8	0.044	①	①	30–45	①	①	Hyd.	Hyd.
	R	5.8	0.044	①	①	30–45	①	①	Hyd.	Hyd.
	G	7.5	0.044	①	①	30–45	①	①	Hyd.	Hyd.

NOTE: The lowest cylinder pressure should be within 75% of the highest cylinder pressure reading. For example, if the highest cylinder is 134 psi, the lowest should be 101. Engine should be at normal operating temperature with throttle valve in the wide open position.
The underhood specifications sticker often reflects tune-up specification changes in production. Sticker figures must be used if they disagree with those in this chart.
① See underhood sticker
② Engine running

87936c22

GLOSSARY

AIR/FUEL RATIO: The ratio of air-to-gasoline by weight in the fuel mixture drawn into the engine.

AIR INJECTION: One method of reducing harmful exhaust emissions by injecting air into each of the exhaust ports of an engine. The fresh air entering the hot exhaust manifold causes any remaining fuel to be burned before it can exit the tailpipe.

ALTERNATOR: A device used for converting mechanical energy into electrical energy.

AMMETER: An instrument, calibrated in amperes, used to measure the flow of an electrical current in a circuit. Ammeters are always connected in series with the circuit being tested.

AMPERE: The rate of flow of electrical current present when one volt of electrical pressure is applied against one ohm of electrical resistance.

ANALOG COMPUTER: Any microprocessor that uses similar (analogous) electrical signals to make its calculations.

ARMATURE: A laminated, soft iron core wrapped by a wire that converts electrical energy to mechanical energy as in a motor or relay. When rotated in a magnetic field, it changes mechanical energy into electrical energy as in a generator.

ATMOSPHERIC PRESSURE: The pressure on the Earth's surface caused by the weight of the air in the atmosphere. At sea level, this pressure is 14.7 psi at 32°F (101 kPa at 0°C).

ATOMIZATION: The breaking down of a liquid into a fine mist that can be suspended in air.

AXIAL PLAY: Movement parallel to a shaft or bearing bore.

BACKFIRE: The sudden combustion of gases in the intake or exhaust system that results in a loud explosion.

BACKLASH: The clearance or play between two parts, such as meshed gears.

BACKPRESSURE: Restrictions in the exhaust system that slow the exit of exhaust gases from the combustion chamber.

BAKELITE: A heat resistant, plastic insulator material commonly used in printed circuit boards and transistorized components.

BALL BEARING: A bearing made up of hardened inner and outer races between which hardened steel balls roll.

BALLAST RESISTOR: A resistor in the primary ignition circuit that lowers voltage after the engine is started to reduce wear on ignition components.

BEARING: A friction reducing, supportive device usually located between a stationary part and a moving part.

BIMETAL TEMPERATURE SENSOR: Any sensor or switch made of two dissimilar types of metal that bend when heated or cooled due to the different expansion rates of the alloys. These types of sensors usually function as an on/off switch.

BLOWBY: Combustion gases, composed of water vapor and unburned fuel, that leak past the piston rings into the crankcase during normal engine operation. These gases are removed by the PCV system to prevent the buildup of harmful acids in the crankcase.

BRAKE PAD: A brake shoe and lining assembly used with disc brakes.

BRAKE SHOE: The backing for the brake lining. The term is, however, usually applied to the assembly of the brake backing and lining.

BUSHING: A liner, usually removable, for a bearing; an antifriction liner used in place of a bearing.

CALIPER: A hydraulically activated device in a disc brake system, which is mounted straddling the brake rotor (disc). The caliper contains at least one piston and two brake pads. Hydraulic pressure on the piston(s) forces the pads against the rotor.

CAMSHAFT: A shaft in the engine on which are the lobes (cams) which operate the valves. The camshaft is driven by the crankshaft, via a belt, chain or gears, at one half the crankshaft speed.

CAPACITOR: A device which stores an electrical charge.

CARBON MONOXIDE (CO): A colorless, odorless gas given off as a normal byproduct of combustion. It is poisonous and extremely dangerous in confined areas, building up slowly to toxic levels without warning if adequate ventilation is not available.

CARBURETOR: A device, usually mounted on the intake manifold of an engine, which mixes the air and fuel in the proper proportion to allow even combustion.

CATALYTIC CONVERTER: A device installed in the exhaust system, like a muffler, that converts harmful byproducts of combustion into carbon dioxide and water vapor by means of a heat-producing chemical reaction.

CENTRIFUGAL ADVANCE: A mechanical method of advancing the spark timing by using flyweights in the distributor that react to centrifugal force generated by the distributor shaft rotation.

CHECK VALVE: Any one-way valve installed to permit the flow of air, fuel or vacuum in one direction only.

CHOKE: A device, usually a moveable valve, placed in the intake path of a carburetor to restrict the flow of air.

CIRCUIT: Any unbroken path through which an electrical current can flow. Also used to describe fuel flow in some instances.

CIRCUIT BREAKER: A switch which protects an electrical circuit from overload by opening the circuit when the current flow exceeds a predetermined level. Some circuit breakers must be reset manually, while most reset automatically.

COIL (IGNITION): A transformer in the ignition circuit which steps up the voltage provided to the spark plugs.

COMBINATION MANIFOLD: An assembly which includes both the intake and exhaust manifolds in one casting.

COMBINATION VALVE: A device used in some fuel systems that routes fuel vapors to a charcoal storage canister instead of venting them into the atmosphere. The valve relieves fuel tank pressure and allows fresh air into the tank as the fuel level drops to prevent a vapor lock situation.

COMPRESSION RATIO: The comparison of the total volume of the cylinder and combustion chamber with the piston at BDC and the piston at TDC.

CONDENSER: 1. An electrical device which acts to store an electrical charge, preventing voltage surges. 2. A radiator-like device in the air conditioning system in which refrigerant gas condenses into a liquid, giving off heat.

CONDUCTOR: Any material through which an electrical current can be transmitted easily.

CONTINUITY: Continuous or complete circuit. Can be checked with an ohmmeter.

COUNTERSHAFT: An intermediate shaft which is rotated by a mainshaft and transmits, in turn, that rotation to a working part.

CRANKCASE: The lower part of an engine in which the crankshaft and related parts operate.

CRANKSHAFT: The main driving shaft of an engine which receives reciprocating motion from the pistons and converts it to rotary motion.

CYLINDER: In an engine, the round hole in the engine block in which the piston(s) ride.

CYLINDER BLOCK: The main structural member of an engine in which is found the cylinders, crankshaft and other principal parts.

CYLINDER HEAD: The detachable portion of the engine, usually fastened to the top of the cylinder block and containing all or most of the combustion chambers. On overhead valve engines, it contains the valves and their operating parts. On overhead cam engines, it contains the camshaft as well.

DEAD CENTER: The extreme top or bottom of the piston stroke.

DETONATION: An unwanted explosion of the air/fuel mixture in the combustion chamber caused by excess heat and compression, advanced timing, or an overly lean mixture. Also referred to as "ping".

DIAPHRAGM: A thin, flexible wall separating two cavities, such as in a vacuum advance unit.

DIESELING: A condition in which hot spots in the combustion chamber cause the engine to run on after the key is turned off.

DIFFERENTIAL: A geared assembly which allows the transmission of motion between drive axles, giving one axle the ability to turn faster than the other.

DIODE: An electrical device that will allow current to flow in one direction only.

DISC BRAKE: A hydraulic braking assembly consisting of a brake disc, or rotor, mounted on an axle, and a caliper assembly containing, usually two brake pads which are activated by hydraulic pressure. The pads are forced against the sides of the disc, creating friction which slows the vehicle.

DISTRIBUTOR: A mechanically driven device on an engine which is responsible for electrically firing the spark plug at a predetermined point of the piston stroke.

DOWEL PIN: A pin, inserted in mating holes in two different parts allowing those parts to maintain a fixed relationship.

DRUM BRAKE: A braking system which consists of two brake shoes and one or two wheel cylinders, mounted on a fixed backing plate, and a brake drum, mounted on an axle, which revolves around the assembly.

DWELL: The rate, measured in degrees of shaft rotation, at which an electrical circuit cycles on and off.

ELECTRONIC CONTROL UNIT (ECU): Ignition module, module, amplifier or igniter. See Module for definition.

ELECTRONIC IGNITION: A system in which the timing and firing of the spark plugs is controlled by an electronic control unit, usually called a module. These systems have no points or condenser.

END-PLAY: The measured amount of axial movement in a shaft.

ENGINE: A device that converts heat into mechanical energy.

EXHAUST MANIFOLD: A set of cast passages or pipes which conduct exhaust gases from the engine.

FEELER GAUGE: A blade, usually metal, of precisely predetermined thickness, used to measure the clearance between two parts.

FIRING ORDER: The order in which combustion occurs in the cylinders of an engine. Also the order in which spark is distributed to the plugs by the distributor.

FLOODING: The presence of too much fuel in the intake manifold and combustion chamber which prevents the air/fuel mixture from firing, thereby causing a no-start situation.

FLYWHEEL: A disc shaped part bolted to the rear end of the crankshaft. Around the outer perimeter is affixed the ring gear. The starter drive engages the ring gear, turning the flywheel, which rotates the crankshaft, imparting the initial starting motion to the engine.

FOOT POUND (ft. lbs. or sometimes, ft.lb.): The amount of energy or work needed to raise an item weighing one pound, a distance of one foot.

FUSE: A protective device in a circuit which prevents circuit overload by breaking the circuit when a specific amperage is present. The device is constructed around a strip or wire of a lower amperage rating than the circuit it is designed to protect. When an amperage higher than that stamped on the fuse is present in the circuit, the strip or wire melts, opening the circuit.

GEAR RATIO: The ratio between the number of teeth on meshing gears.

GENERATOR: A device which converts mechanical energy into electrical energy.

HEAT RANGE: The measure of a spark plug's ability to dissipate heat from its firing end. The higher the heat range, the hotter the plug fires.

HUB: The center part of a wheel or gear.

HYDROCARBON (HC): Any chemical compound made up of hydrogen and carbon. A major pollutant formed by the engine as a byproduct of combustion.

HYDROMETER: An instrument used to measure the specific gravity of a solution.

INCH POUND (inch lbs.; sometimes in.lb. or in. lbs.): One twelfth of a foot pound.

INDUCTION: A means of transferring electrical energy in the form of a magnetic field. Principle used in the ignition coil to increase voltage.

INJECTOR: A device which receives metered fuel under relatively low pressure and is activated to inject the fuel into the engine under relatively high pressure at a predetermined time.

INPUT SHAFT: The shaft to which torque is applied, usually carrying the driving gear or gears.

INTAKE MANIFOLD: A casting of passages or pipes used to conduct air or a fuel/air mixture to the cylinders.

JOURNAL: The bearing surface within which a shaft operates.

KEY: A small block usually fitted in a notch between a shaft and a hub to prevent slippage of the two parts.

MANIFOLD: A casting of passages or set of pipes which connect the cylinders to an inlet or outlet source.

MANIFOLD VACUUM: Low pressure in an engine intake manifold formed just below the throttle plates. Manifold vacuum is highest at idle and drops under acceleration.

MASTER CYLINDER: The primary fluid pressurizing device in a hydraulic system. In automotive use, it is found in brake and hydraulic clutch systems and is pedal activated, either directly or, in a power brake system, through the power booster.

MODULE: Electronic control unit, amplifier or igniter of solid state or integrated design which controls the current flow in the ignition primary circuit based on input from the pick-up coil. When the module opens the primary circuit, high secondary voltage is induced in the coil.

NEEDLE BEARING: A bearing which consists of a number (usually a large number) of long, thin rollers.

OHM:(Ω) The unit used to measure the resistance of conductor-to-electrical flow. One ohm is the amount of resistance that limits current flow to one ampere in a circuit with one volt of pressure.

OHMMETER: An instrument used for measuring the resistance, in ohms, in an electrical circuit.

OUTPUT SHAFT: The shaft which transmits torque from a device, such as a transmission.

OVERDRIVE: A gear assembly which produces more shaft revolutions than that transmitted to it.

OVERHEAD CAMSHAFT (OHC): An engine configuration in which the camshaft is mounted on top of the cylinder head and operates the valve either directly or by means of rocker arms.

OVERHEAD VALVE (OHV): An engine configuration in which all of the valves are located in the cylinder head and the camshaft is located in the cylinder block. The camshaft operates the valves via lifters and pushrods.

OXIDES OF NITROGEN (NOx): Chemical compounds of nitrogen produced as a byproduct of combustion. They combine with hydrocarbons to produce smog.

OXYGEN SENSOR: Used with the feedback system to sense the presence of oxygen in the exhaust gas and signal the computer which can reference the voltage signal to an air/fuel ratio.

PINION: The smaller of two meshing gears.

PISTON RING: An open-ended ring which fits into a groove on the outer diameter of the piston. Its chief function is to form a seal between the piston and cylinder wall. Most automotive pistons have three rings: two for compression sealing; one for oil sealing.

PRELOAD: A predetermined load placed on a bearing during assembly or by adjustment.

PRIMARY CIRCUIT: The low voltage side of the ignition system which consists of the ignition switch, ballast resistor or resistance wire, bypass, coil, electronic control unit and pick-up coil as well as the connecting wires and harnesses.

PRESS FIT: The mating of two parts under pressure, due to the inner diameter of one being smaller than the outer diameter of the other, or vice versa; an interference fit.

RACE: The surface on the inner or outer ring of a bearing on which the balls, needles or rollers move.

REGULATOR: A device which maintains the amperage and/or voltage levels of a circuit at predetermined values.

RELAY: A switch which automatically opens and/or closes a circuit.

RESISTANCE: The opposition to the flow of current through a circuit or electrical device, and is measured in ohms. Resistance is equal to the voltage divided by the amperage.

RESISTOR: A device, usually made of wire, which offers a preset amount of resistance in an electrical circuit.

RING GEAR: The name given to a ring-shaped gear attached to a differential case, or affixed to a flywheel or as part of a planetary gear set.

ROLLER BEARING: A bearing made up of hardened inner and outer races between which hardened steel rollers move.

ROTOR: 1. The disc-shaped part of a disc brake assembly, upon which the brake pads bear; also called, brake disc. 2. The device mounted atop the distributor shaft, which passes current to the distributor cap tower contacts.

SECONDARY CIRCUIT: The high voltage side of the ignition system, usually above 20,000 volts. The secondary includes the ignition coil, coil wire, distributor cap and rotor, spark plug wires and spark plugs.

SENDING UNIT: A mechanical, electrical, hydraulic or electromagnetic device which transmits information to a gauge.

SENSOR: Any device designed to measure engine operating conditions or ambient pressures and temperatures. Usually electronic in nature and designed to send a voltage signal to an on-board computer, some sensors may operate as a simple on/off switch or they may provide a variable voltage signal (like a potentiometer) as conditions or measured parameters change.

SHIM: Spacers of precise, predetermined thickness used between parts to establish a proper working relationship.

SLAVE CYLINDER: In automotive use, a device in the hydraulic clutch system which is activated by hydraulic force, disengaging the clutch.

SOLENOID: A coil used to produce a magnetic field, the effect of which is to produce work.

SPARK PLUG: A device screwed into the combustion chamber of a spark ignition engine. The basic construction is a conductive core inside of a ceramic insulator, mounted in an outer conductive base. An electrical charge from the spark plug wire travels along the conductive core and jumps a preset air gap to a grounding point or points at the end of the conductive base. The resultant spark ignites the fuel/air mixture in the combustion chamber.

SPLINES: Ridges machined or cast onto the outer diameter of a shaft or inner diameter of a bore to enable parts to mate without rotation.

TACHOMETER: A device used to measure the rotary speed of an engine, shaft, gear, etc., usually in rotations per minute.

THERMOSTAT: A valve, located in the cooling system of an engine, which is closed when cold and opens gradually in response to engine heating, controlling the temperature of the coolant and rate of coolant flow.

TOP DEAD CENTER (TDC): The point at which the piston reaches the top of its travel on the compression stroke.

TORQUE: The twisting force applied to an object.

TORQUE CONVERTER: A turbine used to transmit power from a driving member to a driven member via hydraulic action, providing changes in drive ratio and torque. In automotive use, it links the driveplate at the rear of the engine to the automatic transmission.

TRANSDUCER: A device used to change a force into an electrical signal.

TRANSISTOR: A semi-conductor component which can be actuated by a small voltage to perform an electrical switching function.

TUNE-UP: A regular maintenance function, usually associated with the replacement and adjustment of parts and components in the electrical and fuel systems of a vehicle for the purpose of attaining optimum performance.

TURBOCHARGER: An exhaust driven pump which compresses intake air and forces it into the combustion chambers at higher than atmospheric pressures. The increased air pressure allows more fuel to be burned and results in increased horsepower being produced.

VACUUM ADVANCE: A device which advances the ignition timing in response to increased engine vacuum.

VACUUM GAUGE: An instrument used to measure the presence of vacuum in a chamber.

VALVE: A device which control the pressure, direction of flow or rate of flow of a liquid or gas.

VALVE CLEARANCE: The measured gap between the end of the valve stem and the rocker arm, cam lobe or follower that activates the valve.

VISCOSITY: The rating of a liquid's internal resistance to flow.

VOLTMETER: An instrument used for measuring electrical force in units called volts. Voltmeters are always connected parallel with the circuit being tested.

WHEEL CYLINDER: Found in the automotive drum brake assembly, it is a device, actuated by hydraulic pressure, which, through internal pistons, pushes the brake shoes outward against the drums.

DISASSEMBLY
ALTERNATOR 5-24
CAMSHAFT BEARINGS 5-37
CAMSHAFT 5-37
CORE (FREEZE/OIL GALLERY) PLUGS 5-44
CRANKSHAFT AND MAIN BEARINGS 5-42
CRANKSHAFT PULLEY (VIBRATION DAMPER) 5-34
CYLINDER HEAD 5-28
DISTRIBUTOR 5-24
ENGINE FAN AND FAN CLUTCH 5-27
ENGINE OVERHAUL TIPS
  INSPECTION TECHNIQUES 5-2
  OVERHAUL TIPS 5-2
  TOOLS 5-2
EXHAUST MANIFOLD 5-26
IGNITION COIL 5-24
INTAKE MANIFOLD 5-26
OIL PAN 5-33
OIL PUMP 5-33
PISTONS AND CONNECTING RODS
  PISTON AND ROD DISASSEMBLY 5-40
REAR MAIN OIL SEAL
  TWO PIECE SEAL 5-46
ROCKER ARMS AND PUSHRODS 5-25
ROCKER COVERS 5-24
THERMOSTAT 5-26
TIMING CHAIN FRONT COVER AND OIL SEAL 5-35
TIMING CHAIN 5-36
VALVES 5-29
WATER PUMP 5-28
ENGINE INSTALLATION
1966-85 FORD AND MERCURY MID-SIZED CARS, INCLUDING
  MUSTANG AND COUGAR 6-7
1966-86 PICKUPS AND BRONCO
  EXCEPT 460 6-2
  W/460 6-2
1968-88 FORD, MERCURY AND LINCOLN FULL-SIZED
  CARS 6-5
1971-96 FULL-SIZED VANS
  5.0L, 5.7L 6-4
  7.5L 6-5
1979-88 MUSTANG AND CAPRI 6-7
1983-96 THUNDERBIRD AND COUGAR 6-8
1987-96 PICKUPS AND BRONCO
  7.5L 6-4
  8-5.0L, 8-5.8L 6-3
1989-93 MUSTANG 6-8
1989-94 FORD, MERCURY AND LINCOLN FULL-SIZED CARS
  4.6L 6-6
  5.0L, 5.8L 6-6
BREAK-IN PROCEDURE 6-9
FASTENERS
BOLTS AND SCREWS 3-28
LOCKWASHERS 3-29
NUTS 3-28
SCREW AND BOLT TERMINOLOGY
  LENGTH AND THREAD LENGTH 3-30
  MAJOR DIAMETER 3-29
  METRIC BOLTS 3-31
  MINOR DIAMETER 3-29
  PITCH OR THREADS PER INCH 3-30
  THREAD CLASS 3-30
  TYPES OR GRADES OF BOLTS AND SCREWS 3-30
STUDS 3-28
INSPECTION
CAMSHAFT
  CHECKING CAMSHAFT 5-56
CRANKSHAFT 5-60
CYLINDER HEAD 5-52
MAIN BEARINGS
  CHECKING MAIN BEARING CLEARANCES 5-61

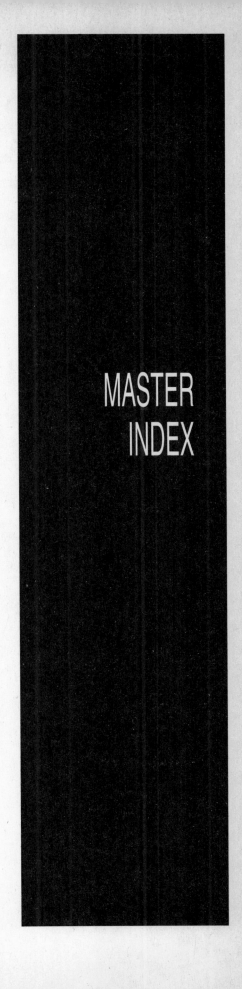

MASTER
INDEX

PISTONS AND CONNECTING RODS
  CONNECTING ROD BEARING INSPECTION 5-59
  MEASURING THE OLD PISTONS 5-59
  PISTON RING END-GAP 5-57
  PISTON RING SIDE CLEARANCE CHECK 5-58
  SELECTING NEW PISTONS 5-59
TIMING CHAIN
  CHECKING TIMING CHAIN DEFLECTION 5-55
VALVES
  HYDRAULIC VALVE LIFTER 5-54
  VALVE SPRING INSTALLED HEIGHT 5-54
  VALVE SPRINGS 5-53
  VALVE STEM-TO-GUIDE CLEARANCE 5-54
PARTS CLEANING
  BLOCK 5-48
  COLD SPRAYING 5-47
  COLD TANK IMMERSION 5-47
  CRANKSHAFT 5-48
  CYLINDER HEAD 5-48
  HAND CLEANING 5-47
  HOT TANK IMMERSION 5-47
  MAIN BEARINGS 5-49
  PISTON AND ROD 5-48
  STEAM CLEANING 5-47
  VALVES 5-48
PRELIMINARIES
  ACCESSORY DRIVE BELTS
    INSPECTION 1-18
  AIR CONDITIONING
    DISCHARGING, EVACUATING AND CHARGING 1-24
    GENERAL SERVICING PROCEDURES 1-22
    SAFETY PRECAUTIONS 1-21
    SYSTEM INSPECTION 1-23
  CAN YOU DO IT? 1-2
  DOES THE ENGINE NEED REBUILDING?
    ISOLATING ENGINE PROBLEMS AND DETERMINING THEIR
    SEVERITY 1-4
    PERFORMANCE LOSS PROBLEMS AND POSSIBLE
    CAUSES 1-8
    USING TEST INSTRUMENTS TO DETERMINE ENGINE
    CONDITION 1-8
  FORD ENGINES
    335 SERIES SMALL BLOCK 1-3
    385 SERIES BIG BLOCK 1-3
    90° V SMALL BLOCK 1-3
    FE SERIES BIG BLOCK 1-3
  GETTING AN ENGINE 1-3
  HOSES
    INSPECTION 1-18
    REMOVAL & INSTALLATION 1-18
  IS THE ENGINE WORTH REBUILDING? 1-4
  LOCATION 1-2
  PARTS 1-4
  PREPARING THE WORK AREA 1-2
  SPARK PLUG WIRES
    TESTING 1-17
  SPARK PLUGS
    CHECKING SPARK PLUGS 1-13
    INSPECTION 1-12
    REMOVAL 1-11
    SPARK PLUG HEAT RANGE 1-10
  TIMING BELTS
    INSPECTION 1-18
  TO REBUILD OR NOT TO REBUILD 1-2
  WHAT TYPE OF ENGINE? 1-2
PUTTING IT ALL BACK TOGETHER
  ALTERNATOR
    BELT TENSION ADJUSTMENT 5-101

CAMSHAFT AND BEARINGS 5-84
CORE (FREEZE) PLUGS 5-73
CRANKSHAFT AND MAIN BEARINGS 5-74
CRANKSHAFT PULLEY (VIBRATION DAMPER) 5-89
CYLINDER HEAD 5-92
DISTRIBUTOR 5-98
ENGINE FAN AND FAN CLUTCH 5-98
EXHAUST MANIFOLD 5-94
FLYWHEEL/FLEXPLATE 5-101
INTAKE MANIFOLD 5-98
LIFTERS 5-89
OIL PAN 5-85
OIL PUMP 5-84
ONE PIECE REAR MAIN OIL SEAL 5-101
PAINTING 5-73
PISTONS AND CONNECTING RODS
  PISTON AND CONNECTING ROD ASSEMBLY AND
  INSTALLATION 5-80
ROCKER ARMS AND PUSHRODS
  CLEARANCE ADJUSTMENT 5-96
ROCKER COVERS 5-101
THERMOSTAT 5-98
TIMING CHAIN FRONT COVER AND OIL SEAL 5-88
TIMING CHAIN 5-84
VALVES 5-91
WATER PUMP 5-94
REPAIR AND REFINISHING
  BLOCK
    CYLINDER HONING 5-71
  CYLINDER HEAD
    CRACK REPAIR 5-65
    HEAD RESURFACING 5-65
    VALVE LAPPING 5-67
    VALVE SEATS 5-66
  OIL PUMP 5-71
  ROCKER STUDS 5-64
  VALVE GUIDES
    KNURLING 5-70
    REAMING THE GUIDES 5-69
    REPLACEMENT GUIDES 5-71
    VALVE GUIDE INSERTS 5-70
  VALVES AND SEATS 5-65
SPECIFICATIONS CHARTS
  1961-71 TRUCK TUNE-UP SPECIFICATIONS 6-31
  1964-71 FORD/MERCURY COMPACT CAR TUNE-UP
  SPECIFICATIONS 6-19
  1964-71 FORD/MERCURY FULL-SIZE CAR TUNE-UP
  SPECIFICATIONS 6-21
  1971-79 TRUCK TUNE-UP SPECIFICATIONS 6-32
  1972-76 THUNDERBIRD TUNE-UP SPECIFICATIONS 6-30
  1972-79 FORD FULL-SIZE CAR TUNE-UP
  SPECIFICATIONS 6-26
  1972-79 FORD/MERCURY COMPACT CAR TUNE-UP
  SPECIFICATIONS 6-22
  1972-79 FORD/MERCURY MID-SIZE CAR TUNE-UP
  SPECIFICATIONS 6-24
  1972-79 MERCURY FULL-SIZE CAR TUNE-UP
  SPECIFICATIONS 6-28
  1980-86 TUNE-UP SPECIFICATIONS — ALL MODELS 6-33
  1987-93 TUNE-UP SPECIFICATIONS — ALL MODELS 6-35
  ENGINE MECHANICAL SPECIFICATIONS 5-102
  STANDARD (ENGLISH) TO METRIC CONVERSION
  CHARTS 1-25
  TORQUE SPECIFICATIONS 5-102
SUPPLIES AND EQUIPMENT
  CHEMICALS
    CLEANERS 3-2
    LUBRICANTS AND PENETRANTS 3-2

SEALANTS 3-2
SHOP TOWELS 3-3
FLUID DISPOSAL 3-2
THE HARD WORK STARTS
BEFORE DISASSEMBLY 4-22
BUDGETING YOUR TIME 4-22
CLEANING THE ENGINE 4-21
CLEARING THE WAY
CARBURETOR OR THROTTLE BODY 4-4
CONDENSER 4-5
POWER STEERING PUMPS 4-6
RADIATOR 4-4
STARTER 4-6
ENGINE REMOVAL
1966-85 FORD AND MERCURY MID-SIZED CARS, INCLUDING
MUSTANG AND COUGAR 4-18
1966-86 PICKUPS AND BRONCO 4-6
1968-88 FORD, MERCURY AND LINCOLN FULL-SIZED
CARS 4-16
1971-96 FULL-SIZED VANS 4-15
1979-88 MUSTANG AND CAPRI 4-19
1983-96 THUNDERBIRD AND COUGAR 4-20
1987-96 PICKUPS AND BRONCO 4-11
1989-93 MUSTANG 4-21
1989-94 FORD, MERCURY AND LINCOLN FULL-SIZED
CARS 4-17
FASTENERS
REPAIRING DAMAGED THREADS 4-3
REPLACING FASTENERS 4-2
FLYWHEEL/FLEX PLATE AND RING GEAR 4-21
STORING PARTS 4-2
THE ENGINE DOLLY 4-21
THE WORK AREA
FLOOR SPACE AND WORKING HEIGHT 2-2
SHOP SAFETY
DO'S 2-5
DON'T'S 2-6
SAFETY EQUIPMENT 2-7
STORAGE AREAS
ELECTRICAL REQUIREMENTS 2-5
HEATERS 2-5
LIGHTING 2-4
SHELVES 2-2
TOOL CHESTS 2-2
VENTILATION 2-5
WORK BENCHES 2-2
TOOLS
AIR TOOLS AND COMPRESSORS 3-21

ELECTRIC POWER TOOLS 3-21
ENGINE TOOLS 3-22
HANDS TOOLS
AUTOMOTIVE TOOLS 3-15
DIAL INDICATORS 3-19
GAUGES AND TESTERS 3-16
HAMMERS 3-13
MICROMETERS AND CALIPERS 3-17
OTHER COMMON TOOLS 3-13
PLASTIGAGE® 3-20
PLIERS 3-11
SCREWDRIVERS 3-13
SOCKET SETS 3-6
TELESCOPING GAUGES 3-20
WRENCHES 3-11
SHOP CRANES, DOLLIES, JACKS AND ENGINE STANDS
ENGINE DOLLY 3-22
ENGINE STANDS 3-22
JACKING PRECAUTIONS 3-24
JACKS AND JACKSTANDS 3-23
SHOP CRANES 3-22
SPECIAL TOOLS 3-20
TUNE-UP PROCEDURES
BREAKER POINTS AND CONDENSER
INSPECTION 6-11
REPLACEMENT 6-11
DWELL ANGLE
ADJUSTMENT 6-13
IDLE SPEED AND MIXTURE ADJUSTMENTS
CARBURETED ENGINES 6-14
FUEL INJECTED ENGINES 6-17
IGNITION TIMING
IGNITION TIMING ADJUSTMENT 6-14
SPARK PLUG WIRES
CHECKING AND REPLACING SPARK PLUG CABLES 6-10
SPARK PLUGS
INSTALLATION 6-9
VALVE LASH
ADJUSTMENT 6-17
UNDERSTANDING THE BASICS
ADD-ON ELECTRICAL EQUIPMENT 2-13
BATTERY, STARTING AND CHARGING SYSTEMS
BASIC OPERATING PRINCIPLES 2-12
UNDERSTANDING ELECTRICITY
BASIC CIRCUITS 2-9
TROUBLESHOOTING 2-10